# CHILDREN'S LITERATURE

# Children's Literature

## A READER'S HISTORY, FROM
## AESOP TO HARRY POTTER

## Seth Lerer

*The University of Chicago Press*   Chicago and London

SETH LERER is Avalon Foundation Professor in the Humanities and professor of English and comparative literature at Stanford University. His most recent books are *Error and the Academic Self* and *Inventing English*.

The University of Chicago Press, Chicago 60637
The University of Chicago Press, Ltd., London
© 2008 by The University of Chicago
All rights reserved. Published 2008
Printed in the United States of America

17  16  15  14  13  12  11  10  09          3  4  5

ISBN-13: 978-0-226-47300-0 (cloth)
ISBN-10: 0-226-47300-7 (cloth)

Library of Congress Cataloging-in-Publication Data

Lerer, Seth, 1955–
    Children's literature : a reader's history, from Aesop to Harry Potter / Seth Lerer.
        p. cm.
    Includes bibliographical references (p. ) and index.
    ISBN-13: 978-0-226-47300-0 (alk. paper)
    ISBN-10: 0-226-47300-7 (alk. paper)
    1. Children's literature—History and criticism.    I. Title.
    PN1009.A1L44 2008
    809'.89282—dc22

                                                                2007046708

FOR MY MOTHER

# Contents

# Illustrations

# Introduction

Ever since there were children, there has been children's literature. Long before John Newbery established the first press devoted to children's books, stories were told and written for the young, and books originally offered to mature readers were carefully recast or excerpted for youthful audiences. Greek and Roman educational traditions grounded themselves in reading and reciting poetry and drama. Aesop's fables lived for two millennia on classroom and family shelves. And thinkers from Quintilian to John Locke, from St. Augustine to Dr. Seuss, speculated on the ways in which we learn about our language and our lives from literature.

The history of children's literature is inseparable from the history of childhood, for the child was made through texts and tales he or she studied, heard, and told back. Learning how to read is a lifetime, and life-defining, experience. "We can remember," writes Francis Spufford in his exquisite memoir *The Child That Books Built*, "readings that acted like transformations. There were times when a particular book, like a seed crystal, dropped into our minds when they were exactly ready for it, like a supersaturated solution, and suddenly we changed."[1] Mine is a book about such transformations. It offers more than just a chronicle of forms of fiction or the arts of illustration. It charts the makings of the literate imagination. It shows children finding worlds within the book and books in the world. It addresses the changing environments of family life and human growth, schooling and scholarship, publishing and publicity in which children—at times suddenly, at times subtly—found themselves changed by literature.[2] Mine is, therefore, a reader's history of children's literature: a study of the figurations of the reading child from antiquity to the present; but a report, as well, on my own life of reading and the critical interpretations that my literary scholarship brings to the texts of childhood.

But what is childhood? Ever since Philippe Ariès sought to define its modern form, scholars have sought to write its history. For Ariès, childhood was not some essential or eternal quality in human life but was instead a category of existence shaped by social mores and historical experience. In his *Centuries of Childhood* (first published in France in 1960), he argued that the periods before the modern age had no concept of childhood as we understand it: that the child as an emotional, or economic, investment is a modern phenomenon, not in keeping with earlier periods' neglect, abuse, or indifference to children as individual beings.[3] While Ariès's work did much to dispel the sentimentalism that attended the work on children and the family before him, it has come under scrutiny by scholars who have illustrated a more finely textured cultural condition to the child in history.[4] Childhood was not invented by the moderns—whether we associate them with John Locke, the Puritans, Jean-Jacques Rousseau, the Romantics, or the Victorians—but is a shifting category that has meaning in relationship to other stages of personal development and family life. Greeks and Romans, Byzantines and Anglo-Saxons, Renaissance and Revolutionary cultures all had clearly defined concepts of the child and, in turn, canons of children's literature. Children are or become, in the words of the twentieth-century philosopher Marx Wartofsky, "what they are taken to be by others, and what they come to take themselves to be, in the course of their social communication and interaction with others."[5] So, too, is children's literature: books that are taken into childhood, that foster social communication, and that, in their interaction with their readers, owners, sellers, and collectors, teach and please.

This book presents a history of what children have heard and read. Their stories, poems, plays, or treatises may well have been composed with children in mind; or they may have been adapted for readers of different ages. I distinguish, therefore, between claims that children's literature consists of books written *for* children and that it consists of those read, regardless of original authorial intention, *by* children. The history I write is a history of reception, and perhaps the best way to illustrate my critical position is to find it in the children's book itself.

At the beginning of Antoine de Saint-Exupéry's *The Little Prince*, the narrator recalls how, as a six-year-old, he came across a picture of a boa constrictor swallowing an animal. "I pondered deeply," he remembers, and he made his own drawing. Showing it to the grown-ups, he asked if it frightened them, but they responded, "Why should anyone be frightened by a hat?" Of course, this was not a hat, but a boa constrictor digesting an elephant. The boy redrew the picture, showing the inside, but the grown-ups were not impressed. And so, the boy gave up a career as an artist. "Grown-ups never understand anything by themselves, and it is tiresome for children to be always and forever explaining things to them."[6]

This episode represents two ways of reading literature. On the one hand, we may look for what it seems to us; on the other, we may look for what its author meant it to be. The unimaginative will always see the ordinary in the strange, a hat where there may really be a snake digesting an elephant. Part of the challenge for the literary critic, therefore, is to balance authorial intention and reader response. But part of the challenge for the children's literary critic is to recognize that texts are mutable—that meanings change, that different groups of readers may see different things, and that what grown-ups find as ordinary items of experience may transform, in the child's imagination, into monstrous brilliance.

Some readers have found children's literature to be a rack of hats: didactic, useful books that keep us warm or guard us against weather. I find children's literature to be a world of snakes: seductive things that live in undergrowths and that may take us whole. Like the Little Prince, I have come upon volumes that have swallowed me. My book is full of animals, whether they be the creatures who fill Aesop's old menagerie or the islands and continents of the colonial imagination. But my book, too, is full of hats, from Crusoe's crude goatskin head covering to the red-and white-striped topper that covers, only barely, the transgressions of Dr. Seuss's famous Cat. Each item is a subject of interpretation. Each becomes something of a litmus test for just what kind of reader we may be.

Much recent work in literary criticism has articulated these distinctions with, if not the charm of *The Little Prince,* then at least with equal vigor. Studies of authorial intention have, over the past three decades, lost ground to histories of reception that show how the meaning of a literary work often lies in the ways in which it may be used, taught, read, excerpted, copied, and sold.[7] In the mid-1980s, the critic Victoria Kahn distilled these approaches into her claim that "the aim of literary studies should be, not the interpretation of individual texts, but the study of the conventions of interpretation, and thus of the production and reception of texts in different historical periods."[8] Children's literature retells a history of the conventions of interpretation and the reception of texts in different historical periods. But children's literary works themselves take such a problem as a theme. Often, a book instructs the child in the arts of reading. It may tell tales about its own production, or it may—more figuratively—show us how we transform our lives into books and texts. What characterizes many of the works I study here is precisely this instruction in the ways of making sense of signs and symbols, life and letters.

I am thus fascinated by the transformations of key books and authors over time. The trajectory of Aesop's fables, for example, writes a history of Western education, of family life, of languages, translations, manuscripts, printing, and digitization. The reception and recasting of Defoe's *Robinson Crusoe*, too, illustrates the changing visions of adventure and imagination, not just in the English-speaking countries and their colonies, but throughout Europe, Asia, and the Americas. The schoolroom has remained the setting for children's literature from Greek and Roman antiquity to the present. St. Augustine recalled, in his *Confessions*, how he had to memorize parts of the *Aeneid* as a schoolboy. Medieval and Renaissance classrooms filled themselves with Aesop. Eighteenth-century girls found their experience recast in Sarah Fielding's *The Governess*, subtitled *The Little Female Academy*. Boys from Tom Brown to Harry Potter found their most imaginative adventures in the classroom, the library, or the playing field.

In the course of these tales, I find images and idioms that mark defining moments in literary history. Lists and catalogues, for example, seem to govern everything from the excerpts of Homer in Hellenistic papyri, to the medieval and Renaissance alphabets, to Crusoe's inventories, Scrooge's double-entry bookkeeping, and the contents of the "great green room" of *Goodnight Moon*. A narrative can inhere in any juxtaposition of recorded events or items. Simply repeating lists of things—ranged alphabetically, chronologically, or topically—can offer unexpected associations. The literary critic Hayden White, in a now-classic study of the place of lists in Western narrative, avers: "Could we ever narrativize without moralizing?"[9] Every list is, potentially, a reckoning, and in the history of children's literature lists offer an accountancy of growth. Children's books often illuminate or criticize an actuarial approach to life. What Scrooge learns in *A Christmas Carol*, for example, is to stop making accounts—to recognize that moral reckoning is not the same as monetary, and that inscription in the book of life is not to be confused with entries in the ledger. By contrast, many twentieth-century children's books teach the idea of list-making.

What is *Goodnight Moon* but a catalogue of things: a list of properties both real and fanciful that mark the progress of the evening and the passageway to sleep? Dr. Seuss transforms the list into a wild burlesque of reckoning itself, imagining an alphabet "on beyond zebra," or a fauna far beyond the categories of Linnean classification.[10]

If children's literature seems full of lists, it also seems full of theater. The schoolroom from the age of St. Augustine to Shakespeare was a place of performance, as boys memorized, recited, and enacted classic texts and rhetorical arguments for the approval of the master. The playing fields of Rugby or the battlefields of Africa were, for the nineteenth century, great stages for the masculine imagination. Young women, too, put on their shows—but here, the audiences were more often domestic than martial. *Spectacula theatrica*, the spectacle of theater, captivated young Augustine. It also captivated young Louisa May Alcott, who had aspired to an actress's life and who began her *Little Women* with a little holiday play put on by the March sisters. The theater enticed Pinocchio, too, whose puppet life is derailed by the strange seductions of the showcase (the Disney version of the story even has its Fox, duded up like some vulpine David Belasco, sing, "An actor's life for me"). "Don't put your daughter on the stage, Mrs. Worthington," sang Noël Coward in the 1930s. But it seems that we have always done so, and part of my interest here lies in the ways in which the literary child performs for others.

If there has been a theater of childhood, especially in the modern era, it has been due in large part to Shakespeare. Plays such as *A Midsummer Night's Dream*, characters such as Juliet and Ophelia, and figures such as Caliban had a great impact on the makings of children's literature. Shakespeare was everywhere, and his figurations of the fairy world, his presentations of young boys and girls, and his imagination of the monstrous gave a texture to those works of children's literature that aspired to high culture. By the mid-nineteenth century, childhood itself could take on a Shakespearean cast: witness the popularity of Mary Cowden Clarke's fanciful recreations in *The Girlhood of Shakespeare's Heroines*; witness Anne Shirley in L. M. Montgomery's *Anne of Green Gables*, acting out like Juliet; witness the weird soliloquies of Captain Hook, who comes off in Barrie's play of *Peter Pan* as a Shakespearean manqué.

The world was a stage, but it also was a book, and in particular it was a book of nature. Technology and science had an impact on the child's imagination long before the chemistry sets and Edison biographies of my own childhood. Medieval bestiaries, herbarics, and lapidaries often offered illustrated guides to God's creation (each item pictured, described, and then allegorized into moral meaning). The great explorations of the seventeenth and eighteenth centuries prompted new places of imagined transport—there is a direct line from Crusoe's island to Sendak's *Where the Wild Things Are.* In the nineteenth century, the work of Charles Darwin had a deep impress on the narratives of childhood. Did children now evolve? Could they devolve, by contrast, left to their own uncontrolled devices? And who knew whether and where new species would be found? From Charles Kingsley and Edward Lear, through Rudyard Kipling and H. G. Wells, to Dr. Seuss, the endless wonder of the world transformed itself into new creatures, new adventures, and new timelines of development.

I am, by training and profession, a philologist: a scholar of word histories, of medieval myths, and of the history of scholarship itself. Philology, too, finds its way into the children's literary imagination, from the Grimm brothers' fairy tales, through Tolkien's Middle Earth and Lewis's Narnia, to Philip Pullman's Miltonic *His Dark Materials.* The tradition of the fairy tale is part and parcel of this philological tradition. The Grimms had originally begun to collect their *Märchen* as part of their larger project of recovering the sources of Germanic linguistic and literary culture. Tolkien, the Oxford etymologist, found sources for his magical vocabulary in the roots of English. There is a mystery to meanings in the dictionary, and fairy tales and folklore share in larger national and scholarly projects that imagine a childhood for the European peoples.

Philologists were dictionary makers, but they were also historians of literature, and any literary history (like any dictionary) must decide what to put in and what to leave out, what to stress and what to shadow. There was a time when books like mine would have aspired to the *grand récit,* the big tale of development or progress told with equal scholarly attention to all moments of the history. That time, for literary historians, has largely passed. Traditional narratives of progress or development have given way to accounts that revel in details of the everyday. The epic history has yielded to assemblies of fragments, individual texts, and local analyses. Works such as *A New History of French Literature* and the companion volume, *A New History of German Literature,* break up their narratives into distinctive, at times year-by-year entries, some focusing on texts, some on events, some on authors.[11] Such an approach fits with a broader, recent turn in literary history to find value in works not just of high culture, but also of popular expression, technical history, or personal account. Such an approach, too, recognizes that the study of literary history remains less a study of progress toward a goal than an attempt to grapple with, and make narrative sense out of, disparate moments in the lives of readers, writers, and their books. "It is impossible to say," writes Denis Hollier, the editor of *A New History of French Literature*, where literature "starts and where it ends. . . . Literature wants to be everything—but beside itself. As a result, the question today is no longer . . . 'What is literature?' but rather, 'What is not?'"[12]

For a long time, what was *not* literature was the ephemeral, the popular, the feminine, the childish. National literary histories tended to ignore women writers, to slight the role of the popular press or the folktale, and to brush aside works of wide circulation that nonetheless did not seem to match the greatness of known authors. In response to these critical traditions, histories of children's literature have tended in the opposite direction: instead of analyzing, they celebrate; instead of discriminating, they list. There is a sense one gets, in reading through the bulk of children's literary history and criticism, that some precious truth has been irrevocably lost, as if the disciplines of theory or the skepticisms of the modern world have kept us from a wholeness from which we have been estranged. Just as we seek to find anew the innocence of childhood, so we have sought a golden age of children's literature.[13]

In spite of what such histories may tell us, there is no single golden age, no moment when the literature for and of children is better, more precise, or more effective than at any other moment. Children's literature is not some ideal category that a certain age may reach and that another may miss. It is instead a kind of system, one whose social and aesthetic value is determined out of the relationships among those who make, market, and read books. No single work of literature is canonical; rather, works attain canonical status through their participation in a system of literary values.[14] At stake is not, say, why *Alice in Wonderland* is somehow better than the books of Mrs. Molesworth; or why the many imitations of Defoe's *Robinson Crusoe* never quite measure up to their famous model. What is at stake, instead, is how successive periods define the literary for both children and adults, and how certain works and authors were established in the households, schools, personal collections, and libraries of the time.

If my history of children's literature builds on current cultural and theoretical concerns, it also speaks to commerce. Even before Newbery set up shop in the mid-eighteenth century, there was a book trade, and scribes, publishers, and editors included books for children in their inventories (it is significant that virtually every early printer throughout Europe published an Aesop as one of his first volumes). Newbery himself grounded his booklist in the educational theories of John Locke, and the British and American trade in children's books kept up his emphases for decades. In France, the city of Rouen became a center for the children's book trade in the eighteenth century, and by the late nineteenth the Paris firm of Pierre-Jules Hetzel set a standard for the making and the marketing of books for younger readers (Hetzel was Jules Verne's and Alexandre Dumas' publisher, and he put out the French translations of Scott's *Ivanhoe* and Cooper's *Last of the Mohicans*).[15] And in America, once public libraries became established, once prizes for children's literature were funded, once children's authors became arbiters of taste and tie-ins, children's literature became a public business.

Children's books are now the most profitable area of publishing, and links between traditional and innovative media establish younger readers as the prime market for imaginative writing. European and American demographics, too, point to a rise in the number of school-age children and a corresponding interest among parents not just for new books to read, but for a sense of history to children's reading. Hardly a day goes by when I do not read of somebody rediscovering a "classic" book or author for a new audience. Such accounts reveal, too, how the categories of the children's book are codified not just by writers and readers, but by book sellers, librarians, and publishing houses. To a large degree, the twentieth-century history of children's literature is a story of those institutions: of debates among librarians concerning audience and appropriateness; of medals and awards, reflecting social mores and commercial needs; of tie-ins, toys, and replications, in a range of media, of characters from children's books. Such media phenomena attest not only to the governing commodity economy in which the children's book now sits. They also constitute a form of literary reception in their own right. The marketing of Pooh or Pocahontas in the late twentieth century may not be too different from the harlequinades of the eighteenth, when booksellers sought ways of augmenting their readerships by offering these single-sheet, illustrated selections from well-known stories. The history of reading perennially links together commerce and interpretation.

The history of reading is also the history of teaching, and children's literature is an academic discipline.[16] Beginning in the 1970s—with the founding of such university-press journals as *Children's Literature* (Yale

University Press) and *The Lion and the Unicorn* (Johns Hopkins University Press)—children's literature became the object of formal study and the subject of professional inquiry. Part of this rise was spurred by the new modes of social history of the time. The emergence of family history as a discipline worked in tandem with the emphasis on first-generation feminist scholarship to seek out texts and authors unmarked by the traditional canon, as well as to rewrite traditional diplomatic narratives as stories of familial relations.[17] The women writers exhumed from historical neglect were often writers on the family, and on occasion writers and compilers of imaginative and didactic works for children.[18] So, too, as motherhood came to be understood as a form of labor, the acts of telling stories, writing books, or entertaining and instructing children came to be appreciated as acts of authorship.[19] These developments in social history had a profound impact on the direction of children's literature in the academy. As Jack Zipes, one of the leading critics of this field, summarizes, "Whereas the majority of academic books on children's literature written before 1972 tended to be bland literary histories that celebrated the good nature and intentions of children's literature with positivist methods and a paternalizing ideology to match, the more recent studies have probed the ulterior motives of children's literature and explored its socio-political and psychological ramifications."[20] Written in 1990, at the close of two decades of theoretical and political ferment, Zipes's review essay rightly notes the maintenance of the "radical efforts of different critical schools" in children's literary study, almost in the face of the politically conservative swing of American and European society. Two decades later, it can be perceived that children's literature as a university discipline reflects not just the theoretical preoccupations of the academic, but the technological manipulations of an information culture. The study of children's literature *is* cultural studies, not just in that it draws on literary, socio-historical, and economic methods of analysis, but in that it may serve as a test case for the syntheses of current cultural criticism. The discipline of children's literature now flourishes in the academy, and a goal of this book will be to provide a resource for its scholarship and a goad to future study.

Another goal of this new history of children's literature is to realign what has become a largely Anglophone focus for children's literary study.[21] All cultures have found ways of writing for their children: classical antiquity and medieval and Renaissance Europe; modern nations; pre-industrial societies. There remains something unique, however, about English-language traditions. The Puritan concern with childhood—the future of families, the question of the spiritual condition of the child, the emphasis on literate and catechismal education—dovetailed, in the course of the eighteenth century, with John Locke's theories of child-rearing and his philosophical commitment to the study of nurture and education to foster a distinctive place for children and their books in English literary history. John Newbery established the first press devoted to providing books for children in mid-eighteenth-century England. By the nineteenth century, English and American booksellers were investing heavily in marketing to families. American literary culture had developed a controlling metaphor of breaking with a British and paternalistic past, and childhood and children's development became controlling themes for many novels, plays, and poems, even if they did not have the young specifically as audiences.[22] In the late nineteenth century, the rise of Darwin's theory of evolution and the establishment of a British colonial empire also contributed to English-language children's literature: questions of human development, notions of political relationships of colonized and colonizer, and theories of racial identity all became subjects of a growing body of writings designed to instruct and entertain young readers.[23]

Across the arc of such an English literary history, writings for and about children have a unique status when compared with other European traditions. But this is not to say that other cultures have not had their children's books. In Germany, for example, *Struwwelpeter* and *Max und Moritz* lived beyond their nineteenth-century origins to influence the rise of comics in the early twentieth century. The Grimms' *Kinder- und Hausmärchen* spurred German-language interest in the social function of the children's book, and German organizations were founded long before those in Britain or America to promote children's literature.[24] The French *livre d'enfance et de jeunesse* had been a recognized category of book production since the eighteenth century, and French scholarship and criticism on the nature of these books predate *Babar* or Jules Verne.[25] In fact, the first major study of children's literary traditions published after the Second World War was by a scholar of French literature, Paul Hazard.[26] The *eventyr* of Hans Christian Andersen participate in a much broader Scandinavian tradition of the fable, fairy tale, and children's book. In the last decades of the twentieth century, Japanese anime and manga so recast the pictorial imagination of the child that it is now almost impossible to think of children's books, films, cartoons, and graphic narratives without seeing images from Pokémon or the work of Hayao Miyazaki.

Children's literature, in short, is world literature, and it would take another book at least as long as this one to account for all its current, global transformations.[27] And so, what this book may offer, in the end, is a prehistory of children's literary life in world culture. Because I am by temperament a scholar, I have attended primarily to scholarly, rather than popular, ways of engaging with the literatures of and for childhood. But I have attended, too, to the ways in which children's books often took scholarship as their theme. Reading and writing, list-making and literate organization become the central actions of the heroes and heroines of these stories. A wooden tablet from the Byzantine Egyptian town of Antinoopolis from about the fifth century AD has a text, in Greek: "Letters are the greatest beginning of understanding."[28] I have always believed this, and have followed this belief throughout this history of children's literature. But belief is not enough. Underneath this text, the teacher has signed his name, and underneath that signature, a student has attempted to copy the teacher's line. Badly spelled and poorly written, it is almost sad to see—a mangled version of a maxim about literacy. A millennium and a half later, Frederick Douglass recalled, in his autobiography, how he learned to write by copying the letters in between the lines of his young master's notebook.[29]

Moments such as these reveal something about the status of the discipline of children's literature. It is as if its story must be written in between the spaces of the masters, as if it remains but a cramped or simplistic version of "adult" writing. Nothing, of course, could be further from the truth. Recent criticism has made clear that children's literature exists *as literature*: that it has forms and genres, an imaginative scope, a mastery of figurative language, an enduring cast of characters, a self-conscious sense of authorship, a poetics, a politics, a prose style. This book may be read as a study of literature and literary culture in the broadest sense, one that centers on texts written for and read by children, but one that asks some basic questions: What is the social function of reading and writing? How do communities create themselves around audiences and readerships? What is the public role of authorship? Are people made, in essence, through the books they read?

*Docere et delectare*: to teach and to entertain. I hope I have done both here—or, at the very least, have shown how children's literature itself does both, and how we may find in the stories of our social past and personal present an illustration of how books shape our lives. To that end, there remains a personal, even autobiographical cast to this book. All critical accounts are personal: they rely on the tastes of readers and the constraints of the forms in which they are expressed. But anyone who has had children knows that reading (especially reading together) lies at the heart of familial bonding. As I have worked on this book, I have watched my son grow from a toddler to a teenager. I have studied his books and games, his fantasies and factual obsessions. This is a personal history, shaped by the tastes we two share, by memories of my own reading, by the syllabi I present for my students, and by the more than half a century I have lived as a father, son, American, and Jew.

Some readers may be disappointed that their favorite book is not included here, or not discussed in great enough detail. Some may object to the fact that there is scholarship and criticism at all, as if seeking to say something about any book destroys it. Some may object that at times, I write about books not traditionally classed as children's literature. Whatever their objections, at the very least I hope that readers will find templates for their own work: ways of reading books I have not discussed, ways of bringing texts into the ambit of the child's imagination, ways of understanding how a parent and a college professor adjudicates between the love of learning and learning how to love.[30]

No single volume has attempted the tasks I have set myself. Early histories, such as F. J. Harvey Darnton's *Children's Books in England* (originally published in 1932 and reprinted frequently thereafter), were specific, single-country accounts, often calibrated more to celebration than analysis. More recent general works, such as Perry Nodelman's *The Pleasures of Children's Literature*, tend to exhort the reader to accept the genre rather than to understand it fully, while the Oxford University Press book *Children's Literature: An Illustrated History*, though compiled by leading scholars in the field, retains the popularizing format suggested by its title (and also limits itself to English-language writing in the modern period). Many works of criticism focus on a single period or author. Several are encyclopedic in format. And many volumes offer selections from the great works of children's literary fiction, poetry, and drama. But this book is not quite like any of them, and the reasons may be personal as well.[31]

I began my career as a medievalist, and the move from medieval studies to the history of children's literature remains, for me, a critically coherent and a culturally central one. Far from being an age that had no perception of or investment in the child, the European Middle Ages was in many ways an *aetas puerorum*—an age preoccupied with the childhood of Christ and with his powerfully affecting infantility; one full of stories

of boy and girl saints, precious children often painfully constrained or
even tortured into holiness; a period concerned, too, with contemporary
children as the vehicle for the inheritance of wealth, land, and title, as
the mode of social and commercial advancement, and all too often as
the figurehead of kingdoms ruled by regents. The study of the Middle
Ages was, for me, a study of the cipher of the child in its political, artistic, literary, and economic environs.[32] But the child was, too, a metaphor
for much that later periods considered "medieval" in itself. Renaissance
and Enlightenment historians saw medieval Europe as a childish time, a
kind of cultural formation moment in the history of the West that they,
more modern figures, had outgrown. The educators of the sixteenth and
seventeenth centuries perceived such genres as romance and saint's life
as childish. So, too, the elaborate rituals of the pre-Reformation church
were viewed as somehow childish. Victorian historiography only confirmed this attitude, as medieval culture came to be represented in the
popular imagination as a world of fools and boy kings. Mark Twain, in his
*Connecticut Yankee in King Arthur's Court*, distills a generation of historical perception as he limns an Arthurian world—and in turn, a history of
medieval literature—in these terms. The world to which his Hank Morgan has been transported is populated by a "childlike and innocent lot,"
"great simple-hearted creatures" among whom "there did not seem to be
brains enough in the entire nursery," a group above whom Hank feels he
could establish himself as "a giant among pigmies, a man among children,
a master intelligence among intellectual moles."[33]

It is a short step from this view to the medievalizing of children's literature itself. Tales of romance or adventure were the stock in trade of
boys' or girls' books not simply because these tales were romantic or adventurous. Rather, it is the cultural location of a literature for children
in an earlier historical period that makes the pre-modern so essential to
an understanding of the history of children's books. In something like
the *Boy's King Arthur* (1880), cobbled together by Sidney Lanier from
Malory's *Morte d'Arthur*, we can see the inheritance and the anticipation of a medievalized child's reading. In the work of J. R. R. Tolkien and
C. S. Lewis, we see professional medievalists transforming philological
research and allegorical interpretation into moral tales for postwar England (whether that be the First or Second World War). A range of historical novels—often written in the spirit of Scott's *Ivanhoe*—drew not
just on medieval content but on the imagined speech of medieval English men and women, to coat their adventures with the patina of the

exotic. In movies from *Robin Hood* and *Ivanhoe* to *Excalibur* and *Braveheart*, in comics from *Prince Valiant* to *Beowulf 3000*, in computer entertainments from *Doom* and *Myst* to *Age of Empires*, we may witness the construction of a fantasy medieval culture for the popular, youthful imagination.

But the role of medieval culture in the history of children's literature is more complex than simply offering a mine of escapist matter. In many ways, the forms of children's literature are distinctively pre-modern, as they sustain the techniques of allegory, moral fable, romance, and symbolism. Such narrative devices—central to the literatures of classical, medieval, and Renaissance Europe—were abandoned, even denigrated, by the post-Enlightenment theorists of literature and by modern practitioners of poetry and fiction. Realism, history, social critique, and psychological depth have long been accepted as the common currency of "literature" in the modern period. Indeed, anything that seemed to depart from such literary forms and indulge in the allegorical, the fantastic, or the ostentatiously symbolic or romance-like would be labeled, in effect, subliterary: in a word, childish. The history of literary forms, written in the redefinition of the "modern," helps us understand the ways in which the pre-modern not just inflects but governs what we think of as a children's literature. To be a medievalist is to be granted a unique access to children's books, as one finds old techniques sustained to make new moral, educational, or social claims.

If I am a scholar, I am also a parent. To read to a child is to experience not just the pleasures of instruction or the warmth of entertainment, but the immense importance of quite simply *reading*. The bonds of literacy are the bonds of parenting, and the imaginative lives of children develop both in reading and in listening. In *The Braid of Literature*, Shelby Wolfe and Shirley Brice Heath urge the development of "one or another method of teaching reading or promoting children's literature [that] center on the moment of reading and its primary importance for the reader in making meaning from the text." They continue: "The words, images, attitudes, norms, and contradictions of the text spring up far beyond the actual episode of reading in new shapes and in other contexts and readings of different books. We see here how the initial reading of a literary text gives itself up to children's rereadings in the world. . . . The experience of reading lives on far beyond the act of reading."[34]

There may be no better literary case of such experience than when Marcel's mother reads to him in bed at the opening of Proust's *Remembrance of Things Past*. Calming the distressed boy, she sits down and reads George Sand's *François le Champi*—an odd choice for a little boy, as it describes the story of a woman who adopts an orphan and then has an incestuous relationship with him. Nonetheless, Marcel's mother excerpts and abbreviates: "When it was Mamma who was reading to me aloud she left all the love-scenes out." Mamma, the narrator goes on, "supplied all the natural tenderness, all the lavish sweetness which they demanded to phrases which seemed to have been composed for her voice, and which were all, so to speak, within her compass. She came to them with the tone that they required, with the cordial accent which existed before they were, which dictated them, but which is not to be found in the words themselves." She "breathed into this quite ordinary prose," he concludes, "a kind of life, continuous and full of feeling."[35]

Even the most ordinary prose becomes magical when read aloud at bedtime. And even the simplest-seeming of our children's books teaches something elegant and deep. Perhaps the first book I read to my son was *Goodnight Moon*, and in its catalogue of little objects, its repetitive idiom, and its lulling rhythm I found something that I later learned others had seen within it. Leonard Marcus, writing in his biography of that book's author, Margaret Wise Brown, suggestively analyzes the book's form and power in ways I had felt palpably.

> A little elegy and a small child's evening prayer, *Goodnight Moon* is a supremely comforting evocation of the companionable objects of the daylight world. It is also a ritual preparation for a journey beyond that world, a leave-taking of the known for the unknown world of darkness and dreams. It is spoken in part in the voice of the provider, the good parent or guardian who can summon forth a secure, whole existence simply by naming its particulars. . . . And it is partly spoken in the voice of the child, who takes possession of that world by naming its particulars all over again, addressing them directly, one by one, as though each were alive, and bidding each goodnight. . . . The sense of an ending descends gradually, like sleep.[36]

And yet, that ending is also a beginning. Marcus calls attention, in his analysis that follows, to relationships between the children's catalogue and the structures of fiction generally, alluding in particular to Twain's *Huckleberry Finn*. What I have come to realize is that our own acts of reading are thus educations in the arts of language: in the ways in which our words construct, reveal, or occlude the world of experience; in the power of words read and spoken to present a room familiar and yet always richly strange.

As a parent and a teacher, therefore, I argue for the continuance of books in an age marked by visual technology. There remains nothing like the feel of the book in the hand, nothing like the security offered by a book in the bed (an experience recorded in the West from at least the twelfth century).[37] "For young children," aver Wolfe and Heath, "entering the world of story through books is a sensory experience."[38] As the historian Roger Chartier puts it, "Reading is not just an abstract operation of intellect: it is an engagement of the body, an inscription in space, a relation of oneself and others."[39] If there is a future to children's literature, it must lie in the artifacts of writing and the place of reading in the home. To understand the history of children's literature is to understand the history of all our forms of literary experience. The children's book informs the adult narrative. The grown-up's novel becomes abridged or adapted for the child. Even such a simple rhyme as *Goodnight Moon* can teach the parent and the child about the nature of the elegiac and the act of reading that enhances our ending and beginnings.

*Goodnight Moon*, like many classics of the genre, ends with sleep. Lullabies make bedtime the locus of personal imagination and family bonding. The book as bedtime story, or as place of dreaming, is itself the lesson of the lector. Such are the ruses of the children's book, and such, too, are its joys. And who is to say which one of us, on closing stories and retiring to bed, will have the better dreams?

# Speak, Child

## CHILDREN'S LITERATURE IN
## CLASSICAL ANTIQUITY

From the beginnings of recorded culture, people have grown up with the books they learned and loved. Each stage of childhood marks itself through new curricula. Familiar stories are read again, and new authors added to the syllabus. For ancient Greece and Rome, the progress of the child was measured through the book, and if there is a "children's literature" for classical antiquity, it lies in the texts and tales adapted from the canons of the Greek and Roman lives and libraries.

For nearly a millennium, the life of children centered on performance. The two poles of early learning were memorization and recitation. Students would be given passages from poets and dramatists and would be expected to learn and then recite them. The teacher would call attention to correct pronunciation and accent. But more than simply spewing back remembered texts, the student would soon be expected to generate performances of his (or, on rare occasions, her) own. Literary study led to a proficiency in rhetoric, and law, politics, and military leadership were all rhetorical activities in Greek and Roman culture. To look for children's literature in classical antiquity, therefore, is to look at the history of rhetoric and education.[1]

But it is to look, too, at the history of childhood itself. Greek children had the stages of their lives measured in discrete levels of instruction. First there would have been the elementary teacher, called the *grammatistes* or *didaskalos*; then there was the *grammatikos*, charged with grammar and literature; and finally, the *rhetores* and *sophistai* would instruct in rhetoric and oratory. The goal for students, especially those of well-born families, was public life.[2] This was the goal for Roman students, too, though with some shifts from the Greek model. For what the Romans really did was to invent childhood as a distinctive social and cultural category. They celebrated, memorialized, cared for, and taught children in ways central to maintaining Roman ideology.[3] Virgil's *Aeneid* codified these claims in its representation of the hero as a son and father. "The image of Aeneas," writes Beryl Rawson, "rescuing father Anchises and son Ascanius from the burning city of Troy, a symbol of family devotion, became ubiquitous."[4] Pius Aeneas is, in large part, who he is because his *pietas* stems from devotion to the family. True, Hector shows affection for his son Astyanax, in a particularly touching moment in Homer's *Iliad* (6.466–502), and Greek literature is rich with episodes of filial devotion. But it was Rome that linked the child explicitly with civic (and ultimately imperial) politics.

The history of children's literature in antiquity is, therefore, interlinked with the differing histories of Greece and Rome. The Greeks may have loved their children, but the Romans celebrated them. Indeed, they came up with the birthday party for such purposes. In Roman civic life, time marked itself through annual celebrations, for which poems were written and rites performed. The child became the center of a civic life in which the state and family were closely connected. In his policies and patronage, the emperor Augustus Caesar linked together national and family history. The colonies of Rome were explicitly likened to the children of the fatherland—a *patria* now reinvested with the etymological resonances of that word.

Antique children's literature goes beyond the lists of texts that children read or an account of fables, excerpts, and instructions we may gather from them. It centered on the making of the child as citizen. The young Roman orator grew up to be, ideally, a senator, a defender, a prosecutor, or a judge. Declamation was a complex art, not just of speaking publicly, but also of impersonating others. Declamatory training focused on imagining particular legal situations in which a student could take up a prosecuting or defending role. Often, the student would be asked to speak in the voice of the accused or the accuser.[5] Declamation trained the young in an art of impersonation—a kind of fiction-making.

As nascent fiction-makers, Romans would have learned their artistry from reading other fictions. Homer's *Iliad*, Hesiod's *Theogony*, the tragedies of Euripides, the comedies of Menander, Virgil's *Aeneid*, the odes of Horace, the epigrammatists in Greek and Latin—these were mined not just for maxims or morality or examples of style, but for the personae of power. These works would have been excerpted into manageable sections. Different passages would be read at different ages. And, always, texts would be prepared for recitation. Education trained the student to put on new roles: the parent, the teacher, the god, the ruler. So, too, in his or her own life, the child would be expected to perform, whether it be as a student in the classroom or as a *filius* in the family. All the world was, indeed, a stage, and in his or her life each person played many roles. Horace's *Ars Poetica* had voiced this view long before Shakespeare appropriated it into his *As You Like It*.

And for the Greeks, too, education was performance. To read through the papyri, notebooks, tablets, and surviving shards of the Hellenic schoolroom is to read great speeches, dramatic displays, theatrical expostulations.[6] The thought of little boys pretending to be Homer's gods or heroes may bring smiles to modern faces, but to the Greeks these were the educative lines of power. For there were moments when the little child would certainly perform like a god (or, for that matter, like a parent). Slaves were the omnipresent extras of Greek and, later, Roman life. Nursemaids were often slaves; so were many teachers. Aesop, that father of the fable, was himself a slave, and the fables and the tales that circulated of his own life are rife with stories of the servant who upsets the master, or the child who dupes the parents.[7] Slavery is central to the history of children's literature, and it is nowhere more apparent than in classical antiquity. The *pedagogus* was the household servant who made sure the student made it to class and back. Well-born Roman children might have an entire entourage, from pedagogue to *capsarius* (the book bag carrier). From miming figures out of fiction, children learned how to order others, how to affirm a superior place in the social and familial world.[8]

Performance, reading, writing, slavery—all are the contexts for an understanding of the children's literature of classical antiquity. There are, of course, distinctions between Greek and Roman life and between the Hellenistic and the late antique classroom. But there are also powerful consistencies, traditions that extend into the early Christian environs of St. Augustine's Africa or Ausonius's Gaul. The study of children's literature of this period is not the study of particular works written for children, but instead the study of how preexisting texts were adapted for children: how Homer gets excerpted into schoolbooks, how Virgil was parsed, how plays and lyric poems could be reread and retaught with increasing complexity of grammatical, stylistic, and ethical analysis. "Studies, like men, have their infancy," wrote Quintilian in the first century AD (est sua etiam studiis infantia).⁹ Does children's literature have an infancy? To answer such a question, I begin with infants and the etymologies that illustrate just how the lives of children centered on the staged performances in schoolrooms and the fictional imaginations of their poets.

Midway through book 9 of the *Iliad*, Achilles seems to falter in his heroic resolve. Debate about continuing the war rages in the Greek camp, and the hero turns to his companion Odysseus to answer claims that have been made for staying on and fighting. If we fight and die, Achilles notes, home is gone but fame will be everlasting. But if we leave now, there will be a long life in the land of our fathers. The Greeks are stunned at these words. Is Achilles really leaving Troy? Soon, old Phoinix speaks up, calling Achilles his "dear child" and recalling how, when Achilles was a "mere child," he accompanied the boy to tutor him. That mere child, he says, "knew nothing yet of the joining of battle nor of debate where men are made pre-eminent." He goes on: "Therefore he [that is, Achilles's father] sent me along with you to teach you of all these matters, to make you a speaker of words and one who is accomplished in action."¹⁰

The Greek word for "child" that Phoinix uses is *nepion*, a word that means not simply child or boy (there were many options in the Homeric vocabulary), but specifically "the one who does not speak." *Nepion* comes from *ne + epos*, "no word" (the root *epos*, it should be added, is the source of *epic*). It is thus the Greek equivalent of the Latin term for a young child that would pass into the Romance languages, *infans* (*in + fans*: again, "not speaking"). That Greek and Roman cultures should define the earliest phase of childhood as a period without speech reflects not just an observational awareness of how children develop; it also reflects social and literary concerns. The life of the child was one of recitation. Literary works and public speeches were both forms of public performance; scholarship and heroism were linked as verbal actions. At this moment in the *Iliad*, when key decisions must be made, Phoinix recalls that moment in Achilles' life before he was a hero and a man: that is, before he knew anything of debate, before he had learned to be a speaker of words.

Speech and action, debate and battle are joined here much as they would be joined in Greek and Roman theories of education, and the image of old Phoinix would become, for later educators, an ideal of pedagogy. Quintilian, in his *Institutes of Oratory*, relies on his example on several occasions. "The teacher," he writes early in book 2, "should be as distinguished for his eloquence as for his good character, and like Phoinix in the *Iliad* be able to teach his pupil both how to behave and how to speak"

(2.3.12; see also 2.17.8). It was through skill at recitation (*recitatio*) that the pupil learned the culture's blend of eloquence and action. As Tacitus would put it, in his *Dialogue on Orators*, through this process the child comes to know about the things of this world, the nature of humankind, and public life (*res, homines, tempora*).[11]

To be a *nepion* or *infans* was thus to be before speech: to be not quite a person at all. It was as if selfhood emerged through linguistic performance. Children, almost as soon as they could talk, would be called on at family gatherings or public festivals to share in games or recitations. As early as the fourth or fifth century BC, Greek girls performed songs and games; one famous, enigmatic one was the so-called tortoise game, where the girls would sing a verse or two about the animal and then leap on one another. Roman children, too, were well known for their performances, on occasion offering up songs, poems, and bits of drama to their families at dinner. A document from 105 AD records a public festival in which young children were expected to compete in recitation—children who were chosen not only for their family's political connections, but also for their literary achievements. The Latin of this document describes these children as descending from *summi viri* (the best of men) and *magna ingenia* (men of great imagination or invention).[12] Manliness and intellect: such qualities recall the relationship between action and word as advised by old Phoinix, or between character and eloquence as taught by Quintilian.

These words describe not only the people who performed, but the quality of texts themselves. Epics and lyrics, tragedies and comedies were subject to close analysis precisely for their presentations of the character of people and their mental feints. A remarkable papyrus fragment from the third century AD contains portions of a poem on the labors of Hercules, complete with colored illustrations. The story of the hero and the Nemean Lion appears in what Raffaella Cribiore describes as an "elementary text written in simple style and diction and crude meter."[13] Text and illustration are arrestingly marked out for the untrained eye. Words are written separately (an unusual thing in either Greek or Latin) to facilitate not simply reading, but oral recitation as well. And there is still enough color in the pictures to evoke the realism of the scene: Hercules is blond, the grass green, the lion tawny.

The labors of Hercules had long been seen as something of an allegory of the education or development of the young. Each task was an assignment, each accomplishment a test passed with flying colors. The myth resonates with student experience, and the details of this fragmentary

Fig. 1. Papyrus text of the labors of Hercules. Oxyrhynchus papyrus 22.2332,
3rd c. AD. Reproduced from Raffaella Cribiore, *Gymnastics of the Mind*
(Princeton, NJ: Princeton University Press, 2001), p. 139.

version would as well. It is a dialogue, as far as we can tell. Some "inarticulate country bumpkin" (*deinos agroikos*) comes up to the hero: "'Speak,
child of Olympian Zeus, tell me what was your first labor,' I said. And he
teaches me: 'I first did this . . .'."[14] It is a dialogue of instruction, a twisting
of the roles of student and teacher. Hercules appears here not generally
as hero or as man but specifically as *pai Zenos Olympiou*, child of Olympian Zeus. His paternity, his status as a son, is paramount. But then, in
answering, he becomes the teacher, telling the fool of the great exploits.
The language is colloquial; the meter, in Cribiore's words, "crude." It is
not so much a high literary text for students as it is, perhaps, something
of a children's book itself: a little illustrated drama for the reader weary
of rhapsodes and grammarians. And in its thematic attention to speech
itself—an attention evidenced even in its fragmentary state—this story
goes back to the traditions of performative, rhetorical culture. "Speak,
child": that is the great injunction of all of these texts, and if that speech
is handled well, one may be thought if not heroic, then at least better than
an inarticulate bumpkin.

"Speak, child." St. Augustine recalled such an injunction when, in his
*Confessions*, he recounts a boyhood in which he was compelled to memorize and recite classic texts.[15] In a memorable moment in book 1, he remarks that were it not for a certain passage in one of Terence's comedies,

we should never have heard of certain key words of the poetic vocabulary. But then he goes on:

> Terence brings on the stage a dissolute youth who excuses his own fornication by pointing to the example of Jupiter. He looks at a picture painted on the wall, which "shows how Jupiter is said to have deceived the girl Danae by raining a golden shower into her lap." These are the words with which he incites himself to lechery, as though he had heavenly authority for it: "What a god he is! His mighty thunder rocks the sky from end to end. You may say that I am only a man, and thundering is beyond my power. But I played the rest of the part well enough, and willingly too."[16]

It is, of course, a passage about moral wickedness, one that Augustine will moralize here and in several of his other writings. But it is also a passage that concerns theatrical performance—imitating action and imagining a role beyond that of the mere man. It is a story of the boy placed on stage; as such, it resonates profoundly with the picture Augustine will paint immediately afterward of how, as a boy, he had to recite the goddess Juno's speech from the opening of the *Aeneid*: "We were compelled to make believe and follow the flight of the poet's fancy by repeating in prose what he had said in verse. The contest was to be won by the boy who found the best words to suit the meaning and best expressed feelings of sorrow and anger appropriate to the majesty of the character he impersonated" (1.17, p. 37). Exercises such as this one were played out in Roman schoolrooms for at least three centuries before he wrote. Quintilian, for example, advocates assignments in which students recast verse into prose in a way that preserves the passage's poetic sense. This is not simply recitation, but creation: the student forms himself as both a reader and a writer, much as Augustine throughout the *Confessions* shows himself transforming both Virgilian and scriptural verse into expressive Latin prose.

The character from Terence played his part well and willingly. So, too, did Augustine. He recognized that being a child is in large part being a performer—following the dictates of the teacher, living up to the expectations of the parent, taking on the public dares of peers. The early books of the *Confessions* are famously filled with theater pieces: from the explicit account of his adolescent obsession with the plays at Carthage to the more figurative story of the theft of the pears (a staged performance if ever there was one).

The *Confessions* is a good guide to the survival of an educational tradition well into the late colonial period and, geographically, far from Rome itself. Cicero, Virgil, Terence, and Sallust all appear early in the autobi-ography, illustrating the impress of these four basic school authorities on the young Augustine.[17] But Homer came first, as he had for nearly a thou-sand years—even if it was to Augustine's displeasure: "Why did I dislike Greek literature, which tells these tales, as much as the Greek language it-self? Homer, as well as Virgil, was a skillful spinner of yarns and he is most delightfully imaginative. Nevertheless, as a boy, I found him little to my taste. I suppose that Greek boys think the same about Virgil when they are forced to study him as I was forced to study Homer" (1.14, p. 34).

Young boys had been forced to study Homer as a model of style, as a repository of myth, as a cultural encyclopedia, and as, quite simply, the poetic author *par excellence* of the classical world. Greek education (and, in turn, Roman education grounded in Greek models) began with the memorizing and parsing of Homeric scenes. A millennium of evidence survives: papyri and wooden boards covered with school texts, exercises, and notes.[18] To read through them is to see the hands of teacher and student forming letters and recording passages. Sometimes the texts are written out with each word separated into syllables (for easy reading, one assumes). Sometimes the texts come with grammatical or stylistic commentary. Words find their glosses, sentences their parts of speech, in both the assured writing of the master and the scrawl of the child. On a wooden tablet from the third century AD, a teacher has written out a portion of the *Iliad* for student study. The letters are large and clear, the initials even larger. The text is book 2, lines 132–62, a passage rich with alternating speeches, brilliant epic similes, and—at the start—a reference sure to stir the heart of any child. Agamemnon is speaking:

> Already have nine years of great Zeus gone by, and lo, our
> ships' timbers are rotted, and the tackling loosed; and our wives,
> I imagine, and little children [*nepia tekna*] sit in our halls awaiting us.[19]

Whatever child was reading and reciting from this tablet would have waited in a hall not for the heroic return of the father-king, but for the appearance of the teacher. As in the Phoinix scene from book 9, children stand as infants before scenes of martial speech. The Greek adjective *nepia* in this passage comes from *nepion*—the *nepia tekna* are not simply little children, but unspeaking infants. And from the silence of these imagined waiting infants, Homer moves to tell of the effect of Agamemnon's speech: a rousing of the hearts of men.

And even as when the West Wind at its coming stirs a deep cornfield
with its violent blast, and the ears bow under it, even so was all
their gathering stirred, and they rushed to the ships with loud shouting.[20]

This is the rhetorical Homer, the Homer of the great speeches, great similes, great outbursts. Little wonder that book 2 was one of the favorite instructional sections of the *Iliad*. There was, of course, the catalogue of ships, valued by ancient teachers for its specificity of detail and its geographical and genealogical instruction. But there were also scenes such as the one held on this tablet: scenes of pathos and drama couched in epic simile. Evidence from early papyri strongly suggests that teachers favored the great similes of the *Iliad* not only for teaching poetic technique, but also for illustrating how such similes evoked the humble and the everyday experience of common life (here, the wind coming through a cornfield) juxtaposed against the drama of a heroic past. In memorizing and repeating such scenes, the ancient student could display his skills at oral recitation and, in the process, gain idioms for and insight into the kinds of rhetorical and forensic displays he might make as an adult.

The drama of Homeric epic shared space with the language of the dramatists themselves in many early student papyri and notebooks. A Greek scroll from Egypt in the third century BC keys its texts to oral recitation and the thematics of public performance. It begins with lists of letters and syllables, followed by sets of numbers, lists of proper names (mythological figures, places, rivers), and then words of three, four, and five syllables. What follows this little primer is a miniature poetic anthology—a collection of passages that constitute a kind of canon of children's literature for the Hellenistic student. Central is a Homeric text, lines 116–24 from book 5 of the *Odyssey*. Preceding it are passages from Euripides' *Phoinissai* and *Ion*, and following it are sets of epigrams (one on a fountain, another on a monument to Homer) and poetic fragments from comic plays centering on humorous caricatures of cooks. The roll ends with a set of basic mathematical exercises.[21] The literary selections here are graded for difficulty. They have a moral content and epigrammatic flavor. They emphasize the details of both mythological and everyday life. These are texts full of new words for the student, and, read in sequence, they present examples of the major literary genres of the age: tragedy, epic, epigram, and comedy.

Look closely at the opening literary selection from the *Phoinissai*. Written out in separated syllables, this scene presents a powerful maternal figure

(Jocasta) offering moral advice to her son, Eteocles. In modern translation, it reads:

> No, experience
> Can plead more wisely than the lips of youth.
> Why, son, do you grasp at ambition,
> Worst of deities? Do not: she is the queen of wrong.
> She enters many homes and happy cities,
> But she does not leave until her votaries are ruined.[22]

It is an important passage, not just for its moral content, but for its dramatic voice. For what we have here is not just some disembodied set of maxims, but a theatrical moment—a performance in which the text speaks directly to the youthful student, a performance in which the young reader becomes inextricably involved.

It is no accident that this is a woman's voice, for female figures of authority stand prominent in classical instructional literature, from Plato's Diotima to Boethius's Lady Philosophy. It is also no accident that the passage from the *Odyssey* that follows the Euripidean fragments gives the words of another powerful female—Kalypso, here complaining to Hermes that she must let Odysseus go.

> So he [Hermes] spoke, and Kalypso, the beautiful goddess, shuddered, and she spoke and addressed him with winged words: "Cruel are you, O you gods, and quick to envy above all others, seeing that you begrudge goddesses that they should not mate with men openly, if any takes a mortal as her dear bedfellow. Then, when rosy-fingered Dawn took Orion to herself, you gods that live at ease begrudged her, till in Ortygia chaste Artemis of the golden throne assailed him with her gentle shafts and slew him."[23]

The passage fascinates for many reasons. Embedded in it is the larger myth of Eos and Orion, of Artemis and her killing arrows, and of strange places such as Ortygia. There is the fantasy of female domination, of the seductions of goddesses and men. But there is, as in the selection from the *Phoinissai*, the larger moral sense that men are men and have their missions, that the temptations of ambition or desire only waylay or ruin them. Two female voices—vibrant and dramatic—address the student reader, instructing him in the details of myth and the moralities of human action.

This *is* a volume about speech and action, a collection of performances that provoke the student to engage in dramas of instruction and delight.

Homer himself appears in a fragmentary epigram in this collection not just as a poet, but as a warrior too. And at the close of the literary section of this scroll, Homer's words show up, but now in comic mouths. The final literary selection comes from Straton's *Phoenicides*, a dialogue that features a character complaining that a certain cook is using a rare, and thus confusing, Homeric vocabulary. The passage centers on an argument about sacrificial ritual, and it deploys a string of unusual, technical words for that ritual (for example, certain specialized terms for the cuts of meat or their preparation). The words are so weird that one of the characters says that he needs to get the books of Philitas (the author of a list of rare words) to figure them out. In a modern translation, the concluding lines of this passage read: "But I begged him, changing my tone, to say something normal. But Persuasion herself could not have persuaded him even if she was standing right there. I think this scoundrel has been a slave from childhood of some sort of rhapsode, to be filled up with the words of Homer."[24] This is a remarkable literary moment. Aside from the humor of the passage, aside from the words it would have taught the student reader, it reflects directly on the very processes of learning that this volume is designed to reproduce. For it is, in effect, a volume of weird words, a collection of literary and, especially, Homeric idioms designed to fill up the student with both literary and cultural awareness. Have all our students been mere slaves of childhood to some sort of rhapsode? Is our education little more than the ingestion of exotic language—a language much like a feast of foreign delicacies?

This passage, like the ones that immediately precede it, has to do with cooks. The cook was a stock figure of New Comedy, in both Greek and Latin. With his recipes and spices, he often came off as something of a walking lexicon of culinary exotica. He could please his master and seduce the young, sate and amaze. He brought together disparate things into well-crafted wholes. Much like the poet or the playwright, the cook was servant and savant, and cooks stood throughout the comic tradition as figures for poetic creativity. The cooks that fill the sides of this papyrus are no different, and their speeches ripple with weird words and brilliant flourishes.

Not just comic cooks, but comic actors could be models for the education of the young. Quintilian, writing in the Roman first century AD but deeply influenced by centuries of Greek tradition, advocates the comic actor (*comoedus*) as a model for the future orator. True, the student should avoid the excesses of the stage; but in seeking to learn "how narrative should be delivered," how tone should be authoritative, or how excitement should be measured, the student should turn to the *comoedus* for example. Passages should be memorized and performed, and they should be selected, Quintilian states, for their appropriateness in training the orator. The student "should have a careful and efficient teacher at his side not merely to form his style of reading aloud, but to make him learn select passages by heart and declaim them standing in the manner which actual pleading would require: thus he will simultaneously train delivery, voice and memory" (1.11.14). In this papyrus scroll, with its dramatic and Homeric passages, its comic scenes, and its epigrams, we find the teacher's hand preparing texts for training students in delivery, voice, and memory.

The Greek traditions of instruction I have represented through these texts survived well into the Roman world. Quintilian argued that the first language of the well-born child should be Greek precisely to allow him access to these educational traditions. Why, he asked, "since children are capable of moral training, should they not be capable of literary education" (1.1.17)? The primary texts of that education remained largely Greek: Homer, the lyrics, the tragedies and comedies (we can assume, too, that when Quintilian speaks of Aesop's fables, he is referring to their Greek transmission; see 1.9.2). Of course, there was Latin literature too, especially the works of Virgil, Horace, and Cicero (1.8.5ff.). But Roman literary models, at least for children, do seem to have been largely grounded in their Greek antecedents. Even the reading of Virgil, as early as the first century AD, centered to some extent on identifying the Roman poet's debts to Homer and the Greek tragedians. Centuries later, the late antique commentaries on the *Aeneid* still concerned themselves with noting parallels between Virgil's text and Homer's.

Like Homer, Virgil had become a schoolroom author. With its great speeches, set-piece similes, and epic range, the *Aeneid* had become a staple of study and recitation long before Augustine had been "obliged," as he recalled in the *Confessions*, "to memorize the wanderings of a hero named Aeneas" (1.13). Augustine "wept for Dido," much as schoolboys had been weeping for her over the previous three centuries (even in Ovid's day, the story of Dido and Aeneas was the most popular). Schoolboy scribblings drawn from the *Aeneid* seem to have begun almost as soon as the poem was put in circulation. Virgilian graffiti have been found on Roman Forum walls, and such famous phrases as the poem's opening, "Arma virumque cano," can still be read on the ruins of Pompeii.

Virgil was taught in the schools in much the same way that Homer was. Grammatical and stylistic analysis predominated. Selections from his text were set for recitation.[25] But it was not simply that the poem offered students object lessons in behavior or occasions for extracting moral precepts from its lines. It was that the *Aeneid*, in the large, recounted a story of paternal care and filial devotion. Anchises, Aeneas, Ascanius—in these three generations lay the Roman ideologies of national and family history. To teach the *Aeneid* in a world filled with the statues, coins, and friezes of Roman fatherhoods was to associate the *patria* with the *paternitas* of teaching. Study became moral growth, an argument played out in the late antique and medieval commentaries on book 6 of the poem, where Aeneas's descent into the underworld was understood as an allegory of education. The encounters with the enigmatic Sibyl, with the golden bough, and with the shade of Anchises himself in that book stood, for nearly a thousand years, as set pieces of (and for) instruction. Anchises lectures Aeneas among the dead: he instructs him in the origins of human life, gives him a sense of ancient history, and predicts the future of their yet unborn descendants and the future of Rome's power. Aeneas comes upon *pater Anchises* in the underworld as if the old man were some aged sage, some scholar "lost in thought, ... studying the souls of all his sons to come."[26] And the son listens to the lectures, asks his questions, hears the story of his future. Anchises says: I will teach you of your fate. It is a fate of future sons, a history of Rome expressed in terms of children.

One of the most publicly mourned of those children would be Marcellus, the beautiful yet doomed son of Augustus Caesar and Octavia, who would die at nineteen.[27] The Romans mourned their dead children with a passion unmatched by almost any other culture, and the statues, plaques, and stelae to their memory reflect their parents' sense of loss over unfulfilled dreams. "O nate" (O son), Anchises begins at line 868, do not seek out that great sorrow of your people—in other words, do not ask about the fate of Marcellus. For twenty lines we get Anchises' speech about this boy, a model elegy for Rome's unrealized hopes. He was the golden boy, the son of Octavia and the nephew and son-in-law of Augustus Caesar, on whom Rome had placed its dynastic hopes. He died in the year 23 BC. Donatus records that when Virgil, in his recitation of book 6 before Augustus and Octavia, came to the words "Tu Marcellus eris," Octavia took it so hard she had to be revived.[28] Servius commented on how the whole Roman citizenry lamented Marcellus's death, how Augustus himself spoke at the funeral, and how Octavia wept silently throughout Virgil's recitation of this passage.[29]

Virgil's performance would inspire others. Cicero, for example, in his *De Oratore*, used the texts of epic and tragedy to illustrate how the young student could give voice to emotion.[30] Much like the passage from book 6 of the *Aeneid*, or for that matter like the selections from Homer in the Hellenistic papyri, Cicero's selections are thematically concerned with childhood, parenting, and power. Take, for example, Cicero's first example, from a play by Accius on the house of Atreus (recalling the horrible scene of eating one's children):

> Why, my very brother bids me miserably chew up
> My own children.
> (3.58.217; translation modified by me)

Or this line from Ennius's *Andromache*:

> O father, O my country, O Priam's palace!
> (3.58.217)

Or the last in Cicero's sequence of quotations, from Pacuvius's *Iliona*:

> What time did Paris mate with Helen, wedlock that no wedlock was,
> I was with child, and now the months were ended and my time was near;
> 'Twas at that season Hecuba gave birth to Plydore, her last.
> (3.58.219)

In the words of the historian Stanley Bonner, scenes such as these "must have been read aloud by schoolboys and would leave a lasting impression in their minds."[31] But these are not just scenes of rhetorical or dramatic display. They call attention to the overwhelming pathos of the parent-child relationship in time of crisis. They invite the reciting student to take on parental roles. In the process, such a student may imagine, or impersonate, the kind of adult he may well become—or, at the very least, the kind of adult dramatized in Roman literature.

But just what kind of adult was the Roman? Surely, everyday life was far from the Homeric or Virgilian idiom. Things happened; people woke up, ate, went off to school or public service, and came home. In such a world, the sites of childhood power lay not with subverting parental control, but with mastering the servants. The slaves were everywhere, and nowhere more apparent to the reader of an ancient children's literature than in the texts known as the hermeneumata. These were colloquies—

little dialogues, sometimes in Latin, sometimes in both Greek and Latin, that reveal daily life and daily lessons. Lists of words and bits of literary texts make up the beginning readings for the child. Most of their content is either adorable or trivial, but every now and then something emerges to reveal the relationships of literary education and social control central to Roman and colonial life.[32]

These hermeneumata survive in late (often medieval) manuscript copies. In several such manuscripts, scholars have found a colloquy in various forms—a bilingual narrative in which the child speaks, often giving orders to the slave or describing what he himself would do throughout his day. It probably originates from Gaul in the third or fourth century AD, and thus it shows us something of the life of the child in the late colonial Roman world.[33] I love the opening, in which the child wakes up and commands the nursemaid: "Dress me and put my shoes on; it is time, it is the hour before dawn, so that we should get ready for school." This episode is filled with lists of words for different kinds of clothing. Each article is fetched, gets put on, and is recorded. All of the different family and household members are duly catalogued. And when the child gets to school, he warmly greets the teachers, and they greet him back. He calls for his book and tablets. He lists all the terms for reading and writing, calculating and reciting. He lists all the forms of speech, all the constituents of words. And he lists all the texts he reads: first, selections from the *Iliad* and then the *Odyssey*; then all the subjects for discussion (for example, the causes of the Trojan War); and then all the major authors in both Greek and Latin: Cicero, Ovid, Lucan, Statius, Terence, Sallust, Theocritus, Thucydides, Demosthenes, Hippocrates, Xenophon. The student recites, and he takes notes. Then he goes home for lunch.

This colloquy reveals how the child could be educated as a master. Slaves and servants are the objects of attention here. Get me this, get me that. The child becomes a figure of mastery, a kind of proto-adult, through mimicry of grown-up order-giving. Now, slavery loomed large in antique childhood for philosophical as well as social reasons. Greek writers often portrayed children as little more than slavelike. Plato noted in the *Republic* that "the great mass of multifarious appetites and pleasures and pains will be found to occur chiefly in children and women and slaves."[34] But unlike slaves, children (especially well-born children) could be educated to outgrow their foolishness or ineptitude.[35] Thus, many of the stories I have surveyed here—tales of heroic action, speeches of divinities, comic interludes with servants—illustrate the ways in which the child could learn to grow. Ventriloquisms of the parent become voicings of the master, and whether a student takes on the role of a god or a hero, he is taking on the pose of power.

The slave was never far from children's literature.[36] Slaves and servants live in its fictions and its maxims. Recall the papyrus collection of Greek literary excerpts that concluded with the speeches of the cooks, which show just how such slaves were figures central to the comic imagination. Or think, now, of Aesop's fables, filled with bad slaves, indentured servants, and their varied masters.[37] There is the fable of the man who falls in love with an ugly and ill-natured slave girl and gives her everything she wants. Dressed and adorned in this finery, she argues incessantly with the mistress of the house. The slave girl believes Aphrodite is the one behind her master's largesse. But one night the goddess comes to her and says, "Do not thank me, as if I were the one making you beautiful; I'm angry with your lover for thinking you beautiful." The moral of this story, in the version passed down into the Greek of the fabulist Babrius, reads: "Every man who rejoices in ugly things as though they were fair and good is god-cursed and blind of heart."[38] It is a fable that affirms the lowliness of slaves—their ugliness and foolishness. But it is also a fable of instructions to the young and inexperienced: cherish the beautiful; do not deceive the simpleminded; don't be a besotted fool.

Consider, too, the fables of the runaway slave. One Aesopic tale tells of an owner who finds his fugitive slave hiding in a mill: "Where would I have rather found you than here?" (p. 510). What better place, in other words, to catch a slave than in a site of servitude, a mill where harnessed animals turn the grindstones? Where does the slave belong? these fables ask. Another one concerns Aesop himself and a runaway. The slave confides in Aesop, complaining about his master's bad treatment, even though he himself has done nothing wrong. Aesop counters: "Now then, listen, these are the hardships that you suffer, according to your account, when you have done no wrong; what if you commit an offence? What do you think you will suffer then?" The slave thinks about it and returns home (pp. 401–3). Be content with your station, the fable advises. But this fable, more than just advising servile life, has to have resonated with the life of the young student, who was often beaten, badly treated, and ill-handled by his pedagogic masters (stories from Roman life, in particular, are full of mean-spirited old teachers, the most notorious of whom, Orbilius, was remembered famously by Horace as a flogger and a crank).[39] How much these stories of the runaway slave must have piqued the imagination of the student, seemingly indentured to capricious teachers.

These tales, like so many fables, are tales of power and control. The moral of the fable lies invariably with status, class, and birth: be content with who you are; do not aspire to rise above your station; respect those above you; keep things in the order of nature. But Aesop himself was a slave, and an ugly one at that: "potbellied, misshapen of head, snub-nosed, swarthy, dwarfish, bandy-legged, short-armed, squint-eyed, liver-lipped."[40] Slaves *were* ugly, to Greek and Roman eyes; and for some writers (Quintilian, Pliny) they were incapable of artistic or literary expression. The worst thing a beginning orator could do, Quintilian notes, was to take on the posture of servility (11.3.83). But again, slaves were the teachers, the experts in technical professions, and the keepers of the young. The paradoxes of the slave emerge most clearly in the Latin verse of Phaedrus (himself a freed slave, a *libertus*), a compiler of Aesopica in the early first century AD. At the close of book 2 of his collection, we have an epilogue about the author, Aesop himself: "The Athenians set up a statue in honor of the gifted Aesop, and by so doing placed a slave on a pedestal of everlasting fame, that all men might know that the path of honor lies open and that glory is awarded not according to birth [*nec generi*], but according to merit [*sed virtuti*]."[41] These verses may stand as something of a little fable of their own: a moral story illustrating a condition of life. *Nec generi, sed virtuti*, not through birth but according to merit: such may well be the epigraph for a tradition of children's education that—paradoxically, but always practically—sought to maintain the class lines of inheritance and power and, at the same time, to espouse an ideal of instruction that could raise the child above himself. Those little dead in Beryl Rawson's *Children and Childhood in Roman Italy* got their fame and their statuary. Indeed, she opens her book with a picture and discussion of Q. Sulpicius Maximus, dead at age eleven—a "budding orator" shown holding his school scroll, with his epitaph and his own poetry inscribed beneath him. Rawson's analysis of his name and of the contexts for this statue reveals that he was a first generation freeborn citizen; his parents were most likely slaves. "Through education," she notes, "they hoped to help their son build on his superior status to achieve social standing, wealth, and influence higher than their own."[42]

Phaedrus's poem on Aesop and this sad statue come together at my close to illustrate what I had presented, at my opening, as the environments for understanding children's literature in classical antiquity: performance, reading, writing, and slavery. The child lived on the stage set of familial and public life. Recitation lay at the core of literary instruction, and the texts copied on papyrus scrolls or waxed tablets often provided performative models from great literature. And what these texts taught were not simply moral maxims, but habits of control. Children could be masters in the house; yet children of the slaves, too, could achieve beyond their birth to gain a path of honor through their merit. Phoinix advised Achilles to become a speaker of words and a man of action; children performed in Rome, drawn from families of *summi viri* and *magna ingenia*; and Aesop's fame lives on, much like that of little Q. Sulpicius Maximus, *nec generi, sed virtuti.*

These oppositions will govern the legacies of antique children's literature. Character and wit, birth and learning—these are the axes along which we may chart children's reading. And when they read Aesop, in particular, they will find a menagerie of actors trying to make sense of fears and foibles. The Aesopica, as we shall see, brings together all the strands of antique children's literature, not just for the students of the ancient world, but for those of the Middle Ages, Renaissance, and modern ages.

# Ingenuity and Authority

## AESOP'S FABLES AND THEIR AFTERLIVES

No author has been so intimately and extensively associated with children's literature as Aesop. His fables have been accepted as the core of childhood reading and instruction since the time of Plato, and they have found their place in political and social satire and moral teaching throughout medieval, Renaissance, and modern cultures.[1] We know almost nothing of the historical Aesop, yet we know a great deal about the transmission and transformation of his tales—the making of what modern scholars call the Aesopica. Much recent scholarship has detailed this complex history. But much recent literary criticism has come anew to fable as one of the defining genres of Western literature. Studies of classical and medieval educational practice have proliferated; critical accounts of early modern translations have grown; and theoretical responses to the form have inflected literary study in the large. In reading through this literature, one realizes that fables long ago escaped the confines of the nursery and the schoolroom. Their readerships have included parents as well as children, masters as well as slaves, rulers as well as subjects.

But fables still remain a defining form of children's literature. Their narratives return, again and again, to central episodes in childhood life: learning to read and write, learning to please and fool the parent, learning to chart a moral path through temptation. Whatever purposes adults have put them to, they remain at the core of children's reading. In addition to their local morals or their specific injunctions, the fables teach ideas of authorship, notions of audience, ideals of verbal action—in short, literature itself.

Though fables have appeared in virtually all recorded languages, the literary language of the Aesopica remains the vernacular. Its language was, in origin, the language of the slave—that of Aesop himself, or of the nursemaids and servants who would later tell them to the young under their charge. Our word *vernacular* comes from the Latin *verna*, a female household servant, and we might well say that the history of the fable *is* the history of the vernacular. This is the language of the subordinate, and it is significant that fables were associated with the serving classes from earliest antiquity. Later fabulists always make a point of how they translated or transformed their sources from this world—how they made something literate out of an oral tale, something poetic out of prose, something fit for privilege out of the base clay of fools. Aesop always existed to be translated, and the history of his fables is a history of language change and textual transmission.

But language change and textual transmission are what fables are about. The Latin word *fabula* comes from the root *fari*, to tell. Fables are told things. Quintilian, in the first century AD, acknowledged as much when he relegated them to the purview of nursemaids. But this is precisely the point. The story of the fable is the story of the shift from oral performance to writing. The pupil, Quintilian argued, "should learn to paraphrase Aesop's fables, the natural successors of the fairy stories of the nursery, in simple and restrained language and subsequently to set down this paraphrase in writing with the same simplicity of style [*stilo*]."[2] Compare this advice with a remarkable scene from the *Golden Ass* of Apuleius, composed less than a century later. Having heard a fantastic story told by a crazy, drunken old woman to a captive girl, the story's narrator laments: "I stood far off, grieving by Hercules that I had no tablet and pen to note down so pretty a fable."[3] These passages show the desire to transform popular speech into written form. They dramatize the shift from fables' origin with women, nurses, the illiterate, and the crazed to their reception by men, teachers, the literate, and the sane.

Such is the history of the fable and the story of Aesop's place in the worlds of children's literature. My purpose here is not to trace the history of his fables and their critical reception as a whole (that would demand a book all its own). Nor is it even to describe all of the ways in which the fables have become a part of children's literature (again, another dissertation). Instead, I show how the fables constitute a literary system, a world through which the child may reimagine the institutions, individuals, and idioms of everyday experience. And in the course of tracing that imagining, we may recover not just children's notions of the world, but our own adult fantasies of what that world might be.[4]

Aesop's impact on Greek education was almost immediate. In addition to works by Homer, the dramatists, and the epigrammatists, the fables were at the heart of early reading and writing. A telling moment appears early on in Aristophanes' *The Birds* (first performed in 414 BC). The Athenian Pisthetairos is trying to explain to the bird Koryphaios how the birds once ruled the world. The birds are older than men, older even than the gods. How does he know? From reading Aesop, of course, whose fable of the lark affirmed that it was the oldest thing in the world. Pisthetairos chides the bird: "You are without any education and completely without interest in many things, and you haven't even read Aesop."[5] *Amathes* is Pisthetairos's first word, Greek for "without learning or schooling." The line implies that Aesop was already in the schools by Aristophanes' day—that anyone who did not know his Aesop had not even started class. "The Athenian," writes one modern scholar, "lived in the world of the Aesopic Fable. From it the child learned reading and writing and the Greek way of life."[6]

Fables rely on figurative language. They take parts for wholes, draw on particulars for generalizations, make mute creatures speak. Their status in the nursery or in the classroom rests not simply on their moral or didactic goals, but on their metaphorical enchantment. They are, quite simply, literature at its most simple and direct, and instruction in the fable is a lesson in the arts of the literary imagination. Socrates recognized this quality. In Plato's *Phaedo*, Socrates' friends appear and ask him why, in prison on the day set for his execution, he is turning Aesop into verse. He reports that he had a dream in which he was told, "Make music and work at it." And so, he says, "since I was not a maker of myths, I took the myths of Aesop, which I had at hand and knew, and turned into verse the first I came upon." And he goes on, reflecting on the nature of pleasure and pain:

> They will not both come to a man at the same time, and yet if he pursues the one and captures it, he is generally obliged to take the other also, as if the two were joined together in one head. And I think . . . if Aesop had thought of them, he would have made a fable telling how they were at war and god wished to reconcile them, and when he could not do that he fastened their heads together.[7]

Aesop becomes a touchstone for an understanding of life itself. Socrates recognized that the heart of the Aesopic fable is a form of impersonation: of animating the inanimate, of turning abstractions into realities.

Such metamorphoses are everywhere in the fables, but perhaps nowhere more central to the youthful reader than in those concerned with education and its implements. Take, for example, the story of the thief and his mother (Perry 200). A schoolboy stole a writing tablet from another student and took it home to his mother. Instead of scolding him for stealing, she praised him. So, soon afterward, he stole a cloak and gave it to her. She praised him again. As he grew up, he continued to steal, and she continued to praise. One day he was caught in the act and sentenced to death. Just before his execution, he went to whisper to his mother, but instead bit off her ear. To her denunciation he replied, "If you had punished me long ago, when I gave you that stolen school tablet, I would never have progressed as a thief to the point where I would be led to my death here."

The moral of the story seems transparent—nip bad behavior in the bud—but the imagery is telling. Notice that it is a writing tablet that the boy first steals. The fable locates action in the schoolroom, making this not just a tale for the school but *about* the school. It is an orally transmitted story about writing, about stealing instruments of learning and development. But it is, too, a story in praise of those instruments, as if the writing tablet were as valuable as a cloak. Learning is a precious thing here.

Or take the story of the boy on the wild horse (Perry 457). The narrator announces, "You are in the same trouble they say a boy had when he got on a wild horse. The horse ran away with him, of course, and he couldn't get off while it kept on running. Someone saw him and asked him where he was going. The boy pointed to the horse and said, 'Wherever he likes'." Like the tale of the thief, this is a story of youth out of control. Childhood is in many ways like riding a wild horse. We need to find our right direction, not be driven by the whims of wildness. Like this wild child, other boys are constantly in trouble in Aesop. The drowning boy (Perry 211) calls for help, yet gets only a reprimand from a passerby. "Come help me now," the boy calls out; "you may scold me later when I have been saved." In another fable, a boy is collecting locusts and is about to pick up a scorpion, which he mistakes for a locust (Perry 199). The scorpion calls out, "Would that you had done that; then you would have lost the locusts that you already have."

These fables evoke a world of children and its challenges to the rituals and rigors of adulthood. They take parent-child relationships as their theme. Many focus on those relationships of power and control central to childish fantasy. It is not simply that Aesop offers up a world in which beasts speak, or that his simple morals seem appropriate for younger ears. It is that his fables are about the child. This feature is what made the Aesopica so apposite for education, so central to the nursery and the classroom. Aesop appeals to children because the subjects of his fables remain childlike protagonists in an adult world ripe for rip-off.

And so it is important for the educator to appeal to children's taste, but at the same time to control that taste: to limit childish urges and use fables for both positive and negative example. One fable in particular shows up with striking frequency in late antique papyri—but with a telling difference from its origin in the Aesopica. The story of the murderer who meets his own death (Perry 38) had an obvious and popular appeal. Here is Aesop's version:

> A man who had committed murder was being pursued by the relatives of his victim. When he came to the river Nile and encountered a wolf, in his fright he climbed a tree that stood beside the river and hid in it. There he saw a snake opening its jaws at him and flung himself into the river. A crocodile in the river caught him and ate him.

The moral of the tale asserts that "we must watch out most particularly for men who do not even refrain from doing wrong against those who are close to them."[8] Everything is here: the crime, the animals, the retribution. It is as if the whole Aesopic menagerie (the wolf, the snake, the crocodile) conspires to enact a moral judgment. Animals work their wiles here not through speech, but through action.

The papyri, however, which range in date from the fifth to the seventh century AD, reveal a tale subtly recast into a conflict between father and son:

> A son who killed his own father, fearing the law, took refuge in a desolate place, but when he reached the mountains, he was pursued by a lion. Since the lion chased him, he mounted a tree. But he saw a serpent lying on it and, unable to climb further, he was killed. The evil man never escapes from God, for the divine leads evil people to justice.[9]

Notice the transformations here. First, this is a story of a patricide. The murderous son is not pursued, but seeks refuge in a "desolate place"—a place not simply geographical but moral. Desolation is the spiritual condition of the killer, and the lion in pursuit now stands as something far more allegorically significant than the beast of Aesop's fable. So, too, do the tree and snake. This is a tale about the moral life, a bit of Aesopica recalibrated for a Christian readership. The whole feel of the story changes, as the old beast fable becomes something approaching a biblical parable. Death comes through the serpent; the tree is a tree of knowledge gained too late. The resonances startle.

But there is more to this comparison than observing the transmutation of a classical fable into a Christian allegory. The father-son motif now takes on an additional religious aura. For in the Bible, it is always fathers who test their sons. Abraham and Isaac, God and Jesus: these were the *figurae* of belief. A God the Father always makes true believers into children, and a literature of childhood in the Christian world cannot but chime with this controlling idiom. Aesopic fables in that Christian idiom make children's literature into something different from what it had been before. Now we are faced not with the *patria* of Rome or the *paternitas* of emperors, but with the fatherhood of God.

Aesop's fables thus take on a unique position in the education of the Christian child. Church teachers and, later, monastic schools sustained to varying degrees the older Roman traditions of rhetoric and grammar. St. Augustine had shown—not only in his *Confessions*, but in his many manuals of doctrine—how instruction in the arts of oratory led to arts of preaching, and how the techniques of close reading could be transferred to the study of the scriptures. His interest in the fable, too, was part of his concern with Christian education. Horace, Augustine writes in his treatise *Against Lying*, can have "mouse speak to mouse, and weasel to fox," and still make important points through such fictions. As to the fables of Aesop, Augustine notes that "there is no man so untaught [*ineruditus*] as to think they ought to be called lies: but in Holy Writ also, as in the book of Judges, the trees seek a king for themselves, and speak to the olive, to the fig, to the vine, and to the bramble."[10] Horace, Aesop, and the Book of Judges stand here as fabulous narratives that convey a basic truth. They form the core of education, and it seems significant to me that Augustine should refer to someone as so untaught as to think that Aesop's fables should be called mere lies. *Ineruditus*: not erudite, not schooled in language or interpretation. Teaching, Augustine suggests, begins with Aesop, and the central lesson of scriptural narrative—that the literal level of a story conceals a deeper truth—can be found even in his fables.

St. Augustine, of course, was not alone among late antique commentators on the fable, and he was far from alone in seeking a place for the Aesopic tradition in emerging Christian intellectual environments. Macrobius, best known for his extensive, philosophical commentary on Cicero's *Dream of Scipio* (a commentary of immense impact on medieval and Renaissance readers), remarked that fables, for all their falsehood, could have good effects:

> They delight the ear as do the comedies of Menander and his imitators, or the narratives replete with imaginary doings of lovers in which Petronius Arbiter so freely indulged and with which Apuleius, astonishingly, sometimes amused himself. This whole category of fables, which promise only to gratify the ear, a philosophical treatise avoids and relegates to children's nurseries. In [such fables] both the setting and the plot are fictitious, as in the fables of Aesop, famous for the elegance of his fictions.[11]

Here we have not only a defense of the fable, but a canon of children's literature. Menander, Petronius, Apuleius, Aesop: these are the authors of the schoolroom.

But while students who read Menander, Petronius, and Apuleius would have read these authors' own words, for most of history children who read "Aesop" were not reading Aesop at all. In Hellenistic and Roman times, they would have been reading compilations put together by the scholar Demetrius of Phalerum in the fourth century BC. In the first centuries AD, they would have read versifications by Babrius (in Greek) and Phaedrus (in Latin). Babrius was most likely known already to Quintilian, and fragments of his poems survive in papyri from Byzantine Greece. Phaedrus, who called himself a freedman of the emperor Augustus, was similarly popular. Known to Martial, his Latin verses stimulated many imitators; and his work, like that of Babrius, was read and copied in medieval manuscripts. Babrius and Phaedrus, though, were more than versifiers. They transformed the Aesopic fables into a collection of unified stories, each with a certain moral point or literary interpretation. In their hands, the fable moves from a freestanding, popular form of applicable folk wisdom into a systematic body of literature. Both writers are acutely conscious of their authorial roles in shaping such a system—a role they acknowledge as having inherited from Aesop himself. Aesop was *auctor* of the tales, begins Phaedrus. He came up with the *materia*, the substance, of the fables, "but I polished them into verses of six feet."[12] Babrius, too, acknowledges Aesop as a source and, like Phaedrus, comments on his own role in transforming the fables' original "free manner of prose," their oral form, into rhetorical verse: "I shall adorn each of those fables with the flowers of my own Muse. I shall set before you a poetical honeycomb, as it were, dripping with sweetness."[13]

The history of the fable is, again, the history of its translation—but it is clear that Phaedrus is translating Aesop not just into Latin, but into Latin literature. His evocative images bring the diction of high-culture poetry to bear on Aesop's popular tales. In fact, Phaedrus describes his literary process much as the great Roman poet Catullus described his own. In the first of his poems, Catullus offers up his new volume of verses (what he calls his *libellus*, or little book) with the edges of the papyrus roll smoothed with pumice ("arida modo pumice expolitum"). These are polished verses, both literally and figuratively. So, too, Phaedrus has polished his verse (his Latin word is *polivi*) into a little book (his word is *libelli*).[14] Babrius's Greek phrasing also makes his Aesopic transformations into higher literature, hearkening back to Hellenistic poets such as Callimachus.[15]

Phaedrus and Babrius, in short, make literature out of lore, and their versions of the individual fables often stress the themes and images of artistic creation, poetic patronage, and verbal wit. Look, for example, at Phaedrus's fable of King Demetrius and the poet Menander. Demetrius usurps the throne of Athens. The mob can't wait to praise him; even the first citizens kiss his hand. Finally, Menander comes out of retirement to pay his respects. Sashaying in, overdressed and clearly effeminate, he provokes the king's ire. "Who is that little queer [*cinaedus*]?" he sneers. That is Menander, the writer (*scriptor*). Well, then, the king responds, immediately changing his tune, "no man could appear more fair" (pp. 350–53). The joke lies, of course, in the king's own need to curry favor from the famous. But the joke lies, too, in the reversal of authority. Kings kowtow to great writers—note that Menander here is *scriptor*, not *auctor*. His literacy is foremost. And whatever his sexual orientation, he wrests control from a ruler who has come to power wrongly (*improbo*). This is, in short, a fable about power wrongly gained and about the real power of the writer to restore the proper hierarchies of obeisance.

By the Middle Ages, Babrius and Phaedrus were no longer the primary bearers of the Aesopic tradition.[16] Not only was the language of their poems difficult for medieval students to read, but they also lacked the explicit Christian morals that had come to be appended to the fables by the third and fourth centuries AD. A new set of fabulists emerged as pedagogues and poets to the young. Most prominent among them were Avianus, a late fourth-century Roman who translated Babrius's fables into Latin verse, adding some of his own; Romulus, another late antique Latin writer who rendered Phaedrus's poems into prose, in the process altering the details and providing later readers with a different, prefatory context for studying the Aesopica; and a certain "Walter of England" (also known as the Anonymous Neveleti, after his work's Renaissance editor), who in the twelfth century compiled a set of Latin versified fables, based largely on versions of the Romulus collection. Taken together, these writers synthesized the inheritance of the Aesopic tradition and further stimulated recensions, translations, and adaptations throughout the Middle Ages. Theirs was the material studied in the medieval school, and theirs were the versions eventually translated into the European vernaculars in the fourteenth, fifteenth, and sixteenth centuries. For a thousand years— until the texts of Babrius and Phaedrus were rediscovered in the sixteenth century, and until the Greek text of the Aesopica was recovered in the seventeenth—these medieval Latin versions were "Aesop."

As with many medieval school texts, the Aesopica was passed down in manuscripts complete with gloss and commentary. Between the lines, the scribe or schoolboy would write in simpler Latin synonyms for unfamiliar terms, or even translate them into his own vernacular. Along the margins, philosophical and literary commentary would illuminate the deeper meanings of the fable. The old animals now acted in imaginative allegories, each one taking on a moral quality or aspect of the human character. In the famous fable of the crow and the urn, the bird comes upon a pitcher partly full of water and figures out that by dropping stones into the pitcher, it can raise the water level enough to drink from it (Perry 390). Avianus transformed this prose fable into elegiac Latin couplets: a poem of ten lines, rich with weird vocabulary and twisted syntax, designed to test the student's skill at reading. Medieval manuscripts encrust this poem with glosses and explanations. In some, the fable is transformed back into Latin prose, clarifying its essential moral; for example, in one commentary in a fifteenth-century manuscript from Prague, the summary begins, "Here the author demonstrates that wisdom is better and greater than strength."[17] A thirteenth-century manuscript from Wolfenbüttel similarly presents the fable as having an authorial intention: "In this fable, the author teaches that cleverness is more useful than might and wisdom is more useful than exertion, and he seeks to prove this with the example of a raven."[18]

These medieval commentaries, like their counterparts for Virgil, Ovid, and the range of classical *auctores* studied in the schools, fit the Aesopica into a literary theory grounded in the search for the *intentio auctoris*—not so much "authorial intention" in the modern sense, but rather the larger purpose of the text. That purpose could be to instruct, to pose a moral, or to illustrate a particular habit of mind. The purpose could have an ethical force, too, as in this version from a manuscript in Budapest: "The Allegory: by the thirsty crow we understand the sinner, who desires to please God with his intelligence, through confession, sincere contrition, and penance."[19] Or take this comment from a manuscript in Erfurt: "Allegorically the heart of man, which rests in the body as if in an urn, is understood by the water in the urn. By the crow the devil is understood, who places stones, that is to say, wicked thoughts, in the human heart because of his deception and wiliness, so that he might drink the water, that is to say that he might distract the human heart from good works."[20]

There remains in these collections, whatever their allegorical specificity, a guiding focus on instruction in the arts of literacy. The figures of invention or craft, such as the figure of the crow, become models for a student similarly taxed to find grammatical or intellectual solutions that will demonstrate that, in the words of a Vatican Library manuscript, *ingenium superat vires*: cleverness beats force.[21]

In fact, all of these are fables of *ingenium*, whether it be the cleverness of creatures or the wit of the fabulist himself. In some of them, the parent-child relationship explicitly becomes the grid on which to plot the growth of intellectual ability. One fable in the Walter of England collection is titled "Bos maior docet arare iuniorem" (The big ox teaches the little ox to plow). The fable is a simplified version of a text attributed to Phaedrus and is similar to one from the Romulus collection titled "De patre monente filium."[22] A father has an ill-mannered, vagrant son who needs to be taught good behavior and responsibility. To this end, the father is told a story about an old ox yoked together with a young one. The old ox asks to be removed from the yoke, for the young one is struggling against it. The farmer explains to the old ox that he has yoked the two together so that the old may teach the young. In the Phaedrean version, it is Aesop who steps in and tells the story to the father. In the medieval versions, the narrator himself tells it. In all cases, this is a kind of fable within a fable: a framed story that appealed in particular to the medieval taste for allegorical interpretation. The poem sets up fable-telling as a form of figurative instruction. It mirrors the structure of the classroom, while at the same time recalling those older idioms of labor that had made the tales of Hercules so popular among earlier children. In Walter of England's version, the sentences are short, there is almost no elision, and the vocabulary is relatively simple (though still heavily glossed in the manuscripts). The *doctrina*, or teaching, of the fable is as follows, in the commentary to the Walter of England manuscript: "It is the duty of the parents to teach their children such that they follow them in morality and virtue through their example. The old teach the young through example and explicit instruction."[23]

But there is more to this little fable than old men and oxen. Plowing the field had long been a controlling metaphor for writing (it is as old as the ancient Greek term *boustrophedon*, lines cut back and forth by oxen at the plow). The furrows of the field recalled the lines ruled on the page or letters written into the wax tablets of the schoolroom. The Latin verbs *arare*, "to plow," and *exarare*, "to plow up," connoted writing; in a wonderful example from Martial's *Epigrams*, the poet writes to his little book that if it is condemned by the critic Apollinaris, it would be only "fit for schoolboys to plough your backside" (*inversa pueris arande charta*).[24] It would, he means, be suitable only for schoolboys to scribble on the back of the roll. For the child, writing was a kind of plowing: working laboriously over parchment with the pen, or digging into waxed boards with the stylus. Phaedrus himself wrote of his project, "Whatever may come of it . . . I will plough up a third book with Aesop's stylus" (Quodcumque fuerit . . . librum exarabo tertium Aesopi stilo).[25] Medieval Latin writers picked up on this idiom. To plow became not just to write, but to compose literature itself—a tradition that reached its English vernacular apogee in Chaucer's *Canterbury Tales*. At the beginning of *The Knight's Tale*, the Knight remarks on the big narrative ahead of him and on his own limitations as a tale-teller: "I have, God woot, a large feeld to ere, / And wayke been the oxen in my plough" (A.886–87). So, too, in the prologue to the following *Miller's Tale*, the drunken Miller announces that he has enough to talk about: "Yet nolde I, for the oxen in my plogh, / Take upon me moore than ynogh" (A.3159–60).[26] As the plowman states in Walter's fable, "With celebration, plow joyfully, you who have been tamed to the habit of plowing." What better tale for young boys, learning the skills of writing, plowing the fields of parchment, yoked to their old masters? And this is a lesson to the masters, too: you may not want to work either, the fable says, but only through your example are the young to be instructed.

Aesopic fable had become the field through which the medieval writer plowed, not just in Latin but in Old French, Middle High and Low German, Spanish, and (by the late fifteenth century) English. The fables were among the very first works of classical literature to be systematically turned into the European vernaculars, not only because of their simplicity, but because Aesop's fiction is *about* translation. His fables' own concerns with teaching, the tradition of pedagogical adaptation, and the larger literary history of transformation all make linguistic change a theme for the tradition.

Sometime in the last decades of the twelfth century, the poet Marie de France turned more than one hundred Aesopic tales into her *Fables* in French verse.[27] A writer of remarkable range and facility, Marie produced a set of poems that get at the heart of the Aesopic idiom. In her verses, beasts speak in the powerful colloquialisms of the vernacular. Morals appear not with the heavy hand of the schoolteacher but the wit of the courtier. Throughout, there emerges an authorial identity whose self-awareness stands on par with that of Babrius and Phaedrus, authors who had imagined themselves working not just with but also against the authority of Aesop.

Marie begins her *Fables* with an appeal to the literacy of her audience and the authority of her sources.

> Cil ki seivent de lettruüre,
> Devreint bien mettre cure
> Es bons livres e escriz
> E as essamples e as diz
> Ke li philosophe troverent
> E escristrent e remembrerent.
>
> [Those persons, all, who are well-read,
> Should study and pay careful heed
> To fine accounts in worthy tomes,
> To models and to axioms:
> That which philosophers did find
> And wrote about and kept in mind.]
>                          (Prologue, lines 1–6)

The most basic texts would be the Aesopica. The job of teachers and writers is to take what they have heard and write it down: "Par moralité escriveient / Les bons proverbs qu'il oieint" (The sayings which they heard, they wrote, / So that the morals we would note; lines 7–8). Marie establishes again the central premise of Aesopian transmission: the shift from hearing to writing. The ancient fathers did just this, she says—"Ceo firent li ancien pere" (11)—much as Romulus wrote fables for his son, or Aesop wrote for his master. These fables were translated from Greek into Latin ("De griu en latin translates"; 20), and now Marie will put them into French verse ("A me, ki dei la rime faire"; 27).

Translation is transmission. The etymology of the Latin word *translatio* is "carrying over," and Marie's work begins with a set of genealogies that mark the inheritance she holds. Literature is a kind of paternal bequest; literary history is a family romance. The ancient fathers are not only fathers of the church, but all writers who establish their paternity through literary making. And though Marie writes self-consciously as a woman—and though many of her fables have struck modern readers as being acutely sensitive to female social status and having a female literary sensibility—her opening account articulates a literary history bequeathed by fathers to their children or commissioned by masters from their slaves.

Within the Aesopic tradition, and in Marie's *Fables* in particular, beastly illiterates hold a mirror up to errant youths, and few of these animal figures were more popular than that of the wolf at school. An early medieval Latin version (Perry 688) has the wolf being instructed by a priest. The priest writes an A, and the wolf repeats the letter. The priest writes a B, then a C, and the wolf repeats them both. "Now put the letters together and make syllables of them," says the priest. The wolf replies, "I do not know how to make syllables." "Pronounce whatever seems best to you." So the wolf says, "It seems to me, these letters spell 'lamb' [*agnus*]." To this the priest replies, "Quod in corde, hoc in ore": what lies in the heart is also in the mouth.[28]

This fable, though not original with Aesop, was nonetheless compellingly incorporated into the Aesopica, and it had a remarkable afterlife throughout the Middle Ages, appearing in a range of vernaculars and employed for a wide variety of pedagogic ends. It was so popular that Pope Urban II could rely on it in an edict of April 14, 1096, in which he criticized the clergy of Poitiers for their complaints against the monks:

Indeed, as I realized that they were not pleading for spiritual but for fleshly privileges, I spoke in seriousness a certain proverb that ought to have shamed them, if they wanted to heed it, about the wolf set to learn the alphabet: when the teacher said A, he would say "lamb," and when the teacher said B, he would say "pig." They did the same, because when we promised psalms and prayers, they in response demanded things which are not beneficial to the profit of souls.[29]

Urban manipulates the tale somewhat, cutting directly to the moral chase rather than spelling out—in all senses of that phrase—the pedagogic resonances of the fable. Marie de France, however, transforms it into a reflection on intention and expression.

> Un prestre volst jadis aprendre
> A un lu letters fere entendre
> 'A' dist le prestre; 'A' dist li lus,
> Que mut ert fel e enginnus.
>
> [A preacher long ago was set
> To teach the wolf the alphabet.
> 'A' said the preacher; 'A' wolf said,
> Who very crafty was, and bad.]
> (82.1–4)

But this wolf is more than just bad and crafty. He is "enginnus," ingenious, and this word recalls that whole tradition of *ingenium* (from which it descends) at the heart of the Latin schoolroom fables. What difference lies between the crow who puts pebbles in the pitcher and the wolf who cannot spell? Recall how medieval pedagogues allegorized the fable of the crow and the pitcher as a moral on *ingenium*, on cleverness over brute strength. With the wolf, *ingenium* is subtle craft, designed not to get what is needed (water to quench thirst) but to voice what is craved (illicit food).

The wolf, now in not sheep's but student's clothing, reappears again and again to symbolize *ingenium* gone wrong—wit and instruction pressed into the service of cupidity or vice. Those wolves are everywhere, filling the fables with their slyness. Sometimes their significance is bluntly put: one medieval Latin commentary on the fable of the wolf and the goat states, "Allegorically by the wolf the devil is understood."[30] At other times it is more subtly worked, as in the great twelfth-century Latin beast epic the *Ysengrimus*, whose hero is a wolf-monk and whose scope extends beyond the purview of the schoolroom to embrace ecclesiastical and political satire with an edge not seen again in poetry until Chaucer. And at other times, the wolf's significance is downright elliptical, as in the brief Aesopic fable of the wolf and the actor's mask.

This little story was originally couched as an encounter between a fox and the mask, but by the Middle Ages the wolf had replaced his cousin to make this into another story of *ingenium* gone awry. Phaedrus is the earliest text for the tale:

> A fox, after looking by chance at a tragic actor's mask (*persona tragica*), remarked, "O what a face is here, but it has no brains!" This is an example for those to whom Fortune has granted rank and renown, but denied them common sense.[31]

By the twelfth century, when this fable reappeared in Latin schoolroom texts and commentaries, the wolf (*lupus*) had replaced the fox (*vulpis*), but another change had taken place as well. The old traditions of the classical stage had vanished. Actors no longer acted with the masks of tragedy and comedy (the Latin word *persona* originally referred to the actor's mask and thus to the character enacted in the fiction of the play; hence our modern rubric *dramatis personae*). Medieval drama had been relocated into moral exemplum or biblical story. The original premise of this fable would have been lost to medieval readers, and so the wolf now comes upon not a mask but a disembodied head. In the version ascribed to Walter of England, it is a head ornately embellished, with jewelry and curled hair, the face colored with makeup. This splendid head now has neither voice nor thought; the wolf addresses it thus: "O sine voce gene, o sine mente caput" (O cheeks without a voice, O head without a mind). The prose commentary following the poem in its manuscript first clarifies the meaning of the wolf's exclamation (I translate: "O head with great beauty and ornamentation, your cheeks proud, but without voice. Your head made up with rouge and hair curled, as if to say, beauty is a lie"). It then glosses this encounter by comparing the beauty of certain books with the inanity of their readers. "Sunt enim multi qui libros pulcherrimos habere volunt sed in eis studere nolunt":[32] there are many who would want to have very beautiful books, but they will not study them. Such people, obviously, are like heads without minds.

A fable about honor and common sense is now a lesson for the student. But the theme of artifice was not lost on the medieval reader. A later version of this poem, incorporated into one of the bilingual Latin–Old French Ysopets of the fourteenth century, is retitled "De lupo qui invenit quoddam caput pictum" (About the wolf who found a painted head). The head is now a piece of sculpture, and the wolf's line takes on a new resonance: "O cheeks without voice, O head without mind." The

Latin poem now comes with an "Addicio" remarking on the vanity of appearance and, in a brilliant analogy, stating that physical appearance is merely a brother to the chimera ("Apparens species fratres sunt atque chimera").[33]

The Old French rhymed translation, which follows the Latin together with its additional poetic *moralité*, now makes clear that this is a fable about art itself: about relationships between beauty and truth, about the labor that goes into artifice. King David, the psalmist, is here the source of authority, and the aphorisms in the Old French lines take on a power that transcends the schoolroom. "Biauté ne vaut riens sans bonté" (Beauty without goodness is worthless). There is no value in artistry without the labor that goes into making it meaningful.

A fable about fortune has become a lesson about art. In the little illustration that accompanies the Latin and Old French poems in this manuscript, we see the wolf coming upon the sculpted head—a weird little moment, as if he were coming upon some bit of food, or as if this severed head lay now like that of Orpheus, still singing, perhaps, as it floated down the river. Even modern readers unfamiliar with this fable may recall a comparable scene in literature, when Hamlet comes upon the disinterred skull of the jester Yorick. He picks it up and turns it in his hands, much as the wolf turns the head in his paws.

> Alas, poor Yorick! I knew him, Horatio, a fellow of infinite jest, of most excellent fancy. He hath borne me on his back a thousand times. And now how abhorred in my imagination it is! My gorge rises at it. Here hung those lips that I have kissed I know not how oft. Where be your gibes now? Your gambols, your songs, your flashes of merriment that were wont to set the table on a roar? Not one now to mock your own grinning? Quite chapfall'n? Now get you to my lady's chamber, and tell her, let her paint an inch thick, to this favor, she must come. Make her laugh at that.[34]

The history of the Aesopic imagery is here: the cheeks without a voice, now "chapfall'n"; the painted head, now transferred to the lady; the verbal performances that are the mark of acting.

The fable of the wolf and the actor's mask provides more than just a local image for a comic scene. It stands behind the narrative of Hamlet's play itself. What is this story but a succession of lupine, vulpine characters coming upon tragic masks? Polonius recalls his student performance as Julius Caesar; Hamlet gives advice to player kings; heads without reason govern Denmark. The Aesop that Shakespeare would have encountered in the later sixteenth century was both a school text and a guide to life: a figuration of the ways in which a literary author could embrace the world. It was the base text for grammar and rhetoric, and in this most grammatical and rhetorical of plays—a play about a student come home from the classroom—Aesop's fables guide our understanding of its episodes.

Hamlet's recovery of Yorick's skull enacts the cultural recovery of childhood recitation and performance. It is a fable of remembrance, a recollection not just of an earlier experience in the tragic persona's life, but of an earlier experience in literary history: a time before estrangement. As with so many of the other moments of theatrical self-reference in the play, this episode reflects on what has passed—older performance styles; texts out of fashion; recitations of the schoolroom, or the university, or the Inns of Court, or the marketplace scaffolds, rather than of the public stage. It out-Herods Herod. It looks back to patterns of theatricality that by the 1590s appeared provincial or antiquated. We come upon the shards and leavings of the Middle Ages (the time that the Renaissance would dub as childish, immature, and foolish) and find ways of reincorporating them into modernity. Where be your gibes now?

And so the history of the Aesopica remains a paradox: it was a literary form born out of social challenge, yet one designed to constrain resistant behavior and shape children's lives to social norms. Aesop may have begun life as a slave, but in his literary afterlife he is the master. By the time of Robert Henryson, who offered Middle Scots poetic versions of the fables in the middle of the fifteenth century, he is in fact a scholarly master, appearing to the poet in a dream bearing

> A roll of paper . . .
> And a swan's feather pen sticking behind his ear;
> An inkhorn, with a pretty gilded pen case.[35]

He comes accoutered with all the instruments of writing and the school. "Esope I hecht" (I am named Aesop) he avows; "my writing and my werk / Is couth and kend [known far and wide] to mony cunning Clerk" (lines 1375–76). As something of a cunning clerk himself, Aesop is now the "Maister," worthy to be called, by Henryson's narrator, "Poet Lawriate" (1377). As such a laureate, he shares, in the late medieval English literary consciousness, a place with Petrarch (the original poet laureate) and Chaucer (so dubbed by his successors). And for the earliest of European printers   seeking sanctioned authors for their presses' first productions—that laureateship gives him primacy of place in their print shops.

Europe's first printers used Aesop's fables not just to sustain a literary heritage or offer guidance to the young, but to affirm their own authority as makers of the texts of culture. Among the very first books printed in any European vernacular (during the 1470s and 1480s) were Aesop-inspired volumes, many with elaborate illustrations. Such volumes stand as encyclopedias of culture and of craft. The illustrations of these late fifteenth- and early sixteenth-century books reveal the range of every skill, profession, action, and experience. In early printers' hands, the fables become illustrations of the world: guides not just to morality, but to a reading of the everyday. The ancient Greek landscape or the medieval Latin idioms of instruction are here transformed into familiar things. Tables, food, clothes, animals, kings, slaves—all stand on these pages as representations of a lived reality. The Aesopica of the first decades of print become guidebooks to local life, and their vernacularity presents landscapes and households as legends of belonging.

Those legends percolated throughout all the European languages. French poems fill early printed books; old German verses transform ancient creatures into everyday domestic characters; and English prose shows up on some of the first pages set in movable type. The French Ysopet fables would be copied well into the fifteenth century, and their elaborations on the birds and beasts would find their most familiar expression in Chaucer's Middle English *Nun's Priest's Tale* or the adventures of Reynard the Fox. Throughout German-speaking Europe—from Switzerland to Vienna to Silesia—the fables reappear with detailed vernacular commentary. They are among the first texts to be printed in the German language, and if Ulrich Bonner's *Edelstein* or the so-called Wroclaw Aesop are less well known than Marie de France, it is not for any lack of literary skill on their part, but more likely because of the hegemony that Old French studies held over medievalists in the nineteenth and twentieth centuries. Like their French counterparts, these German texts develop the laconic Latin of the fables into long, poetic excurses. A little couplet that concludes the fable of the old ox and the young bullock (told within the fable of the father and the ill-mannered son) offers, "Proficit exemplis merito cautela docendi / Maiorque sua credit in arte minor" (The lesson of the teacher is effective when properly accompanied by examples / And so let the young man rely on the knowledge of his elder). This sentiment expands into the following German verses, found in the Wroclaw Aesop of the middle fifteenth century:

> Snelle bessert sich des menschen mut
> Wo man gut beyspel thut.
> Ouch sal der iungen gehorick seyn
> Yn der kunst dez meyster syn.
>
> [The mind of men is quickly improved
> Where one provides a good example.
> The young should be obedient
> To the master in matters of skill.][36]

The word *beyspel* meant moral saying, proverb, good example. But it also connoted the Aesopic genre itself. The fable both tells and is a *beyspel*, and the reading of these fables has an educative purpose. What follows is an appeal to the authority of all examples, Aristotle himself:

> Aristoteles, du meyster yn kunsten weyt,
> Gesprochen hostu wor langer czeit:
> So wir gute exempel gebeu,
> So merken vm dy iunger ebin.
> Wil der selbir recht syn gelert,
> So mus her dor czu seyn gekert
> Gancz czu glewben des meysters ler,
> Do won wachs kunst, dy lengir . . . mer.
>
> [Aristotle, you master renowned in skill,
> long ago said: "When we provide good examples, our
> students learn well. If our pupil wants to be erudite himself,
> he should be intent on accepting the teacher's teaching; from
> that, knowledge will grow the more."][37]

The details of translation are significant. With the invocation of Aristotle's authority, the poet shifts, if only momentarily, from the familiar German to the learned Latin. Aristotle does not give good *beyspel*, he gives good *exempel*. The Latin word replaces the German at this moment in order to call attention to the quality of classical instruction, to the unassailable authority of Aristotle, and, perhaps most pointedly, to the translator's awareness that not all concepts can be translated. If this is children's literature, it is for children very much aware of living in a multilingual world, where translating from one language to another is part of daily life (at least in school), and where the Aesopica teaches not merely local moral lessons, but the larger *exempel* of learning as a social ideal.

German Aesops had an impact far beyond their borders. Heinrich Steinhöwel, an Italian-educated German, drew on Aesop, Avianus, Isidore of Seville, and a host of medieval fabulists and commentators to produce one of the first printed editions of the fables, published in a German and Latin text of 1476 or 1477. This book, known as the *Esopus*, formed the basis for the French prose *Esope* by Julien Macho of Lyons, which was published there in 1480. William Caxton, England's first printer, used this French translation as the basis of his own volume. Caxton's "book of the subtle histories and Fables of Esope" appeared, as the book is dated, on March 26, 1484, and it offers a supple version of the life of Aesop together with 167 fables, tales, and anecdotes. This book, much like those upon which it was based, is not so much an edition of the Aesopica as it is an anthology of learned writings stimulated by the Aesopic tradition: a book that testifies to humanism's fascination with the exemplary fiction, with the enduring popularity of beast tales, and with English readers' obvious desire for a vernacular version of the texts familiar to them from their school days.[38] Reading through Caxton's assembly, one sees different moments in the history of the Aesopica emerge, like strata from a road cut. Folktale, sermon, grammatical exercise, moral exemplum, scurrilous story—all are there.

By the time these things reach Caxton, mutated through translations and commentaries, they are at times radically different from how they began. Take, for example, the thief and his mother. In Caxton and his source, Macho, there is no mention of the writing tablet that the boy steals from school. They say only that the boy began to steal as a child and brought his booty to his mother.[39] Or take the story of the father and the son that adumbrates the tale of the ox and the bullock. At one level, it all seems to be there, but the tone has changed. Now it has the flavor of a biblical parable, a kind of saying of Jesus:

As to vs reciteth this fable / Of a fader of famylle / which had a sone / the whiche dyd no thynge that he oughte to haue done but euer was goynge and playing in the toune / And the fader for the cryme and mysrewle of his sone brawled [i.e., berated him] euer and bete his meyne [i.e., beat his companions] / And sayd to them such a fable.[40]

It has become a story about the country and the city, and the moral fable of the father-laborer and the oxen represents the ideals of a rural, working life when set against the nightmares of an urban dissipation. Caxton enhances his French source with additional detail: there is not just a "crime," as in Macho, but "misrule," a word central to the fifteenth-century English vocabulary of moral behavior. In the process, he makes this very much a local tale fit for very English readers faced with wayward sons.

Though Caxton is remarkably close to his French source, his occasional enhancements give the fables something of the flavor of a biblical parable, a preacher's exemplum, or a popular sermon. His idiom recalls the fifteenth-century English *Alphabet of Tales*, a collection of moral exempla for medieval sermonizers and their congregants. Among the many sources for this volume—each little narrative arranged in alphabetical order according to its key moral lesson—Aesop is explicitly acknowledged in three of the tales. One of them tells the story of the ass and the horse, under the rubric "Gloria mundi parum durat" (Worldly wealth is transitory). The *Alphabet of Tales* version is brief and perfunctory, and opens thus: "Esopus in 'Fabulis' tellis how ther was a hors that was arrayed with a brydyll of gold and a gay saddll, and he mett ane ass that was ladyn; and this ass made hym no reverens, bod held evyn furth his way." The horse is angry and demands room to pass. The ass gives in. But time passes, and the horse "that was so gaylie cled, was wayke and lene," and the ass has become fat and healthy. "Whar is now thi gay array at thou was so prowde of?" he asks the horse.[41] In Caxton, the horse is not just old, but also "lene." He is also "arrayed" with the golden bridle. This is a distinctively English phrasing not corresponding to anything in Caxton's source, Macho. It is as if a little bit of the *Alphabet of Tales* bleeds into Caxton—as if the printer, for all his European erudition, cannot escape the sounds of an English, popular tradition.

But this is more than just a fable about pride. Medieval literature is rich with stories of array, in which courtiers disguise themselves as common folk, or in which ordinary people find themselves "translated" into elevated settings. The famous story of Griselda—told in Italian in Boccaccio's *Decameron*, turned into Latin by Petrarch, and then into English by Chaucer in his *Clerk's Tale*—is a story of translation. "Whan she translated was in swich richesse," when Griselda was transformed by her husband, Walter, from the poor girl into a princess, she is barely recognizable. "Of her array," says the narrator, "what sholde I make a tale."[42]

Aesop, the *Alphabet of Tales*, and Caxton have all made a tale of such array: a tale about the ways in which the ordinary can be clothed in golden trappings, about how texts can be transmuted to bear a new burden of meaning. Medieval writers had long viewed translation as a form of dressing up. Petrarch notes how he took Boccaccio's story and reclothed it, much as Griselda was reclothed in new finery. And like that severed head the wolf found, beautifully coiffed and colored, objects that we find must be perceived not for the beauty of their surface, but for the goodness of their hearts. This is the lesson of the medieval Aesopica: the importance of going beyond glittering surfaces to substance. This is the lesson, too, of a good deal of medieval education, and the young boys that Quintilian imagined as the audience for Aesop have now mutated into a congregation, led by the paternalistic preacher along moral ways. If Aesop is a children's writer in this world—a "father Aesop" from Phaedrus to Robert Henryson—then all who read him become children in the face of his authority.

What does it mean to write a history of Aesop? It means to trace the transformations of a fabulist into an author. It means to chart the acts, as well as the themes, of translation throughout a history of reception. It means to illustrate how fables, born of slavery, can be applied to reinforce the hierarchies of the master and the student. We come upon the fables, perhaps, much as Hamlet comes upon that skull, or the wolf upon the head: scattered fragments of an old tradition. Babrius noted how he took the elements of Aesop and put them "in a new and poetic dress," covering them, like an old warhorse, "with trappings of gold."[43] How can we not here recall the gay finery described in the tale of the horse and the ass? These texts—mute manuscripts and battered books—still speak, to those who can read them. Where be your gibes now? They remain for those who, unlike that wolf before the priest, can read their letters. Knowledge is a treasure ("Scientia enim thesaurus est"), says the medieval commentator on Walter of England's fable of the wolf and the head, a treasure "which it is not possible for a thief to steal, a mouse to gnaw through, a maggot to demolish, water to wash away, or fire to burn up."[44] Among all the transitory things in the world, knowledge survives. But note how all of those things that beset knowledge are themselves the creatures of the fables: thieves, mice, maggots, water, and fire all live in the menagerie of the Aesopica, confined to their fictions, allowed to speak to those who can unearth their bones.

# · 3 ·

# *Court, Commerce, and Cloister*

## THE LITERATURES OF MEDIEVAL CHILDHOOD

Was there a literature for medieval children? Three decades of research into the culture of the child, the habits of the school, and the practices of Latin and vernacular literacy have revealed a richly textured verbal and imaginative world for children throughout medieval Europe.[1] The church absorbed the old traditions of the Roman schoolroom, adapting instruction in *grammatica* to the precepts of Catholic doctrine. Classical texts continued to be read and annotated, parsed and understood, but with new goals. Moral allegories were found in pagan narratives; poetic and prose styles shaped newer religious writing. The Aesopica was always there, but now new genres entered into school and home. The emergence of distinctive social structures—feudalism, courtly service, urban mercantile ambition, civic consciousness—fostered forms of children's literature different from those of the classical inheritance. In particular, courtesy and conduct manuals instructed children in proper behavior and speech and helped boys and girls take on social and familial roles. Popular poetry and tales in the vernaculars emerged, some of it indebted to Aesop, some of it developing local folk motifs and myths.

The structure of the family, too, was changing in the thousand years after the Romans pulled back from their British and Continental colonies. Patrilineage and primogeniture became the ways of passing on wealth and land, title and power. Marriage took on a sacramental value in the church, and the practices of baptism, communion, and confession, together with the conventions of naming children after biblical or holy figures, transformed the medieval family—at whatever social level—into something not just social or economic but spiritual as well. The "holy family" was always in the background; while real, live families could hardly emulate the piety or sacrifice of Mary, Joseph, and Jesus, medieval Christianity was, in many ways, a religion grounded in a sacral sense of home life, and the Christ child omnipresently remained for anyone who read a book, looked at a picture, or attended church.

The presence of that Christ child helped make medieval Europe into something of an *aetas puerorum*, an age of children. At times poignant, at times powerful, images of the baby Jesus show everything from the child lying in the manger or suckling at the Virgin's breast to symbolic, even surreal, visions of the child emerging out of the raised host at the Mass.[2] Little Jesus dolls became the toys of girls and even older women, enabling them to play-act the Virgin Mother and in the process to model their own future maternity along devotional lines. Other children, too, filled medieval art and literature. The sacrifice of Isaac had long been viewed as a kind of typological anticipation of the crucifixion of Christ, and so pictures, poems, plays, and stories based on this biblical episode fill medieval books.[3] Little saints, with their suffering and martyrdom, populated the devotional and the political imagination. Most famous of these was Hugh of Lincoln, the boy who was allegedly martyred by Jews in 1255 and whose legend influenced Chaucer's *Prioress's Tale*. Romances and heroic legends also often focused on the childhood of their subjects, from *Havelok* and *Tristan* to *Bevis of Hampton*, *Guy of Warwick*, and the *Horn Child*. Central to these narratives is the hero's progress from foundling through education and accomplishment. Children show up, abandoned by their parents or lost; they are recovered and reared, and eventually come home through deeds of action or ingenuity. Even the stories of King Arthur hinge on childhood: the future king, a bastard child raised by others, reveals his inheritance in one dramatic move (pulling the sword from the stone) and then is set under Merlin's tutelage.

But in addition to these literary fictions and religious forms, real medieval politics were also powered by the young. "Woe to thee, O land, when the king is a child." This tag line from Ecclesiastes (10.16) was invoked throughout the Middle Ages by royal subjects and royal aspirants faced with child monarchs. Kings came to thrones early in their lives, and it is remarkable how young medieval rulers really were. In England, for example, Henry III was nine when his father, King John, died in 1216. Richard II of England was ten when he inherited the throne in 1377. Henry VI was only a few months old when his father, Henry V, died in 1422, and he was formally crowned king at seven. In France, Philip IV, known as "the

Fair," became king at seventeen in 1285, while Louis IX (later St. Louis) was eleven when he ascended the throne in 1226. At times, the youthfulness of kings was an advantage. St. Louis' biographer, Jean de Joinville, records how "from his childhood the King was very compassionate to the poor and suffering," a habit that lasted throughout his reign.[4] At other times, it was a curse. To French diplomats of the 1430s, Henry VI seemed childlike, *un très beau fils* and *ung tres bel enfant*, comments that were designed not to express his beauty but his simplemindedness and inexperience.[5] And other children filled the courts of these child-kings. Young boys would be sent as pages to a ruler or nobleman by the time they were ten years old. Girls would begin their training as maids in waiting at a similarly young age. Great households had children working everywhere, from kitchen, to stable, to chapel, to bedchamber. In 1445, Henry VI had sixty-two children in service, and lesser households had nearly as many in proportion.[6]

If children seemed to fill the medieval court, they also filled the medieval workshop. Guilds had developed in the towns and cities to control the production and delivery of goods and services, and central to guild structure was apprenticeship. A young boy, or sometimes a girl, would be apprenticed to a guild, and by entering the master's household he or she would participate in an extended family that embraced both personal and commercial possibilities. Apprentices would be schooled, fed, and trained. In England, though, the apprentice structure was not for just anyone. A child had to come from a family of at least some social status and means. Parents had to pay the master to take in the child, and the child had to have spent his or her earliest years in a house where good manners were the rule.[7]

All of these social roles had their own literature. The *speculum principis* (mirror for princes) evolved as a way of teaching rulers how to rule. Their moral content, collections of aphorisms, and assembly of religious and classical quotations made such writings veritable encyclopedias of noble ethics, and they proliferated in both Latin and the vernaculars. Poetry and prose survive that describe for apprentices the conditions of guild life and also offer guidelines for moral and social behavior. Such writings fit into the larger genre of parental advice literature, where fathers or masters address their children and where the goals of good behavior dovetail with ideals of Christian charity. For children in the monastery or the convent, works of classical and religious Latin taught the rudiments of grammar, the techniques of verbal style, the standards of an aesthetic value, and, of course, the virtues of the devotional life. Much like their Roman ancestors, the children in religious houses read Virgil, Ovid, and Horace; knew the major myths; and could deploy vocabularies ranging from the fluid and familiar to the arcane and the pedantic.

Within these worlds of court, commerce, and cloister, many of our most familiar genres of children's literature emerged. The lullaby, perhaps the form we most intuitively associate with early childhood, developed in the European vernaculars. Such songs obviously had had a long performance life before they were transcribed into the manuscripts of the thirteenth and fourteenth centuries. A form of written literature from the Middle Ages, though, was the primer. The term *primer* (which seems unique to England) was originally used to describe prayer books for the laity, but the form developed in the late thirteenth and early fourteenth centuries to include basic alphabetic education. Lists of letters would be followed by simple prayers. Sometimes primers were more elaborate, containing psalms and scriptural readings. Whether they were specifically called primers or not, the basic tool for teaching children how to read was strikingly similar to the wooden boards and papyri that had filled the late antique classroom.

But in addition to their obvious Christian content, these early books were charged with a characteristic medieval way of thinking. Writing in the early twelfth century, Hugh of St. Victor asserted, in the course of his instructional manual the *Didascalicon*, that this whole visible world was a book written by the finger of God. For the medieval child, the world *was* a book, full of signs and symbols in need of interpretation. Social success, moral growth, and economic security all hinged on successful understanding. But the book itself was also a world, as illuminated manuscripts came to incorporate the range of creatures on their pages. To look at a pictured page from Anglo-Saxon and Carolingian Europe, or from the twelfth-century schools and fourteenth-century courts, is to look at the range of all creation, bordered by—or, at times, seeming to escape—the margins. Even Jesus himself came to be read as something of a book. The marks of mutilation on his crucified body were viewed as letters of instruction. One English poem of the early fifteenth century strikingly associates Christ's body and the book. On the outer cover of the volume, the poem states, are written "five paraphs [paragraph marks] great and stout, / Boled [embellished] in rose red." On the cross, Christ himself was similarly inscribed: "On tree he was done full blithe / With great paraphs, that be wounds five, / As you may understand."[8]

Medieval children read and wrote, prayed and played, at the nexus of the body and the book, the world and the text.[9] The study of medieval children's literature not only tells us something of their daily lives; it also illuminates the imagination of medieval society. Filiation, fatherhood, the mother tongue—such images from family life inflect the literary and linguistic consciousness of medieval Europe. Notions of inheritance and authority inform literary as well as social history. This chapter's goal, therefore, is to explore what medieval children read (and sometimes wrote) as they gained mastery of verbal, social, and spiritual literacy.

Medieval children learned to read and write from alphabets and prayer books, Psalters and primers. Unlike their antique counterparts, the boys (and to a lesser extent the girls) who began their instruction, either in the church school or the home, would find their ABCs imbued with Christian teaching from the start. In the margins of a manuscript from the eleventh century, someone has written out the alphabet immediately followed by the opening words of the Lord's Prayer.[10] The word *amen* often follows lists of alphabets in manuscripts, and sometimes, too, the letters are arranged in the form of the cross. Alphabetic poems with religious themes abound. Such abecedaria have biblical precedents, one of the most notable of which is Psalm 118, where the twenty two stanzas of the poem use the twenty-two letters of the Hebrew alphabet in order. This kind of verbal tour de force may have inspired late antique and medieval writers to produce poems on a range of topics, but with structures governed by the order of the alphabet or keyed to acrostic patterns.[11]

The Anglo-Saxons, in particular, loved the play of letters. Manuscripts from the ninth through the eleventh centuries testify to their fascinations with acrostics and wordplay. Their manuscripts are rich with elaborate initials: snakes curl into the letter Q, a lion's head pokes out of a J, and birds bristle out of A's. They are rich, too, with annotations: glosses that reveal to us how students learned their Latin and their English, how they gained a knowledge of history, mythology, and doctrine. To read through classbooks and anthologies from this age is to be struck by the range of the material. Religious works are there, of course; so, too, are grammatical treatises. But on occasion, we find such things as Ovid's *Art of Love*, complete with annotations. We also find collections of riddles, in Latin and Old English, that must have challenged early students to make sense of grammar and of grace. Collections such as the so-called Exeter Book of Old English Poetry (probably written in the early eleventh century and kept in the Exeter Cathedral Library since its original donation in 1072) contain riddles on just about everything, from natural phenomena, to earthly animals and plants, to human artifacts.[12]

These riddles bring all creation together. They assemble a set of puzzles whose individual answers contribute to an understanding of the world and of the ambiguities of linguistic experience. Even the most mundane of objects can appear remarkable (*wrætlic*). A hen and a rooster coupling in a barnyard are a "wrætlic" twosome. A "wrætlic" thing hangs by a man's thigh. Pierced in the front, it is stiff and hard. It has a good place when the man lifts up his garment to set it in its proper hole. It is . . . a key. But, of course, it is also not a key. Such an object is *wrætlic* in the eye of the poetic beholder, whose double entendre can make this household object seem proudly phallic (much as the riddles elsewhere make the leek or the sword similarly tumescent, or make the bread rising in a bowl come to resemble a pregnant woman's swelling womb). But not all the riddles are so earthy. Riddle 24 in the Exeter Book takes as its solution a great book, probably the Bible itself. Told in the first person, it begins by recounting how a thief ripped off flesh and left skin, treated the skin in water, dried it in the sun, and then scraped it with a metal blade. Fingers folded it, and the joy of the bird (that is, the feather) was dipped in the wood-stain from a horn (that is, the ink in an inkwell) and left tracks on the body. Wooden boards enclosed it, laced with gold wire. Ask what I am called, the riddle concludes. No mere little book, this object is made up of all other parts of creation. The natural world and human artifice come together here to affirm that the book is a kind of cosmos, and that it contains all knowledge. If the children of men will use me, it avows, they will be safer and surer, bolder and more blessed, wiser and more full of friends. The reader will receive *arstæfum*—support, benefit, or grace. This word is a compound: *ar* means grace, favor, help; *stæf* means staff, or support. But Old English *stæf* also meant character, letter, or penstroke. *Bocstæf* was the word for "letter." *Stæfcræft* was the Old English word for the Latin *grammatica*: the study of language, of literacy itself. In his *Grammar*, written for his pupils at Eynsham in the early eleventh century, Bishop Ælfric (c. 955–1020) wrote: "Þe stæfcræft is seo cæeg, ðe ðære boca andgit unlicð": knowledge of letters is the key that unlocks the meaning of books.[13]

Ælfric had spent his career unlocking the meaning of books. In his *Grammar* and his *Glossary*, he explained Latin and Old English to monastic children. In his *Colloquy*, he used situations drawn from everyday experience to enhance the student's command of Latin syntax and vocabulary. But about a generation after he composed it, an Old English interlinear gloss was added, most likely by one of his disciples. And so, whatever Ælfric's original intentions, the manuscripts of his *Colloquy* survive as testimonies to bilingual education—to the mapping of vernacular experience onto learned life.[14]

The *Colloquy* is a dialogue between master and students. Each student plays a role, taking on the voices of particular professions, crafts, or callings, and the master asks each one in turn just what they do and how they do it. At one level, then, the *Colloquy* stands as an education in the arts of everyday existence. It is a kind of list, a survey of Anglo-Saxon laborers and their instruments or subjects. The hunter lists his animals, the fisherman lists his fish, the fowler lists his birds, and so on. As in the riddles of the Exeter Book, everything is here, and for the English-speaking student—whether of the eleventh or the twenty-first century—the value of the *Colloquy* at its most basic lies in its assembly of vocabulary terms for all these things. But as a work designed for students in monastic schools, the *Colloquy* has a doctrinal purpose and an allegorical flavor. How can a Christian reader not find spiritual allegory in, for example, the story of the hunter who sets out his nets for unsuspecting game? How can such a reader not go through the story of the fisherman without the image of the apostles as fishers of men, or without a weird frisson of remembrance at the following exchange?

> MASTER. Would you catch a whale?
> STUDENT FISHERMAN. No.
> MASTER. Why?
> STUDENT FISHERMAN. Because it is a dangerous thing to catch a whale. It is safer for me to go to the river with my boat than to go with many boats hunting whales.

Leviathan may lurk for any foolish Jonah. It is a dangerous thing to catch a whale. And for each laborer or craftsman, there is a political as well as a moral imperative. "What do you do with your catch?" the master asks the student playing the hunter. "I give the king whatever I get because I am his hunter." Social activity participates in fealties to power, and the hunter's obedience to his king mirrors the oblate's obedience to his monastic master, or the monk's obedience to the abbot, or the Christian's obedience to God.

But throughout Ælfric's *Colloquy*, as well as throughout the many other examples of this genre in the Middle Ages, there is performance and play-acting. Students take on roles. They learn not just the facts of life but life's language, and the *Colloquy* makes much of teaching students not just how to read, but how to speak correctly. The text begins with the students' plea: "We children bid you, Master, that you teach us to speak correctly (*recte*), for we are unlearned and speak corruptly (*corrupte*)." These idioms recall the language of the Benedictine Rule (that guide to monastic behavior set down by St. Benedict in the sixth century and central to the so-called Benedictine Revival of the English tenth century, of which Ælfric himself was a product): if anyone makes a mistake in pronouncing a psalm, responsory, antiphon, or lection, let him be punished; "for such a fault children shall be flogged." Similarly, the master of Ælfric's *Colloquy* asks his charges, "Will you be flogged in order to learn?" What this tradition illustrates is the deeply performative quality of learning and devotion in early medieval monastic education. Learning your lines is what matters, and the dramatic quality of this pedagogy looks back to St. Augustine's reminiscences of his own boyhood in his *Confessions*. Much like Augustine, schoolboys of the following millennium would have to recite passages from classical texts, paraphrase verse into prose, transform prose into verse. There was a theater to the medieval schoolroom—and a schoolroom quality to medieval theater.

By the twelfth century, this theatricality emerged in fully formed dramatic productions throughout Europe. Medieval drama evolved out of many traditions: from the Mass and liturgy, with their antiphonal calls and responses, their elaborate movements throughout the church interior, their high theater of communion; from the folk traditions of game and play, with their communal moments of impersonation and with such carnivalesque performances as the feast of fools or the boy bishop; from the public display of justice, as executions became forms of theater, set up so that the populace could witness, cheer, and recoil; and from the Bible, as the stories of the Old and New Testaments formed the core of cycle plays put on by urban guilds as part of festivals for Christmas, Easter, and the feast of Corpus Christi.

Some of the surviving dramatic texts clearly have elements of schoolroom playfulness, and a few in particular were expressly designed for (and perhaps even written by) students themselves. The twelfth-century *Play of Daniel (Danielis Ludus)*, from Beauvais in northern France, brilliantly exemplifies the kind of children's theater at work in the European medieval church school.[15] Written and performed by the young (*invenit hunc juventus*, "young people wrote it"), it has the perfect subject for the schoolroom:

a biblical account of reading hidden signs and the mastery of *grammatica*. But it is a story, too, about theatricality itself. Balthazar's feast becomes, in this play, a set piece of performative excess. The king adorns himself in rich costumes; all Babylon applauds (*ridens plaudit Babylon*). And the reward for deciphering the handwriting on the wall will be a similar theatricality:

> He who shall read this writing
> And decipher its meaning,
> Under his power
> Babylon shall be placed;
> And, arrayed in purple,
> He shall enjoy a golden neck-chain.
>
> (lines 67–72)

Costume becomes the prize for learning, as Balthazar becomes something of a generous schoolmaster offering the goodies to the best student. And Daniel, in this play, becomes that prize student. Stepping up to the head of the class, he reads, but also admonishes the king:

> O king, I do not desire your gifts;
> Without fee the writing will be interpreted.
> Here is the answer:
> Disaster threatens you.
> Your father before all other powerful ones
> Once was powerful;
> Swollen with too much pride,
> He was cast down from glory.
> For, not walking with God,
> But acting as if he himself were God,
> He snatched away the vessels from the temple
> And put them to his own use.
>
> (lines 147–58)

Nebuchadnezzar's downfall, in Daniel's interpretation here, lies in his theatricality. His pride led him to act as if he were God: *sese Deum simulans*.

Latin remains the language of this play, and the interpretation of God's handwriting remains firmly ensconced in the idiom of Latin education:

> The king calls before him wise men [*sapientes*]
> Who might reveal to him the hidden meaning
> of the message written by that right hand [*gramata dextrae*].
>
> (lines 15–16)

Letters are *gramata*, and Daniel's challenge is to unlock them (the Latin word throughout the play is *solvere*, not just "solve," but unlock, untie, open up). How similar this is to Ælfric's injunction from an Anglo-Saxon England two centuries before: his word *stæfcræft* is the Old English for *grammatica*, the key that unlocks (*unlicð*) the meaning of books. But how different is the execution, for in Beauvais, Latin gives way not to English but to French. King Balthazar is very much a French monarch, and when the princes call him before the king, they do so in a macaronic set of verses that make French the language of secular rule:

> Vir propheta Dei, Daniel, vien al roi
> Veni, desiderat parler a toi.
> Pavet et turbatur, Daniel, vien al roi.
>
> [O man and prophet of God, Daniel, come to the king.
> Come, he desires to speak with you.
> He quakes with fear and is troubled, Daniel, come to the king.]
>
> (lines 112–14)

One may learn in Latin, but one comes to a king in French here, and the use of French half-lines throughout the play affirms, linguistically, the difference between sacred and secular powers. But it affirms, as well, the place of linguistic difference in the making of the literate child. "Genvois al roi" (I go to the king; line 268), Daniel avers before he sets out, and the king relies, for all his own Latin, on the language of the French law courts to affirm his legal power:

> Ego mando
> et remando
> ne sit spretum
> hoc decretum.
> O hez!
>
> [I charge
> And repeat my command
> That this decree
> Be not flouted.
> Hear ye!]
>
> (lines 306–10)

That final "Hear ye!" still chimes in the modern ear for anyone attuned to the traditions of French law behind English and American judicial and political ritual.

The *Play of Daniel*, much like the pedagogic colloquy, shows people acting as if they were others, and it emphasizes the importance of the kind of spoken language used to pray, obey, and explicate a text. It is one thing, though, to impersonate a fisherman or hunter, or even a king; it is another to play-act as if one were a biblical hero, or a saint, or for that matter God. The *Play of Daniel* illustrates just how difficult it is to draw the line between imagining oneself as other (i.e., acting) and believing oneself to be the other. The play goes on, from this point, through a series of set pieces of performativity: processions, mimes, legal trials, public prophecies. The play not only exposes the theatricality inherent in the biblical story; it reveals the church to be a theater of its own, a place of acting in which all performances of ritual need to be assessed for their precise place on the line between devotion and drama. Of course the Mass is a performance; of course the church is rich with costume, prop, and ceremony. But, the play argues, if we snatch away the vessels of the temple for our own use, we take objects imbued with religious significance and transform them into mere stage props. Theatricality controlled, the play avers, can be good: it can inspire the young, stimulate the soul, and lead to spiritual awareness. But uncontrolled, it leads to pride, self-absorption, and vanity.

Such was the lesson of a good deal of medieval drama, a lesson perhaps nowhere as humorously taught as in the mid-fifteenth-century English play *Mankind*.[16] Long thought of as a moral drama played by itinerant actors, the play more recently has been examined as a document of youthful mockery and fun. Chunks of classroom Latin and pedagogical assignments pepper its diction, and it may even have been acted out by schoolchildren.[17]

*Mankind* imagines its eponymous hero beset by the temptations of the world. Characters with the names Mischief, New-Guise, and Nowadays embody the corruptions of everyday life, while the character Titivillus (literally, "all the vices") stands as a Satanic misleader working hard to stanch the lessons of the play's good pedagogue, Mercy. The play is full of jejune wit. Scatology predominates; jokes about castration and sex circle around the sophomoric double entendre of the word "jewels"; and throughout, scenes of reading and writing mock the pedagogic practices of the day. The imagery of note-taking and account-making, of proclamations and contracts, fills the play with what could only be an adolescent's imagination. Compare, for example, the *Play of Daniel*'s use of the French legal call "O hez!" with the character Nowadays' parody of the same idiom: "Oyyt, oy-yit, oyet! All manere of men and comun women / to the court of

Mischiff othere cum or sen!" (lines 667–68). But it is early in the play, when the rogues enter, that explicit parody of classroom work appears. Mercy enters speaking a Middle English dialect rich with French vocabulary and learned Latinate diction. New-Guise retorts, "Ey, ey, yowr body is full of Englisch Laten! / I am aferde it will brest." Nowadays chimes in:

> Ye are a strong cunning clerke;
> I prey yow hertily, worschippfull clerke,
> To have this Englisch made in Laten:
> "I have etun a disch-full of curdys,
> Ande I have schetun yowr mowth full of turdys." —
> Now, opyn yowr sachell with Laten wordys
> Ande sey me this in clerical manere!
>
> (lines 124–30)

Nowadays mimics the language of one of the most widely used textbooks of the fifteenth century, John Leland's *Informacio*, where he writes, "What schalt thow doo whan thow has an Englysch to make yn Latin?" Other lines parody other school exercises.[18] But the simple identification of sources cannot convey the explosive juvenile humor of this scene. Go translate this, Nowadays says, and gives us obscenity. And later on, in a mockery of both liturgical and political Latin, he offers the ultimate curse: "Osculare fundamentum!" (Kiss my ass!).

More than mere bawdry, *Mankind* offers up another lesson in the limits of theatricality. The rogues here, by their names and by their character, remain figures of impersonation, dress-up, and performance. They are quite literally in the new guise, that is, in the costumes of contemporary decadence—indeed, at one point New-Guise offers Mankind "a fresh jakett, after the new guise" (line 676), as if to costume him in sin. And at the play's end, with the tempters defeated, Mercy will lecture Mankind on the delusions of the flesh, fable, and fancy. The moral life should be lived not among the dramatis personae of the theater, but with the "play-ferys" of the "angellys above": *play-ferys*, meaning not simply "companions" (as the modern editor glosses it) but, more pointedly, playmates—a delightfully affecting way of seeing heaven as that greatest of all play-dates, with the angels in that schoolyard of eternal life.

The drama of the medieval stage was full of children—as actors, as representations of the Christ child or little saints, as mischievous imps. Whatever sources we may find in schoolroom parody or everyday experience would come to inflect, too, the more elaborate dramas of the Renaissance theater. Boys' plays filled the court of Henry VII and Henry VIII. Christmas and festival pageants, ceremonial affairs, and mythological lessons were all possibilities for performance. In 1487, for example, Henry VII celebrated the birth of his first son, Prince Arthur (who was to die in 1502), with a miracle play performed by the boys of St. Swithin's Priory and Hyde Abbey of Winchester.[19] Under Henry VIII, such performances became familiar staples of royal ceremony. His master of the revels, William Cornish, led the children of the Chapel Royal in a performance of a play called *Troylous and Pandor* for Twelfth Night, 1516 (a fascinating glimpse at how canonical literary material, here Chaucer's *Troilus and Criseyde*, could be adapted for the child actor).[20] Even the great Thomas More acted as a boy. His son-in-law, William Roper, recorded this reminiscence: "Thoughe he was of younge yeares, yeat wold he at Christmas tyde sodenly sometimes steppe in among the players, and neuer studying for the matter, make a parte of his owne there presently among them, which made the lookers on more sporte than all the plaiers beside."[21] Years later, would Chancellor More remember such a moment as he took the scaffold's stage? And would other courtiers recall, much later in the sixteenth century, their own childish dramas when the players enter in Shakespeare's *Hamlet*, or when the rustics in *A Midsummer Night's Dream* put on their bad play of Pyramus and Thisbe, in which the foolishness of Wall or the inanity of poorly scanned lines evokes schoolroom farce or parodies by "play-ferys"? Whatever fictions Shakespeare's theater offered, there were real boys on stage, boys playing female roles but always boys. So Cleopatra imagines her literary afterlife as one of "scald rhymers" and "quick comedians," as she sees a future "squeaking Cleopatra boy my greatness" (*Antony and Cleopatra*, 5.2.220). A history of children's theater and of the theater of childhood come together at the close of this great tragedy, as the Egyptian queen (played, of course, by a boy) takes the asp to her breast and with her death evokes the newborn: "Dost thou not see my baby at my breast, / that sucks the nurse asleep?" (5.2.308–9).

And for the baby at the breast, the earliest of childhood's rhymes and songs would come.

> Lullay, lullow, lully, lullay,
> Dewy, bewy, lully, lully,
> Bewy, lully, lullow, lully,
> Lullay, baw, baw, my barne,
> Slepe softly now.[22]

This fourteenth-century example looks as modern as any lullaby, and at the same time looks as old as song itself (the Romans used the syllables *lalla* in their cradle songs, too). The mid-thirteenth-century encyclopedist Bartholomaeus Anglicus heard lullabies throughout the nursery. In the words of his late fourteenth-century English translator, John of Trevisa, nurses "usen to singe lullinges and other cradil songs to plese the wittis of the childe." Many such songs survive, from verses charged with simple, soothing repetition of a syllable to more complex lines full of wit and poignancy. A poem from 1500 advises, "Euery modyr sekyrly yt can here cradyll kepe, sche most syng lullay / To bring here child on slepe." Mothers clearly did "sing lullay," though the literary evidence we have for lullabies may record not the actual practice of singing children to sleep but rather idealized cradle scenes, especially those of the Virgin and the baby Jesus. In fact, many medieval English lullabies are really Virgin Mary songs, and their survival testifies to the impress of the Nativity on the popular imagination of child-rearing.[23]

So, too, the earliest evidence of children's rhyming comes filtered through the church. Preachers would allude to children's games and childish ditties in their sermons to their flocks.[24] Monastic scribes, trying out new pens, would scribble down the vestiges of verse from their own childhood.[25] Even the great scholar Gabriel Harvey, writing in the 1590s, slipped scraps of what he called "Children's Songs" into his books.[26]

> When pucketts away, where shall we go play?
> When the puckett is asleep, then we may go sow our wheat.
>
> My dame hath a hutch at home
> A little dog with a clog;
> Hey, dogs, hey.

Harvey's "puckett" goes back to the Middle English *pouke*, a sprite or evil spirit of the woods (and, of course, the source of Shakespeare's Puck of *A Midsummer Night's Dream*). When the evil spirit is away, where shall we play? When he is asleep, then we may sow our wheat. This little *pouke* shows up throughout Middle English verse, often in couplets of folk wisdom or puerile wit. But he also has sway over the schoolroom. One poem from the fifteenth century, titled by its modern editor "The Schoolboy's Wish," imagines the teacher beaten with his own staff and condemned to the devil (called here by the amusing euphemism "Sir Robert"): "And thow

Sir Robert, with his cloak, / Would thee help and be thy pouke."[27] Let the devil himself, the students pray, help the teacher with his cloak, and may that devil be the teacher's own tormenting sprite. The *pouke* of childish fantasy infected older readers, too, as in this bookplate to a volume of homilies and Gospels:

> He that stelys this booke
> Shulbe hanged on a crooke;
> He that this booke stele wolde
> Sone be his herte colde:
> That it mow so be
> Seith amen, for cherite.
>> Qui scripsit carmen Pookefart est sibi nomen
>> Miller jingatur qui scripsit sic nominatur.[28]

He who wrote this poem, his name is Pookefart—as if now the impishness of poukery controls not just the landscape but the literary page. Gabriel Harvey's "pucketts" are the late descendants of these creatures: shards of a childhood lived in song.

This philological arcana may seem marginal to children's literature. But children's verse lives in the margins. Gabriel Harvey may have scribbled down some memories of childhood, but schoolboys themselves filled notebooks with remembered songs or bits of nonsense—in fact, "The Schoolboy's Wish" survives written between two Latin works by the scholar John of Garland.[29] Other marginal poems are tongue-twisters, clearly calibrated to enhance the elocution of the student, such as a stanza beginning, "Three gray greedy geese." Some have a riddlic quality, not unlike the Old English riddles of the Exeter Book and their Latin forebears: "What is higher than is the tree? / What is deeper than is the sea?" Others trade on superstition and magic:

> By street or way if thou shalt go,
> From these two things thou keep thee fro:
> Neither to harm child nor beast
> With casting, turning west nor east.[30]

The marginal status of this poetry, however, should not simply be construed as accident. Nor should we take these annotations out of the contexts of their books and simply see them as freestanding poems, fit for an anthology or witness to a kind of universal lore of childhood. These are, instead, the verbal equivalent of what the art historian Michael Camille has called the "images on the edge": the marginal materials to medieval manuscripts that, in their often obscene, grotesque, or merely mundane content, served as a kind of counterweight to the serious, and often Latin, prose of their pages.[31] These images, Camille notes, offer worlds "at the edges of the world," examples of how medieval men and women experienced both the sublime and the ridiculous, the sacred and the powerfully profane, together. In medieval manuscript illuminations, margins are crowded with weirdnesses such as knights tilting at attacking snails, monkeys reading books, monks defecating before nuns—and children at play.

These marginalia hold a brilliant mirror up to the adult world of martial prowess and political control (the subject of the *Roman d'Alexandre*). They show not battles between men, but childish rituals of aggression: puppets, cocks, and play knights. Camille's work on courtly manuscripts illuminates this childish world. He illustrates in great detail how marginalia, often jejune or scatological, playful or silly, invert the stereotypes of court and epic. They may have been the venues for court artists to critique the culture that employed or patronized them. Like the Aesopic fable, Camille argues, marginalia provide the means for servants to critique the masters—always within the safety of the fiction or the image.[32] They make possible the placement of the romance imagination in the world of real things. Do we take Alexander's exploits with a grain of salt when looking at a picture of two boys poking wooden lances at a quintain?[33] And can we also see that, in the fears and fantasies of childhood, hares may become hunters—a dreamlike twist not only on the social facts of hunting, but on the tradition of the hunter in such educational manuals as Ælfric's *Colloquy*? For Gabriel Harvey, writing down his childish songs, the dogs and pucketts function much like earlier medieval marginalia: strange witness to a world out there that no manuscript border or printed page can seal off. We need to understand these scraps of children's verse or illustrations of the child within the larger frame of adult life—to recognize that children and adults live side by side, and that the meaning of a "children's literature" for medieval Europe lies inextricably linked to its ideals of literature for adults.[34]

What happened, then, when adults wrote for children in the Middle Ages? Parents and teachers, masters and journeymen composed reams of advice for their young charges, and forms of didactic writing flourished—both in Latin and the European vernaculars—for more than five hundred years. One of the best-known products of this didactic tradition is

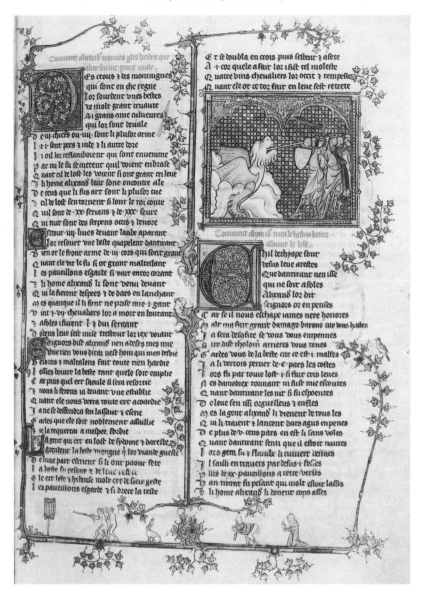

Fig. 2. Nature on the margins. From *The Romance of Alexander* (13th c.).
Bodleian Library, University of Oxford, MS Bodl. 264, folio 56r.

Geoffrey Chaucer's *Treatise on the Astrolabe*, a scientific manual composed
for his ten-year-old son Lewis. The astrolabe was a device used to observe
the sun and stars. It could locate the angle of the sun against the horizon
and thus determine the time of day. It could locate the angle of stars in

the night sky and thus determine the time of night. It could also use the positions of the stars to locate the latitude of the observer, determine the places of the constellations along their seasonal paths, and find the positions of the planets throughout the year. It was, then, a device enabling the determination of physical location, and Chaucer—always the poet of the spatial and the temporal, always the poet seeking our place in the world—wrote a treatise designed to teach Lewis not just how to use the instrument, but how to find himself on earth and in the stars.[35]

"Lyte Lowys my sone," he begins, and continues by explaining how he designed the *Treatise* to be comprehensible to someone of "thy tendir age of ten yeer." He has divided the work into five parts and written it in "naked wordes in English, for Latyn canst thou yit but small my litel sone." Still, Chaucer claims, English is as good a language as any other for this textbook—for God knows, he says, that people learn in all their languages, "right as diverse pathes leden diverse folk the righte way to Rome." He begs excuse in case he has written too much (a "superfluite of wordes"), in part because this is difficult material for a child to learn and in part because "me semith better to written unto a child twyes a god sentence, than he forgete it onys."

Chaucer seeks a national, as well as a paternal, identity not by looking around, but by looking up; not by surveying outwardly the landscapes of experience, but by directing vision upward to the heavens. Knowing where you are necessitates an instrument of stellar understanding: "our orizonte, compowned after the latitude of Oxenforde." Location is both physical and intellectual, a way of life and a habit of study. Locate yourself in your degree, Chaucer avers, and you know where and who you are.

Finding yourself in the world meant many things. It meant locating yourself newly in a city; seating yourself at a dinner table; presenting yourself at court; apprenticing yourself at the workbench or the wharf. From the late fourteenth through the mid-sixteenth centuries, such works as *The Book of Curtesye*, *Stans Puer ad Mensam*, *Urbanitatis*, *The Book of Nurture*, and *The Book of Kervynge* taught boys (and, to a lesser extent, girls) how to behave. In the mid-fifteenth century, the gentryman Peter Idley drew on much of this material when he composed his poetic *Instructions to His Son*. Its catalogue of counsels would have been familiar to any reader of this body of writing: respect your elders, watch your tongue, be patient, shun vice, and follow the examples of historical figures.[36]

Many amateur versifiers tried their hand at such instructional writing. A manuscript now in the Huntington Library in San Marino, California

(HM 140), offers an assembly of didactic and religious texts.[37] It was most likely put together in the late fifteenth or early sixteenth century by members of a London merchant family, and many of its contents would have spoken directly to the literary tastes and social aspirations of this kind of readership. One of the poems in this volume is John Lydgate's *Testament*, a verse autobiography by one of the most popular poets of the fifteenth century. Here the poet recounts his childhood, and in his catalogue of boyish misbehavior, the older narrator pointedly addresses the codes of conduct for the young boy in commercial, social, and religious spheres of action. Lydgate tells stories of neglect of schoolwork, petty thefts, and the disrespect of elders with such vigor and detail that many of the poem's modern readers have taken its autobiographical content as unadulterated truth and have relied on its descriptions to construct a history of education at the close of the Middle Ages.

One of the poem's fifteenth-century readers, however, clearly recognized the *Testament* as raw material for his own essay on advice. In the verses now known as the "Poem to Apprentices," preserved in the HM 140 manuscript, an amateur poet applies the ideals of social behavior learned from the *Testament* and from the other texts in the manuscript to counsel patience under stress.

> Childrenn and yonge menn that comme to this citee
> And purpose youre self apprentices to be
> To lerne crafte or connyng
> I counsaille yow alle doo after me
> And than ye shalle not reprovid be
> Yf ye use my doctryne sikerly.
>
> (lines 1–6)

What follows is a string of specific injunctions on timely rising, responsible work, good service at table, and moral virtues in general, with a range of other lessons modeled on Lydgate's stories of his own youthful indiscretions.

> Ffyrst that ye rise in the mornyng erly
> And that ye serve god devoutly
> With pater noster Ave and crede
> Arraye your self lightly
> Be with your maister in the mornyng tymely
> And doo that he you bidde.

Speke to your maister reverently
And answere hym ever curteisly
See your arraye be clene
Suffer maister and maistresse paciently
And doo their biddyng obediently
And loke noo pride in yow be sene.

(lines 7–18)

This poem may not seem terribly "literary" to our eyes and ears, but it is, I want to stress, made up of literature. It responds directly to those texts that medieval readers took as literary, and it appears in a manuscript compilation keyed to the literary tastes of a commercial family at the close of the fifteenth century. Together with its companion pieces, notably a versified version of the story of Job, a truncated version of Chaucer's *Clerk's Tale*, and Lydgate's hagiographical *Saint Albon and Saint Amphibalus*, the "Poem to Apprentices" imagines English literature as didactic in purpose. The goals here are to teach patience and obedience, especially now in civic contexts, not just courtly ones. Note in particular how St. Albon in Lydgate's poem becomes a patron of commerce: "Pray for marchauntis and artificers / To encrese by vertu in their businesse." And the tale of Job, for late medieval readers, came to refer less to the prefiguration of the Passion of Christ (its older medieval resonance) than to a newer fear of losing one's possessions. Job as a children's story emerges, in the words of the art historian F. Harth, "along with the rise of the bourgeois class in northern Europe."[38]

Children's literature at the close of the Middle Ages is, in these civic and urban settings, inseparable from new ideals of family life and commercial success. It is inseparable, too, from the rise of vernacular literacy and the book trade. To this point, all the texts I have considered here are manuscripts; medieval children's literature survives in copies made by hand. But by the close of the fifteenth century, the advent of printing was to change dramatically the making and dissemination of what children read. English printers such as William Caxton and his successors Wynkyn de Worde and Richard Pynson published much of this old, manuscript material, making it accessible to a purchasing public. Children's literature became a commercial item—in fact, for the first time we may talk of children's books.

Among the first of them was *The Book of Curtesye*. Printed in 1477 or 1478, it is a stanzaic poem of advice, much of which had clearly been circulating during the fifteenth century. Two manuscript copies of the poem also survive, one of which appears in the commonplace book of the Londoner Richard Hill, whose personal volume contains many other poems and prose pieces keyed to children's education or entertainment. It was obviously a popular text, and Caxton's decision to print it early in his English career makes clear his understanding of the pedagogic market. The poem is filled with familiar advice (including, once again, a guide to table manners, drawn from the tradition of Chaucer's Prioress); but it also counsels the child to "excersise your self also in redynge."[39] Books teach and entertain, but they also provide the child with examples of good topics of conversation and models of eloquence with which to shape his speech. The *Book of Curtesye* specifies just whom to read and why: John Gower, whose moral writings "shal gyue you corage / He is so ful of fruyt. Sentence and langage" (lines 323–29); Geoffrey Chaucer, founder of eloquence in English, whose works are "ful of pleasaunce" and of "sentence" (lines 330–50); Thomas Hoccleve, especially his book of advice to rulers called the *Regiment of Princes* (lines 351–64); and John Lydgate, whose long and comprehensive works are full of "sadnes of sentence" but also great rhetorical display (lines 365–99). Concluding its account of these writers, the *Book of Curtesye* avers, in language that recalls the ancient idioms of Bishop Ælfric, "For of our tunge / they were both lok and kaye" (line 406).

This book fascinates both as a guide to children's literature and as a model for its early publication. First, it makes clear that there was a canon of children's books: that is, a set of authors and works keyed to the maintenance of certain moral values, patterns of social behavior, and ideals of verbal performance. Second, it makes clear that certain medieval English authors, whatever their original audiences, had become children's writers by the late fifteenth century. This is, of course, not to say that Chaucer or Lydgate were exclusively read by children. But certain of their works did fit in the purview of a child's literate education. Chaucer in particular was edited and recast for children throughout the late fifteenth and sixteenth centuries. Certain of his tales were cut down; some of his poetry was copied into family anthologies for younger readers; and his reputation generally embraced the paternal and the advisory. For late medieval and Renaissance readers to dub Chaucer the "father" of English poetry was not just to consider him the origin of a literary tradition. It was, most pointedly, to stress his fatherly, instructional role: his stance as teacher to the young. Works such as the *Treatise on the Astrolabe*, therefore, could be incorporated into a late medieval and Renaissance understanding of

Chaucer's fatherly authority. Stories of parents and children in the *Canterbury Tales* could be appreciated as expressions of Chaucerian paternalistic understanding. The Chaucer of this age and audience is not, as we see him now, the political satirist or the ribald entertainer. He is domesticated, tamed in his complexities for childish readers and reserved for the indoctrination of domestic values.

Caxton's successors—Wynkyn de Worde, Richard Pynson, and others—continued many of his educational and entertaining projects. They printed didactic manuals and romances. But they also reached into the folk heritage of English narrative to find children's tales. Pynson printed *A Little Geste of Robin Hood* in 1500; de Worde printed it in 1506; and printers in other cities published it throughout the first two decades of the sixteenth century.[40] We tend to think of tales of Robin Hood as an obvious kind of children's literature. With their straightforward heroics, colorful characters, and simple morals, the stories fit what many modern readers seek in children's books. The poetry of Robin Hood similarly fits our expectations: with their short lines and ballad stanzas, such poems have long been thought of less as literature than as mere "rhymes." Now, it is clear that Robin Hood survived in a range of folktales and popular rhymes throughout the fourteenth and fifteenth centuries. And it is clear, too, that much of this verse was dismissed by learned writers or vernacular poets of courtly aspiration. In William Langland's *Piers Plowman* (written in the last decades of the fourteenth century), his allegorical character Sloth announces, "I can noughte perfitly my paternoster as the prest it syngeth, / But I can rymes of Robyn Hood and Randolf erle of Chestre" (B text, 401–2). Sloth clearly has not been a good student, for the Pater Noster was one of the very first texts, following the alphabets, in medieval primers. One imagines Langland's character as some sleepy adolescent whose eyes cannot focus on the page and whose mind wanders to the orally transmitted verse of exploits.

Robin Hood and adventure verse were thought of as corrupting to the child. Whatever plans Wynkyn de Worde or Richard Pynson had in mind, the pedagogues and moralists who succeeded them denounced these stories. William Tyndale, best known for his English translation of the Bible, condemned Robin Hood, along with a range of other literatures, in his 1528 *Obedience of a Christian Man*. When the common people were forbidden to read the Bible in their vernacular, Tyndale asks, why then were people permitted to read "Robyn hode and bevies of Hampton / Hercules / hector and troylus with a [th]ousande histories and fables of

love and wantones and of rybaudry as fylthy as herte can thinke / to corrupte the myndes of youth with all"? (C iiii r). Many other writers of
the sixteenth century voiced similar sentiments, and they have long been
taken as testifying to an inherent association between romance, folklore,
and childishness.[41]

But this tradition of condemnation does not reflect on medieval
habits of reading or on the constructions of a children's literature for
medieval England. Rather, it is reformist in purpose. By the time the
Reformation had ensconced itself in England under Henry VIII, medieval
literature was widely viewed as not just idle or corrupting, but as papist.
Statutes of the 1540s prohibited the reprinting of all literature (with the
exception of Chaucer and Gower) of the earlier period: "printed bokes,
printed balades, playes rymes songes and other fantasies."[42] By the reign
of Queen Elizabeth I, medieval literature was seen as retrograde, he-
retical, vile. Roger Ascham's complaints in his *Scholemaster* (1570) represent contemporary opinion: "In our forefathers' time, when papistry
as a standing pool covered and overflowed all England, few books were
read in our tongue, saving certain books of chivalry, as they said, for pas-
time and pleasure, which, as some say, were made in monasteries by idle
monks or wanton canons."[43] For post-Reformation England, medieval literature *became* children's literature. It was associated with childishness,
error, sloth, idleness, and foolery.

So what happened when medieval books fell into early modern children's hands? In Cambridge University Library, a set of early printed
quartos reveals the imaginations of two brothers, Robert and Anthony
Doe, children of a recusant (i.e., post-Reformation Catholic) family in
England in the late sixteenth and early seventeenth centuries.[44] The books
are full of scribbles, pictures, announcements of ownership, cryptic pen
trials, and occasionally quotations from other works. Take, for example,
this snatch of verse written by Anthony Doe on the margins of the book
*The Extripation of Ignorancy*, by Paul Bush (printed in 1526): "And in the
miste of my house walke." This line comes from Psalm 101 in the widely
circulated Sternhold-Hopkins Psalter. Containing metrical translations
of the Psalms, together with a variety of other devotional materials, this
Psalter was the work of Thomas Sternhold, John Hopkins, and others,
and it evolved through a series of editions from 1533 until 1562. From that
year until 1600, the book went through thirty editions. The Psalter had
long been a central text in the education of the English young, and the
Sternhold-Hopkins translation makes its pedagogic purposes explicit on

the title page of the 1562 edition: "Very mete to be vsed of all sortes of people priuately for their solace & comfort, laying apart all vngodly songes
and ballades, which tende only to the norishing of vyce, and corrupting
of youth." It is a Psalter appropriate for the young, and one that clearly
had been read by the children of the Doe family.

Later on the margins of *The Extripation of Ignorancy*, the influence of
this Psalter is palpable in Anthony Doe's own attempt at psalmistry. On
one page, he has made the following unfinished inscription: "O Lord my
god I cum to thee in this my grif and paine now turn to me in my destris
and." This text fits perfectly into the metrical model of the Sternhold-
Hopkins psalm translations. It can be lineated thus:

> O Lord my god I cum to thee
> In this my grif and paine
> Now turn to me in my destris
> And . . .

I can find no text that precisely corresponds to these lines. There are
echoes of other versified psalms of the period, but there is nothing exactly like them. They are a form of metrical psalmistry in the style of the
age—the fragment of a poem, an imaginative response to a printed text
in a child's hand.

Medieval literature thus had its impact not just on medieval children,
but on early modern ones as well. We think of it as romance and adventure, Robin Hood and magic, lullabies and folk rhymes. But as I have illustrated here, it is a literature of literacy and power, where monastic
students may find schoolroom performance echoed in the handwriting
on the wall, and where the earliest of printers may see markets for new
generations aspiring to grow up into courtesy. And on the margins of the
pages, we may see the shards of childish reading or, on rare occasion, children acting like the authors of their age.

# From Alphabet to Elegy

## THE PURITAN IMPACT
## ON CHILDREN'S LITERATURE

It is easy to demonize the Puritans. The very term has long connoted extremes of behavior, whether it be the revolutionary regicide that spawned the age of Oliver Cromwell, or the severity of dress and decorum that we think of when we imagine the early American settlers. And yet the Puritans clearly adored their children. Their progeny fascinated them: their growth, their education, and their lives as readers. Under the aegis of the Puritans, children's books became a new and separate kind of literature. They emerged as an expression of Puritan culture itself, an extension of larger publication projects keyed to spiritual education and moral growth. These were stories of redemption and conversion, tales designed to teach that, even during childhood, life has a spiritual goal.[1] A child was, in the words of James Janeway's *Token for Children* of 1671— perhaps the most popular book of the seventeenth century, after Bunyan's *Pilgrim's Progress*—"a precious Jewel" committed to the parent's charge.[2] Children were the future of the family, but they were also the future of the Puritan movement itself.

Puritanism was a movement for the future, and the children of the Puritans figured both socially and imaginatively in that movement. At times, Puritans thought of themselves as children breaking with the family, challenging the paternalistic inheritance of British Anglicanism and the church and king. Their own rebellion voiced itself in a rebellion about naming. Acts of naming fill Old Testament narratives, and acts of renaming, as in the story of Abraham and Sarah, marked the turning points in such figures' lives.[3] So, too, the Hebrew Bible was filled with stories of significant naming, where personages would receive allegorically transparent appellations keyed to character or experience. The English biblical translation of 1560—the so-called Geneva Bible, which would become the scriptures for the Puritans—took the time to explicate these many names into the vernacular, and in these names and narratives the Puritans would find a template for their own signifying selfhood. An early Puritan document of 1565 advises against baptizing children with "the names of God, or of Christ, or of Angels, or of holy offices, . . . nor such as savour of paganism or popery: but chiefly where there are examples in the Holy Scriptures in the names of those who are reported in them to have been goodly and virtuous."⁴ Such injunctions led the Puritans to mine the Bible for virtuous characters. Ichabod, Ebenezer, Ezekiel, Nathaniel, Zerrubabel—such were the names of their children. But often, too, they dubbed their children with the English translations of biblical monikers: Hopeful, Silence, Learn-Wisdom, Hate-Evil, Do-Well, Increase, Thankful, Accepted. Such names created a community of the truly goodly and virtuous—a community that from our modern perspective seems more allegorical than alive. It is as if they lived, in real life, in the world of *Pilgrim's Progress*—and this may be precisely the point. For Bunyan's characters were no mere flat-dimensioned allegories of the medieval tradition. They were living figures of the Puritan world, illustrations of how figural the life on earth could be.⁵

This figural existence had not just a literary consequence, but also a political one. Whether in England or America, the Puritans imagined themselves living in a landscape of transcendent meaning, and their fascination with the family transformed that landscape into images of parent and of child. The paternalism of Oliver Cromwell, for example—the "Great Protector"—gave way to a vision of a harsher fatherhood when the king and the Anglican Church were restored in 1660. In the late seventeenth century, the Puritans began to see themselves as an oppressed sect, as suffering children at society's cruel hands. In this perception they were not alone—the Anabaptists, Presbyterians, Dissenters, and Quakers all, to some degree, considered themselves persecuted. But where they were almost unique was in their transformation of this sense of persecution into narratives of children's literature. The stories of the pain and death of children, so popular in the last quarter of the century, grew out of this political environment.

In America, too, the Puritan settlers rejected the old image of a "fatherland" to embrace a new world of rebirth and childhood.⁶ Such imagery would fill the writings of the early settlers, and the rise of children's literature in the colonies remains inseparable from the familial imagery that dominated the colonists' relationship to England. Such a relationship would eventually define the early American literary and political experience as a whole. Obedience to God the Father matched obedience to a paternal England, and the great tension in children's literature of the Puritan cast lay between this need to reinforce authority and the stress on individual development. Eventually, the childhood of the colonies would stand (in the words of Jay Fliegelman) not as "an apprenticeship or a period of growth, education, and preparation for adulthood," but as "a permanent relationship to external authority."[7]

The children's books of Puritan England and America allegorically enacted these social and political relationships, and to understand that allegory—not just on the page but in the world—was to learn the art of reading. Alphabetic education was designed for success not simply in commerce or in culture, but in spirit. There was a kind of moral literacy to the Puritan movement, a sense that books could shape lives. Only through reading, through performing the catechism, and through reflecting on exemplary narratives could the child be prepared for heaven, whenever the invitation might come.

For death was everywhere. Cotton Mather could sum it all up thus: "Yea, you may be at play one hour; dead, dead, the next."[8] Writing, speaking, preaching, and reading about death became the constitutive experience of Puritan literacy. Funeral elegies abound; deathbed confessions filled booksellers' catalogues.[9] The fear of death gripped even the youngest of readers. *The New England Primer*, the most popular and long-lived of the alphabet books of the Puritan inheritance, brought death to almost every letter.[10]

> The Cat does play,
> And after slay.
>
> As runs the Glass
> Man's Life doth pass.
>
> Time cuts down all
> Both great and small.
>
> Youth forward slips,
> Death soonest nips.

The elegy was more than just an idiom for children's literature. The Puritans recognized that writing about childhood is an elegiac practice. All children's literature recalls an unrecoverable past, a lost age before adulthood. And all children die—they must, to become grown-ups. "As runs the Glass / Man's Life doth pass." And when we recall the rhymes and fables of our childhood, we bring back, if only momentarily, the child in all of us. The Puritans saw childhood as a vital but passing phase of life, and in their promulgation of a children's literature, they not only looked ahead to futures for their sect, they looked back to their own individual lost innocence.

The list and the elegy lie at the heart of children's literature, but they are not just arbitrary categories. List-making always has an elegiac quality to it, as if we reckon up accomplishments or failures for the book of life. But list-making also forestalls the elegy. It becomes a way, in this life, to take up time, to keep us busy and defer that final reckoning. In a sense, then, all of our modern writings for the child are "Puritan." John Newbery's selection of his booklist in the middle of the eighteenth century still reflected the double focus of the inventory and the elegy, the content of social behavior and salvation. In America, *The New England Primer* reinforced the habits of interpretation of the early Puritans, and its alphabetic imagery would govern educational practice well into the nineteenth century.

Early children's books organized material in alphabetic ways. One of the first was Johann Comenius's *Orbis Sensualium Pictus*, a picture book that, after its initial publication in 1658, went through hundreds of editions and translations and would influence a host of later textbooks.[11] Comenius's volume ranges the sounds of animals, for example, in alphabetic order, each with a picture of the bird or beast making its sound. It also offers pictures of key virtues and vices, also ranged in alphabetic order, as a way of compiling a kind of moral dictionary. Comenius's innovation was to strip the alphabet of its overt religious aura (A is not for Adam here) and stress how it was a graphic system for representing the sounds of human speech. By organizing knowledge alphabetically, Comenius could illustrate how the order of letters mimed the order of the world.[12]

Comenius's book was central to much of later alphabetic education. But it also shared in a larger metaphorics of the letter governing the nature of the child. The "character" of children was apparent from their characters, the letters of their handwriting, and this play on the double sense of that word governed a great deal of humanist inquiry into the nature of the self and educational development. For thinkers such as More, Erasmus, and Juan Luis Vives, and for their later followers among schoolmasters, tutors, and philosophers, a student's handwriting remained a key to moral character. Forming the letters properly became an exercise in what might be called ethical legibility. Instructions and illustrations on both how to form the letters and how to hold the pen were, in effect, part of the legacy of the old manuals of courtesy. So, too, were instructions in the making and care of pens: cutting the quill, filling it with ink, keeping the penknife sharp and clean. Even the choice of a penknife could reveal the student's inner quality, his class, and his taste.[13]

This fascination with character, in all senses of the word, led to the rise, too, of the prose genre of character studies: brief accounts of emblematic professional, social, or moral types. Such works proliferated in the late sixteenth and seventeenth centuries, and one of the most popular was the *Microcosmographie* of the Anglican churchman John Earle.[14] Published originally in 1628, the *Microcosmographie* went through more than a dozen editions by the century's end. What fascinates me about Earle's work, and what clearly fascinated early readers, too, is not just its succinct limnings of familiar personages (the Antiquary, the Church-Papist, the Cook, the Pretender to Learning, the Shop-keeper, the Plodding Student, and the like), but its brilliant alphabetic conceit of "The Child" in his opening chapter.

> A Childe is a Man in small Letter, yet the best Copie of Adam before he tasted of Eve, or the Apple; and hee is happy whose small practice in the World can only write this Character. Hee is natures fresh picture newly drawn in Oyle, which time and much handling dimmes and defaces. His Soule is yet a white paper unscribbled with observations of the world, wherewith at length it becomes a blurr'd Note-booke.... His father hath writ him as his owne little story, wherein he reades those dayes of his life that he cannot remember; and sightes to see what innocence he has out liv'd.
>
> (B1r–B2v)

A is indeed for Adam here—and for apple—and the character of the child is explicitly to be compared to the characters on the page. Children are to adults as small letters are to capitals. The soul is a blank sheet—the old image of the *tabula rasa* now transformed into a schoolboy's smudged notebook. The father here does not merely sire the child; he has "writ him as his owne little story, wherein he reades those dayes of his life that he cannot remember"—an image of such poignancy and brilliance that the modern reader cannot but recall Charles Dickens's transformation of this sentiment at the beginning of his *David Copperfield*: "Whether I shall turn out to be the hero of my own life, ... these pages must show."

Children become the books of our imagination here. And if the child is kin to letter or to page, then the sustained study of the letters and the pages of the world becomes the key to understanding childhood. This process is precisely what the Puritans would gather from an argument like Earle's—and though Earle himself was no dissenter from the Church of England or the king, his book had such wide popularity throughout the period of Puritan activity in England (even during the Interregnum, there were three separate editions published) that we cannot but see it as part of the trajectory of character inquiry that shaped the Puritan alphabetization of childhood. Reading and writing, recognizing the letter and correctly forming its character, were the poles of its pedagogy. For Elisha Coles, whose *Nolens Volens*, a Latin grammar followed by an alphabetical arrangement of key terms from the Bible (published in 1675), even everyday words have their scriptorial power.[15] Under the word "Iron," Coles supplies these biblical quotations:

> Oh that my words were now written, oh that they were printed in a book.
> That they were graven with an iron pen and laid in the rock for ever.
>
> [Job 19:23–24]

> Take thou unto thee an iron pen, and set it for a wall of iron between thee
> and the city and set thy face against it, and it shall be besieged.
>
> [Ezekiel 4:3]

Such quotations would inform the child that even behind simple terms lie arts of writing. Indeed, Job's verses may well stand for the desires of any author who would wish his letters printed or engraved in stone forever. Cotton Mather, too, found pedagogic writing in the Bible. In his *A. B. C. of Religion* (published in Boston in 1713), he notes: "You have here a Psalm, of lessons to be learn'd by children; even as soon as they learn their letters. In the Hebrew, every verse begins with a new letter, according to the order of the alphabet. Perhaps, that so the Hebrew children might have it as early as they had their alphabet. Children are here called upon" (A3r). The order of the alphabet controls the order of the Psalms; the education of the ancient Hebrew child anticipates that of the contemporary Puritan. Behind every lesson is, etymologically, the *lectio*: the act of reading. And behind *scripture* lies the essence of that word: the scripting of the letter.

The alphabet was everywhere, but it was in the Bible in particular. Scripture itself was an encyclopedia of knowledge, and the early primers often offered alphabetic lists of biblical words. Coles's *Nolens Volens* is such an example, as is the earlier *English Schoole* (1635) by the now almost forgotten mathematician John Pell (1611–1685).[16] As part of the circle around the educator Samuel Hartlib, Pell came in contact with Comenius's ideas of alphabetic instruction, and *The English Schoole* took its young readers through lists of biblical words, first of single syllables and all the way up to seven syllables. Pell's book has been seen as the inspiration for a far better known, and similarly titled, compendium of biblical vocabulary. Tobias Ellis's *English School* first appeared in 1680, and, like Pell's book, it relied on the Bible for its basic lists of words.[17] But Ellis went beyond his source. He added "All the proper Names of Scripture in an Alphabetical Order," running from names of two syllables to those of six. He offered pictures for the words of one, two, and three syllables, keyed to alphabetical order. And at its close, his book presented facsimile models of handwriting, running from the book hand for the student to the secretary hand of the professional. Each of these model script sheets begins with an alphabet—first in small letters and then in capitals—and then offers biblical quotations. Blocked off and framed on their respective pages, these concluding sheets are much like hornbooks for the writing child: guides to character-building in both senses of the term, as they provide a template for writing the characters of English and for living out the character of the good Christian.

Were all of these books, strictly speaking, Puritan products? Some of their authors, such as Coles, were Puritan divines. Others, such as Pell, moved in reformist circles (he was Cromwell's envoy to Switzerland) but came back into official life after the Restoration. All we know of Ellis is his appellation "minister of the Gospel" on the title pages of his books (whatever his Interregnum affiliations, he did dedicate his *English School* to Charles II). What they all share, regardless of their specific sectarian affiliation, is their deeply reformist sense of scripture and an attitude toward imagery far different from that governing the older, Catholic iconography of sainthood or salvation. Everyday objects stand side by side with the things of biblical history in these books—not so much to popularize the Bible, but to make clear that all life is, ultimately, scriptural.

The epitome of this tradition was the famous *New England Primer*, a book that probably originated in the 1680s and 1690s but took on its familiar shape in the edition of 1727 (which is the earliest surviving edition as well).[18] The *Primer* was, throughout its long life, many things. It embraced alphabets and emblems, proverbs and prayers, poetry and moral tales. Though its main contents remained stable, its tone shifted markedly in the middle of the eighteenth century, becoming more evangelical and richer in hymns and prayers (all probably in response to the religious climate change spurred by the so-called Great Awakening). But in its earliest form, the *Primer* reflects the controlling idioms of Puritan children's literature and, in the process, acts as something of a gloss on the inventories and the elegies that filled the books of this literature.

The *Primer* begins with lists. Its hornbook-like opening presents the alphabet in both roman and italic print and then, on the next page, both the "great" and "small" English letters in black letter and in roman type. From the start, then, the *Primer* is not only an instruction manual for spiritual literacy; it is an inventory of typography as well. The bookishness of prayer is central to its argument: in the famous picture alphabet, the letter B stands for "Thy Life to Mend / This Book Attend," and even H reveals "My Book and Heart / Shall never part." And so, when the child moves past these letters to the section titled "The Dutiful Child's Promises," it is to "learn these and such like Sentences by Heart"—to put the book precisely in the heart. The Alphabet of Lessons, the Lord's Prayer, the Creed, the Ten Commandments—all are, as the Commandments end, "words which I command thee this Day shall be in thy Heart." The heart is now a kind of book, a page or tablet on which lessons should be written. Such is the lesson of the poem attributed to the martyr John Rogers that comes toward the end of the *Primer*.

> Give ear my Children to my words,
>> whom God hath dearly bought,
> Lay up his Laws within your heart,
>> and print them in your thought.
> I leave you here a little Book,
>> for you to look upon;
> That you may see your Fathers face,
>> when he is dead and gone.

The poem offers an anatomy of literacy. Ear, heart, and eye become the operative organs of the child's understanding. And in contrast to the earlier, pre-Reformation habit of meditating on the wounds of Christ or the tortured crucifixion of his body, this poem exhorts the child to look upon the face of God. That act of seeing is an act of reading. The act of knowing is an act of printing. "Lay up his Laws within your heart"—the phrase "lay up" meant, in the print shop, the activity of washing the forme, or composed page.[19] God's laws are always in the form of an inscription, whether it be in the tablets of the Ten Commandments or on the printed page of text.

The *Primer* thus taught many things: the child's place in the family, society, and creation; the need to obey the parental law, whether it be set out by living fathers or by God the Father; and the habits of controlled expression central to religious and civic life. One did not speak without consideration, and the *Primer* stresses (as did many other manuals of Puritan instruction) the importance of governing one's utterances. Oral catechizing, notes David H. Watters in his study of the *Primer*, "initiated the child into a discourse which is controlled in form and content." It "prepared the child to approach written texts as if they spoke with the authority of a parent."[20]

But if the *Primer* is a guide to life, it is, as well, a book of death. The dead are everywhere, from the biblical verses that precede the hornbook opening, to the poems at its core, to the story of the martyred John Rogers at its end. "For surely there is an end, and thy expectation shall not be cut off." This bit of Proverbs opens the book, and the end is everywhere. The cat illustrating the letter C plays, but afterward slays. Rachel, in letter R, mourns for her firstborn. Time cuts down all, and as for youth, "Death soonest nips." The verses that follow the Ten Commandments (perhaps written by Cotton Mather himself) note:

> I in the Burying Place may see
> Graves shorter there than I;
> From Death's Arrest no Age is free,
> Young Children too may die.

It is only a short step from this little poem to the tales of the young dead collected in Janeway's *Token for Children*—a book, it is worth noting, that was printed in Boston within two decades of its first English appearance and that remained a mainstay of the American, as well as the British, Puritan library well into the eighteenth century. The telos of the *Primer*, like that of Janeway's *Token*, is the world to come.

That world to come is, in the end, found in the book itself. For the point I want to stress about *The New England Primer*, as I stress about all children's literature, is that it is not just a vessel for instruction but is an artifact itself. The physicality of this small book drives home the imagery from printing and typography that permeates its content. It is an object, held in little hands. But like all objects in this world, it breaks up, decays, wears out. As the poem of John Rogers puts it:

> To you my Heirs of earthly Things,
>   which I do leave behind,
> That you may read and understand,
>   and keep it in your mind.
> That as you have been Heirs of that
>   which once shall wear away,
> You also may possess that part,
>   which never shall decay.

Who knows how many versions of *The New England Primer* predate the edition of 1727? Who knows how many copies circulated of that issue, of which but one brittle, damaged book remains? To hold one of these books in our modern hands is to realize not that old texts were lost, but that they were so used and handled, pocketed and plucked out, that they must have fallen apart. Worn away by countless children, these books were, quite simply, read to death.

Books may be read to death, but so, too, may be people. If anyone read himself to death, it might have been John Harvy, one of James Janeway's exemplary children, born in 1654 and dead at age eleven.[21] A prodigy in language, he could speak at two as well as other children did at five; and though restricted by his parents from attending school at such a young age, he himself found a school of his own. "Without the knowledge of his parents," little John attended school "and made a very strange progress in his learning, and was able to read distinctly, before most children are able to know their letters." His story in Janeway's *Token for Children* is a story of the life virtually sacrificed to books. Obsessed by reading, "inquisitive . . . and very careful to observe and remember what he heard," John Harvy emerges as the model child behind what would become the pedagogy of *The New England Primer*. It is as if he lives out all of the injunctions of the *Primer*. His book and heart shall never part. To mend his life, he attends to the book. He models the Puritan ideal of carefully controlled speech, while at the same time illustrating the doctrine of what John Bunyan would call "grace abounding." In Janeway's words, he acts often "without any instruction from his Parents, but from an inward Principle of Grace." He learns his catechism perfectly, in keeping with the instructions to be idealized in *The New England Primer*. But that is not enough for John: "He was not content to learn it himself, but he would be putting others upon learning their Catechism." No one, not even his mother's maids, escapes his attention.

When he was six years old, John Harvy was afflicted with "sore eyes." Instructed by the doctors to rest his eyes and not to read, John could not obey. He would "stand by the window and read the Bible and good Books; yea, he was so greedy of reading the Scripture, and took so much delight in it, that he would scarce allow himself time to dress himself; . . . judging it God's Command that he should give himself up to reading, he could not be beat off from it, till he was so bad, that he had like never to have recovered his sight more." John practically reads himself blind, and this physical self-abnegation appears throughout Janeway's story to show how the boy put words always above things. Learning was "his recreation. He was never taught to write, but took it of his own ingenuity." He ate sparsely, dressed soberly, and prayed earnestly.

If John almost read himself blind, he almost read himself to death, too—or, to put it more precisely, he read to prepare himself for death. Death was the telos of his reading. "He was next to the bible most taken with reading of Reverend Mr. Baxter's works, especially his *Saints Ever-lasting Rest*, and truly, the thoughts of that Rest, and Eternity, seemed to swallow up all other thoughts; and he lived in a constant preparation for it, and looked more like one that was ripe for Glory, than an inhabitant of this lower World." By the time he was eleven, his family had moved to London, and the plague had hit (it was, as Janeway states, "that dreadful year, Sixty Five"). With his family members dying around him, John keeps to his *Saints Rest*, "which he read with exceeding curiosity," even writing "several Divine meditations" of his own. Sickened by the plague himself, John asks his mother—in what must be one of the most curdlingly pathetic moments of pre-Victorian children's literature—"I pray let me have Mr. Baxters Book, what I may read a little more of Eternity, before I go into it." Speech soon fails John, and he dies.

This is a story about language and interpretation, literacy and elegy, the world and the word. John Harvy's is a life of texts, a life lived for the book and the sermon. He would, Janeway notes, sermonize his schoolmates, often taking as his text the biblical sentence "The Axe is laid on the Root of the Tree, and every Tree that bringeth not forth good Fruit, is hewn down and cast into the Fire." Imagine reading this page in one of the many American reprints of *A Token for Children* of the first third of the eighteenth century and then turning to the final alphabet page of *The New England Primer*. There, for the letter T, a skeleton with scythe and hourglass stands beside the couplet "Time cuts down all / Both great and small." And at the bottom, a picture of a tree and the three lines "Zacheus he / Did climb the Tree / His Lord to see." It is as if John Harvy had an almost intuitive grasp of Puritan typology, a sense of what was both narratively and iconographically central to religious pedagogy.

John Bunyan certainly had such a grasp. At the close of the poem that begins *Pilgrim's Progress*, titled "The Author's Apology for his Book," Bunyan enjoins his audience to follow the imaginative landscape of his allegory, to "see a Truth within a Fable."[22] Reading *Pilgrim's Progress*, though, is also reading oneself:

> Would'st read thy self, and read thou know'st not what
> And yet know whether thou art blest or not,
> By reading the same lines? O then come hither,
> And lay my Book, thy Head and Heart together.

(p. 7)

The book and the heart—now joined by the head—shall never part for the attentive reader, and if Bunyan's book is about spirit and salvation, it is also about learning letters. *Pilgrim's Progress* begins with a scene of reading, as the dreaming narrator envisions a man with "a Book in his hand." He looked, "and saw him open the Book, and Read therein; and as he read, he wept and trembled" (p. 8). Experience is inseparable from reading—as when, for example, later in the story, Hopeful comes upon a massive pillar and sees "written above upon the head thereof, a Writing in an unusual hand; but he being no Scholar, called to Christian (for he was learned) to see if he could pick out the meaning: so he came, and after a little laying of Letters together, he found the same to be this, Remember Lot's Wife" (p. 108). Such a scene recalls the encounters with inscribed objects that fill the older, medieval romances of the Arthurian tradition. But here the encounter is pressed into the service of a larger pedagogical and doctrinal goal: to get us all to recognize that life is about laying letters together, that experience is filled with images and allegories, and that biblical typology peppers the landscapes of the everyday.

This emphasis on spiritual literacy dovetailed with the Puritan tradition of the alphabet and the importance placed on scriptural education. It would contribute to the immense popularity of *Pilgrim's Progress* as a book for home and school, as one of the mainstays of early reading for two centuries of British and American children. But there was much more that made it appealing. For all its allegorical and pedagogic heft, it offered an adventure narrative familiar from old folktales and romances. There remains something childlike about its encounters with such characters as Giant Despair, with his castle and his "grim and surly voice," and his "nasty and stinking" dungeon (pp. 113–14). Children were clearly reading the book almost as soon as it appeared: witness the account of a certain young John Draper in Christopher Ness's *A Spiritual Legacy* (1684). Before he had turned seven, Draper was turning to books to help him with his "melancholick" need to pray. "I little minded what I heard, till I read the *Pilgrims Progress*, which made me again grown melancholick . . . to the observation of others; then the good providence of God brought to my hands Mr Baxters *Call to the unconverted* which (through grace) shewed me the necessity of my conversion."[23] Bunyan becomes the goad, though not in this case the instrument, to religious awareness, even for a little boy; and at the end of his life he came to write explicitly for children, publishing *A Book for Boys and Girls: or Country Rhimes for Children* in 1686. Here, in a blend of primer exercise and folk poems, Bunyan seeks to teach children "what the Letters be / And how they may improve their A, B, C" (prefatory poem). As in *Pilgrim's Progress*, there is a fair amount of catechizing in this book. Children are taught through questioning and answering, and the experience of reading the sequence of "Country Rhimes" may be akin to the experience of Christian's journey throughout *Pilgrim's Progress*: we are always coming upon cryptic messages, strange emblems, and representations of ideal and vicious behavior that we need to interpret.

At times, too, *Pilgrim's Progress* could itself stand as one of those very emblems. Benjamin Franklin (as he recounts in his *Autobiography*) comes upon Bunyan's book much as a traveler would come upon a cryptic text. It allures, it attracts, it goads the hero into reading. Like one of Bunyan's peripatetic characters, or even one of James Janeway's book-ridden children, Franklin "from a Child . . . was fond of Reading, and all the little Money that came into my Hands was ever laid out in Books" (p. 1317).[24] His first, of course, was *Pilgrim's Progress*; and, pleased with that work, he sets out to collect the whole of Bunyan's works, "in separate little Volumes." Soon, however, he sells them off to buy a set of history books, and young Franklin apparently moves beyond Bunyan's allegories to embrace Plutarch, Defoe, and Mather. But Bunyan cannot be suppressed. When Franklin sets out to sea, he runs into a drunken Dutchman who asks Franklin to dry off one of his prized possessions.

It prov'd to be my old favourite Author Bunyan's Pilgrim's Progress in Dutch finely printed on good Paper with copper Cuts, a Dress better than I had ever seen it wear in its own Language. I have since found that it has been translated into most of the Languages of Europe, and suppose it has been more generally read than any other Book except perhaps the Bible.— Honest John was the first that I know of who mix'd Narration & Dialogue, a Method of Writing very engaging to the Reader, who in the most interesting Parts finds himself as it were brought into the Company, & present at the Discourse. De foe in his Cruso, his Moll Flanders, Religious Courtship, Family Instructor, & other Pieces, has imitated it with Success. And Richardson has done the same in his Pamela, &c. (p. 1326)

Bunyan always comes first, not just in the history of the child but in the history of literature. *Pilgrim's Progress* was, in every sense of the term, a formative book: one that shaped not just readers but writers. It was the book against which all books could be measured, whether they be the Bible or *Pamela*.

Bunyan, in this account, gives rise to novelistic fiction, much as he gives rise to self-accounts by readers, and his book does so in several ways. First off, it is the story of a family and a life. But what a life it is. Here is no ideal father, homebound with the wife and children. Christian, the book's hero, runs off from the start, apparently for higher goals: "So I saw in my Dream, that the Man began to run; Now he had not run far from his own door, but his Wife and Children perceiving it, began to cry after him to return: but the Man put his fingers in his Ears, and ran on crying, Life, Life, Eternal life" (p. 10). How many fathers had run off for higher things? How many saw their families as a prison, how many had been counseled by friends such as Christian's—here, named Obstinate and Pliable—to come back to comforts? The family is imperiled at the start of *Pilgrim's Progress*, and that peril must have struck the children who read it as a terrifying threat. Bunyan himself had abandoned his family to pursue his preaching. He left his second wife, pregnant and with four children (one of them blind) when he went to prison in 1660. "I was," wrote Bunyan in *Grace Abounding*, "as a man who was pulling down his house upon the head of his Wife and children; yet, thought I, I must do it, I must do it."[25] Little wonder, then, that the one thing that strikes Mark Twain's Huckleberry Finn when he sees Bunyan's book on the shelf of a pleasant family's home is this fact of paternal disappearance: "One was 'Pilgrim's Progress,' about a man that left his family it didn't say why. I read considerable in it now and then. The statements was interesting, but tough."[26] For Huck, whose own father had left his family but didn't say why, the opening feint of *Pilgrim's Progress* has to resonate with personal experience. Whatever he may have found in his considerable reading of the book, he may well have been looking (as generations of children looked) for some compelling reason why the father leaves.

The opening of *Pilgrim's Progress* thus sets out one of the central motifs of the modern novel: the absent parent. Part of the motivation for reading to the end of Bunyan's long book must be the desire to see Christian reunited with his family and the parent-child bond reaffirmed. Such was the business of the book's part 2, a celebration of domestic life, of fellowship, of family togetherness. Part 1 of *Pilgrim's Progress* takes place on the open road; part 2 transpires in the home. Here are the cozy rooms, the enclosed gardens, the welcoming inns of local comfort. This is, in many ways, less Christian's book than it is his wife's, Christiana's, book. If anyone should knock upon its door, notes Bunyan in the poem that opens part 2, "then answer thou, Christiana is here." Within this house of fiction, children's games are played: there are riddles, little songs, and stories. As the innkeeper Gaius explains to Christiana and her children, "Hard Texts are Nuts. . . . Ope then the Shells, and you shall have the Meat" (p. 263). The little game becomes a source of understanding. Food for children is food for the soul. To recall Janeway's tale of John Harvey, these are savory words or moral teaching.

The close of *Pilgrim's Progress* resonates, as well, with the elegiacs of Janeway's *Token for Children*. Christiana dies, called by a written message, a letter from death. Letters from the beyond cluster at the book's end, all accompanied by tokens (this is Bunyan's own word) that the messengers are real. Again and again, characters ask for a "Token of the truth" of the message (e.g., on p. 307). Again and again, allegorical figures congregate as if they were at some post office of death: Mr. Honest, Mr. Valiant, Mr. Stand-fast, Mr. Great-heart. Like Bunyan himself, Stand-fast recounts how he had left his family—"a Wife, and five small Children" (p. 310). The whole feel of this ending recalls the tropes and trappings of the Puritan deathbed—complete with echoes of Ecclesiastes—and the book ends as Bunyan says good-bye both to his fictional children and to his living readers. Both will live on: "As for Christian's Children, the four Boys that Christiana brought with her, with their Wives and children, I did not stay where I was, till they were gone over. Also since I came away, I heard one say, that they were yet alive, and so would be for the Increase of the Church in that Place where they were for a time" (p. 311).

The children of the Puritans had also gone over—not by fording some river of death, but by sailing the Atlantic. The progress of those pilgrims stood as the arch-narrative of national identity, and Bunyan's book was there almost from its first appearance (the first American edition appeared in 1681). So, too, was Janeway's, whose *Token for Children* appeared in Boston in 1700. But now, it is explicitly as an *American* edition. Appended to the stories of its exemplary dead is a new section, "A Token for the Children of New-England." Not lacking in their own ideal youth, the colonists should have their tales told, and so this collection of "notable things" appears "in Imitation of the Excellent Janeway's Token for Children." Notice that word *imitation* here. It is as if New England's *Token* is a child to Janeway's father: a text made in imitation of the model, much as later versions of *Pilgrim's Progress* would be shaped according to the template of Bunyan's literary fatherhood. Recall now, too, John Earle's imaginative formulation in the *Microcosmographie*: a child is a man in small letter, and his soul is a white paper. Literary history is family history, and the early American commitment to a sustained children's literature only reinforces a conception of the childhood of American identity.

Books, like Americans, are children. The commitment not just to reprinting, but to imitating and abridging, illustrating, and adapting books for younger readers makes later writers children to the masters. Recall Franklin's reacquaintance with his old familiar Honest John, now in Dutch. It remains recognizable, though in a different language and appearance: "finely printed on good Paper with copper Cuts, a Dress better than I had ever seen it wear in its own Language." Bunyan was constantly being re-dressed. Illustrated as early as 1680, it was soon paraphrased into verse: *Pilgrim's Progress in Poesie* (1697). This book's opening address, "To the Charitable Reader," so brilliantly blends all the themes of Puritan poetics, family metaphorics, and literary history that it bears quoting in full.

Books in our Studies, share in our Favour, as Children in our Families; some one carries the Belt: And so we please our selves by Habits, or Characters of Distinction.

Either in the first, as Joseph by his Father; or in the second, as Jacob by his Mother, managing her Project even to a stealing of the blessing.

The Lot of Fondness, oft falls upon the lest, or youngest Child; which, tho it may not speak as well as the Elder, yet may have some Marks of a deep Judgment, and Excellent Invention; The very Endowments which drew my Affections to the Pilgrim's Progress. So I took the Pilgrim to my own glass, ambitious to dress him for my own pleasure.

It's well I had no higher Thoughts, for as I went on in the Dressing-Room, Art so often fail'd me, that I was ready to throw up All; as looking far better in his plain Cloaths, than by all the Lacing, Pricking, and Pinning, that I could afford him. Yet sometimes I thought better; and as a beautiful Child, that looks well at one time, and shows Courser at another, so did the Pilgrim in my Eye; Insomuch, I was ready to say, as some Parents, of a worse-favour'd Child; But thou art my own, I could fling thee away. And thus disputing it with my self, what to do, in comes a bold thought, saying, Nay, hold! don't do so. Thou hast had other thoughts of it thy self; and so may another man; tho at first he dislike it, another time it may look better.[27]

Behind the image of the book better dressed lies a genealogy of art and an association of both literary and family history. Someone carries the belt—in some families, one of the children is going to be beaten. There are good children and bad children, young children and old children. The biblical accounts of Joseph and of Jacob here take on a weird new dynamic, as if we were meant to reimagine the Old Testament's founding families in all the pettiness of modern life.

We are asked, too, to reimagine books as errant boys. This little book is the youngest child of literature here, a plaything to be brought before the father's glass. Again, family life, be it historical or figurative, rings with violence. The dressing of the book is lacing, pricking, pinning. The same child can be beautiful or coarse: if you were not my own, I'd throw you out. But wait—in another light, it may look better. *Pilgrim's Progress* is children's literature here because its literary history is inextricably associated with the life of children. It is, in this versifier's handling, not the father of all novels, but the childish plaything of the father. And behind such paternalism lies the ever-present threat of dismissal: but thou art my own, I could fling thee away.

If the child is a man in small letter, then the adapted book is a child to the fatherly original. The eighteenth century would see a spate of adaptations and abridgments: not just of *Pilgrim's Progress*, but of Defoe's *Robinson Crusoe*, Richardson's *Clarissa*, and the Bible itself.[28] Whether in Britain or America, these publication projects spoke to a real, social need for children's books. But they also spoke to the literary need to shape a writing self against the fatherhood of the great authors. All texts remain imitations, whether they be the American *Token for Children* or the English *Pilgrim's Progress in Poesie*. And whatever the precise sectarian affiliations of their makers, such books, too, remain deeply a part of Puritan experience. For the Puritans' literary history, much like their social history, was keyed to family and inheritance. The imitation of exemplary figures governed both the growth of children and the growth of authorship. In this sense, then, the rise of children's literary reading and writing is inseparable from the pursuit of literacy central to the Puritan ideal of education.

That the pursuit of literacy went on in prose *and* verse is central to this Puritan ideal, and few poets have had the impact on the history of children's literature that Isaac Watts did.[29] The son of a Nonconformist minister, Watts grew up in the world of religious dissent. Prohibited from attending university as a non-Anglican, he nonetheless received an education rivaling that of any of his contemporaries, and over the space of fifty years he composed some of the most compelling poetry ever written for children.

Watts's *Divine Songs, Attempted in Easy Language for the Use of Children*, first printed in 1715, was undeniably the most popular book of children's verse ever published. Twenty editions appeared in his lifetime alone, and the impact of his poetry can be felt from Benjamin Franklin (for whom it had the status of moral maxims) to Lewis Carroll (who parodied it throughout *Alice in Wonderland*) to Emily Dickinson (who clearly modeled many of her poems on the hymnal idioms of Watts's songs). His poems speak directly to the themes of literate experience and elegiac feeling that were central to the Puritan imagination. They bridge the allegory of Bunyan and the aphorism of *The New England Primer*. Quite simply, they defined, for generations of parents and children, just what verse *was*.

But Watts's work for children went beyond these little songs. He published a *Logick* in 1725, an *Art of Reading and Writing English* in 1721, and, toward the end of his life in 1741, the *Improvement of the Mind*, a work of such reputation that Samuel Johnson could declaim, "Whoever has the care of instructing others, may be charged with deficience in his duty if this book is not recommended."[30] Watts's poetry is part and parcel of this broader educational project—a project designed not simply to teach good behavior or a moral life, but to stress how both lie focused in the proper reading, writing, and pronouncing of the English language. Watts's work, in short, may be thought of as an argument for the vernacularity of child-rearing and for the cultivation of an English juvenile imagination.

Take, for example, his poem "Praise to God for learning to read," from the *Divine Songs*.

> The praises of my Tongue
> I offer to the Lord,
> That I was taught, and learnt so young
> To read his holy Word.[31]

The poem begins, as so many of Watts's poems do, with a first-person assertion of voice. That voice is everywhere—"Great God, to thee my voice I raise," begins another poem—as Watts's poems take, in effect, the language of the psalms to magnify God's grace. The poem about learning how to read is, therefore, as much a poem about learning how to speak. The eye and tongue, the heart and mouth, conjoin themselves in this anatomy of literacy. Look at the progress of its imagery:

> That I am led to see
> I can do nothing well;
> . . . . . . . . . . . . . . . . . .
> Here I can read and learn,
> . . . . . . . . . . . . . . . . . .
> O may that Spirit teach,
> And make my Heart receive
> Those Truths. . . .

My book and heart shall never part, and Watts anticipates this axiom from *The New England Primer* throughout the arc of the *Divine Songs*. There is "Praise for birth and Education in a Christian Land," followed by "Praise for the Gospel," "The Excellency of the Bible," and then "Praise to God for learning to read." These are encomia to literacy, arguments for a theology of looking. The Bible poem begins:

> Great God, with Wonder and with Praise
> On all thy Works I look;
> But still thy Wisdom, Pow'r and Grace,
> Shines brightest in thy Book.
>
> The Stars that in their Courses roll,
> Have much Instruction given;
> But thy good Word informs my Soul
> How I may climb to Heaven.

Now, turn to the poem titled "The All-Seeing God":

> Almighty God, thy piercing Eye
>> Strikes thro' the Shades of Night;
> And our most secret Actions lie
>> All open to thy Sight.

God is the greatest reader of them all. Watts builds a theory of devotion centered on the act of looking at the page, the word, the letter. We may read the Bible and find in it knowledge far beyond that of the stars, he notes. But when God reads, he sees it all. Our actions lie open like the pages of a book.

> There's not a Sin that we commit,
>> Nor wicked Word we say,
> But in thy dreadful Book 'tis writ,
>> Against the Judgment-Day.

> And must the Crimes that I have done
>> Be read and publish'd there?
> Be all expos'd before the Sun,
>> While Men and Angels hear?

To read through the *Divine Songs* is to be struck again and again by their arresting emphasis on literacy, by their associations among books of men, the book of God, and the book of life.

But it is not enough to read the word or even to praise it. The poet must reveal the many technical possibilities of that praise. Watts offers up the Hosanna and the Gloria in several forms. Each one appears in what he calls long meter, common meter, and short meter. These are technical experiments, tours de force of the poetic imagination, that exemplify what Watts would argue in his *Art of Reading and Writing English*. There, he would show how reading English verse aloud is the epitome of literate ability. Different meters create different effects. Poetry, he writes, allows "a great deal of just Liberty and Variation, . . . without destroying the Harmony of the Verse." Such variation, he goes on, "adds a Beauty and Grace to the Poetry." The goal in reading verse aloud, then, is the expression of "harmony," a technique possible, Watts argues, only if the reader performs with a natural expression—pronounces verse as "common language, without affecting to add new Musick to the Lines."[33]

Control and regulation, however, extend beyond the voice to embrace the written and the printed letter. There is a brilliant clarity in the layout, typography, and simple legibility of Watts's pages. His use of roman and italic typefaces follows precisely his explanations in *The Art of Reading and Writing English*. The pages of the "Dedication" in the early editions of the *Divine Songs* are models of clean printing, with their large roman letters and wide margins. How different are these pages, addressed to the young daughters of Sir Thomas Abney, than those of the preface for the adult reader that follow: there, close-set italic words jostle on the page. But when we finally arrive at the text of the *Divine Songs*, we are back to the large letter and the wide-spaced word. The book remains, in brief, a model of typography for the beginning reader.

At the end of this collection of songs, another poem appears (for the first time in the eighth edition of 1727): "Some copies of the following Hymn having got abroad already into several Hands, the Author has been perswaded at last to permit it to appear in Publick, at the End of these Divine Songs for Children."[34] What follows is perhaps the most famous of Watts's poems, "A Cradle Hymn."

Watts effectively transforms this poem from an orally transmitted, individually copied work into a printed, authorized text. Watts is the "Author" here, rounding up copies that have gotten into other hands. He makes it public by publishing it. "A Cradle Hymn" becomes the capstone to the volume as a whole: not just an address to a little child in bed, but something of an authorial farewell to an audience. The book now ends with bedtime—as all great children's stories really do—and "A Cradle Hymn" becomes the final text for any child to read (or any parent to read aloud) before the dream time.

> Hush! my Dear, lye still and slumber;
> Holy Angels guard thy Bed!
> Heavenly blessings, without Number,
> Gently falling on thy Head.

"A Cradle Hymn" is both an inventory and an elegy. Along the arc of its fourteen numbered stanzas, the reader moves from the child's bed to the holy manger and, in the end, to the Passion. In the quanta of its quatrains, we see something very similar to the alphabet poem of *The New England Primer*: a set of individual encounters with scriptural history, religious imagery, and the things of this world. Much like that poem from the *Primer*, too, each stanza has a focus word, a central term around which the quatrain orbits. Each one is capitalized, each one stands out at the beginning of the stanza: Dear, Babe, Heaven, Cradle, Babe, Manger, Child, Story,

Shepherds, Babe, Manger, Child, Days, Kisses. "It has been," Watts wrote in his *Art of Reading and Writing English*, "the growing Custom of this Age in printing of every thing, but especially Poetry or Verse, to begin every Name of a thing (which is call'd a Noun Substantive) with a Great Letter" (p. 66). "A Cradle Hymn" follows this custom precisely, and the great letters, in their sequence, mark the ABCs of its devotions.

Writing for the *New England Courant* under the pseudonym "Silence Dogood" in 1722, the sixteen-year-old Benjamin Franklin begins his essay on the New England funeral elegy with a quotation from Watts's poetry.[35] Most people, Silence writes, do not think that good poetry can be written in New England. But there is an emerging practice of the elegy, and in the course of his essay, Franklin goes on to measure the ideal form of this poetry against Watts's example. He offers a set of instructions on how to title, address, organize, and pattern the poem. Use a set of "Melancholly Expressions," he advises, such as *dreadful, deadly, cruel cold death, unhappy fate, weeping eyes*, and so on. Then add rhymes, such as *power, flower; quiver, shiver; grieve us, leave us; tell you, excel you; expeditions, physicians; fatigue him, intrigue him*. And in the end, "you must spread all upon Paper."

From the first hornbooks through *The New England Primer*, from Janeway through Bunyan to Watts, from prose to verse, from alphabet to elegy, the Puritans spread all upon paper. Franklin, at this moment himself barely out of childhood, recognizes all the tricks and tropes of Puritan poetics. Even in his choice of pseudonym, he recalls the Puritan habits of nomenclature. "Silence Dogood" is as much a satiric jab as Washington Irving's later "Ichabod Crane" or Dickens's "Ebenezer Scrooge." But Franklin's choice recalls not so much the characters of the Geneva Bible as the injunctions of the *Primer*: be quiet and do good works. There were, in fact, attested examples of children named "Silence" and "Dogood" in the seventeenth and early eighteenth centuries.[36] Franklin's witty moniker returns us to the generations of those Puritans who would break with the old paternalistic past and name their children anew.

The Puritans were always making up receipts and recipes from the account books of their moral lives to their textbooks for good behavior, proper reading, and good writing. There is a primer-like aura to all these writings, as if Franklin could write his own "New England Primer" for the public ode. But all these works are not just elegies for others. Janeway's little children, or the Christ child, or Bunyan's fictive family, or Watts's little readers—in the end, all pale before the true subject of elegiac writing: the elegist himself, or herself. Franklin's parodic "Panegyrick" concludes with this couplet:

> Then least what is your due should not be said,
> Write your own Elegy against you're Dead.[37]

We all write our own elegies before we die, and in a sense the children's books we read and write are all obituaries for ourselves. "I could give thee a thousand Kisses," says the speaker in the final stanza of Watts's "Cradle Hymn."

> Hoping what I most desire:
> Not a Mother's fondest Wishes,
> Can to greater Joys aspire.

I *could* give you a thousand kisses—but I don't. I hope, I wish, I aspire. This is a poetry of what has not happened, of what the speaker wishes for or thinks of doing but does not. Like all tales for children, Watts's "Cradle Hymn" hovers in that middle world between a memory of the past and anticipation of the future: between nostalgia and anxiety. We reckon up the tokens of our time and convince ourselves that we may find in such accounts a meaning for the lives we have lived and some inkling of what is to come.

And in America, a country always living between memory and anticipation, these strains of children's literature have a unique command. We're always wondering, like Huck Finn, why the father left and whether he will return. We're always imitating models, whether they be the literary tokens of the British or the moral templates of the biblical. "From a Child I was fond of Reading," wrote Franklin in his *Autobiography*. To be a child is to be fond of reading: to be the man in small letter, whose book and heart shall never part.

# *Playthings of the Mind*

## JOHN LOCKE AND
## CHILDREN'S LITERATURE

"Children," wrote the early eighteenth-century educator John Clarke, "are Strangers in the World." They are born without ideas, and what they learn comes to them through their experience. Their "first Acquaintance . . . is with sensible Objects. Those must store the yet empty Cabinet of the Mind with a variety of Ideas." It is, he goes on, "the business of Education to watch over that weak and tender Age, that the yet unwary thoughtless Mind, uncapable of feeling into Nature and the Consequences of things, be not too much led away, and entirely possessed by the deluding Pleasures of Sense." The end of education is the "forming of the Mind to Virtue," and the syllabus of study (language, history, mathematics, rhetoric, and so on) calibrates itself to that end. One would think, Clarke continues, that given the centrality of education to the growth of the young mind and body, there would be a "great Variety of Books" on the subject. But there are few, and in the end, "I know not of any in our Language that are worth the Perusal but Mr. Locke's."[1]

John Clarke and his many peers in pedagogy have been long forgotten. But John Locke has not. In his *Essay concerning Human Understanding* (1690) and, more pointedly, *Some Thoughts concerning Education* (1692), Locke offered a philosophically grounded theory of education. With its governing convictions that the human being has no innate ideas at birth; that the child learns from the experience of the external world; that pictures, toys, and models can assist in teaching words and concepts; and, finally, that the goal of education should be both instruction and delight—with all this, Locke's theory has had perhaps more impact on tutoring and teaching than that of any other educator in the past three hundred years. Not just in Britain, but in France, Germany, Holland, and America, Locke was revered as the defining figure (dare we say the father?) of educational theory and practice.[2]

If his writings helped shape children's schooling, they helped, too, to shape their literature. Mrs. Sarah Trimmer, writing in 1802, noted that before Locke's time there were hardly any books for children, but "when the idea of uniting amusement with instruction was once started by . . . Mr. Locke, books for children were soon produced."[3] Throughout the eighteenth century and well into the nineteenth, children's books took on the focus of Locke's philosophy and taste. His belief, for example, that the child is born a blank slate—a *tabula rasa*, whose mind's cabinet is empty—influenced a way of representing knowledge and experience in literary narrative. Indeed, one could well argue that the governing epistemology of children's literature has been, since the early eighteenth century, deeply Lockean. By denying the possibility of innate ideas, Locke and his followers transformed the child into a product of his or her education. And by focusing that education on sensible experience, writers of children's literature could tell stories of growth as encounters with the things of this world.

Unlike in the older medieval romances or Bunyan's *Pilgrim's Progress*, the sequence of experience was not designed to confirm some preexisting condition or belief. And unlike in the manuals of courtesy that were the earlier basis of much social education, behavior in Locke's world was not keyed simply to adhering to set models of decorum. The Lockean narrative revealed the child responding to, absorbing, or reacting against things and actions. A book such as *Little Goody Two-Shoes*, for example (first published by John Newbery in 1765), tells the story of a little girl who learns her lessons and grows up to be a teacher. At one point in the story, she attempts to help her neighbors who were unable to harvest their hay, "which had been for many Years greatly damaged by wet Weather." So she "contrived an Instrument to direct them when to mow their Grass with Safety, and prevent their Hay being spoiled."[4] The grown-up Goody has invented the barometer—a device that, with its deployment, leads some to consider her a witch. Skill here is not the measure of intelligence but of demonism. This seemingly small detail remains central to the novel's drama, as it reveals Goody Two-Shoes as a mistress of empiricism: an observer of the world, a maker of the tools of measurement, a rejecter of the superstitions and the old wives' tales of folklore.

Of course, Locke had an immense impact on the history of English literature in the large. Long before *Goody Two-Shoes*, Defoe's *Robinson Crusoe* followed many of Locke's principles—from its overarching emphasis on the particulars of knowledge through its narrative of Crusoe's mastery of technical ability, even to the details of that hero's need to set up a written, contractual relationship with those who would later appear on his island.[5] The traditional conception of the "rise of the novel" has Locke (as well as the Puritans) at its center. As Ian Watt has summarized it:

> To begin with, the actors in the plot and the scene of their actions had to be placed in a new literary perspective: the plot had to be acted out by particular people in particular circumstances, rather than, as had been common in the past, by general human types against a background primarily determined by appropriate human convention. This literary change was analogous to the rejection of universals and the emphasis on particulars which characterizes [Locke's] philosophical realism.[6]

In Locke's own words: "In Particulars, our Knowledge begins."[7] For children's literature, as much as for adults', this fundamental conviction motivates tales of moral growth centered on the sensory perception of the outer world. We are, along with Robinson Crusoe or Goody Two-Shoes, effectively "emplotted" in the particulars of life; and early education provides, as Locke argued, the guidance for our navigation of that plot.

And the plotlines of that life were full of things. The children's spaces of the Lockean universe are not filled with "tokens," or with signs of subsequent salvation. They are filled with objects, and Locke uses the word "plaything" to connote not just the toys of the nursery or the bedroom, but the objects of experience that teach sensible and moral action. The word "plaything" had begun to appear in the late seventeenth century to refer to toys, but it becomes in Locke, and in his followers, a term of what we might call recreational epistemology.[8] "Children," Locke wrote in *Some Thoughts concerning Education*, "are never dull or out of humour for want of such Play-things," be they bits of paper, pebbles, or small items found around the house. Making such playthings should be the activity of learning for the child, and even items that may be too complicated for the child to fashion ("Tops, Gigs, Battledors, and the like") should be "used with labour . . . not for Variety, but Exercise" (p. 238). Playthings could also be used to teach the child to read. Letters could be pasted onto dice or polygons; words could become toys; books themselves could become objects of delight (pp. 256–58). So influential was Locke's advocacy of such toys that John Newbery, in the 1740s, offered balls, pincushions, counting stones, and polygons for sale along with his books.[9] So influential, too, was this theory of playthings that children's books themselves could be styled with that title: for example, Newbery's *Pretty Play-Thing for Children*, or Mary Cooper's *Child's New Play-Thing* (1742), the latter offering up letters, syllables, pictures, and words designed to be cut out and pasted onto cards or blocks for help in teaching children how to read. The book becomes one more item in the furnished room of childhood.

Locke's impact on eighteenth- and early nineteenth-century children's literature, then, lies not just in his ideal of an educated life: that character, self-mastery, and hard work were all teachable.[10] It lies, too, in his emphasis on the particulars of sensory experience, his fascination with the playthings of the world, and his creation of a figurative language of such things to explain just what fills the mind. Throughout this literature, we see children faced with their messy rooms, their ill-strewn closets, and a whole world of domestic spaces in need of cleaning and sorting. More than just scenes of simple sloppiness, such episodes make real the imagery of Locke's figures for knowledge. No less a book than Sarah Fielding's *The Governess* of 1749—long recognized as the first full-length novel written explicitly for children—begins with precisely this Lockean encounter of messy furnishings: "When you run through numbers of Books, only for the sake of saying, you have read them, without making any Advantage of the Knowledge got thereby, remember this Saying, 'That a Head, like a House, when crammed too full, and no regular Order observed in the placing of what is there, is only littered instead of being furnished.'"[11] Fielding then goes on to tell a story about the two Watkins girls, who threw their clothes and possessions in "irregular Heaps," who liked to "tumble all the Things in their Drawers," and thus could find nothing when they needed it. The moral of this little story? "Thus will those foolish Children be served, who heap into their Heads a great deal, and yet never observe what they put there, either to mend their Practice, or increase their Knowledge. Their Heads will be in as much Confusion, as were Miss Watkins's Chests of Drawers" (p. xii).

The job of children's literature is to make sense of things, and it was no accident that one of the genres that emerged in the wake of Locke's writings was the fictional biography of inanimate objects. Such books had emerged, early in the eighteenth century, for purposes of social satire. From Charles Gildon's *The Golden Spy* (1709) through Tobias Smollett's *Adventures of an Atom* (1769), Charles Johnstone's *Adventures of a Guinea*

(1760), Thomas Bridges' *Adventures of a Bank-Note* (1770), and nearly countless others, speaking objects filled the stalls of London's booksellers. Like many novels of the time, they were episodic and adventurous, concerned with exposing the workings of particular professions, trades, or crafts. It was as if the things of everyday life could become characters themselves—as if the pen, the coin, the toy, the book, the coach were, in fact, the true agents of our lives, and not we ourselves.[12]

Were these novels children's books? Some modern scholars have discussed them in the context of the rise of children's literature in the mid-eighteenth century.[13] For today's reader, it may be hard to see them as calibrated for the childish reader. Certainly, their political allusions, philosophical debates, and complex sentences seem of a magnitude far different from what is found in, say, *Goody Two-Shoes* or *The Governess*. And yet, some of these novels clearly address problems of paternity, inheritance, and education; some have the feel of simple language for the younger reader. Bridges' *Adventures of a Bank-Note*, in particular, has almost a Dickensian quality to its opening: a mystery about the speaker's father.[14] "As it is usual for the hero of either a true tale or a romance to give an account of himself and family, in compliance with an old custom I shall do the same" (p. 1). And soon we learn the story of the father and the bank; the "roguery, which is pretty sure to descend from father to son for endless generations" (p. 5); and finally the revelation: "Not to keep you longer in suspense, . . . my father was a poet" (p. 6).

*The Adventures of a Bank-Note* is a story about "pedigree," a word that we today associate almost exclusively with domestic animals. And it is no accident that novels of the eighteenth century, too, associate the house pet with the inanimate object as a speaker of its own fabulous autobiography. Such titles as *The Life and Adventures of a Lap-Dog, The Life and Perambulation of a Mouse*, and *The History of the Robins* (among many others) guided readers through the fantasies of a nonhuman, but experiential, sensibility. Such tales owed much to the old techniques of romance, to the emerging genre of the picaresque novel, and to the beast fable.[15] But their pedagogical and philosophical scaffolding was all Locke. For Locke was fascinated by animals. In *Some Thoughts concerning Education*, he lamented the familiar sight of children tormenting their pets. Boys and girls, he argued, should be taught to care for creatures. "I cannot but commend both the Kindness and Prudence of a Mother I knew, who was wont always to indulge her Daughters, when any of them desired Dogs, Squirils, Birds, or any such things, as young Girls use to be delighted with:

But then, when they had them, they must be sure to keep them well and look diligently after them." How children treated animals was something of a moral test for Locke, a measure of the child's inner self. Anyone who would "delight in the Suffering and Destruction of inferiour Creatures, will not be apt to be very compassionate, or benign to those of their own kind." Locke's arguments, at one level, grew out of his larger philosophical commitment to the idea of universal preservation as a natural law. "The World would be much quieter, and better natur'd than it is," if we took care of all sensible creatures (*Some Thoughts*, pp. 225–26). In his *Essay concerning Human Understanding*, he went so far as to claim that animals could reason, remember, and perceive (though not as fully as humans). Were animals but lesser versions of the human, or were they something akin to biological machines—incapable of thought, "mere Mechanism," in the words of one mid-eighteenth-century philosopher?[16]

These were the larger questions motivating an important strain of Enlightenment philosophy, and they were the questions motivating children's literature at that time. But they were, in particular, the questions motivating an Aesopic revival sponsored in large part by Locke himself. The fables had long been the mainstay of both schoolroom instruction and popular reading. Translations, commentaries, and editions had proliferated throughout Europe after the first printed versions appeared at the end of the fifteenth century. In *Some Thoughts concerning Education*, Locke singled out Aesop's fables as "the best . . . Stories apt to delight and entertain a Child" (p. 259). Repeatedly, he stressed the clarity and force of the Aesopica: not only did these stories offer entertaining forms of moral instruction, their use of simple language (whether the fable was read in English or Latin) was ideally suited to the beginning student. But there was more than that. Locke advocated writing out translations of Aesop interlinearly (p. 271). And he thought that the fables were ideally suited, too, to illustration. If the student's Aesop "has Pictures in it, it will entertain him much the better, and encourage him to read, when it carries the increase of Knowledge with it. For such visible Objects Children hear talked of in vain. . . . And therefore I think, as soon as he begins to spell, as many Pictures of Animals should be got him, as can be found, with the printed names to them" (p. 259). In 1703, Locke himself prepared just such an edition: an interlinear translation with labeled portraits of each of the fables' central animals.[17] With its clear pictures, pressed into the service of his particularist theory of knowledge, and with its recasting of many of the fables into tales—not of *ingenium* or wit, but of self-mastery—Locke's

Aesop played out in practice the ideas behind *Some Thoughts*, as the animals encounter not just challenges for food or pleasure, not just challenges from other beasts or humans, but fields and households full of things that they must order into meaningful landscapes.

The modern legacy of Locke's work may be, in the end, that fascination with the two sides of the child's playthings—tales of the toys that come alive, and stories of the animals that talk and feel. It would be no exaggeration to say, for example, that *Winnie the Pooh* remains a profoundly Lockean book: one keyed to narratives of mental growth, focused on the ways of reading texts, and centered on the habits of a bear "of little brain." In Pooh, or in the range of eighteenth-century works written in Locke's shadow, we have all the central questions of children's literature. What is the moral and rational condition of the child? Is the child a thinking creature? What things are like children? Are animals or toys akin to newborns? What happens when those animals or toys take on lives of their own? How do they challenge our perceptions of the unique nature of humanity, and in turn our perceptions of the child in all of us? Such are the questions raised by Locke's theories of knowledge and education, and such are the questions answered by the children's writers of his orbit.

And these remain the questions of Locke's Aesop. At first glance, this book looks little different from the many early published versions of the fables. There are all the old familiar tales and characters, illustrations of the major figures, and the guiding pedagogic purpose of instruction in both language and moral behavior. But on close inspection, Locke's edition differs markedly from its predecessors. For one thing, there is no Life of Aesop at its start. The story of the fabulist, so much a part of medieval, Renaissance, and seventeenth-century editions, does not appear, nor does an illustration of Aesop himself. Locke's illustrations, moreover, do not illuminate the actions of the fables; they are but portraits of the actors in them. And while English translations abounded, and even interlinear versions had appeared before, Locke's versions are keyed explicitly to the particulars of print and to a way of reading that fulfills the specifics of his educational theories.

At the end of the seventeenth century, the fable genre had long been a mainstay of not just children's literature but adults' as well. The stories of the ingenuity of animals, and of the slave Aesop himself, were pressed into the service of political reform and social satire. From John Ogilby's *Fables of Aesop, Paraphrased in Verse* (1651) through Francis Barlow's *Aesop's Fables*, *with his Life* (1666) to Roger L'Estrange's *Fables of Aesop* (1692) and many others, the Aesopica had functioned as a way of making social commentary under the guise of simple story. Kingship and commonwealth, dynastic rule and constitutional reform—all could be the veiled subjects of these fabulists. Central to many of these collections was the Life of Aesop and the vision of the slave who, through imagination and interpretation, undermines the power of the master, gains his freedom, and ultimately achieves both social and literary esteem.

Locke's goal, in part, is to reclaim Aesop for the child. He makes the fables fit texts for instruction. He shears them of their elaborate details, subplots, and descriptions. Instead, we get mostly linear narratives: direct statements that address the actions of one particular character. This method of attention leads, then, to the way in which the book is illustrated. Rather than offering pictorial representations of the actions of the fables, as many previous editions had, Locke's book begins with pictures of the seventy-seven central figures (almost all of them animals) in the fables, ranged in the order in which they appear in the collection. There is nothing particularly imaginative about these pictures. In fact, they look little different from the kinds of illustrations that would fill *The New England Primer*. These are the visual devices of the illustrated alphabet displaced into the fable. If ranged in their alphabetical rather than compilatory order, these illustrations would appear identical to anything coming out of the Puritan tradition of the alphabet book.

The look of Locke's Aesop is, then, from the start, the look of the abecedarium   a look that finds its way into the text of at least one of the fables itself. The story of the thief and his mother, so central to the late antique and medieval Aesopic collections (as I showed in chapter 2), begins with a child who steals a writing tablet. The early versions of that story attended to the notion of learning itself as something of a treasure: of letters as, in the words of one Hellenistic maxim, "the greatest beginning of understanding." In Locke's version of this fable, the boy becomes a contemporary student who steals not a writing tablet but a "horn-book" (what the interlinear Latin calls *tabella alphabetaria*). The vehicle of alphabetic instruction here becomes the object of theft. The particular realities of a contemporary schoolroom enter into the old verities of the Aesopic fable.

Locke's is an Aesop for the hornbook world, and the job of hornbooks—like the job of primers—was not just to teach the letters, but to teach the letter forms as well. Handwriting and typography could shape each letter

Fig. 3. Letters and pictures of animals in [John Locke], *Aesop's Fables in English and Latin, interlineary* ... (London: A. and J. Churchill, 1703).

differently (this was, recall, the lesson of the opening of *The New England Primer*). An education in the arts of literacy had to include education in the typographic arts. The subject of the children's book became, in essence, the book as an object in itself.

This emphasis on letter forming had become a part of the Aesopic tradition by the close of the seventeenth century. Locke's preface to his Aesop focuses not so much on the moral content of the fables as on their typographical appearances. In the English and Latin parallel lines, the "words which answer one another, being placed over another," are "always printed in the same Character, to shew their correspondence." Certain phrases that are similar in Latin and English are also "Printed in the same Character." Where the words from one language do not correspond exactly to the words in the other, "every other word is printed in a different Character." And when there is the need to add words in English, in order to complete the sense of a sentence where the Latin offers only implication or case ending, "these are printed in the Old English Character, or between Crotchets, different from the other two."

Locke's text is thus as much a picture as the pictures of the animals themselves. The visual appearance of the fables is as central as their subject. When he states, therefore, that the pictures are added "to make it still more taking to Children, and make the deeper impression of the same upon their Minds," he unites printed word and sculpted image into nothing less than physical impressors on the tablet of the reader's mind. The mind becomes the blank page upon which ideas are impressed, or printed. Even on the first page of Locke's text, all the characters can be seen at work—and in play. There is the roman and the italic type, the Old English black letter, the uppercase and lowercase forms. Recall how the writers of an earlier tradition had imagined children as but the small letter of the capital adult; or how Benjamin Franklin, synthesizing generations of a Puritan poetics, could present his recipe for a New England funeral elegy: "You must spread all upon Paper." Now, in the world of Lockean epistemology, that paper becomes the clean slate of the mind. All the letters now are there, and by the time we get to the story of the thieving schoolboy (331 pages into the volume), we can see that what he takes can no longer be the empty *tabula* at the beginning of the class but the *tabella alphabetaria*.

Locke's Aesop synthesizes these traditions of the alphabetical with a new preoccupation with print culture to produce a book of fables that unites the character of letters with the character of people. His birds and beasts are characters as well: figures from alphabetic illustration now enlivened into Aesopic encounter. It is as if the static portraits of the ABCs took wing into the fictions of the fabulist. And in those fictions, old familiar stories take on new attentions and new details to give voice to an epistemology of the particular.

For what, in fact, gives voice at all? In one particularly telling case, Locke splits the old story of the fox and the actor's mask into two stories. First, it appears as the story of the wolf and the painted head:

The Wolf turns about and admires a humane Head found in the Shop of a Carver, perceiving (as indeed it was) that it had no sense. Quoth he, O fair Head, there is in thee much of Art, but nothing of sense.[18]

Then, 250 pages later, it reappears as the story of the fox and the wolf's head:

A Fox going into a Musitians house whilst he gazed upon all the instruments of musick, and all the Furniture of the House he found a Wolf's head Skilfully and workman like made, which he had taken into his paw, he said, O head that wast made with a great deal of wit, yet hast no wit at all.[19]

Though the morals of these fables are similar (both enjoin us to beware of superficial beauty), their narratives brilliantly reflect on the epistemology behind Aesopic fable itself. These are tales of the blank slate, of created objects that have only the outward appearance of a head, but no mind within. The wolf's tale seems straightforward enough, but the fox's has a bizarre twist, for what he finds is an artistic representation of a wolf. His is a kind of meta-fable: one about the ways in which the fabulist shapes characters with wit and skill. The fox enters a house of music and art, a kind of domesticized version of the imagination itself. The mind was a cabinet, a house of furniture, a collection of instruments of intellection.[20]

Art without wisdom is worthless here—but more striking than the moral is the range of the particulars. Music was not a high priority for Locke. True, he states, some value "a good Hand, upon some Instruments"; but by and large, Locke felt that, given the "List of Accomplishments" for a young student to fulfill, music might be in "the last place" (*Some Thoughts concerning Education*, p. 311). For a man's head may be filled with many things: not only trivial accomplishments, but "Scraps of Authors," bits of literary learning, small details. "When a Man's Head is stuffed" with such things, "he has got the just Furniture of a Pedant" (ibid., p. 285). Or, as Locke put it elsewhere in *Some Thoughts*, when one "has emptied out into his Pupil all the Latin, and Logick, he has brought from the University, will that Furniture make him a fine Gentleman?" (p. 190). The fable of the fox is now the fable of the child distracted: of the student who confronts the instruments and furniture of superficial accomplishment; of the head made skillfully but without the real wit of prudence in it.

"Art and Wisdom" should be brought together in the child's development, an argument Locke makes throughout *Some Thoughts* and one that forms the moral of the very first of his Aesop's fables. To the story of the cock who finds a jewel in a dunghill, Locke moralizes: "Understand by the

Jewel, Art and Wisdom." And it is through the unity of these two faculties that mastery is achieved. For what Locke's Aesop is about is not so much the wit or ingenuity of creatures, but the mastery that knowledge grants the world. The purpose of education, Locke writes in *Some Thoughts*, is "to teach the Mind to get the Mastery over it self" (p. 174), and he concludes the book by enjoining that the child be taught "to get a Mastery over his Inclinations, and submit his Appetite to Reason" (p. 314). Children, when they grow up together, "often strive for Mastery, whose Wills shall carry it over the rest" (p. 212). Mastery in all its forms was one of Locke's central concerns throughout his philosophical writings. Reason, freedom, education—all focus on the mastery of the self, control of the mind, and willingness to work with others. As Peter Schouls distills it, in the opening of his study of Locke and the Enlightenment: "Human beings, for Locke, are born to be masters. They are born to be masters because it is their nature to be rational and free, and it is through deliberate exercise of their reason in all the exigencies of life that they achieve mastery."[21]

From this point of view, Locke's fables become essays in the exigencies of life: stories about creatures attaining their mastery over the world, over others, over themselves. Tales of animals, workers, or servants and their masters fill the Aesopica, and Locke selects from this storehouse stories of control with the design of illustrating the ways in which "mastery of mind" (to use the language of *Essay concerning Human Understanding*) remains the true "freedom of understanding."[22]

And thus it is that Locke's Aesop remains a book about self-mastery. Not only in its fables but in its larger pedagogic goal, the book imagines students working on their own. The title page makes all this clear: the book is "for the benefit of those who not having a master would learn either of these tongues." The student reader grows in mastery, much like the cock in the first fable in the volume: the precious stone he finds is now the book itself—not just a plaything for the eye and hand, but Art and Wisdom yoked together. "Neither Fools love the Liberal Arts," runs the moral of this story, "when they know not the use of them." Locke's Aesop offers a compendium of liberal arts, designed to get the student reading, acting, and knowing.

Other Aesop collections throughout the eighteenth century had similar goals, but few were as explicitly Lockean in their form and purpose as John Newbery's *Fables in Verse, for the Improvement of the Young and Old* (1758). Throughout his many publications, from *A Little Pretty Pocket-Book* of 1744 to *The History of Little Goody Two-Shoes* more than twenty years later, Newbery put into practice Locke's theories of mental development, his arguments for playful education, and his condemnation of cruelty to animals. The preface to *A Little Pretty Pocket-Book* distills the program of *Some Thoughts* into manageable aphorisms—complete with attribution to "the great Mr. Locke."[23] In its later alphabetic lessons, the *Pocket-Book* plays out the vision of Locke's letters turned into "playthings," while in *Goody Two-Shoes*, scenes of kindness to animals refract the character of Margery Two-Shoes herself and, in the process, show her as a teacher of compassion and character.

Newbery's Aesop fits into these forms as well. To start, its preface ripples with a Lockean vocabulary: these are "lessons in prudence and morality"; they are the "most entertaining" ways of making "a lasting impression on the mind." Reading is recreation, a means of invigorating the mind, much as exercise invigorates the body. Locke's emphasis, early in *Some Thoughts*, on the child's healthy mind and body finds its voice in Newbery's vision of reading as a form of "exercise." At the conclusion of the preface, Newbery synthesizes Locke's pedagogic vision into an argument for fiction: "The virtue and instruction, which we gather from a fable or allegory, is like the health we get by hunting, as we are engaged in an agreeable pursuit that draws us on with pleasure, and makes us insensible of the fatigues with which it is attended."[24] Aesop's fables, of course, are filled with scenes of hunting, whether of animals pursued by men, or beasts preying on other beasts. The fox and the wolf epitomize the venatory self, and in their search for food, they might come upon such strange things as a severed head. Locke, as I have shown, split this particular fable into two, but Newbery collapses them to offer up "A Fox and a Carved Head." Here, instead of the old Aesopic field or Locke's musician's studio, the fox comes upon a carver's shop. We see the samples ranged before us in the illustration, as the fox fondles not some broken head (as in the earlier versions of the tale), but what is obviously a complete bust. He looks upon it with the eye of a connoisseur.

> A Fox one day, who chanc'd to pop
> His head into a Carver's shop,
> A beauteous bust admir'd;
> And having turn'd it round and round,
> And ev'ry feature perfect found,
> He with a sigh retir'd.
> Reflecting on the object seen,
> So calm, so simple and serene,
> He said, departing thence,
> What pity 'tis so fine a face,

> Possess'd almost of ev'ry grace,
> Should want a grain of sense!
>
> (pp. 59–60)

The whole tone of this poem remains one of quintessential eighteenth-century middle-class experience. The very verb of its first line, "pop," would have been brand-new in the middle of the century—the *Oxford English Dictionary* cites Richardson's *Pamela* (1741) and Sterne's *Tristram Shandy* (1759) as containing the first uses of the word, meaning "to come upon abruptly" or "to light upon by chance" (*OED*, s.v. "pop," v. 1, def. 8b). Newbery's fox is not some hungry beast, but an urbane assessor of the arts. Even the sigh with which he retires has a perfectly voiced, be-wigged ennui to it.

But behind the patina of the social grace lies Lockean epistemology. Knowledge comes from reflecting on seen objects. An understanding of the world comes from examining its features. As Locke put it in *Some Thoughts*, not by rote memorization but by reflection will the child learn: "The Custom of frequent Reflection will keep their Minds from running adrift, and call their Thoughts home from useless unattentive roving" (p. 287). Indeed, such "unattentive roving" had been the downfall of many an Aesopic character—from the boy who found himself upon a wild horse, to the slave who left his master, and beyond. But for our fox, now, his is an attentive roving, a reflection on the objects of artistry.

And in good Lockean fashion, Newbery offers not just morals to his fables but extended "Reflections" too, and here the reflection calls attention to the meaning not just of this little fable, but of everyday experience itself.

> With human life you all may see
> The Fox's notion will agree;
> For without contradiction,
> The world is but one spacious street,
> In which carv'd heads and all sorts meet,
> And verify the fiction.
>
> (p. 60)

The world is indeed a spacious street, as Locke himself could verify in a strange tale he tells in *Some Thoughts*. In a certain town, there were boys who used to tease "a Man of a disturb'd Brain." This man, "one Day seeing in the Street one of those Lads, that used to vex him, step'd into a Cutler's Shop he was near; and there seizing on a naked Sword, made after the Boy." For the rest of his life, Locke notes, this boy would never enter a doorway without thinking of "this Madman." Here, on the street of life, all sorts of heads may meet, be they the cruel heads of little boys or the disturbed minds of men. "This frightening Idea made so deep an Impression" on the boy that he never forgot it. More to the point, the boy went on "telling this Story when he was a Man" (p. 243). Life becomes narrative. The particulars of experience impress themselves upon the mind. Telling tales becomes an act of verifying fiction—that is, of finding truth in fable.

But in both Aesop and Locke, the telos of these tales lies in turning everyday objects into pedagogic playthings. We encounter all things on the street; our task is to take each as a tool for teaching. Such is the lesson, really, of the fable of the fox and the head. For here, that sculpted head is something of a Lockean plaything: an object that becomes a toy to teach a lesson. So, too, are the fables themselves; and so, too, were Newbery's other books. *A Little Pretty Pocket-Book* presents its little lessons to impress. Each one comes with an alphabetic marker: there is "The great A Play," then "The little a Play," and so on through the letters. But these letters have little relationship, apparently, to what they title (each poem, tale, or game does not, in fact, begin with or highlight its titular letter). Instead, the sequence of games and letters offers parallel systems of understanding: the one along the pages' running heads keyed to the alphabet; the other, in the texts, keyed to moral learning.

But when Newbery gets more than halfway through the alphabet, the structure seems to change. The games, beginning with "little p," center on forms of writing and reading. That "little p Play," for example, is a game of Hop-Scotch:

> First make with Chalk an oblong Square
> With wide Partitions here and there;
> Then to the first a Tile convey;
> Hop in—then kick the Tile away.

The picture shows the numbers ranged from one to ten on such an "oblong Square"—and it looks for all the world like a hornbook or battledore, with numbers now instead of letters. The following "great Q Play" describes the game of Squares:

> This well-invented Game design'd
> To strike the Eye and form the Mind.
> And he most doubtless aims aright,
> Who joins Instruction with Delight.

This quatrain offers nothing less than versified Locke. Invention and design, the eye and mind, instruction and delight—these are the poles of the polemic of *Some Thoughts concerning Education*. Later games are more explicitly alphabetical, as the letters themselves participate in play. For example:

> Great E, F, and G,
> Come here follow me,
> And we'll jump over
> The Rosemary Tree.

The lines between the game, the text, the plaything, and the book gets blurry here, and this, it seems to me, is precisely the point. For now it is the book that is the thing. The very titles of Newbery's publications define life or people through the things we have: *The Pocket-Book*; *The Lottery Book*; *The Fairing, or A Golden Toy*; *Nurse Truelove's Christmas-Box*; *A Pretty Book of Pictures*; *The Pretty Play-Thing for Children*; *The Valentine's Gift*. In these and many other books published by Newbery and his successors at his press, the titles call attention to the book as a thing. They tell us nothing of the content of the books; rather, they tell us of their social function in the habits of exchange (they are gifts) or the experience of sense perception (they are pocket-books, boxes, toys; they are pretty). Even the title of Newbery's most famous publication, *The History of Little Goody Two-Shoes*, defines its heroine according to something she has, rather than something she is.

Goody Two-Shoes lives among the things that are designed to see the world. Long before she invents a barometer to help her neighbors harvest their hay, she gets her shoes and then her skills in reading. No longer a poor child with just one shoe—she gets two of them from a shoemaker—and proud of her new possessions, she "obtained the Name of Goody Two-Shoes" (p. 21). Only when she has been renamed can she go on to learn and teach, and in this sequence of events Newbery tells not just a story of a young girl's education, but a larger tale of rebirth through knowledge.

As Margery learns her letters (chapter 4), she cuts them into pieces of wood, arranges the lowercase and uppercase letters in sequence, "and having got an old Spelling-Book, she made her Companions set up all the words they wanted to spell" (p. 26). There is Margery, teaching her students under a tree. This illustration cannot but recall the older images from *The New England Primer*, from the Puritan spellers, and even earlier from the medieval and Renaissance allegories. This is a kind of primal moment, a scene of education in the garden, a moment when the tree of knowledge offers not the temptations to sin but the locus of learning. Margery takes bits of wood with letters on them and makes them into a game of learning—a game familiar from Newbery's own *Pocket-Book*, or from Mary Cooper's earlier *Child's New Play-Thing* speller, or from Locke himself. The scene in which she teaches a young boy to learn the alphabet by "throwing down" the blocks of letters and having him arrange them could be right out of Locke's *Some Thoughts*—that moment when he suggests cutting letters on the sides of dice and "throwing" them (pp. 256–57).

The world is made of things. Each letter, syllable, and word takes on a physical identity. It is not simply that words represent things in the world, or that the schoolbook uses pictures to teach children how to read. It is that words themselves take on a kind of tactile quality. When Goody Two-Shoes visits a small cottage to teach children how to read, she uses the dining table where they had been eating to spell out the foodstuffs of their day. And then, "the Letters being brought upon the Table" (p. 37), the children make up sentences of basic religious devotion. This is, quite literally, food for thought, set up now on the table cleared for learning—the physical representation of that *tabula rasa* of Locke's theory of the mind.

The lessons and the life of Goody Two-Shoes show us a character defined by her possessions and the characters of writing turned into possessions themselves. It is but a short step to transforming such possessions into literary characters themselves. By the middle of the eighteenth century, biographies of things and pets had become one of the most popular of genres, both for children and adults. They share an educative purpose and a story of personal growth. Charles Johnstone's *Chrysal, Or The Adventures of a Guinea* (1760), for example, begins with a lesson, as the narrator lectures us on how he could talk with such an object. "How this communication though is made, I cannot so well inform you: whether it is by the oscillation of the nervous fibres, or by the operation of a certain invisible fluid.... no more than I can explain to you, how my touching these marks, on this material substance the brain, can raise ideas in the immaterial mind." And after all these debates on understanding, personal identity, and knowledge, we find an asterisk to this blunt footnote at the bottom of the page: "Locke."[25]

Locke was everywhere in these strange volumes. In Francis Coventry's *History of Pompey the Little, or The Life and Adventures of a Lap-Dog*

(1751), Locke is forever on the bookshelf and in conversation. Of the transparently named Lady Sophister, the narrator notes: "Mr. Locke had the Misfortune to be her principal Favourite, and consequently it rested chiefly upon him to furnish her with Quotations, whenever her Ladyship pleased to engage in Controversy."[26] Locke "furnishes" quotations, and I think that verb stands out as the most pointed of satiric jabs against the ill-informed. If the mind of Lady Sophister is so ill ordered, so cluttered with half-read books and half-digested notions, how can Locke do anything to organize her mental furniture?

The crazed debate in *Pompey* hinges on the question of the immortality of the soul, and in the midst of it Lady Sophister recreates the system of the world through catalogues of things:

> "My opinion," resumed she, "is exactly the same with Mr. Locke's.—You know, Mr. Locke observes there are various Kinds of Matter—well—but first we should define Matter, which you know the Logicians tell us, is an extended solid substance—Well, out of this Matter, some, you know, is made into Roses and Peachtrees—the next step which matter takes is Animal Life, from whence we have Lions and Elephants, and all the Races of Brutes.—Then, the next step, as Mr. Locke observes, is Thought, and Reason, and volition, from whence are created Man, and therefore you very plainly see, 'tis impossible for the Soul to be immortal."[27]

To which Dr. Rhubarb replies, "Roses and Peach-trees, and Elephants and Lions! I protest I remember nothing of this Nature in Mr. Locke." But this is clearly what readers such as Lady Sophister remember; or, to put it more precisely, these things are the inhabitants of childish worlds for childish readers. There remains something not just vain and silly but underdeveloped about Lady Sophister, as if she were a child who gets hold of grown-up books and makes them into something else. Roses and peach trees, lions and elephants are in Aesop, Newbery, the primers, and the Play-Things. They fill the landscape of the children's book, and at a moment such as this one, *Pompey* becomes not just a book *for* children, but most profoundly and wittily a book *about* children. It takes as its central theme the matter of the childish reader and the legitimacy (in all senses of that word) of knowledge. *Pompey* and many of its eighteenth-century compeers tell stories about genealogies—how ideas get developed, how children grow, how things originate. Lady Sophister's crazy reminiscences of Locke come off, now, as not so much a bad reading of the philosopher as a bad version of creation itself: in the beginning was the thing, and then there were Roses and Peachtrees, and then Lions and Elephants, and then Man.

Among such stories of inheritance and genealogy, few stand out for their brilliance and their humor as vividly as Thomas Bridges' *Adventures of a Bank-Note* (1770). Its style is unencumbered by epistemological digression, its vocabulary is simple, its sentences are straightforward. And its central claim is one of childhood. This is a book about the nature of the child, about relationships of parenting and birth, about responsibilities to adults, and about the very origins of our experience.

The book begins with good advice to children: as "the grandmother of Sir Robert Walpole us'd to say to him, when he was but a little boy. . ." Although the banknote "never had the happiness of knowing my grandmother," it will, still, "give a full and true account of my birth, parentage, life, and education" (p. 2). It is a brilliant story. An impoverished poet one day receives thirty guineas for his writing. After paying his debts—for sundries, food, supplies, and so on—he is left with "twenty-one pounds six shillings and ninepence three farthings" (pp. 7–8). What will he do with the money? At first, he thinks to buy himself a noble title from the king. But no sooner does this grand thought come to mind than the poet-father is reduced to burlesque comedy. Bridges sets us up and knocks us down: "The goddess Aurora had no sooner given notice that Phoebus was oiling his harness . . . than my father instantly threw a tattered night-gown over his shoulders." He runs downstairs for some milk, but when he sets out to pay the milkmaid, "my poor father (whose mind was in high conversation with Phoebus and the Nine) forgetting he had no breeches on, opened up his night-gown and . . . fell to rummaging his naked thigh to find his breeches pocket." Offended by this action, the milkmaid "let fly the bason [of milk], with all its contents, at the part that offended her eye the most" (pp. 9–12).

There is a vertiginous, jejune comedy to this moment: a scene of fatherhood unmanned. Our poor banknote seeks out some way of rescuing this failed dad. He shows how, through the inspiration of the Muses, the poet goes to the bank and gets himself a note for twenty pounds, "payable to Timothy Tagghrime, Esq. After the Bank has dubb'd you an esquire, no man will dare to say a word against it; you may then boldly add the title esquire to your name the very next work you publish" (p. 14). By siring the banknote, the poet gives birth to his new self. "Away went my father to the Bank, directly, and in an auspicious hour begot—I mean, got me" (p. 16).

And so, dear reader, I am born. How many children thought themselves such banknotes—ciphers to be passed along, from parent's pockets into hostile worlds? The adventures of our hero, like all the adventures of the child, go on in secret spaces: in the purses, pockets, tills, and palms of life. Notice, in fact, how many of these books live in such spaces—books such as Newbery's *Pocket-Book*, or the *Adventures of a Lap-Dog* (what does it mean to be defined as living in a lap?), or the *Adventures of a Hackney Coach* (with its secure interior), and on and on. These are the pocket-worlds of childhood, the little-boy and little-girl equivalents of Locke's great cabinet of mind. It is as if these stories play out Locke's own imagination of some other worlds, a kind of eighteenth-century equivalent of science fiction stories in which other universes house strange beings, like and unlike us.

> He that will not set himself proudly at the top of all things; but will consider the Immensity of this Fabrick, and the great variety, that is to be found in this little and inconsiderable part of it, which he has to do with, may be apt to think, that in other Mansions of it, there may be other, and different intelligent Beings, of whose Faculties, he has as little Knowledge or Apprehension, as a Worm shut up in one Drawer of a Cabinet, hath of the Senses or Understanding of a Man. (*Essay concerning Human Understanding*, bk. 2, para. 2)

What we might call the "it-tales" of the eighteenth century play out this possibility. What would it mean to see the world as if one were a worm, a pincushion, or a pet? And, shut up in the drawer, the pocket, or the toy box, what worlds could we imagine?

Tales such as *The Adventures of a Bank-Note* or the *Adventures of a Lap-Dog* play out this epistemology for literary ends. They illustrate how novels are really stories of the child, stories of how narrators emerge from influential parents, how the adventurer is but a child departing home. Lemuel Gulliver, Robinson Crusoe, Tristram Shandy, David Copperfield—how different are they, really, from that little banknote, loving yet embarrassed by his father, compelled to set his adventures on the axes of "birth, parentage, life, and education"?

And how different are they, too, from such a note in the commercial world? It is no accident that many of these eighteenth-century books about inanimate objects are about money: banknote, guinea, rupee, penny, sovereign, shilling.[28] For any reader of the century, they would have offered lessons in the quality of credit. But they would have offered lessons, too, in how we *invest* in children. Our offspring are our banknotes. We put stock in them, we hope they redeem us. They have value, they are money in the bank. What an emerging middle class had realized was just how children were investments—how the social and financial achievements of the child would publicly redound to parental attention. Teaching children to succeed becomes as much a hope for sons and daughters as for fathers and mothers. The payoff (to use both a financially and a socially laden term) is mutual.

Locke knew all this. He knew that in a world of cash and credit, managing accounts could help the child "preserve the Estate he has." It is "seldom observed, that he who keeps an Accompt of his Income and Expences, and thereby has constantly under view the course of his domestick Affairs, lets them run to ruine" (*Some Thoughts*, p. 319). Accountancy has both social and moral, as well as financial, implications. Money management is akin to other forms of ordering the life—like keeping the mind's furniture well situated. At stake is not just making sure that sons do not bankrupt their fathers. At stake is realizing that parenting is always a commercial enterprise; that "what the Father allows [the child], he ought to let him be fully Master of" (p. 320).

The adventuresome banknote sees a father ill-equipped to manage his own accounts. He is not master of his money; he is not even master of his pocket. "I lay in the pocket of this father of mine" (p. 16). So do all children, really. And the spaces in which children live are little pockets of experience.

For Sarah Fielding, pockets of experience and pocket money come together to interrogate the nature of the children's book itself. "My young Readers," she begins *The Governess*, "before you begin the following Sheets, I beg you will stop a Moment at this Preface, to consider with me, what is the true Use of Reading; and if you can once fix this Truth in your minds, namely, that the true Use of Books is to make you wiser and better, you will have both Profit and Pleasure from what you read" (p. vii). Profit and pleasure fill the pocket at, for example, that moment early in the novel when the students of Mrs. Teachum's school have fought over some apples and, in an attempt to make amends, the head girl, Jenny Peace, brings in a new basket of fruit. "Miss Jenny now produced a Basket of Apples, which she had purchased out of the little Pocket-money she was allowed, in order to prove, that the same Things may be a Pleasure, or a Pain, according as the Persons to whom they are given are good or bad" (p. 21).

As the book begins, one summer evening in a garden, Mrs. Teachum brings out a bunch of apples for all of her nine students. Soon called away, she leaves the fruit in charge of Jenny Peace, "with a strict Charge to see that every one had an equal Share of her Gift" (p. 5). Alas, there is one extra apple, and each of the girls pleads for it: one on the basis of her age, another on the basis of her youth, another because of her meekness, another because of her strength, and so on. In a vain attempt to quash this rebellion, Jenny throws the extra apple over the fence. No good. The girls quarrel, Mrs. Teachum returns, and little is accomplished. This is the moment when Jenny returns with her new, personally purchased apples, places them in the middle of her troupe, and invites all of them to eat. "And now they were so changed, that each helped her next Neighbour before she would touch any for herself" (p. 21).

Eden now has a price. The pocket money of the eighteenth-century middle class can, it would seem, buy manners and self-mastery at once. Like Newbery's Goody Two-Shoes, Fielding's Mrs. Teachum teaches in a garden. A, it seems, is always for apple. By opening with this scene—redolent of biblical typology and alphabetic pedagogy—Fielding turns the old familiar images of basic education into templates for social behavior. Her goals are not so much to teach the memorizable, the factual, the list; but, more like Locke, to inculcate a social judgment in the student. Good manners and self-mastery, the hallmarks of Locke's educational ideals, become the curriculum of Mrs. Teachum's school.

But that curriculum, also in good Lockean fashion, is a syllabus of particulars. As Jenny puts it to her charges, after the fruit quarrel has been settled: "I will, if you please, relate to you the History of my past Life .... And after I have given you the Particulars of my Life, I must beg that every one of you will some Day or other, when you have reflected upon it, declare all that you can remember of your own" (pp. 22–23). Jenny becomes her own best narrator, a kind of Gulliver or Crusoe of local girlhood. The English novel had grown out of such attentions to particulars, and "The Life of Miss Jenny Peace" that follows this moment in *The Governess* reads like a novel in miniature. Here we may find all the familiar trappings of the self-telling narrator: the death of the father, the scene of learning how to read, the sorrow at the death of the first pet, the mother's death, and then the shipping off of Jenny not to sea, but to Mrs. Teachum's.

But let us not forget the apples. In Locke's world, learning from particulars is learning from the start: "The child, when part of his Apple is taken away, knows it better in that particular instance, than by this General Proposition, the whole is equal to all of its parts; and that if one of these have need to be confirmed to him by the other the general has more need to be let into his Mind by the particular, than the particular by the general" (*Essay concerning Human Understanding*, bk. 4, para. 7). The apple, for Locke as much as for Fielding, is the emblematic fruit of childhood. It is the source of knowledge—here, not of good and evil but of wholes and parts. For Fielding, what her students need to understand is how the parts of a life contribute to its whole. This is a story of particulars, but it remains, too, a story of first things. Jenny's words cannot but echo the experience of Genesis: obey commands, attend to precepts, remember yourself.

*The Governess* sets out to teach many things, but what I think it teaches most is the practice of novelizing the self: the recognition that all children are the central characters in books about their lives and that the act of learning how to grow is, in the end, the act of learning how to tell.[29] Locke recognized this, too. In *Some Thoughts concerning Education*, he makes clear that the reflection on experience, not just the memorization of rules, makes for a better child. Recall how Locke had argued for reflection as a way of keeping children from an "unattentive roving," how things worth remembering "call their Thoughts home" (p. 287). Jenny Peace gives her fellow students something worth remembering. She calls them home to inward thoughts, to self-reflection and self-telling. And like the characters of the Aesopica, or like those out of Locke's own anecdotes, she teaches that the telling makes the person. Here, however, life is not like the "spacious street" of such a fable, but like the garden of our origins. Recall, too, Locke's wild story of the disturbed man teased by the boys, who attacked one of them with a sword, and how the boy, even as a grown man, could not get the incident out of his mind. The madman had chased the young boy up to his father's house. The door is latched, the boy undoes it, and he gets home just in time to miss the madman's blow: "he had just time to get in and clap to the Door to avoid the Blow, which though his Body escaped, his Mind did not." Locke goes on: "For, telling this Story when he was a Man, he said, That after that time till then, he never went in at that Door (that he could remember) at any time, without looking back" (*Some Thoughts*, p. 243). The incident lives on in the telling; and this is Sarah Fielding's point as well. Poor Jenny Teachum cannot get out of her mind the way a group of schoolboys captured, tortured, and eventually killed her cat.

When I was about Eleven years old, I had a Cat that I had bred up from a little Kitten. . . . In return for my Indulgence, the Cat seemed to have changed its Nature, and assumed the Manner that more properly belongs to Dogs than Cats; for it would follow me about the house and Gardens, mourn for my Absence, and rejoice at my Presence. . . . But one Day the poor little Creature followed me to the Door; when a Parcel of School-boys coming by, one of them catched her up in his Arms, and ran away with her. . . . The cruel Wretches, for Sport, as they called it, hunted it the next Day from one to the other, in the most barbarous manner; till at last it took Shelter in that House that used to be its Protection, and came and expired at my Feet. (p. 32)

There are doors of remembrance we can never enter without looking back. Both Locke's anecdote and Jenny's reminiscence illustrate how childhood trauma lives on: how the act of telling is the act of living through. But both of these little stories also reflect on the fundamental questions of nature. Can one really change one's nature? Can a cat be bred to be a dog? Can a madman grow into a sane one? Can the child truly become something other than it was—through reading, education, reminiscence, or self-mastery? "Boys will be boys" seems to emerge as the moral of Jenny's story. But if cats can, in some sense, become dogs, can girls, too, become boys?

These are the questions central to Locke's theories of mind and education, and central, too, to Fielding's *Governess*. For if that mind is like a furnished house or cabinet, then entry into thought or memory is through a door. These tales of doors are therefore tales of knowledge: ways of ordering the stuff inside the head into a meaningful arrangement. The doors in these two tales are both doors of home: in Locke's, the door to the father's house; in Jenny's, the door to the mother's. But doors lead also into rooms of terror. Take, for example, the story of the giant Barbarico, which Jenny tells in *The Governess*. "And now, by their united force," she reports, "they dragged the ponderous Key from under the Monster's Head; and then descending, they all went to the outer Door of the Cave, where, with some Difficulty, they set wide open the folding Iron Gates" (p. 59). Mrs. Teachum, much like Locke himself, sets little store by such fairy tales. Their purpose, she says, is only "to amuse and divert" (p. 68). But surely Locke's story of the madman and the boy is, in effect, as much a tale of monsters and midgets as might be Jenny's story of Barbarico or her remembrance of the schoolboys and her cat. The point is that we have to tell these stories, and in the process of telling, we become ourselves.

I began with the playthings of the nursery and I end with the terrors of the tale. Aesopic beasts find sculpted heads. Teachers make toys out of letters. We rummage through our memories like people rummaging through pockets. And sometimes, to our undying parental embarrassment, we find we have no pants on. All of us have been terrified by taunting bullies or by madmen. Childhood is no Eden, even if it was filled with apples. Locke's impact on the literatures of and for children lies in this world of the particulars: blocks and battledores, cats and dogs, roses and peach trees, and lions and elephants.

# Canoes and Cannibals

*ROBINSON CRUSOE* AND ITS LEGACIES

Almost from its original publication in 1719, Daniel Defoe's *Robinson Crusoe* had an immense impact on literature for children and adults. It has been widely seen as one of the first major novels in English; as the stimulus for a range of adventure stories; as the kernel for abridgments and adaptations; and as the marker for particular personal and political experience.[1] The novel brings together the two major early modern philosophical and social strands that contributed to children's literary culture: Puritan devotion and Lockean epistemology. *Robinson Crusoe*'s emphasis on self-inspection, its preoccupation with lists and inventories, and its overarching concern with salvation, Providence, and the right reading of the world all associate it with the Puritan legacies of Bunyan, Janeway, and the seventeenth century divines. In addition, the novel's fascination with particulars, its catalogues of experiences and technologies, and its commanding faith in a knowledge gained about the physical world through the senses all place it squarely in the heritage of Locke. As Robinson himself puts it, in an exclamation that yokes both traditions together, "How strange a Chequer-work of Providence is the Life of Man! And by what secret differing Springs are the Affections hurry'd about as differing Circumstances present!"[2]

In effecting this synthesis, *Robinson Crusoe* did something new, as if it gave voice to the childhood of the English novel itself. And indeed, this is a novel about children. Robinson begins with his genealogy. He gives the etymology of his last name, and in so doing links inheritance with spiritual journey. "Crusoe" is an Anglicized version of the German name *Kreutznaer*—one who approaches the cross (compare the German word

*Kreutzfahrt,* "crusade"). Crusoe is a crusader, and the novel traces the defining Catholic journey of salvation into a Reformation, Protestant journey of self-discovery. Robinson himself is the third son (note that Swift's Lemuel Gulliver is also a third son), and this condition compels him to make his own way in the world. Unlike in *Pilgrim's Progress,* where it was the father who resolved to run away on spiritual missions, in *Robinson Crusoe* the son runs off on an emotional and economic mission.

But Robinson is not the only child in the book. Friday is childlike, and in his servile affections, in his willingness to learn his master's language, and in his physiognomy, he appears the little boy to Robinson's parent. "His very Affections were ty'd to me, like those of a Child to a Father" (p. 151). When Robinson teaches his found child, he does so through the familiar Puritan exchanges of question and answer. "I always apply'd my self in Reading the Scripture, and let him know, as well as I could, the Meaning of what I read" (p. 156). There is the spirit of James Janeway here: the "token for children" is now the instructional manual for this island schoolroom.

In the schoolrooms of Europe, *Robinson Crusoe* was everywhere. A year after its English publication, it appeared in French.[3] Chapbooks, abridgments, and translations abounded. Forty such *Robinsonaden* appeared in German between 1722 and 1769.[4] By then, the French philosopher Jean-Jacques Rousseau had already made *Crusoe* the centerpiece of his vision of education in his treatise *Emile* (1762): "Since we absolutely must have books, there exists one which, to my taste, provides the most felicitous treatise on natural education. This book will be the first that my Emile will read. For a long time it will alone compose his whole library. . . . What, then, is this marvelous book? . . . It is *Robinson Crusoe.*"[5] For Rousseau, Defoe's novel teaches self-sufficiency. Its hero represents man in a state of nature, outside the boundaries of civil society, unaffected by what others do or think. He teaches children to imagine themselves in potentially real situations. For Rousseau, importantly, Robinson does not foster a fantastic or imaginative place for the child. Instead, he offers a model for particular experience, and in experience lies education. In this approach, Rousseau may seem to bear Locke's impress, but there is something more: the measure of a child not so much in terms of moral growth or rational behavior, but in terms of feeling. Throughout *Emile,* Rousseau appears less interested in virtues and vices as the heart of human happiness than in sincerity and authenticity. The experience of the senses nurtures a feeling individual. It also nurtures a technological individual, for *Robinson*

*Crusoe* presents a vision of society before the division of labor. It reveals the possibilities of one man's mastering the arts and sciences. Such mastery frees the individual from social constraints. The book instructs the reader in the skills of self-sufficiency: agriculture, pottery, woodworking, metalworking, and so on.

Rousseau's vision was immensely influential on the novel's early reception. It contributed to the abridgments and imitations that gave rise to the so-called Robinsonade tradition: the story of adventure, island exile, and return that occupied young readers from the late eighteenth through the early twentieth century. It may have influenced, as well, the place of the novel in early American self-definition. As Jay Fliegelman has illustrated in his study of Revolutionary American literary culture, this Rousseau-inflected Robinson helped shape a literary vision of colonial response to a paternalistic British rule. Robinson's decision to leave his parents, Friday's guilt about the father he himself had left behind, and the location of the island "off the coast of America" all encouraged, in Fliegelman's words, "colonial readers to perceive an analogy between the fate and significance of Crusoe's island and their own Atlantic nation."[6] Parenting and politics stretch out the Robinsonian tradition—not just through the obvious imitations of, say, John Stockdale's *The New Robinson Crusoe* (1788) and Johann Wyss's *Swiss Family Robinson* (1812), but across a whole arc of island tales: R. M. Ballantyne's *The Coral Island* (1858), Robert Louis Stevenson's *Treasure Island* (1883), and Jules Verne's *The Mysterious Island* (1874). *Robinson Crusoe* still governed many of the classics of twentieth-century children's literature: A. A. Milne's *Winnie-the-Pooh* (whose Christopher Robin synthesizes, in his name, the two great explorers of new worlds, Christopher Columbus and Robinson Crusoe); E. B. White's *Stuart Little*; and Maurice Sendak's *Where the Wild Things Are.*[7] In all these books, there are adventures and enislements, parents and children, runaways and returns. But there are also two things that, I think, directly distill Defoe's influence and that encapsulate his novel's literary scope, its social vision, and its hold on the childhood imagination. These things are *canoes* and *cannibals*.

Years into his island exile, Crusoe comes upon a human footprint. Was there someone else on the island, too, or was this simply the mark of one of his own feet? Perhaps, he meditates, there's little strange in seeing other footprints. "I should easily have known, that nothing was more frequent than for the Canoes from the Main, when they happen'd to be a little too far out at Sea, to shoot over to that Side of the Island for

Harbour; likewise as they often met, and fought in their Canoes, the Victors having taken any Prisoners, would bring them over to this shore, where according to their dreadful Customs, being all Canibals, they would kill and eat them" (p. 119). *Canoe* and *cannibal* are fascinating words. Both come originally from North American languages, and they entered English in the seventeenth century in ways that say much about British attitudes toward culture and society, education and identity.[8]

*Canoe* comes from *canoa*, a word that entered Spanish with the earliest explorers. It described a boat made from a hollowed-out tree and was, throughout the eighteenth century, associated with the native peoples of America (and then, by extension, with Pacific islanders). It was a boat crafted by individuals, something that somebody could make himself. It was not a product of group labor or its divisions; it was not a ship, in the European sense; and when Robinson eventually constructs his own little sailboat, he is amazed to find that Friday, "tho' he knew very well how to paddle a Canoe, . . . knew nothing what belong'd to a Sail and a Rudder" (p. 165). This sailboat is something that, though not much like a canoe, was measured against it as a model. "The Boat was really much bigger than I ever saw a Canoe . . . that was made of one Tree, in my Life" (p. 165).

Read *Robinson Crusoe* for its canoes and you find scenes of individual accomplishment, moments of observation, and narratives of the encounter between European and savage. The canoe stands as a project not just of maritime mechanics, but of the literary imagination: the thing we make ourselves, to take us places we have never been. Little wonder that much later children's literature is full of canoes or small canoe-like craft. Stuart Little seeks out a canoe for his romantic idyll with the two-inch-tall Miss Ames—but he leaves it overnight, only to return with her to find it damaged beyond all repair. In *Where the Wild Things Are*, the wolf-suited Max takes his small craft off to the island full of terrifying creatures.

And the most terrifying of those creatures, throughout Western literature, are cannibals. Perhaps no practice (short of incest) morphed into as overwhelming a taboo as cannibalism. The word itself probably emerged into the European languages as a corruption of *Carib* (or *Canib*), an indigenous people that Columbus first found in the West Indies. Almost immediately, their name became associated with the eating of human flesh, and ultimately with an uncontrolled savagery that the colonizer feared in the colonized (Shakespeare's Caliban from *The Tempest* owes his name to a rearrangement of the letters of *cannibal*). Crusoe assumes that all the islanders he might encounter will be cannibals, and among the first things that he tries to teach Friday is to lose the taste for human flesh. Even at their first encounter, Crusoe reveals his disgust at the idea that he and Friday dig up the dead islanders to eat them ("at this I appear'd very angry, express'd my Abhorrence of it, made as if I would vomit at the thoughts of it"; p. 149). Even so, Friday remains "still a Cannibal in his Nature" (p. 150), and it takes much teaching to get him to affirm that "he would never eat Man's flesh any more" (p. 154). By the time they capture Friday's father, along with another European sailor, Crusoe can create a kind of hierarchy of social identities and, in the process, locate cannibalism only slightly below Catholicism.

> My island was now peopled, and I thought my self very rich in Subjects; and it was a merry Reflection which I frequently made. How like a King I look'd. . . . It was remarkable too, we had but three Subjects, and they were of three different Religions. My Man Friday was a Protestant, his father was a Pagan and a Cannibal, and the Spaniard was a Papist. However, I allow'd Liberty of Conscience throughout my Dominions. (p. 174)

Canoes and cannibals stand as the two poles of island adventurism, the features that distinguish civilized and savage.

But they are also landmarks on a political landscape. Crusoe's fantasy of rule admits the cannibal, but only insofar as this contributes to his own sense of royal largesse. But is there something of the cannibal in kings? Crusoe's subjects would "lay down their lives" for him (p. 174). The king is an instrument of death. So, too, a would-be nursery king, young Max of *Where the Wild Things Are*, threatens to eat his mother up. Sent to his room unfed, Max travels in a boat of his desire—a little thing with a little sail, yet garnished with his own name on the side. Max: the maximum, the biggest, the best. And in the maximal reign of his imagination, this boy travels to a land of wild things, only to command them: "BE STILL!" How like a king he looks, and his subjects   still cannibal in their nature— respond with the love only a cannibal could offer: we will "eat you up— we love you so."[9]

The arc of *Where the Wild Things Are* remains, as with *Crusoe*, the arc of cannibal and canoe. Both books propel us not just to new landscapes, but to new questions. What does it mean to be a human being? Are there certain patterns of behavior that are so taboo that they exile us from the family table? Is the goal of adventure really, in the end, the goal of conquest? Between these two books lies a history of island tales and terrors, and the beginnings of that history lie with the chapbook adaptations of *Robinson Crusoe* itself.

The word *chapbook* refers to a short, cheaply made pamphlet sold originally by the chapmen, or itinerant merchants, of English and European cities.[10] It was designed to offer literary culture to those who could often least afford it, and while chapbooks were not originally designed as venues for children's reading, they became, by the middle of the eighteenth century, the vehicle for popular abridgments of the classics. *Robinson Crusoe, Gulliver's Travels, Pilgrim's Progress*, and many fairy tales and nursery rhymes appeared in cheap, abridged editions for the young. They illustrated what certain readers, merchants, parents, and teachers thought was most instructive or entertaining about certain books. Read in the larger context of the Robinsonian tradition, however, they contribute to a deeper understanding of just what literary and aesthetic techniques were deemed teachable to children: techniques of description, of appreciation, and of rhetorical address.[11]

What did children get from *Robinson Crusoe*? Rousseau may have thought that they would get a sense of independence, or a lesson in mechanics, or a vision of the feeling person in a state of nature. But many eighteenth- and nineteenth-century readers had more modest goals. In fact, many were afraid of the book. Sarah Trimmer, best known for her survey of children's books, *The Guardian of Education*, warned in the first decade of the nineteenth century that "children of very lively imaginations accustomed to indulge their fancy without control in their infantine amusements, may undoubtedly be led by it into an early taste for a rambling life, and a desire for adventures."[12] Others were equally wary. Stockdale's *New Robinson Crusoe* (1788) thought that Crusoe's woes stemmed from his early lack of parental control. Mother and father "suffered their dear child to do whatever he pleased; and as this dear child liked better to play than to work or to learn anything, they let him play almost the whole day long, by which means he learned little or nothing."[13]

Throughout the early imitations and abridgements, this moral cast predominates. A cut-down edition of 1786 concludes: "Now as many of my readers, from a wild inclination of their own, or from the advice of bad children, may wish to ramble from one country to another, they may rest assured by me, that it will only bring them into distress, for every word of my father's advice, when he called me into his chamber, I fatally found strictly to be true."[14]

It would be easy to go through these books and lament their limitations. Many critics have already done so, noticing, as Samuel Pickering has, the negative impact that English pedagogues would find in tales of travel. Disobedience, displacement, disaffection—these were the things stern teachers found in Crusoe's actions. Rousseau's paean to the life unfettered lay far from their ken. More telling than a simple catalogue of crankiness, it seems to me, would be an attentive reading of some of these chapbooks. Two examples come to mind, not simply for their intrinsic interest, but for what has been made of their exemplary value.

The first I choose is *The Adventures of Robinson Crusoe*, an 1823 chapbook recently reprinted in *The Norton Anthology of Children's Literature*.[15] The editors of the *Anthology* describe this version as paring "down the novel to its essence as an adventure tale" (p. 1633), but I think it is much more. For a start, we have to notice what is pared away. The chapbook version begins without the etymology of Crusoe's name, without the long debate between the hero and his father, and without the reflections that make the novel's beginning so complex and tantalizing. Here is its entire first paragraph:

> I was born of a good family in the city of York, where my father, who was a native of Bremen, settled, after his having got a handsome estate by merchandise. My heart was very early filled with rambling thoughts; and though, when I grew up, my father persuaded me to settle to some business, while my mother used the tenderest entreaties, yet nothing could prevail upon me to lay aside my desire of going to sea. I at length resolved to gratify my roving disposition, notwithstanding the uneasiness my father and mother showed at my leaving them. (p. 1634)

The story begins only partly in Defoe's words. Phrases such as "good family," "in the city of York," and "estate by merchandise" come right out of the novel, though not necessarily in this order (Defoe originally wrote "got a good estate by merchandise"; clearly, the chapbook author found the word "handsome" more compelling for his readers). But almost immediately, diction changes. The second sentence simply states that Crusoe's "heart was very early filled with rambling thoughts." This statement makes it seem as if Crusoe's life is a matter of his inner self, his disposition— indeed, at the paragraph's conclusion, the narrator avers his "roving disposition." In the original novel, Crusoe makes clear that his "rambling thoughts" are a direct consequence of being "the third son of the Family, and not bred to any Trade." Rambling is a social and an economic problem for the seventeenth-century child. It is a moral problem for the early nineteenth-century one. In fact, nowhere in Defoe's novel does the phrase "roving disposition" appear.

This opening paragraph rewrites *Crusoe* into the judgmental terms of moral criticism. "Rambling" is the word that Sarah Trimmer and her predecessors had picked up on immediately, and this chapbook is, in effect, written through their lens. And as their lessons were to shun adventure for diligence, so this chapbook Crusoe becomes a model of industry. As we read through the story on the pages of *The Norton Anthology*, we see the emphases on the plantation in Brazil and, after the shipwreck, the careful attention to learning how to make things, plant things, and control domestic life. Friday's footprints appear, and then Friday himself, as little more than object lesson for the English master; and by the end (almost all too quickly), they are rescued. Crusoe returns to England and then goes to Lisbon, where he finds himself rich from his plantation's returns.

Adventure, yes, but economics, value, industry, and teaching fill these pages more than ripping yarns. In this brief space (the whole text takes up only ten pages of *The Norton Anthology*), what stands out are not dramatic encounters, but careful accounting. Prices in pounds abound; details of craftsmanship stand out (it fascinates me that in such a short version of the novel, more than a dozen densely printed lines are devoted to Crusoe's pottery). Crusoe is industrious, but he is also even more strangely alone than in Defoe's novel. For there, the castaway had made himself a home; even before Friday appears, he sits in royal majesty with his family pets.

> It would have made a Stoick smile to have seen, me and my little Family sit down to Dinner; there was my Majesty the Prince and Lord of the whole Iland; I had the Lives of all my Subjects at my absolute Command. I could hang, draw, give Liberty, and take it away, and no Rebels among all my subjects.
>
> Then to see how like a King I din'd too all alone, attended by my Servants, Poll, as if he had been my Favorite, was the only Person permitted to talk to me. My Dog, who was now grown very old and crazy, and had found no Species to multiply his Kind upon, sat always at my Right-Hand; and two Cats, one on one Side the Table, and one on the other, expecting now and then a Bit from my Hand, as a Mark of special Favour. (p. 108)

Now, compare the chapbook version of this scene:

> Certainly a Stoic would have smiled to have seen me at dinner: there was my royal majesty, an absolute prince and ruler of my kingdom, attended by my dutiful subjects, whom, if I pleased, I could either hang, draw or quarter—give liberty, or take it away. When I dined, I seemed a king, eating alone, none daring presume to do so till I had done. Poll was the only person permitted to talk with me. My old but faithful dog, now growing exceedingly crazy, continually sat at my right hand; while my two cats sat on each side of the table, expecting a bit from my hand, as a princely mark of my royal favour. (p. 1637)

Set side by side, these passages reveal something more than mere abridgment. It is not that the children's version is simpler, or shorter, than the original. At times, the chapbook develops Defoe (for example, "a Mark of special Favour" expands into "a princely mark of my royal favour"). What has changed here is the *tone*. Defoe's self-consciously theatricalized idiom, the almost manic self-attention that his narrator displays, has flattened out to mere description. Defoe's "how like a King" anticipates that later moment in the novel when Crusoe reflects on his lordship over Friday, his father, and the Spaniard: "How like a king I looked." Behind these phrases, I believe, is a Shakespearean histrionics—the voice of Lear at his most mad, garlanded with flowers in Act IV of his play. Blind Gloucester hears something and asks, "Is't not the king?" and Lear replies:

> Ay, every inch a king.
> When I do stare, see how the subject quakes.
> I pardon that man's life. What was thy cause?
> (*King Lear*, 4.6.107–9)

This is most certainly the voice of Crusoe, and Poll sits there, much like Lear's Fool, a favorite.

The chapbook will have none of this. Crusoe's oratory, his crazed family fantasy, is sifted into bald declaratives. This version offers nothing of the family conflict that so permeates Defoe's book. The extended opening arguments between Crusoe and his father are gone; Friday's father gets but one sentence; and the whole exchange between Crusoe and Friday, capped by Crusoe's statement that Friday's "Affections were ty'd to me, like those of a Child to a Father," has been excised. There really are no families in this chapbook, and I think the reason is that this is a version pared down to emphasize not so much adventure as industry and independence. There is no place for histrionics here, no place for extended filial guilt or anger (on either Friday's or Crusoe's part). Crusoe ends up, in the chapbook version, an old man of seventy-two, having "been taught sufficiently the value of retirement, and the blessing of ending my days in peace" (p. 1643). That lesson is the lesson for the child as well: to live one's days in peace and not to trouble the retirement of elders with despair or disobedience. This chapbook ends with a Crusoe for middle-class, familial England—an England recovering from decades of Napoleonic war, from the loss of North America, from the death of kings. George III (the most Lear-like of the modern English kings) had lingered on in madness until 1820. George IV's dissipated rule would stretch another decade. In such an age of insecurity, ideals of good behavior and directed energy trump fantasies of rambling or of rule.

Two decades after this chapbook appeared, another version showed up, out of the town of Banbury, which by the mid-nineteenth century was the center for cheap publishing in Britain. This version came to my attention in the collection *The Other Print Tradition: Essays on Chapbooks, Broadsides, and Related Ephemera*, edited by Cathy Lynn Preston and Michael J. Preston. The focus of this collection lies in calling new attention to a tradition of cheap print: to see how, throughout history, people read not just the "elite" published versions of canonical literature, but often unauthorized and reworked transformations of high-culture texts. Michael Preston's essay in this volume focuses on chapbook versions of *Robinson Crusoe* and *Gulliver's Travels*, and he finds in a circa 1840 version of the former an instructive "moral story" that relies on simple language, woodcuts, and changed narrative perspective to address a popular, and perhaps childhood, readership.[16]

As in *The Norton Anthology*, a chapbook *Crusoe* serves an argument about the history of literature. And just as the *Anthology*'s chapbook is, as I have sought to show here, more concerned with tone and texture than with simple plot, so, too, the one that Preston reproduces and retells is a fascinating document of narrative manipulation. Right away, something is amiss. The book begins not in the first person but in the third: "Robinson Crusoe was born of a respectable family in York." This opening conditions us to hear far less a personal tale than a bedtime story. It is a story told, now, in the voice of a soothing yet still judging parent—a voice that relies not just on Defoe's story, but on a range of languages running from those of Bible tales to nursery rhymes. Crusoe comes off as something of a sorry Jonah: "The waves appeared ready to swallow him, and he vowed that if it should please God to spare his life this voyage he would return to his father and mother, and live with them" (p. 2). But then we get this bizarre bit of doggerel:

> When his sickness wore off,
>> He was jeer'd by the crew so;
> Till a storm did arise,
>> Then in prayer was Crusoe.
>>> (p. 3)

A few lines later, when Crusoe goes off to South America, builds his plantation, and is taken by pirates (all of this described in a single sentence), we get another stanza:

> He was ta'en by a pirate,
>> In slavery too, so
> Zury pushed off the ship's boat,
>> And escaped with Crusoe.
>>> (p. 3)

For a modern reader, stanzas such as these are laughable (the rhymes on "Crusoe" seem particularly close to either lunacy or ineptness). And yet I think that what this chapbook aspires to is a translation of Defoe's novel into the languages of childhood reading—languages still shaped, in the early nineteenth century, by rhythms of Isaac Watts or the Aesopic fable. Beasts fill this version of the story, as they fill the fables: "A large lion was swimming towards the boat, when Crusoe shot him, and he swam back wounded to the shore, where they dare not land, because of the noise of wild beasts, which came to drink of the water and wash in the stream" (p. 4).

Whatever is going on here, it all changes in the next sentence: "During the day time we filled our jars with water . . ." Without any warning, the book shifts from third to first person, and the bulk of the story is told in Crusoe's voice. That voice runs through the whole of his adventures in a scant half dozen small pages. There is the shipwreck, the landing on the island, the recovery of materials from the ship, the collection of animals, the making of the hewn canoe, the footprints on the beach, and finally Friday, who appears out of the group of savages that Crusoe subdues. "This happened to be my man Friday, who afterwards lived with me as a faithful companion and servant for years. I taught him to speak to me, which was a comfort I had not enjoyed for a long period" (pp. 11–12). And then the story breaks, and we return to the third person: "Friday became a good Christian and wished Crusoe to go to his country to teach vile mans to be good, sober, tame mans." The grammatical irregularities here mime Friday's voice, and for a few sentences we continue in third-person narrative. But again the story shifts back to first person, as Crusoe himself tells the tale of the fight with the savages and the Spaniard. "I had an apparent kingdom, with three dutiful subjects": that is all we get of the great exposition in Defoe's original, or, for that matter, in the still extended version of the earlier chapbook. Then it is back to third person, and a quick review of the return, the reestablishment of Crusoe's economic security, and his retirement "to an estate in the country" (p. 16).

Is this chapbook merely inept, or is there something more to these shifts of narration, tone, and tense? Whatever the aptitude of this chapbook's assembler (and I do think that this is a slapdash piece of work), it does reveal a series of experiments in tone. For what readers and writers learned from *Robinson Crusoe* was how to tell a story. There is a difference between first- and third-person narration. Poetic interruptions can be used for special effect. Word choice, syntax, diction—all contribute to a history of literary tone and an awareness that tone—far more than content, moral, or example—makes a work appropriate for children. How do you describe features of a place? How do you notice faces, forms, and bodies? How do you string individual experiences into a narrative?

These are the questions that Defoe asks, and answers. Those answers form the origins of English literary fiction. Reading through the Robinsonian tradition, we can see Defoe's lessons take hold. Few writers took those lessons to heart as much as Robert Louis Stevenson, whose *Treasure Island* takes the Crusoe story and transforms it into an adventure for the child narrator as well as for the reader.[17]

Part 3 of *Treasure Island* begins with what young Jim Hawkins calls "my shore adventure." Landing on the island, he is struck by visual appearances, "the look of the island, with its grey, melancholy woods, and wild stone spires, and the surf that we could both see and hear foaming and thundering on the steep beach" (p. 691). This is a language, at first glance, seemingly far from Defoe's English—and yet it is not that far away, for what Stevenson (and many others) learned from Defoe was the power of physical description. That Lockean fascination with particulars gave rise to a high level of attention in descriptive art. Defoe, however, deployed it not so much with his landscapes as with his people. Here is Friday, as he first appeared:

He was a comely handsome Fellow, perfectly well made; with straight strong Limbs, not too large; tall and well shap'd, and as I reckon, about twenty six Years of Age. He had a very good Countenance, not a fierce and surly Aspect; but seem'd to have something very manly in his Face, and yet he had all the Sweetness and Softness of an European in his Countenance, too, especially when he smiled. His Hair was long and black, not curl'd like Wool; his Forehead very high, and large, and a great Vivacity and sparkling Sharpness in his Eyes. The Colour of his Skin was not quite black, but very tawny; and yet not of an ugly yellow nauseous tawny, as the Brasilians, and Virginians, and other Natives of America are; but of a bright kind of dun olive colour, that had in it something very agreeable; though not very easy to describe. His Face was round, and plump; his Nose small, not flat like the Negroes, a very good Mouth, thin Lips, and his Fine teeth well set, and white as Ivory. (pp. 148–49)

That face is a landscape, a territory that evokes a history of humankind. Crusoe measures Friday against all the world: from Europe to Brazil to Virginia to evocations of Africa, this passage takes us on a journey as rich as Crusoe's itself.

Stevenson applies this verbal attentiveness to the physical world. Landscapes, here, are like people, and the island itself takes on something of a physiognomy of fear—to make woods "melancholy" implies that they have a kind of feeling; to call rocks "naked," as he does elsewhere (p. 691), implies a bodily imagination of terrain. "There was not a breath of air moving." And yet, the island is alive. "Nothing lived in front of me but dumb brutes and fowls. . . . Here and there were flowering plants, unknown to me; here and there I saw snakes, and one raised his head from a ledge of rock and hissed at me with a noise not unlike the spinning of a top" (p. 694). A boy's description to the last—for all the strange Edenic feeling of this passage, the snake hisses like a toy out of the nursery.

And when Jim comes upon the mysterious stranger on the island, he describes him as if he were one with the landscape. "Whatever it was, whether bear or man or monkey, I could in no wise tell. It seemed dark and shaggy." "Dark" and "shaggy" evoke the forest. "From trunk to trunk the creature flitted like a deer, running manlike on two legs, but unlike any man that I had ever seen." The island makes the boy question humanity itself. "I began to recall what I had heard of cannibals"—now we get from his mind the legacy of Robinsonian adventure: cannibals on islands, terrifying creatures that would make the European break out his gun. But the only "gun" here is the man himself.

"Who are you?" I asked.

"Ben Gunn," he answered, and his voice sounded hoarse and awkward, like a rusty lock.

The rusty lock of Gunn's voice creaks less like a hasp upon a door than the gears of a flintlock rifle, left to rust in sad neglect.

> I could see now that he was a white man like myself and that his features were even pleasing. His skin, wherever it was exposed, was burnt by the sun; even his lips were black, and his fair eyes looked quite startling in so dark a face. Of all the beggar-men that I had seen or fancied, he was the chief for raggedness. He was clothed with tatters of old ship's canvas and old sea-cloth, and this extraordinary patchwork was all held together by a system of the most various and incongruous fastenings, brass buttons, bits of stick, and loops of tarry gaskin. About his waist he wore an old brass-buckled leather belt, which was the one thing solid in his whole accoutrement. (p. 697)

At this moment, Stevenson returns us to Defoe's world, but with a striking difference. The thick description of Ben Gunn plays on Crusoe's description of Friday. Both offer essays in identification: How do skin tone and hair inform us of the moral character beneath them? How do clothes reveal a level of civilization? Are whiteness and blackness categories of humanity itself? But this is no savage; this is a European man. It is as if the boy had come upon Crusoe himself, marooned on his island and attired in the tatters of his former life. The bits and pieces of his ship and his society hang from his limbs, like a pastiche of civilization. So, too, Crusoe, in his skins and hat, girded (in the famous illustration to the volume) with a belt and carrying his guns, is a king of shreds and patches.

These passages in *Treasure Island* transform the techniques, the images, and the tone of *Robinson Crusoe*. They take the island story and reveal it as a tale not just of geographical adventure, but of inner, mental exploration. Every physical description reflects the state of mind of the describer. Ben Gunn is conjured up here out of the reminiscences of Defoe's novel: a patchwork not of cloth and buttons, but of words themselves.

So, too, the chapbooks may be thought of as a patchwork *Crusoe*, and the history of its reception is the lesson of its hero. When Robinson finds himself wrecked upon the shore, he swims to his ship to reclaim items of necessity. Food, water, ammunition, a book or two—these are the items rescued from the disaster. Reading is like a shipwreck. We recall passages and images, occasionally vivid episodes or necessary morals, much

Fig. 4. Frontispiece to Daniel Defoe, *Robinson Crusoe* (London, 1719).

as Crusoe brings back the essentials from his ship. What chapbooks or abridgments, modern critics or anthologists, and nineteenth-century novelists all do is rescue from the old ship of this novel things that they think are essential. What would you carry to your desert island? What books, what music, what accoutrements could you not live without? The desert-island game comes straight from Crusoe's world—as, in the end, does children's literature itself. It returns us to ships of our imagination, as we cull and carry what we should from books.

And if Max takes his wolf suit and his self-named boat to where the wild things are, so, too, Winnie-the-Pooh takes us to the edge of unease.[18] "One fine day," we are told, as Piglet sweeps away the snow, he finds Pooh tracking something on the ground. "What do you see there?" Pooh asks, and Piglet responds, "Tracks . . . Paw-marks" (p. 36). We read on, watching, too (in the familiar illustrations by Ernest H. Shepard), how Pooh and Piglet track themselves in their own footprints. Perhaps it is a Woozle.

Soon the two creatures find more tracks: three sets, then four. They are terrified. Piglet, pretending to have forgotten a task, runs off, and Pooh is left alone. He looks up and sees Christopher Robin sitting in a tree, watching the whole escapade.

> "Silly old Bear," he said, "what were you doing? First you went round the spinney twice by yourself, and then Piglet ran after you and you went round again together, and then you were just going round a fourth time." (p. 43)

Down on the ground, footprints look different from the way they seem from treetops. Robinson Crusoe himself wonders if the print he sees that fateful day may simply be his own. Pooh does not realize, until another Robin (and himself a son) so informs him, that they really are his own. The footprint scene in *Crusoe* has become so forceful, so familiar (it is one of the very few episodes that appear in all the chapbooks, adaptations, and abridgments I have seen), that it can inform a tale as seemingly simple as *Winnie-the-Pooh*. Perspective is everything, this book now tells us, and your fantasies of monsters can be easily dispelled just by soliciting another viewpoint.

If there remains the threat of cannibals behind Pooh's footprints, there appears the temptation of the canoe to take all the creatures on a journey. The expedition to the North Pole finds them debating how they plan to travel.

> "We're all going on an Expotition with Christopher Robin!"
> "What is it when we're on it?"
> "A sort of boat, I think," said Pooh.
>
> (p. 114)

The word "expotition," a mistake for "expedition," now becomes the name of their imaginary boat (could there be something here, too, of the memory of other boats of great adventure: Captain Cook's *Endeavour*, or Shackleton's *Endurance*?). As this chapter advances, Milne breaks the flow of the narrative with poetry: songs, stanzas, and rhymes far more deft than any in the Crusoe chapbooks. The creatures and their leader travel through dangerous forests—"just the place," Christopher Robin notes, "for an Ambush." "What sort of bush?" asks Pooh of Piglet, and it takes the Owl to explain that an ambush "is a sort of Surprise" (pp. 119–20). Like Pooh and Piglet, or the young boy in *Treasure Island*, or Max, or Crusoe, we are all ambushed by imagination. The rills and streams of the Hundred Acre Wood become, on this journey, great falls and rushing rivers. And when Pooh picks up a wooden pole to get across one of those rivers, Christopher realizes that Pooh has himself found the North Pole.

> They stuck a pole in the ground and Christopher Robin tied a message on to it.

NORTH POLE

DISCOVERED BY POOH

POOH FOUND IT

(p. 129)

This is a journey of discovery, but it is also (like so many journeys in *Winnie-the-Pooh*) a trip through language. *Expedition, ambush, pole*—all of these words have double meanings. Throughout the book, familiar phrases take on strange associations: "under the sign of Saunders" becomes weirdly literalized; "Trespassers W" becomes "Trespassers Will," for "Trespassers William," and we then get a whole genealogy for Piglet; and on, and on. *Winnie-the-Pooh*, like *Robinson Crusoe*, tells tales of reading. How do we understand the signs on this earth? What are the books that we would take to a desert island? And once we get there, will we, like Crusoe, set ourselves to the task of writing all things down—even as we run out of ink?

The writers of the Robinsonian tradition, it would seem, never ran out of ink. Between Rousseau and Milne lies a history not just of English literature, but of world literature itself: the German version of Joachim Campe, the Swiss-German recasting of Johann Wyss, the French fantasies of Jules Verne. How did the European adapt Defoe's Englishness? How did *Robinson Crusoe* travel, much like its fictive hero-narrator, around the world to undergo adventures of its own?

The Robinsonian tradition is not just about adaptation or imitation. It is about completion. *Robinson Crusoe*, with its episodic structure, its long gaps of time without narration, and its emphasis on Providence, invited later writers to fill in the blanks. Defoe himself had published a *Farther Adventures* shortly after the original book appeared and another sequel, *Serious Reflections*, in 1720. Many of the Robinsonades that followed play off the novel's possibilities for endless new invention. Tell me another story about Robinson, one imagines readers asking, and writers obliged.

But if the novel challenged writers to come up with added episodes, or if it offered them the opportunity to shape their adventures to a particular imagination, it also challenged the idea of authorship itself. By writing in the first person and by originally publishing anonymously, Defoe fostered the tension between author and persona that would govern novelistic fiction for two centuries. For what the novel teaches, in addition to the techniques of survival or the details of domestic manufacture, is just how to tell a story—how to describe landscape, people, feelings. This is certainly what later writers found so fascinating and so tempting about writing Robinsonades: the occasion to display technique, the opportunities for virtuosity in drama or description. But this is certainly, too, what made the novel's impact on non-English literature so fascinating. Translated from the Puritan and Lockean world of early eighteenth-century Britain, the Crusoe story could become a vehicle for other ideologies or other forms of cultural expression.

Among the earliest and best-known of those adventures was the story's transformation into *The Swiss Family Robinson*.[19] The Swiss clergyman Johann David Wyss began work on this version in the early nineteenth century, by telling bedtime stories to his sons. Transcribing these tales, he produced a large, unwieldy manuscript that would be edited and organized by his son, Johann Rudolf Wyss. It was this version, published under the son's name, that appeared in German in 1812 as *Der schweizerische Robinson*. Within two years, the book was translated into English by Mary Jane Godwin (second wife of the educational reformer and political activist William Godwin). A French version by Isabelle de Montolieu, *Le Robinson suisse*, appeared in five volumes from 1824 to 1826. Later in the nineteenth century, the book was edited and retranslated into English by W. H. G. Kingston. Each of these versions, and the many others that appeared, modified Wyss's version. My guess is that anyone who has read the book has read something different; are these translations, adaptations, abridgments, or imitations? Each moves us farther and farther away from the original author; each contributes less to a history of literature than a history of myth—as if the story, now, were like some set of bedtime legends to be fixed and formed for each new reader. In the book I have before me, Wyss's name nowhere appears. It simply states, on its title page, "The Swiss Family Robinson, illustrated by T. H. Robinson" (there is no date, but it is clearly an edition from the first decade of the twentieth century). There are color pictures, and the chapters do not correspond to the nineteenth-century versions in German or French (my guess is that the text is based on Kingston's version).[20]

This is very much a children's book, with its big print and simple sentences (though not as simple as in another version I have come across:

*The Swiss Family Robinson, in Words of One Syllable*, also published in the early twentieth century).[21] But like all versions of the novel, this is a story about family cooperation, about hierarchies between men and women, fathers and children. Unlike *Robinson Crusoe*, this is no celebration of the individual alone, no narrative of Providence or Lockean particulars. It is here, in the book I have before me, a tale of late nineteenth-century industry, with the division of labor, the control of a paternalistic boss, and the construction of domestic artifacts that have not only utility but grace. Look, for example, at the way in which the family builds their version of Crusoe's canoe. The father finds a large tree, which the family cuts down and from which they strip the bark. It is a great, mechanical enterprise, with a rope ladder, a saw, and cords and pulleys; all the family members find themselves pressed into the service of preparing the boat's bark shell. "The boys," notes the father, "observed that we had now nothing more to do than to nail a plank at each end, and our boat would be as complete as those used by the savages; but for my own part, I could not be contented with a mere roll of bark for a boat; and when I reminded them of the paltry figure it would make following the pinnace, I heard not another word about the further pains and trouble, and they asked eagerly for my instructions" (p. 240). What emerges from their labors is no mere canoe but a well-proportioned little boat, arched over wooden ribs, glued strongly, nailed together. "In two days she had received the addition of a keel, a neat lining of wood, a small flat floor, benches, a small mast and triangular sail, a rudder, and a thick coat of pitch on the outside, so that the first time we saw her in the water, we were all in ecstasies at the charming appearance she made" (p. 241). This is not just a practical but an aesthetic project. What distinguishes the European from the "savage" here, and throughout the book, is a sense of proportion and a feel for beauty.

Writing a children's book is now like making this small boat. You hunt around for suitable material, bring it before the children of the family, and in the process collectively make something that works, that entertains, that pleases. The idea of authorship embedded in this book is the history of its own authorship: collective performance, bequeathed to the child. And if the book is like a ship—if, in the words of the Emily Dickinson poem I was forced to memorize in grade school, "There is no frigate like a book / To take us lands away"—then that book should be even-keeled, balanced, nicely covered, and charming.

I think what makes *The Swiss Family Robinson* such an enduring tale is that it has escaped its author in these ways: that we read versions of the book, or see movie adaptations, and think not of Johann Wyss and his Romantic Switzerland but of ourselves, placed in the various positions of the father, mother, or child. *The Swiss Family Robinson* decouples author from adventurer; it asks us not to find the Defoe behind Crusoe but, instead, to find the family of humankind creating stories of utility and art.

Jules Verne is very different. Throughout his many writings he was clearly taken by, if not overwhelmed by, Crusoe; and his so-called *Voyages extraordinaires*—the adventure novels he began publishing in 1863—all have their debts to Defoe.[22] "When the impulse came," notes his biographer Herbert Lottman, "he would be ready to write a 'Robinson'."[23] There was an early, and unpublished, *Uncle Robinson*; a midcareer *L'école des Robinsons* (*The School for Robinsons*); and many other echoes of the stories of great rafts, or islands, or boy captains, or strange clipper ships. The best-known and most successful of these books, however, was *L'île mystérieuse* (*The Mysterious Island*), published in three volumes from 1874 to 1875. Within a year of complete publication, it was translated into English by Kingston (the translator of *The Swiss Family Robinson*). It was in its time, and remains today, not just one of the most esteemed of Verne's books, but the most fertile in producing imitations, adaptations, and film versions.[20]

This is no novel of family cooperation. Its hero is the Engineer, Cyrus Smith. He is an author figure of unquestioned control. He has the answers; his compatriots take orders. Whether they are hewing an apartment complex out of solid rock, building a forge or kiln, or synthesizing sulphuric acid out of local minerals, the Engineer's companions follow his command like soldiers in an army, or like students in a lab. In lieu of children, there are animals: Top, the dog who escapes with the men in their balloon; and Joop, an orangutan who joins them on the island and remains a constant source of childlike amusement.

From the tradition of the Robinsonades, Verne developed the scene of technological inventiveness. Not just furniture or boats, but all forms of late nineteenth-century civic and civil life find their creation here. Reading the book is comparable, at times, to reading manuals of manufacture. For Verne establishes his narrative authority not so much in the drama of his tale or the details of his descriptions, but in the accuracy of his instructions. We trust him, as the islanders trust the Engineer. Indeed, I could imagine being shipwrecked with this very book and being able, based on its accounts, to build my own boats, turn and fire my own pottery, demolish mountains, redirect rivers, and electrify my territory.

But there is an alternative to Verne's and the Engineer's authority here. Captain Nemo makes, at the book's close, a cameo return appearance from his earlier and starring role in *Twenty Thousand Leagues under the Sea* (published in 1869–70). Nemo is, like the Engineer, a master of the machinery that runs his world. But unlike the Engineer, he is a solitary, brooding figure; bookish and isolated, he offers an alternative version of intellectual control. At the book's end, he confesses that he is, in fact, an Indian prince, angry at England for conquering his people, willing to disappear in the *Nautilus* with his store of treasures and technologies. Nemo is, in some sense, an anti-author. A sad, brooding figure from the Old World, he stands in sharp contrast to the civic, can-do exuberance of Cyrus Smith (that very name brings together the American commonplace with the exotic conqueror—Cyrus, king of the Persians).

These figures constitute alternative ideals for children. They stand as figures for the father, for the writer, for the adult authority in society. How do you make your way in the world? When cast adrift, do you create society and family (as the Engineer does) or not? How do you shape your bark canoe to expectations of the world? The Engineer and his men make a boat to give them free access to all their island. Nemo lives submerged, only to sink in his *Nautilus*.

And if the Engineer and Nemo offer two versions of authority, *The Swiss Family Robinson* and *The Mysterious Island* may be said to offer two versions of the non-English legacy of *Crusoe*. But in some sense, they never get away from it. The former lives, as literature, far more deeply and lastingly in English than in any other language. And while Verne's work has had a lasting readership in French, *The Mysterious Island* begins in an English-language world: the world of the American Civil War. For here, it is the story of the prison break, of the American experience, that makes this Robinsonade so complex. Smith is a Union officer in a Confederate prison. The plan is to escape in a balloon back across the Union lines, and in that balloon are another imprisoned Northerner, Gideon Spillett, a reporter for the *New York Herald*; Smith's black servant, Nab; a Union sailor; and a fifteen-year-old boy and his dog. But they are blown in the wrong direction, landing somewhere in the Pacific.

It is as if Verne must start his novel in the New World, as if he must return to the shores of the Atlantic on which Robinson himself was beached; recall Jay Fliegelman's assessment of the novel for colonial readers, who would "perceive an analogy between the fate and significance of Crusoe's island and their own Atlantic nation." The idea behind *The Mysterious*

*Island* is not the idea of travel as a mode of exploration or colonial control. The book's inhabitants have no intention of establishing a new world or of gaining monetarily from its exploitation (as those of Wyss and Defoe had). Instead, they are escapees.

Childhood is many things; it is a time of exploration, an arena of adventure. Every shipping box becomes a canoe or a spaceship. Every backyard is an island empire. But childhood is, as well, a prison. How many of us sought to run away, to escape those confederacies of parents who made us toil at chores, who limited our freedom, who took us far away from friendships? Our fantasies balloon into strange skies, and they may take us to new island ports or over rainbows. Wherever we may be, we may find cannibals—wild things that eat us up; inhuman beings who threaten; animals who may eat their own. The Swiss Robinsons see things that drive home "that we were no longer inhabitants of Europe." And in opening these books, we find ourselves shipped into bark canoes or balloons that remind us that we're not in Europe, or America, anymore.

# From Islands to Empires

STORYTELLING FOR A BOY'S WORLD

Almost immediately after *Treasure Island* appeared, Robert Louis Stevenson's friend W. E. Henley praised it in the *Saturday Review*. Calling it a work "touched with genius," "a masterpiece of narrative," and one "rich in excellent characterization," he concludes: "It is the work of one who knows all there is to be known about 'Robinson Crusoe'."[1] Stevenson himself had long acknowledged his debt to Defoe, noting at one point that the parrot in his novel "once belonged to Robinson Crusoe" and offering this reflection at length:

> It is the grown people who make the nursery stories; all the children do, is jealously to preserve the text. One out of a dozen reasons why *Robinson Crusoe* should be so popular with youth, is that it hits their level in this matter to a nicety; Crusoe was always at makeshifts and had, in so many words, to *play* at a great variety of professions; and then the book is all about tools, and there is nothing that delights a child so much.[2]

Central to the popularity of Crusoe is play: the use of tools, the world of things behind the novel. A good part of that world emerged from the Lockean landscape of impressions and particulars. But that world takes on new textures in an age of industry. The mechanics of guns and charts, of locomotive engines and explosives, of cigarettes and canned goods, all fed into a later fascination with the Crusoe-hero's mastery of the mass of material things before him.[3] Nineteenth-century characters from the works of Captain Marryat to those of H. Rider Haggard all had this streak of ingenuity. And for the twentieth century, this fascination with dexterity continued to embrace the resourceful soldiers of wartime and the almost magical abilities of the American television character MacGyver.

Stevenson set *Treasure Island* in the eighteenth century, in part to evoke a swashbuckling, pre-industrial time of adventure, but in part, too, to relocate what was for his own time the growing focus of adventure. Throughout the Victorian age, the boy's imaginative geography was moving from the island to the continent. Empire had displaced exploration as the motive of the ocean voyage. Encounters with non-Europeans took on new detail in Africa, India, or Asia. Adventure heroes appeared less and less to animate a Crusoe-like experience of independence and more and more to exemplify public and military service. The individual engagement of a Crusoe and a Friday gave way to the commanders' control of tribes. The history of boys' books lives along the axes of the island and the continent, and their different locales inform, as well, the presentations of the school, the body, and the family.[4]

What does it mean to be a boy? Aesop's fable of the runaway horse reminds us that boyhood needs to be reined in, and the traditions of classical, medieval, and early modern instruction iterate advice to sons: behave well, keep clean, speak clearly, mind your studies. By the eighteenth century, these patterns of advice had taken on a new flavor. For not only did boys have to act as social, moral beings: they needed a style.

The famous letters of Lord Chesterfield to his illegitimate son—written in the 1730s and 1740s and published, posthumously, as an advice book by his widow—illustrate this shift in focus.[5] Awkwardness, bashfulness, ineptitude: such are the social vices of the child, and Chesterfield advises a behavior keyed to ease with both the word and the body. After a catalogue of all the bad forms of behavior, he summarizes: "From this account of what you should not do, you may easily judge what you should do: and a due attention to the manners of people of fashion, and who have seen the world, will make it habitual and familiar to you." Manners make the man (to evoke an old axiom), though here the manners extend to expression. "There is, likewise, an awkwardness of expression and words most carefully to be avoided; such as false English, bad pronunciation, old sayings, and common proverbs; which are so many proofs of having kept bad and low company." Chesterfield advises verbal ease, a mark of breeding and accomplishment. His claims grow not just out of fatherly concern. They reflect what was happening in the history of the English language in the seventeenth and eighteenth centuries. For the first time in Britain, speech became equated with social status (not just regional origin). Education in the public schools and universities was education in verbal performance. Public style became verbal style. Reading Chesterfield's advice, we can see something of this social history of English—a new concern with accent, a proof of being well-read, an attention to the niceties of grammar. Propriety was coming into being as a social concept, the word having originally meant verb agreement or grammatical concord. When Samuel Johnson, in his great *Dictionary* of 1755, wrote how the low and vulgar "forget propriety" in language, what he actually meant was that they speak ungrammatically.[6] By the end of the eighteenth century, propriety had come to connote social as well as linguistic correctness. Laurence Sterne writes, in *A Sentimental Journey* (1762), of what he calls *propriété*, a kind of Gallic flair for the appropriate. By 1782, Fanny Burney could remark on "such propriety of mind as can only result from the union of good sense and virtue."[7]

Lord Chesterfield's advice fits into an emerging world of social habit as linguistic style—a union of good sense and virtue, spoken well. To be a boy in this age is, increasingly, to be well-spoken. If we turn to the emerging genre of the school story, we can see how this facility with words becomes the key to social mastery. Thomas Hughes's *Tom Brown's Schooldays* is perhaps the best known of these kinds of stories.[8] Set at Rugby school during the days of Dr. Thomas Arnold in the 1830s, the novel (first published in 1857 and continuously in print thereafter) tells the story of a young boy growing up in rural southwestern England who, by dint of chance, hard work, and connections, eventually finds himself at Rugby. From his first day at the school, lessons in verbal style are everywhere.

> Tom by this time began to be conscious of his new social position and dignities, and to luxuriate in the realized ambition of being a public-school boy at last, with a vested right of spoiling two seven-and-sixers in half a year.
>
> "You see," said his friend, as they strolled up towards the school-gates, in explanation of his conduct, "a great deal depends on how a fellow cuts up at first. If he's got nothing odd about him, and answers straightforward, and holds his head up, he gets on. Now you'll do very well as to rig, all but that cap. You see I'm doing the handsome thing by you, because my father knows yours; besides, I want to please the old lady. . . ."
>
> There's nothing for candour like a lower-school boy, and East was a genuine specimen—frank, hearty, and good-natured, well satisfied with himself and his position, and chock full of life and spirits. (p. 1836)

The key to institutional success is how one "cuts up": behaves, cuts a figure, acts and speaks (the idiom seems to have emerged from school and sporting slang in the mid-nineteenth century).[9] Answer straightforward: how you speak is how you are. The ideals of the public-school boy are ideals that match social and verbal life.

But this exchange, like so many in the school-story tradition, is itself a lesson in a verbal idiom. Part of the initiation for the new student lies in learning coded language. Schools all have their slang, and what books such as *Tom Brown's Schooldays* do is educate the reader as they educate their hero. Reading such books becomes a process of socialization. Just as young Tom enters a new and unexpected world, so, too, the reader enters it. We are all Tom Brown, learning the ropes at Rugby. The young boy's fantasy of public-school life lives in mastery of the argot of playing field and common room.

Such mastery takes us back to the world of Crusoe—or at least the Stevensonian imagination of Crusoe. Nothing delights a child so much as tools. But nothing delights a boy so much as new words for those tools— or, for that matter, words themselves as tools. If Crusoe plays at a variety of professions, then the schoolboy plays, too, at a range of roles: the scholar, the athlete, the lover. Tom Brown is a kind of Crusoe of the school, and he finds there the tools of getting by.

> Over the door were a row of hat-pegs, and on each side bookcases with cupboards at the bottom; shelves and cupboards being filled indiscriminately with school-books, a cup or two, a mousetrap, and candlesticks, leather straps, a fustian bag, and some curious-looking articles, which puzzled Tom not a little, until his friend explained that they were climbing irons, and showed their use. A cricket bat and small fishing-rod stood up in one corner. (pp. 1837–38)

School stands here like some ship of the imagination, filled, as Crusoe's was, with the necessities of life. The list of things here compares with Defoe's lists of things—catalogues of particulars, objects whose functions in the world need to be understood. These are the items that enable Tom and his companions to play at a variety of professions: the cricketer, the fisherman, the mountain climber.

If school is a ship, it is also an island. East gives Tom the lay of the land: "And all this part where we are is the little side ground, right up to the trees, and on the other side of the trees is the big side ground, where the great matches are played. And there's the island in the furthest corner; you'll know that well enough next half, when there's island fagging. I say, it's horrid cold, let's have a run across" (p. 1839). Old Rugby really had an island, but the landscape is more metaphorical than mapped out. The bad weather leads not to retreat but to running; all is sport here, all performance, all panache. It is as if the public school is now an island imperium, and East its tour guide. "East was evidently putting his best foot foremost, and Tom, who was mighty proud of his running, and not a little anxious to show his friend that although a new boy he was no milk-sop, laid himself down to work in his very best style. Right across the close they went, each doing all he knew, and there wasn't a yard between them when they pulled up at the island moat" (pp. 1839–40). All friendships ultimately take us back to Crusoe and his Friday: the one old, the other young; the one a teacher, the other the pupil. And in a way, this episode returns us to that island world, where putting your best foot forward leaves a print on history.

If school life is progress across islands, it is, too, control of a continent. Nowhere do verbal skill and bodily performance, tools and techniques, come together better than in sports. Rugby football was that school's enduring legacy. But, as the novel makes clear, what is more important than the game is *narrating* the game. More vivid than experience is the verbal recounting of experience, and this is the lesson of the boy's world. Nowhere is this clearer than in sports reporting. And so, in the midst of Tom Brown's story, we move from the past to the present tense of life.

"Hold the punt about!" "To the goals!" are the cries, and all stray balls are impounded by the authorities....

And now that the two sides have fairly sundered, and each occupies its own ground, and we get a good look at them, what absurdity is this? ...

But now look, there is a slight move forward of the School-house wings....

But see! It has broken; the ball is driven out on the School-house side. ...

Then a moment's pause, while both sides look up at the spinning ball. There it flies, straight between the two posts, some five feet above the cross-bar, an unquestioned goal; and a shout of real genuine joy rings out from the School-house players-up, and a faint echo of it comes over the close from the goal-keepers under the Doctor's wall. A goal in the first hour—such a thing hasn't been done in the School-house match these five years. (pp. 1842–45)

I have extracted these excitements from a span of five pages of the novel, attending to those moments when the book itself becomes the sports announcer. Direct quotations jockey for attention with directed claims: *look, see*. These are imperatives to the reader, ways of getting us to feel the game in progress. Boys' lives live in the present tense. Their drama lies in every escapade told as a competition or a contest. Whether it be in the hushed tones of suspense (now he approaches the ball . . . carefully takes aim) or in the exaltation of success (he shoots, he scores!), the boy's life tells itself as it is being lived.

This rhetoric of present-tense adventure draws on sports reporting, school tales, and team competition. But it also draws on new technologies. If anything made possible a life lived in the present tense, it was the telegraph. By the late 1840s, news could be transmitted almost instantaneously between distant points.[10] Communication took on a magical quality. By the 1870s, Thomas Edison—whose life almost immediately became the subject of boys' books—was "the Wizard of Menlo Park."[11] Mark Twain's *A Connecticut Yankee in King Arthur's Court* (published in 1889) reports how Hank Morgan, transported back to King Arthur's times, could awe the populace with his electrical inventions (telegraph and telephone) and make old Merlin look the fool. Even earlier in the century, the telegraph was almost beyond comprehension.[12] Samuel F. B. Morse, the telegraph's inventor, sent the first message in 1844: "What hath God wrought?" A decade later, Hans Christian Andersen could reflect in his autobiography, *The Fairy Tale of My Life*, on how the telegraph made possible a new link between Europe and America.[13] Telegraph boys were everywhere—for they were boys, taking on the magic of communication, translating the Morse code, messaging great news across the seas and continents (Thomas Edison got his start as a telegraph boy on the railroad in the 1840s). Even at the end of the nineteenth century, when the telephone had displaced the telegraph as the electrical marvel of the age, popular commentary described it in terms of boys' adventure books. The *Electrical Review* of 1889 wrote, of a long-distance call from New York to Boston, "It beat all to smash all the old incantations of Merlin and the magic of Munchhousen [*sic*], Jules Verne, or Haggard."[14]

Electrical communication compressed the time between event and understanding, and in the mid-nineteenth century, telegraph boys throughout the world were soon clicking tales of war. Battle took on a new immediacy with the telegraph. Soon, it was possible to recount warfare in the present tense—as if it were a game of rugby—and war reporting, much like sports reporting, shaped the journalistic idiom of the age. The Crimean War of 1853–56 was the first sustained conflict in which the telegraph and the railroad made possible an immediacy of reportage. Crimea displayed massive new guns, technological advances in firepower, and social innovations (cigarettes, the legend goes, were invented when a soldier got his pipe shot out from under him and started wrapping his tobacco in the empty cartridge paper used for guns).[15] But that war also maintained, in the face of innovation, old ideals of honor. Tennyson's "Charge of the Light Brigade" is but the most famous lesson of an ideal, if outmoded, chivalry, and in literary treatments such as this one, boys' imaginations moved from the sailor and his island to the soldier and his field. There is nothing that delights a child so much as tools, and Crimea made them new.

In enabling the development of new technologies and styles of warfare, Crimea shaped an idiom for boyhood fantasy and literary style. The war contributed to an imperial imagination for the boyish reader, an imagination sustained by successive encounters: the Indian Mutiny of 1857 and the ensuing placement of the subcontinent under direct control of the British crown; the Anglo-Afghan Wars, which continued off and on from the late 1830s until 1919; the search for the headwaters of the Nile by Sir Richard Burton and John Hanning Speke in the 1860s and 1870s; the discovery of David Livingstone by Henry Stanley in 1871; the Zulu War of 1879; the massacre of General Gordon at Khartoum in 1885 and the later retaking of the Sudan by Kitchener at the Battle of Omdurman in 1898; and the Second Boer War of 1899–1902. Central Asia, India, Africa: these were the spaces of colonial emprise and the imaginative spaces for the reader.

These spaces often conjure, for the modern reader, images of Rudyard Kipling and his Kim, his *Jungle Book*, his Mandalay. Kipling has had an undeniable impact on our impressions of this age. And yet, for the late nineteenth century, far more immediate and popular were works by writers such as H. Rider Haggard and G. A. Henty—prolific chroniclers of boyhood fantasy and fascination. Their stories appeared in such publications as *The Boy's Own Paper* and *The Union Jack*—British penny journals blending school tales and adventure, breathlessly told and brilliantly illustrated.[16] To see how sport and war shaped boyhood storytelling, just set copies of these two papers side by side. The first issue of *The Boy's Own Paper* (1879) offers, on its front page, "My First Football Match," complete with a vivid drawing of the scrum. The reader's eye moves from

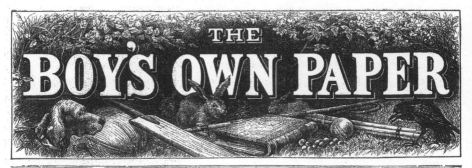

Fig. 5. Front page of *The Boy's Own Paper*, first issue, 18 January 1879. Stanford University Library.

Vol. I.—No. 1.]      Edited by **W. H. G. KINGSTON.**      [Jan. 1, 1880.
[All rights reserved.]

### PADDY FINN;

OR, THE EXPLOITS AND ADVENTURES OF AN IRISH
MIDSHIPMAN, AFLOAT AND ASHORE.

BY THE EDITOR.

CHAPTER I.—THE HOME OF MY ANCESTORS.

" THE top of the morning to you, Terence," cried the major,
looking down upon me from the window of his bed-room.

I was standing in front of the castle of Ballinahone—the seat
of the O'Finnahans, my ancestors—on the banks of the beautiful Shannon ; enjoying the fresh air of the early morning.

" Send Larry up, will you, with a jug of warm water for shav-
ing ; and, while I think of it, tell Biddy to brew me a cup of hot
coffee. It will be some time before breakfast is ready, and my
hand isn't as steady as it once was till I've put something into
my inside."

The old house had not been provided with bells for summon-

" HIS SWORD FLASHED IN THE SUNLIGHT." (See. p. 5.)

Fig. 6. Front page of *The Union Jack*, first issue, 1 January 1880. Stanford University Library.

the text—where the narrator delights in being chosen for his school team, "whose glory it was to fight the battles of [the] school"—to the mass of boys falling on the player with the ball. Now look at the first issue of *The Union Jack* (1880), and the eye moves similarly from the text (recounting "the exploits and adventures of an Irish midshipman") to the picture, as a group of sailors and mounted soldiers clash. The two pictures organize themselves in strikingly similar ways; the eye moves along a swift diagonal of desire.

Recent critics of this kind of literature have made much of the imperial imagination, of the sports ideal, and of the material and social culture that gave rise to easily affordable newspapers, books, and magazines to feed the fantasies of British boys. Joseph Bristow's *Empire Boys* makes clear the relationships of class and culture, market forces and political propaganda governing the arc of reading from the age of Captain Marryat to that of Edgar Rice Burroughs. And yet what interests me, again, is tone: What is the feel of the boy's book? What are the narrative techniques, the idioms and images that give voice to those ideologies of empire or adventure? In what tense is imagination written?

For answers, I start with this remarkable passage from Haggard's *King Solomon's Mines* (1885), narrated by the explorer Allan Quatermain:

Just at that moment the sun came up gloriously, and revealed so grand a sight to our astonished eyes that for a moment or two we even forgot our thirst.

There, not more than forty or fifty miles from us, glittering like silver in the early rays of the morning sun, soared Sheba's Breasts; and stretching away for hundreds of miles on either side of them ran the great Suliman Berg. Now that, sitting here, I attempt to describe the extraordinary grandeur and beauty of that sight, language seems to fail me. I am impotent even before its memory. Straight before us, rose two enormous mountains, the like of which are not, I believe, to be seen in Africa, if indeed there are any other such in the world, measuring each of them at least fifteen thousand feet in height, standing not more than a dozen miles apart, linked together by a precipitous cliff of rock, and towering in awful white solemnity straight into the sky. These mountains placed thus, like the pillars of a gigantic gateway, are shaped after the fashion of a woman's breasts, and at times the mists and shadows beneath them take the form of a recumbent woman, veiled mysteriously in sleep. Their bases swell gently from the plain, looking at that distance perfectly round and smooth; and upon the top of each is a vast hillock covered with snow, exactly corresponding to the nipple on the female breast. The stretch of cliff that connects them appears to be some thousands of feet in height, and perfectly precipitous, and on each flank of them, so far as the eye can reach, extend similar lines of cliff, broken only here and there by flat table-topped mountains, something like the world-famed one at Cape Town; a formation, by the way, that is very common in Africa.

To describe the comprehensive grandeur of that view is beyond my powers. There was something so inexpressibly solemn and overpowering about those huge volcanoes—for doubtless they are extinct volcanoes—that it quite awed us. For a while the morning lights played upon the snow and the brown and swelling masses beneath, and then, as though to veil the majestic sight from our curious eyes, strange vapours and clouds gathered and increased around the mountains, till presently we could only trace their pure and gigantic outlines, showing ghostlike through the fleecy envelope. Indeed, as we afterwards discovered, usually they were wrapped in this gauze-like mist, which doubtless accounted for our not having seen them more clearly before.

Sheba's Breasts had scarcely vanished into cloud-clad privacy, before our thirst—literally a burning question—reasserted itself.[17]

Bristow has made much of this selection, noting how it offers up "the sexual geography of a dark and unexplored continent," and finding in this novel, as well as in Haggard's later *She* (1887), a powerful association between sexual and political conquest. "As Europe is to Africa," he summarizes, "so is man to woman."[18] But what I think is noteworthy here is that this is a story less of action than of remembrance. The narrator is miles and years away from the event. He recalls, in the safety of the study, an encounter so amazing and so awesome that words nearly fail: "I am impotent even before its memory." This is a storyteller who displaces sexual performance onto words. The very massiveness of his description, its piles of nouns and adjectives, its swirling sentences, its constant asides—these are attempts to recreate in words the threat and power of the scene. The subject of this passage is, as we work through it, less and less the landscape that we see than the writer's struggle to describe it. This remains an essay in style.

And that is my point. From Lord Chesterfield onward, the style of manhood was a verbal one. The reader learns from Quatermain how to recall and how to write. The challenge is the challenge of description, as if we are watching him hack his way through a verbal jungle, as if the ascent of mountains pales before the marshaling of sentences. We lose ourselves in the prosody of the passage: the alliteration of "perfectly precipitous" and "cloud-clad"; the self-conscious sublimity of the "majestic sight," the "strange vapours and clouds," the "pure and gigantic outlines," and the image of the mountains "showing ghostlike through the fleecy envelope." *King Solomon's Mines* teaches how to write the story of adventure. It is a tale less of the world than of the book.

The lessons of narration and description fill the books of G. A. Henty, the most prolific of the imperial boys' writers of the late nineteenth century.[19] Such volumes as *With Clive in India*, *With Kitchener in the Soudan*, and *With Roberts to Pretoria* (and more than a hundred others) established a basic pattern. A young boy, often the child of British colonists, finds adventure at the side of a great leader. The boy grows as an ethical participant in the colonial world, and in that growth, his life calls attention to the childishness of a native populace. Recall Crusoe with his Friday: "His very Affections were ty'd to me, like those of a Child to a Father." Colonist and colonizer fit the Crusoe pattern, and Henty's books did more than simply offer escape for readers island-bound in Britain. They made clear that it was those white, British boys who could grow into men, and that their manhood in the empire kept the colonized a child.

Henty's own life embodied all the major nineteenth-century experiences that shaped the boys' book. At Westminster School and at Cambridge, he was an avid sportsman. He boxed, he wrestled, and he rowed. He worked in his father's coal mines. He enlisted in the British Army, serving in Crimea as a member of the Army Hospital Commissariat. He chronicled the soldier's grim experience, and his letters to his father—vivid, detailed, and richly worded—were soon sent to newspapers eager for reports of the conflict. These early publications gained Henty a place as a war correspondent. Throughout the 1860s and early 1870s, he reported from Italy, Spain, France, Serbia, Abyssinia, and West Africa.

This blend of sportsmanship and newspapering gives Henty's prose its immediacy. One of my favorites among his books is *With Buller in Natal, or A Born Leader* (1901), a book not just about white and black but about white and white, English and Boer.[20] Young Chris, the hero of the story, is sixteen when the war breaks out. His opening description brings together all the idioms of sportsmanship and hard work central to the ideals of late Victorian boys' books. But it recalls, too, the outlines of Henty's own life. It is as if Henty has given us a fantasy of his own boyhood—an imaginative recreation of his youth in school, in sport, and in the mines.

> The lad was a fine specimen of the young Uitlander. A life passed largely in the open air, hard work and exercise, had broadened his shoulders and made him look at least a year older than he really was. He was a splendid rider and an excellent shot with his rifle, for his father had obtained a permit from the authorities for him to carry one, and he could bring down an antelope when running at full speed as neatly as any of the young Boers. Four days a week he had spent in the mines, for his father intended him to follow in his footsteps, and he had worked by turns with the miners below and the engineers on the surface, so that he might in the course of a few years be thoroughly acquainted with all the details of his profession.

If Haggard turns Africa into a body, Henty turns the body into Africa. His physical description of young Chris—in its own way as powerfully sexual as Haggard's vision of the mountains—lingers on details of control and dominance. Pity the antelope, or any enemy before his sights.

And in the young man's sights, too, is the strife of southern Africa. "He deeply resented the position in which the British population in the Transvaal were placed, the insolence of the Boers towards them, and their brutal cruelty towards the natives." The Anglo Uitlanders, he goes on, "though forming the majority of the population, and the source of all the wealth of the country, and paying all the taxes, were yet treated as an outcast race, and deprived of every right possessed by people of all civilized nations." And if there were any doubts about the Boers themselves, Henty quickly erases them.

> They were indeed as unsavoury in appearance as they were brutal in manner. Water is scarce in the Transvaal, and is used most sparingly for all purposes of cleanliness. The Boer sleeps in his clothes, gives himself a shake when he gets up, and his toilet is completed, unless on very exceptional occasions when he goes outside the door to the water-cask, fills his hands with water, and rubs them over his face.... In dress the Boer is almost universally slovenly, his clothes hang about him stained and discoloured by long usage. In the majority of cases he is altogether without education, and very many Boers are scarcely able to sign their names. Most of them wear beards and long unkempt hair. But in point of physique they are fine men, tall and powerfully, though loosely, built, but capable of standing great fatigue if necessary, although averse to all exercise save on horseback.... There was no

attempt whatever at uniformity of dress. Most of the men wore high riding boots. Some of the young men from the towns were in tweed suits, the vast majority wore either shooting jackets or long loose coats; some were in straw hats, but the elder men all wore large felt hats with wide brims. They were all, however, similarly armed with rifles of the best and most modern construction. Their general appearance was that of a large band of farmers of the roughest type and wholly without regard for their personal appearance.

In this extended passage, Henty relies on the long tradition of description that lingers over externals to mark internal character. Crusoe's detailed portrait of Friday—his hair, his skin color, his eyes, his overall demeanor—chimes behind this portrait of the Boer. So, too, does the legacy of Lord Chesterfield or Tom Brown. For what this whole tradition teaches is a way of seeing: a method of describing individuals through dress and bearing; an equation of virtue with hygiene, of cleanliness with godliness. How a man cuts up, East had advised young Tom, is everything. And in the cut of Boer clothes lies the stain of inferior character.

Henty's descriptiveness comes less from life than from literature. It is a trope, an invocation of a style of writing and a technique of the novel of encounter going back to *Robinson Crusoe*. And if Crusoe's is a world not just of visual description but of writing (the pen and ink, the need for contracts, the narrator's journal), so, too, is Henty's. In a remarkably self-conscious moment, Henty shows Chris planning an attack on the Boers with his friends. They have enlisted in the army, and they camp before the battle. Chris sets out a plan, but he does so not by extemporizing and orating, but by reading.

> "Very well, then, it shall be so," Chris said. "To-morrow we shall certainly do some scouting, but in a day or two you may be shut up here; and until we get away there will be no scouting to be done. We must have some signals. Suppose we are scattered over two or three miles, we may want to assemble, and must be able to signal. I thought of it before we started from home, and put down in my pocket-book the sort of thing that I fancied would be wanted. I will read it out to you."
>
> He stirred the fire into a blaze and then read:
>
> "One shot followed by another and a third, with ten seconds between them, will mean 'Enemy seen on the right'; with twenty seconds between, 'Enemy seen on the left'; then, after a pause, two shots in quick succession will mean 'Enemy in strength'; three shots will be 'Small party only'; one shot, followed at an interval of ten seconds by two in succession, will

mean 'Retire to the point agreed on before we separated'; followed by three shots in quick succession, will be 'Close in to the centre'. We can think of others afterwards, but I think that will do to begin with. I know that you have all pocketbooks, so take down these signals at once."

Chris runs through the plan, his friends take notes, and then "there was silence and then the books were closed." He then addresses them:

> When we break up into four parties, each party must scatter, keeping three or four hundred yards apart. On arriving at any swell or the crest of a hill, a halt must be made, and every foot of the country searched by your field glasses, no matter how long it takes. You must assure yourself that there are no moving objects in sight. When you get near such a point you must dismount, and, leaving your horse, crawl forward until you reach a point from where you have a good view, and on no account stand up. While you are making your observations any Boers who might be lying in sight would be certain to notice a figure against the skyline, and we know that many of them are provided with glasses as good as our own. We must be as careful as if we were out after game instead of men. You all know these things as well as I do, but I want to impress them upon you. You see, they have captured five of the Natal police, who are a very sharp set of fellows. However, a few days' scouting will show us far better what is required than any amount of thinking beforehand.

This is the language of the correspondent, an account not of a battle lived but of a story written. Chris grows not simply as an active boy, but as a writing boy. His manhood comes through literacy; the Boers, by contrast, "are scarcely able to sign their names." Chris and his fellows live in signs: their battle plans are keyed to signals. This is a war that hinges on the skill of noticing "a figure against the skyline." It is a war of field glasses as much as firearms. Now we are back in *Tom Brown's Schooldays*, where the narrative impels us to behold: "now look"; "but see." "You see," Chris says to get attention—but in this phrase, he conjures up all that this battle is about: seeing and reading, finding figures, learning to discern.

What Henty, Haggard, and the range of school tales, sports reporting, correspondents, and Crusoevians set out to teach was that the boy's life was a world of reading; that it centered on discerning signs and symbols; that the words you spoke were as important as the clothes you wore; and that experience was always lived as if it were a story told. Throughout the works I have explored here, there is very little life unmediated by the book. Allan Quatermain describes his sexualized Africa not as he lives it, but as he remembers it. Chris lays out battle plans from his notebook. Whether on islands or in empires, the tools of literacy are always there, and in the end what makes the colonist or conqueror is his ability to read and write. Remember Benjamin Franklin: "You must spread all upon Paper."

Adventure is the boy's own paper, sheets on which he reads, or comes to write, a life. And if the loci of adventures shift from island sovereignties to continents, then so do books themselves. *Robinson Crusoe* evokes a notion of the book as shipwreck: we return from our island to recover passages or portions that we need. We build houses of our reading memory out of the shards of books, beached on the shores of our imagination. By the late nineteenth century, books are continents. They loom before us, much like Haggard's Africa, daring our conquest. The heroes of their stories model forms of verbal action, and the real heroes of these massive tales are those who read them—for simply completing *King Solomon's Mines* or *With Buller in Natal* is something of a heroic enterprise. The books themselves take on the massivity of land. Look at the late Victorian and Edwardian covers, with their embossed fronts, their engraved lettering, their colored leather stretched over the binding boards. These are hefty volumes, made of leather, gold, and heavy paper, with marbled boards and gilt edges. The boy's book is now a treasure in itself.

The very idea of the treasure came to dominate, by the late nineteenth century, literary tales and literary criticism. Stevenson's *Treasure Island*, Henty's own *Treasure of the Incas* (1903), B. Traven's *Treasure of the Sierra Madre* (first published in German in 1927 and translated into English in 1933)—these are the title templates for adventure. But books were now treasures, too. "I have some treasured books from the 1880s," writes a blogger from 2005.[21] For a century, this idiom has characterized books we love. The *Oxford English Dictionary* records the verb *treasure* as coming to mean "cherish" or "prize" only in the first decade of the twentieth century, but already by the middle of the nineteenth, Henry Wadsworth Longfellow could give voice to the idea of reading as a search for treasure:

> Then read from the treasured volume
> The poem of thy choice,
> And lend to the rhyme of the poet
> The beauty of thy voice.[22]

Few writers were as treasured as Rudyard Kipling, and among the books he wrote for children, few were as effusively valued as *Kim*.[23] The novel, first published in 1901, found immediate critical esteem. Writing in *Black-*

wood's *Edinburgh Magazine* in December of 1901, the reviewer J. H. Millar found it "masterly" and magical, "incomparably fresh and true." It offers a panorama of both empire and adolescence, and Millar writes of its power much as Allan Quatermain had recalled Sheba's Breasts:

> Its secret lies in the wonderful panorama it unrolls before us of the life of the great Peninsula over whose government England has now presided for more than a century. We despair of giving our readers any adequate conception of the glorious variety of the feast here spread before them. The kaleidoscopic quality, if we may venture so to call it, of Mr. Kipling's genius, has never been displayed on so extensive a scale or to such great advantage.[24]

The book is like a landscape, and the reviewer is as intimidated by the scope of Kipling's writing as the explorer would be by the horizon before him. Whether through spyglass or kaleidoscope, the reader surveys a display.

*Kim* was immediately brought into the canon of imperial adventure literature, and it is easy to see why. From its opening sentence, the novel juxtaposes colonized and colonist, the landscape of the open and the tools and weapons of officialdom: "He sat, in defiance of municipal orders, astride the gun Zam-Zammah on her brick platform opposite the old Ajaib-Gher—the Wonder House, as the natives call the Lahore Museum. Who hold Zam-Zammah, that 'fire-breathing dragon,' hold the Punjab; for the great green-bronze piece is always first of the conqueror's loot" (p. 53). Young Kim astride the great gun becomes a symbol for the English boy in India and, in turn, for children reading in an adult world. This gun is a piece of the imagination, named and renamed, in the wonder house of Kipling's book. It is a place, too, of instrumentalized observation, as if the panorama of subcontinental control was to be seen through gunsights. Throughout *Kim*, we see set pieces of such panoramic observation. Kim's waking in the morning toward the close of chapter 4 must have been one of those set passages that readers such as Millar found so magical:

> The diamond-bright dawn woke men and crows and bullocks together. Kim sat up and yawned, shook himself, and thrilled with delight. This was seeing the world in real truth; this was life as he would have it—bustling and shouting, the buckling of belts, and beating of bullocks and creaking of wheels, lighting of fires and cooking of food, and new sights at every turn of the approving eye. The morning mist swept off in a whorl of silver, the parrots shot away to some distant river in shrieking green hosts; all the

well-wheels within ear-shot went to work. India was awake, and Kim was in the middle of it. (p. 122)

As in so many of the books I have studied here, this is a scene of bustling creation: the Aesopic world of animals made eastern and exotic, the noise of the city rich with treasures. It is a diamond-bright dawn; the morning mist is silver. Even in the creaks of wheels and the smells of food, the treasury of India—the economic reasons why the Europeans were there—is palpable. This is a lesson in the rhetoric of the approving eye, in just how to see.

At moments such as this one, Kipling rises to a poetics of place, a heightened preciousness that looks back to Romantic poets such as Coleridge and Wordsworth and ahead to other children's writers working in their wake: to Kenneth Grahame's lush passagework in *The Wind in the Willows*, or to Frances Hodgson Burnett's verdant prose in *The Secret Garden*. What these writers call attention to is the aesthetic life of children, the possibility that youngsters can appreciate the artistry of nature and, in turn, that the verbal artifice of writers can stimulate their sensibility and taste. Kipling, much like Grahame and Burnett, takes us back to questions of the style of childhood and the style of children's literature. He brings us back to Chesterfield and Tom Brown—to a world of both verbal and physical performance.

And he brings us back to Tom Brown when Kim goes off to school. Sent to the English St. Xavier's, Kim starts out as a student in ways that directly recall young Tom Brown at Rugby or, for current readers, Harry Potter at Hogwarts.

> He suffered the usual penalties for breaking out of bounds when there was cholera in the city. This was before he had learned to write fair English, and so was obliged to find a bazaar letter-writer. He was, of course, indicted for smoking and for the use of abuse more full-flavoured than even St. Xavier's had ever heard. He learned to wash himself with the Levitical scrupulosity of the native-born, who in his heart considers the Englishman rather dirty. He played the usual tricks on the patient coolies pulling the punkahs in the sleeping-rooms where the boys thrashed through the hot nights telling tales till the dawn; and quietly he measured himself against his self-reliant mates. (p. 168)

All of those boys have tales, and Kipling lists them: some who were "used to jogging off along through a hundred miles of jungle"; others "who had spent a day and a half on an islet in the middle of a flooded river"; still others "who had requisitioned a chance-met Raja's elephant"; and one boy who "had helped his father to beat off with rifles from the verandah a rush of . . . head-hunters" (pp. 168–69). School is a world of self-narration, and what Kim learns quickly—and what readers are expected to learn, too—is how to tell the story of your own life.

It is this combination of description, narrative, lush imagery, and wonder that held the imagination of *Kim*'s earliest readers. In some sense, it remains a book of yarns, and boys in bunks or around campfires learned much from it about the ways of telling great adventures. Robert Baden-Powell, the founder of the Boy Scouts, learned much too, and in his manual of the movement, *Scouting for Boys* (1908), he summarizes the novel to exemplify the kinds of inspiring stories he wants boys to hear. Kim's progress as a child, his work in school, his entry into the Indian Secret Service, all come together, Baden-Powell concludes, to "show what valuable work a boy scout could do for his country if he were sufficiently trained and sufficiently intelligent."[25]

The founder of the Boy Scouts borrowed much from Kipling (he owed much, too, to a range of late Victorian cultural influences, from Darwin's evolutionary theory to the youth club movements, such as William Smith's Boys' Brigade and the American Woodcraft Indians and the Sons of Daniel Boone). For all its emphasis on action and behavior, the Scouts was a bookish movement—keyed to ideal literary texts and shaped through the many manuals that Baden-Powell himself produced for nearly half a century.[26]

Baden-Powell, after army service in India, found himself a national hero during the Boer War when, during the so-called siege of Mafeking, he and his men survived for more than two hundred days. Returning to England, he founded the Boy Scouts. *Scouting for Boys* is, as much as any novel, an account of personal experience transformed through narrative device. The siege of Mafeking becomes a kind of camp yarn told around the fire. Boys were enlisted in the siege, the Mafeking Cadet Corps, and *Scouting for Boys* recounts their service.

> Every man was of value, and as their numbers gradually got less, owing to men getting killed or wounded, the duties of fighting and keeping watch at night got harder for the rest. It was then that Lord Edward Cecil, the chief staff officer, got together the boys in the place and made them into cadet corps, put them in uniform and drilled them; and a jolly smart and

useful lot they were. We had till then used a large number of men for carrying orders and messages and keeping look-out, and acting as orderlies, and so on. These duties were now handed over to the boy cadets, and the men were released to go and strengthen the firing line.[27]

Set side by side with young Chris's notebook oratory from *With Buller in Natal*, this passage emerges as a literary narrative of seeing and being seen. The soldier's job is both to fight and to keep watch. Lord Cecil takes the boys and dresses them anew (the word "smart" here connotes specifically the clean, brisk neatness of the soldier; compare the usage from 1884 quoted in the *Oxford English Dictionary*: "The Egyptian soldier is . . . smart, clean, and cheap").[28] And when the men go off to the firing line, it is the boys who serve as lookouts.

*Scouting for Boys*, like *With Buller in Natal*, teaches lessons of recognition. To be a scout is, fundamentally, to see (Baden-Powell, while still in India, had published a manual titled *Reconnaissance and Scouting*, in 1884). Scouting becomes a way of looking for and looking at the world. And what the scout should learn to see are not just enemies abroad, but types of people at home.

> When you are travelling by train or tram always notice every little thing about your fellow-travellers; notice their faces, dress, way of talking, and so on, so that you could describe them each pretty accurately afterwards; and also try and make out from their appearance and behaviour whether they are rich or poor (which you can generally tell from their boots), and what is their probable business, whether they are happy, or ill, or in want of help.[29]

Compare this passage with Henty's description of the Boers or, for that matter, Crusoe's view of Friday or the portrait of Ben Gunn in *Treasure Island*. All of these passages teach how to read the face. All offer examples of how to describe—indeed, the goal of noticing the riders on the train or tram in *Scouting* is to conjure up descriptions afterward.

And in those descriptions, scouts and readers should find models for their own deportment. Good appearance is the goal, an ideal reinforced two decades after *Scouting for Boys* in Baden-Powell's *Rovering to Success* (1922). Don't masturbate, the book advises; keep yourself clean; brush your teeth: "It is said that nearly half the ill-health of the nation may be traced to bad teeth."[30] Recall, now, Kim waking in that Indian dawn, "chewing on a twig that he would presently use as a toothbrush"

(p. 122). Good hygiene keeps the empire—a body politic to match the human body.

For these are, in the end, tales of the body. Boys, as Lord Chesterfield advised early on, have a duty to maintain clarity of word and deed and to "cut up" properly. Their dress, their cleanliness, their self-attentions all contribute to an ideal of a healthy, social world. That world, as I have illustrated here, lives in the double narratives of present-tense activity and physical description. And from these narratives emerge the adventures of empire. But from these narratives emerges, too, the idiom of evolution: the imagination of our origins and the fears that underneath the veneer, the good manners, and the pomade of good grooming lie the apes of anarchy. To understand these darker fears and thus to trace the arc of children's literature in what many think of as its golden age, we need to turn from empire to evolution: from Defoe to Darwin.

# · 8 ·

# *On beyond Darwin*

## FROM KINGSLEY TO SEUSS

In *Rovering to Success*, Robert Baden-Powell tells a story about a group of African dignitaries who visit London. Taken by the sights of the great city, they are taken even more by the sight of British military manhood. Arriving at the army school at Aldershot, the Swazi chiefs, dressed up in frock coats and top hats, "were not fully satisfied until they had had the men stripped and had examined for themselves their muscular development. . . . Swazi savages could therefore appreciate manly strength and beauty." Whatever deeper tensions lie in this bizarre moment of cultural confrontation, it remains clear that, on the surface anyway, Baden-Powell's ideal of social life lay in an idea of development. The boy could, whatever his origin, turn himself into a specimen of strength and beauty. Apparently, this conviction did not hold for the chiefs, for whatever their social status in their homeland, they remain on Baden-Powell's pages agape ape-men.[1]

Why was it that the white boy could develop? Why was it that the black man seemed, to European colonists and fantasists, a child? The literary critic Gillian Beer, describing the misplaced impact of Darwin's theories on the colonial imagination, summarizes the condition that could generate Baden-Powell's tales: "The European was taken as the type of achieved developmental preeminence, and other races studied were seen as further back on the chart of growth. The image of growth was again misplaced from the single life cycle, so that whole races were seen as being part of the 'childhood of man,' to be protected, led, and corrected like children."[2]

Darwin's impact on children's literature has long been seen as lying in this fundamental misunderstanding. Writers such as Charles Kingsley,

Rudyard Kipling, and Edgar Rice Burroughs have been assessed for their idioms of evolutionary theory pressed into the service of colonial, class, or racist narratives. Water babies, jungle boys, and ape-men filled the imaginations of the period between the publication of the *Origin of Species* (1859) and the founding of the Boy Scouts (1908)—the period that literary critics have praised as the "golden age" of children's literature. The critical historiography of children's literature itself has something of a Darwinian cast, as most studies see a period of growth and enhancement culminating in the great Victorian and Edwardian fictions of Rudyard Kipling and Kenneth Grahame, Francis Hodgson Burnett and J. M. Barrie, Lewis Carroll and Beatrix Potter. During this period, as Peter Hunt has put it, "children's literature was growing up," becoming more complex, losing its oppressive didacticism, establishing a group of "living classics."[3]

Perhaps we never can escape the evolutionary metaphors that govern our literary and life histories. But we can see a more subtle texture to Darwin's impact on children's books and reading than one that simply juxtaposes white and black or maps stories of biology onto class, race, or nation. Darwin's importance to the history of children's literature lies not only in ideals of fiction, empire, pedagogy, and human development. It lies, too, in his own way of telling his life story—in the memories of childhood lying, in his account of the adventures on the *Beagle*, and in his own complex relationship to his immensely powerful and influential ancestors. Darwin's place in this history is comparable to Locke's: both offered frameworks for explaining growth, both bequeathed metaphors for understanding social life, and both came to stand as intellectual exemplars for their ages.

Childhood is everywhere in Darwin. In his earliest autobiographical sketches, he recalls the pleasure that he took in storytelling. As Gillian Beer describes these reminiscences, "The stories he invented in his childhood were designed to impress and astonish himself and others. His passion for fabulation expressed both a desire for power and an attempt to control the paradoxes by which he was surrounded." She quotes from an autobiographical fragment of August 1838 to illustrate her points, and I find this quotation an effective guide to Darwin's place in children's literary history.

> I was in those days a very great story-teller. . . . I scarcely ever went out walking without saying I had seen a pheasant or some strange bird (natural

history taste); these lies, when not detected, I presume excited my attention, as I recollect them vividly, not connected with shame, though some
I do, but as something which having produced a great effect on my mind,
gave pleasure like a tragedy. I recollect when I was at Mr. Case's inventing
a whole fabric to show how fond I was of speaking the *truth*! My invention is still so vivid in my mind, that I could almost fancy it was true, did
not memory of former shame tell me it was false.[4]

Darwin captures the exhilaration and the fear of all childhood fabulists.
We all want to come home and tell of our adventures, our rare sightings.
And yet many of us really did see pheasants or strange birds—not in our
daily walks, but in our nightly reading. What would it mean to see, in life,
the creatures of our stories?

For Darwin himself, what would it mean to have grown up in a family that made its mark on such imaginations? His grandfather, Erasmus
Darwin, was the most imaginative natural philosopher of his age. A brilliant physician, poet, scholar, and observer of the world, he bequeathed
to his family a body of remarkable writings on plants and animals. That
writing, though, took the form not of prose analysis but of poetic meditation. Works such as *The Botanic Garden* and *Zoonomia* transformed
the latest in late eighteenth-century science into verse.[5] Part Alexander Pope, part William Wordsworth, Erasmus Darwin's poetry reads
much like the imaginations of his grandson: designed (to paraphrase
Beer) to impress and astonish himself and others, to express a desire
for power and an attempt to control the paradoxes by which he was
surrounded. Erasmus bequeathed (in the words of Darwin's biographer
John Bowlby) a "hoard of valuable ideas . . . which [Charles] absorbed
during his student years as part of the Darwin family culture."[6] Read
these lines from *The Temple of Nature* and see just what such a culture
must have given him:

> Shout round the globe, how reproduction strives
> With vanquished Death—and Happiness survives;
> How Life increasing peoples every clime,
> And young renascent Nature conquers Time.[7]

The world of the Darwins was a world of the imagination: a world of
literary narrative, of metaphor, of invention. In fact, as many scholars
have noted, part of Charles's later reluctance to publish, and his defen-
siveness about his claims, may stem in large part from this childhood

wolf-crying. "Believe me," he seems to cry, again and again, throughout the *Origin of Species.*

And yet, the story that the *Origin* tells *is* a story. The point of evolutionary theory is that it narrates natural development. Instead of an instantly created world, where all things came to being at a moment of divine conception, the theory of natural selection posited a world that changed. Fossils could demarcate the strata of the past. Species could morph and mutate and die out. Life was a story, and "the story of life on the earth is a splendid drama," as the nineteenth-century paleontologist William Diller Matthew put it.[8] That story was not only splendid; it was wonderful. Wonder is everywhere in Darwin. In the *Origin of Species* alone, "wonder" appears six times; "wonderful" twenty-seven; "wonderfully" seven; "wondrous" once.[9] It is everywhere, too, in Darwin's successors; witness Stephen J. Gould's *Wonderful Life* of 1989. To read any of these writings is to share in marveling at the fecundity of life, at the seeming randomness of survival, at the adaptive radiation of new species. Here is the young Charles, stepping off the *Beagle* to collect insects in the Brazilian forest:

> If the eye was turned from the world of foliage above, to the ground beneath, it was attracted by the extreme elegance of the leaves of the ferns and mimosae. The latter, in some parts, covered the surface with a brushwood only a few inches high. In walking across these thick beds of mimosae, a broad track was marked by the change of shade, produced by the drooping of their sensitive petioles. It is easy to specify the individual objects of admiration in these grand scenes; but it is not possible to give an adequate idea of the higher feelings of wonder, astonishment, and devotion, which fill and elevate the mind.[10]

As much as evolution or development, as much as social change or species growth, it is this tone of the Darwinian imagination that helps shape the children's literature of the late nineteenth and twentieth centuries. How similar in the expression of amazement is this passage from *The Voyage of the Beagle* to the passage about Sheba's Breasts from *King Solomon's Mines*. It is easy to specify individual objects of admiration, but impossible to give an adequate idea of wonder.

The children's writer most directly linked to Darwin's writings early on, and the one most effusive in his narrative wonder, is Charles Kingsley.[11] Clergyman, Cambridge history professor, amateur anthropologist, and chronicler of science and society, Kingsley moved in the social circles that brought him in contact with not just Darwin himself, but other mid-nineteenth-century luminaries such as Michael Faraday, T. H. Huxley, and Richard Owen. Evolutionary theory fascinated him, though there is some debate still about how complete Kingsley's understanding and commitment were. Nonetheless, he was acutely aware of the theory's impact. "Darwin is conquering everywhere," he wrote to the scholar and clergyman F. D. Maurice in 1863, the same year his novel *The Water-Babies* appeared. By then Kingsley was already corresponding with Darwin himself, whom he had dubbed "his dear and honoured master," and *The Water-Babies* is as much a letter to that master as it is a story for the child.[12]

Immediately upon its appearance, readers appreciated the novel's transformation of contemporary social issues into brilliant fantasy. Part satire, part dreamscape, the novel tells the story of young Tom, a chimney sweep who, frightened by the daughter of a wealthy family whose chimney he cleans, runs off into the woods, falls into a lake, and is transformed by woodland fairies into something like a newt—a water-baby. Tom's adventures with the other creatures of the water take on a fantastic yet sentimental quality in Kingsley's tale, and throughout there are moral lessons calibrated for the listening or reading child. Eventually, Tom is restored to human form and reunites with (but does not marry) the young girl from whom he had long ago escaped. Readers have found in *The Water-Babies* lessons about class and culture, ethical and social life. There is a great deal that offends the modern child and parent (Jews and Catholics, in particular, come in for severe criticism), and yet there is something about the tale that has made it endure as one of the classics of mid-Victorian children's prose.

Part of that endurance comes from the comforting presence of the story's narrator. His is a voice of wonder and assurance:

> Ah, now comes the most wonderful part of this wonderful story. Tom, when he woke, for of course he woke—children always wake after they have slept exactly as long as is good for them—found himself swimming about in the stream, being about four inches, or— that I may be accurate— 3.87902 inches long and having round the parotid region of his fauces a set of external gills (I hope you understand all the big words) just like those of a sucking eft, which he mistook for a lace frill, till he pulled at them, found he hurt himself, and made up his mind that they were part of himself, and best left alone.
>
> In fact, the fairies had turned him into a water-baby. (p. 39)

There is something arrestingly Darwinian about this moment—not so much in its biology as in its rhetoric. There is the balance of amazement and detail, a need in this moment of wonder for a high level of precision and a detail of language. I hope you understand all the big words. The point is not to understand the big words (what child, then or now, would know what the parotid region of the fauces is?), but to recognize the authority of the one who uses them. The point, too, is to recognize that physical detail and scientific fact come all too easily into metaphor and simile. Those external gills are easy to mistake for a lace frill. The business of science is both to measure with exactitude and to express in compelling imagery.

This is the lesson of Darwinian science and the lesson of *The Water-Babies*, too: a lesson in the power of imagination. "But there are no such things as water-babies," says the childish figure from the audience. And so the narrator responds:

How do you know that? Have you been there to see? And if you had been there to see, and had seen none, that would not prove that there were none. If Mr. Garth does not find a fox in Eversley Wood—as folks sometimes fear he never will—that does not prove that there are no such things as foxes. And as is Eversley Wood to all the woods in England, so are the waters we know to all the waters in the world. And no one has a right to say that no water-babies exist, till they have seen no water-babies existing; which is quite a different thing, mind, from not seeing water-babies; and a thing which nobody ever did, or perhaps ever will do.

"But surely if there were water-babies, somebody would have caught one at least?"

Well. How do you know that somebody has not?

"But they would have put it into spirits, or into the Illustrated News, or perhaps cut it into two halves, poor dear little thing, and sent one to Professor Owen, and one to Professor Huxley, to see what they would each say about it."

Ah, my dear little man! that does not follow at all, as you will see before the end of the story.

"But a water-baby is contrary to nature."

Well, but, my dear little man, you must learn to talk about such things, when you grow older, in a very different way from that. You must not talk about "ain't" and "can't" when you speak of this great wonderful world round you, of which the wisest man knows only the very smallest corner, and is, as the great Sir Isaac Newton said, only a child picking up pebbles on the shore of a boundless ocean. You must not say that this cannot be, or that that is contrary to nature. You do not know what Nature is, or what she can do; and nobody knows; not even Sir Roderick Murchison, or Professor Owen, or Professor Sedgwick, or Professor Huxley, or Mr. Darwin, or Professor Faraday, or Mr. Grove, or any other of the great men whom good boys are taught to respect. They are very wise men; and you must listen respectfully to all they say: but even if they should say, which I am sure they never would, "That cannot exist. That is contrary to nature," you must wait a little, and see; for perhaps even they may be wrong. It is only children who read Aunt Agitate's Arguments, or Cousin Cramchild's Conversations; or lads who go to popular lectures, and see a man pointing at a few big ugly pictures on the wall, or making nasty smells with bottles and squirts, for an hour or two, and calling that anatomy or chemistry—who talk about "cannot exist," and "contrary to nature." Wise men are afraid to say that there is anything contrary to nature, except what is contrary to mathematical truth; for two and two cannot make five, and two straight lines cannot join twice, and a part cannot be as great as the whole, and so on (at least, so it seems at present): but the wiser men are, the less they talk about "cannot." That is a very rash, dangerous word, that "cannot"; and if people use it too often, the Queen of all the Fairies, who makes the clouds thunder and the fleas bite, and takes just as much trouble about one as about the other, is apt to astonish them suddenly by showing them, that though they say she cannot, yet she can, and what is more, will, whether they approve or not. (pp. 39–40)

And he goes on and on. Here are the lessons of mid-nineteenth-century science: that the world is changing; that discoveries challenge our understanding of reality; and that what once seemed fantasy could all be real. Explorers had been bringing back things "contrary to nature" for a century—the most famous case, perhaps, being the platypus, which, when a specimen was sent to England by the naturalist Joseph Banks in 1799, was dismissed as a hoax. Many of the luminaries invoked in *The Water-Babies*, Richard Owen and Charles Darwin in particular, weighed in on the nature of this creature. Darwin himself, during the voyage of the Beagle, actually saw a platypus in Australia: "I had been lying on a sunny bank & was reflecting on the strange character of the Animals of this country as compared with the rest of the World. An unbeliever in everything beyond his own reason, might exclaim 'Surely two distinct Creators must have been [at] work; their object however has been the same & certainly the end in each case is complete.'"[13] And so young Tom's transformation into a water-baby is nothing to be scoffed at. The platypus had long been bottled and preserved in spirits; the *Illustrated News* was weekly offering pictures of strange creatures brought from distant riverbanks. Who is to say that water-babies may not show up soon?

What separates the story of the water-babies from the tales of the platypus, however, is the simple fact that Kingsley's book is set in England. No explorer need chart foreign shores. All of this happens right at home. Imagination makes new creatures possible. Just as Darwin could reflect on his own childish fabulations, so, too, Kingsley noted that "man makes fiction ... he invents stories."[14] Darwin's impact on Victorian fantasy lay in this tension between fact and fiction: between scientific observation and the need to make a metaphor; between exact measurements and sense impressions. We are left, both with Darwin and with Kingsley's narrator, apt to be astonished by the suddenness of thunder or the whims of change.

Biology itself was wondrous. "It is a truly wonderful fact," Darwin announced in the *Origin of Species*, "that all animals and all plants throughout all time and space should be related to each other in group subordinate to group, in the manner which we everywhere behold."[15] Classification of creatures proved the principle of natural selection ("On the view that each species has been independently created, I can see no explanation of this great fact in the classification of all organic beings; but, to the best of my judgment, it is explained through inheritance and the complex action of natural selection"; p. 129). The subject matter of the *Origin of Species*, therefore, is the nature of species themselves. What brings living things into affinities, in what ways do they reproduce, and how can we draw lines between, and among, individuated groups?

This is the central set of questions, too, for so much of the jungle literature of the late nineteenth and early twentieth centuries. What are the implications of discovering new species? Can species devolve into earlier forms, and if they can, what does this imply for the European man in contact with and controlling African or Asian others? "We can have no difficulty," wrote the anthropologist Edward Tylor in his *Primitive Culture* of 1871, "in understanding how savages may seem mere apes to the eyes of men who hunt them like wild beasts in the forests."[16] But this impression was, as Tylor notes, a seeming. "Savages" are not apes. But what if the European could become a savage? If he were lost in the jungle, would old instincts return? Would men grow their tails again?

The stories of the wild boys of the forest that filled European literary and scientific fantasy in the late eighteenth and nineteenth centuries fed into this fear of devolution. These stories stand, in part, behind Kingsley's *Water-Babies*, where the group known as the Doasyoulikes regresses into mute beastliness. When the American explorer Paul Du Chaillu (who really did visit the British scientific establishment in 1861 with tales of African "gorilla country") shoots the last of these creatures in the novel, Kingsley notes that the beast "remembered that his ancestors had once been men, and tried to say, 'Am I not a man and a brother?' but had forgotten how to use his tongue."[17]

Am I not a brother? Rudyard Kipling begins his first *Jungle Book* with the story "Mowgli's Brothers," as if to raise the question, once again, of the relationship between species and habit.[18] Just what is Mowgli? Father Wolf first describes him as "a man's cub," as if trying to translate the filiations of the wolf into the lives of human beings. "How little! How naked, and—how bold!" says Mother Wolf (p. 4), describing Mowgli in terms that distinguish his appearance and his social behavior (compare Darwin's observation in *The Descent of Man*: "Man differs conspicuously from all the other primates in being almost completely naked").[19] The jungle animals confront this boy much as a troop of natural scientists would confront an oddity of nature. Like the Europeans trying to define the platypus, the animals try to make sense of Mowgli's species. At one point, they even start calling him "Mowgli the Frog," as if by turning him into a lower species they could gain control. And so, when Mowgli grows up in the wolf pack, he grows up like them: eating and sleeping, learning the signs and sounds of the jungle, caring little for anything "except things to eat." Mowgli, if he could have spoken, even "would have called himself a wolf" (p. 11). But there is something, even this early, that makes him different. Shere Khan questions living in a pack that would be "led by a dying wolf and a man's cub," and he remarks: "They tell me that at Council ye dare not look him between the eyes" (p. 11).

This is an image that will reappear throughout the *Jungle Books*: the belief that animals avert their eyes from humans. One critic considers "its function [as] to give 'biological' legitimation to Mowgli's right to rule," and I think his choice of words is telling.[20] Is there a biological legitimation for ruling? Turn to "The Spring Running" from the second *Jungle Book*. Mowgli is nearly seventeen. "He looked older, for hard exercise, the best of good eating, and baths whenever he felt the least hot or dusty, had given him strength and growth far beyond his age" (p. 303). This blend of outdoor exercise and good hygiene chimes with the vision of the sixteen-year-old Chris in Henty's *With Buller in Natal*, and both descriptions set the heroic boy against a lower group: in Henty's case, the Boers; in Kipling's, the Jungle People. "The Jungle People who used to fear him for his wits feared him now for his strength, and when he moved quietly on his own affairs the mere whisper of his coming cleared the wood-paths. And yet the look in his eyes was always gentle. Even when he fought, his eyes never blazed as Bagheera's did. They only grew more interested and excited; and that was one of the things that Bagheera himself did not understand" (p. 303). Bagheera, the panther, asks Mowgli about it, but he shrugs it off. "Mowgli looked at him lazily from under his long eyelashes, and, as usual, the panther's head dropped. Bagheera knew his master" (p. 303).

The *Jungle Book*s are, in effect, Kipling's *Descent of Man*: an exploration of the nature of the human species; a set of fables about what the human shares with other animals; a narrative that illustrates that even though the boy may grow up in the jungle, he does not devolve into a beast. True, he may pick up patterns of behavior from the animals; true he may adapt according to the climate. But devolution does not happen. Whatever Kingsley's Doasyoulikes presaged, Mowgli remains a human.

If the *Jungle Book*s are Kipling's *Descent of Man*, then the *Just So Stories* are his *Origin of Species*.[21] Part Aesop's fable, part folktale, part bestiary, each *Just So* story imagines an origin: how the whale got his throat, the camel his hump, or the leopard his spots; or how the alphabet originated. The animal tales look to explain a facet of each beast that makes it unique. Physical features have an origin, and origins can be explained here not through natural selection, but through acts of retribution, cleverness, imagination, or control. The camel gets his hump because a genie punishes him for his laziness: the camel's exclamation of dismissiveness, "humph!" becomes the physical "hump" that will enable him "to work now for three days without eating, because you can live on your humph" (p. 18). The rhinoceros gets his wrinkled skin because he stole some of a Parsee's cake, and as payback the Parsee takes the rhino's skin (after the animal unbuttons it to take it off while bathing) and rubs old cake crumbs into it. When the rhino puts it back on, it itches so much that he scratches and rubs it into folds. The leopard gets his spots when he and his Ethiopian friend realize that the other animals of southern Africa adapt to changed environments: the giraffe grows blotches and the zebra grows stripes to hide themselves in trees and bushes. When the Ethiopian and the leopard understand this transformation, the man advises the animal to change as well: change "to a nice working blackish-brownish colour, with a little purple in it, and touches of slaty-blue. It will be the very thing for hiding in hollows and behind trees" (p. 41).

In these tales, Kipling writes out fables for a Darwinian age. Their irony, or humor, or effect lies precisely in how we juxtapose their mythic feel against the force of evolutionary knowledge. For by the end of the Victorian age, all would have known that rhinos got their skin through patterns of adaptive evolution. Darwin singles out the rhinoceros and the elephant as having unique skin quality in the *Descent of Man* (p. 57). And later in that treatise, he spends much time discussing the spots and stripes of mammals (pp. 542–48). There, he advances the argument that ornamental coloring may serve less as a means of camouflage than as an aid in sexual selection. Lions and tigers, zebras and deer, leopards and tapirs—these all show up, and at such a moment, the *Descent of Man* reads like a scientist's corrective to the fantasies of Aesop or the bedtime tales of Uncle Remus.

Such is the backdrop for the *Just So Stories*, and the question now remains how we can tell our children fantasies of origin when facts are known. Each of these stories' titles has an answer by the 1890s. In an age of knowledge, fantasy takes on new social purpose. It provides an outlet for the child's own creative impulses. It offers models for controlling—safely and without threat to empirical reality—the desire to create a world of wild things. Darwin felt this tension all his life; recall his childhood memories of making up animals he had seen. And educators felt this tension, too, especially as scientific teaching took on prominence in schools.

At the close of a little handbook titled *The Preparation of the Child for Science* (1904), the author, M. E. Boole, reflects on the need to foster the child's imagination while maintaining the conviction that the scientific method can explain the world.

> Most children have access to some sort of fairyland in which they spend a good portion of their existence. There is nothing unscientific in that; indeed, every scientific man worthy of the name, every one who is not a mere mechanical adapter of other people's discoveries, spends a good part of his time in that grown-up sort of fairyland, the world of scientific hypothesis. It is from this fairyland of his that he draws the inspirations which guide his researches.

Boole then recalls a conversation he had with a little girl. Standing on the seashore, he hears her implore the local fishermen "to bring her home a mermaid." There are no mermaids, he informs her. Yes, there are, she says, and after much discussion, she asserts: "Oh well, if they are not in this world they must be in fairyland." "What right," says Boole, "had I to say there are no real mermaids?" In this exchange, we may hear, once again, the conversations between Kingsley's narrator and his childish interrupter in *The Water-Babies*—only there, it is the child who speaks up for empirical proof. In an age of science, water-babies, mermaids, talking animals, and jungle boys must live—but they cannot live in our world. "What I ought to have said," Boole reflects, "was that there are no mermaids living under such conditions that fishermen in this world can bring them in boats to little girls."[22]

How can we find those conditions in which mermaids can live? One answer was to go back to the island—not Crusoe's place of self-sufficiency or Stevenson's landscape of adolescent adventure, but the space for imagination unbridled. On such an island we would find Dr. Moreau. There, he would be master of creation, turning men to monsters, much as Circe had turned Odysseus's unsuspecting seamen into swine. There, his creatures would lurk in shadows, only flashes from their eyes revealing their once-human origin. In the forest we might see one, much as Edward Prendick, the narrator of H. G. Wells's *Island of Doctor Moreau*, sees one:

> I distinguished through the interlacing network the head and body of the brute I had seen drinking. He moved his head. There was an emerald flash in his eyes as he glanced at me from the shadow of the trees. . . .
>
> "Who are you," said I. He tried to meet my gaze.
>
> "No!" he said suddenly, and turning, went bounding away from me through the undergrowth. Then he turned and stared at me again. His eyes shone brightly out of the dusk under the trees.[23]

How can we not see Mowgli's eyes here, marking his distinction from the beasts who raised him? And how can we not see the stories of the jungle-man, from Kipling to Edgar Rice Burroughs, in the scene where Prendick is taken in by the Beast Folk and fearful of becoming one of them? In living with the Dog-man, Ape-man, Satyr, and Hyena-swine, Prendick imagines himself becoming "one among the Beast People" (p. 118). "It would be impossible," he notes, "to detail every step of the lapsing of these monsters; to tell how, day by day, the human semblance left them" (p. 123). They give up clothing, loose their bandages and wrappings. Even that unique feature of humankind, our hairless nakedness, disappears as "the hair began to grow over the exposed limbs." He goes on: "I, too, must have undergone strange changes. My clothes hung about me as yellow rags, through whose rents glowed the tanned skin. My hair grew long, and became matted together. I am told that even now my eyes have a strange brightness, a swift alertness of movement" (p. 124). Again, the hair; again, the eyes: such passagework returns us to the image of Ben Gunn, gone wild on Treasure Island. It returns us to the physiognomy of savageness in Haggard and Henty. It chimes with a history of human regression.

Published in 1896, *The Island of Dr. Moreau* is of the age of Kipling, Henty, Stevenson, and Haggard. It gives voice to the scientific questions of the century's turn: questions about the origin of humankind, about the effect of living outside civilization, and about the place of the literary imagination in a world governed by evolution and empiricism. But it gives voice, too, to the idea of the literary voice itself. Throughout all of these novels, fables, tales, and treatises I have explored, there are moments when the narrator fails. Impotent before natural majesty, terrified before the unknown, overwhelmed by beauty or by fecund detail, everyone, at some point, fails. The lush verbiage of natural description or the blow-by-blow reportage of events invariably, at some moment, gives way to silence. What distinguishes the human is the skill of speech. What makes the civilized narrator is his skill at taking in a landscape and describing it in powerful prose. When he fails, when he admits that "it would be impossible," then he is truly overwhelmed by otherness, and we can get an intimation of what jungle, forest, and island really do to us: render us inarticulate.

I, too, may fail before the wealth of literary narratives indebted to the Darwinian revolution. Not only Kingsley, Kipling, and Wells, but surely Lewis Carroll, Frances Hodgson Burnett, Edgar Rice Burroughs, Jules Verne, and countless other, now-forgotten writers felt that revolution's impress (not to mention, too, myriad adult writers: George Eliot, Charles Dickens, Anthony Trollope, Virginia Woolf). But to my mind, no twentieth-century author, whether for children or adults, is more profoundly Darwinian in inheritance and idiom than Dr. Seuss. The rich panorama of alternative zoology, the sense of wonder at the rare abundance of creation, the fascination with the physiognomy of the emotive life, the emphasis on signs and symbols, and the creation of exuberant narrators—all of these qualities recall the world of Darwin, his forebears and heirs. There is something not just like Charles Darwin, but much like Erasmus Darwin in Seuss: poetic paeans to life, the writing of a kind of zoonomia for the modern world.

Take, for example, *On beyond Zebra* (1955).[24] The book begins, as all primers do, by linking letters and animals. From *The New England Primer* to Locke's *Aesop* to the *Just So Stories*, the world of creation finds itself encompassed in the alphabet. In Kipling's "How the Alphabet Was Made," letters took on the very shapes of creatures: the S of the snake, the A of a carp's mouth, and so on. For any child, certain letters exist only for their animals: Z *is* "zebra," for is there any other word that we can conjure at a moment's notice that begins with Z (only "zoo," perhaps, and that itself tells us that with the alphabet's end lies the beginnings of the biota)? But there are more letters, and Seuss's narrator asserts:

> In the places I go there are things that I see
> That I never could spell if I stopped with the Z.

Much as the modern world needed new words to fill the lexica and handbooks of the fauna of the faraway, so Seuss's world needs new letters. "My alphabet starts where your alphabet ends!"

> So, on beyond Zebra!
> Explore!
> Like Columbus!
> Discover new letters!
> Like wum is for Wumbus,
> My high-spouting whale who lives high on a hill
> And who never comes down 'til it's time to refill.

Then there is the Umbus, a cow with ninety-nine teats; there's the Fuddle-dee-Duddle, with the longest tail of anything; and there are sea creatures, air creatures, desert creatures, jungle creatures. As we leaf through the book, we can hear Seuss's narrator, like some manic Moreau, giving us a tour of his hybrid beasts. And as we leaf through the rest of Seuss, we see vast zoos of creatures and cities of people whose existence could not be part of natural selection.

For Seuss's readers, children and their parents, discovery is everywhere, and he invites us to share his Columbian adventures in new letters. His creatures cannot be brought back by fishermen, but they can be drawn by human hands, and Seuss shares with the illustrators of the Darwinian literary tradition something of a physiognomy of the fantastic. Look not just at his animals, but at his people. There are kings and servants, dilettantes and dolts. We learn to recognize the inner character by looking at the outer form, and in this process Dr. Seuss offers a witty critical response to the inheritance of illustration in the older guidebooks. Whatever the original impact of the illustrations to *Scouting for Boys*, it may be hard for any modern reader not to see a Seuss-like character behind them, especially the fool on the left. The curl of the hair, the receding forehead, the big nose and large upper-lip area—these are the marks of devolution (compare Prendick's observation, in *The Island of Dr. Moreau*, of how the island's creatures became less and less human: "their foreheads fell away and their faces projected"; p. 123). This face could come from *Green Eggs and Ham*, as the doltish cover figure peers into the plate; or from that picture in *If I Ran the Zoo*, where mobbing people stare at the Obsk on display.[25]

If I ran the zoo, says Seuss's narrator, there would be lions with ten feet, birds with topknots, hybrids of elephants and cats, and creatures such as the Joats,

> Whose feet are like cows', but wear squirrel-skin coats
> And sit down like dogs, but have voices like goats.

The boy-fantasist of the book imagines his journeys all over the world, collecting animals hitherto unseen. It is a kind of fantasy of conquest, a voyage of the *Beagle* whose goal, in the end, is not science but display. Like Darwin, Seuss's narrators are always faced with the need to display—to justify, explain, make real the products of their fabulous imaginations. Seuss's first book, *And to Think That I Saw It on Mulberry Street* (1937), begins much as Darwin saw himself beginning: confronting the authority of adults who might not believe his fabulations.[26]

> When I leave home to walk to school,
> Dad always says to me,
> "Marco, keep your eyelids up
> And see what you can see."
>
> But when I tell him where I've been
> And what I think I've seen,
> He looks at me and sternly says,
> "Your eyesight's much too keen.
>
> Stop telling such outlandish tales.
> Stop turning minnows into whales."

Evolution, like imagination, lets us see how things turn into other things. And if neither explains the relationships between whales and minnows,

Fig. 7. Types of faces. From Robert Baden-Powell, *Scouting for Boys* (London, 1908).

Fig. 8. Faces in the crowd. From *If I Ran the Zoo*, by Dr. Seuss [Theodor Geisel], TM and copyright © by Dr. Seuss Enterprises, L.P. 1950, renewed 1978. Used by permission of Random House Children's Books, a division of Random House, Inc.

what both can do is explain the fascination we have with wonder, splendor, and beauty in nature.

Darwin had always found birds the most wondrous creatures—from that childhood reminiscence about pheasants, through the finches that absorbed him on the voyage of the *Beagle*, to the *Origin of Species* and *Descent of Man*, where he reflected on their variation and their possible attraction to their own adornments. Do birds, he wonders, admire their own novelty?[27] Darwin marveled at Audubon—and so does Dr. Seuss, whose *Scrambled Eggs Super* (1953) reads like an insane version of *Birds of the World*.[28] This story imagines an on-beyond-zebra-like world of egg-layers who survive, it seems, only to provide the narrator with access to rare omelets.

> I don't like to brag and I don't like to boast,
> Said Peter T. Hooper, but speaking of toast . . .

Peter's assertive voice here is that of the children's author: the voice of the fabulist who makes stuff up, who tells tales of discovery, adventure, and conquest. In contrast to the voice of the late nineteenth-century explorer—always in danger of verbal impotence—Peter's voice, like that of all Seuss's narrators, is one of exuberant mastery. And that is what makes them, for all their weirdness, truly human. Dr. Seuss always measures the human against the imaginary. He illustrates, for all his forays into avian adventure or feline threat, the reassuring stability that common sense and enthusiasm grant us.

That is the legacy of Darwin, too. Armchair ethologists, we turn pages in the *Origin of Species* or the *Voyage of the Beagle* and find not only strange new creatures or new theories, but a new voice. I don't like to brag, and I don't like to boast. That is the voice of literary assurance. Read the introduction to the *Origin of Species* as an essay in developing that voice—a blend of thoughtfulness, apology, and measured conviction: "I am fully convinced that species are not immutable" (p. 6). So, too, is Dr. Seuss, and so too are all the writers I have explored here. Peter T. Hooper does brag of his exploits with the egg, and his search for unheard-of birds makes him into a Darwin of the child's imagination. What we see in both is an engagement with the aesthetics of nature, with the beauty and variety of life, and in turn with the question, Is an appreciation of the beautiful a mark of humankind?

The books I have explored here ask that question, too, as they present their readers with not just descriptions of amazing places, but language that can rise to the beautiful. I have sought to select those passages where language itself is the object of amazement. *Scouting for Boys* may teach the young to see, but it seeks, too, to teach them to describe. And when the child looks not out in the world but into his or her imagination, boards boats not of ordinary fishermen but of extraordinary writers, he or she may come back brimming, like the young Darwin, with a story of a strange bird. Let them give pleasure.

# Ill-Tempered and Queer

## SENSE AND NONSENSE,
## FROM VICTORIAN TO MODERN

Darwin's impact on children's literature went beyond imaginary animals or fantasies of growth or fears of regression. Linguists throughout the late nineteenth and early twentieth centuries found in the ideas of descent and development a set of images for understanding language change. Biologists, too, saw in the study of the history of language an analogy for species adaptation and extinction. The study of language and the study of life went on side by side for half a century or so. Trees of biota mirrored trees of tongues. "Pedigrees" of mammals matched those of the Indo-European languages. The great evolutionary biologist Ernst Haeckel spoke for many of his contemporaries when he announced, in books written in the 1870s and 1880s, that historical philology "anticipated" the methods of paleontology. Language and species worked in parallel.[1]

If part of the influence of evolution was imagining strange creatures, then another was imagining strange languages. Weird ancient tongues and writing systems were being unearthed throughout the nineteenth century. Hieroglyphics had been deciphered by Champollion in 1828; Babylonian cuneiform was being understood by the 1840s; Hittite was legible by the 1910s. There were Mayan glyphs, Mediterranean syllabaries, and Indic pictograms (all of which would not be fully understood until the mid-twentieth century).[2] If there was sense to be made of the animal kingdom, there was sense to be made of language, and if some creatures seemed to be nonsensical aggregations of body parts—whether the real platypus or the fanciful hybrids of Edward Lear—some languages could be nonsensical as well.

This idea of linguistic nonsense takes hold as a force in children's literature in the mid-nineteenth century and never seems to let go. True, there had always been baby talk. Parents must have "goo-ed" and "gaa-ed" at their children for millennia. Lullabies and nursery rhymes hinge on repeated nonsense syllables. But the idea of nonsense as a force of the imagination, of nonsense as a challenge to the logic of adulthood and the laws of civil life—this was a new idea in Victorian England. The masters of that nonsense were, of course, Lewis Carroll and Edward Lear. But there is more to this tradition than the games of Alice or the limericks of a sad cartoonist.[3]

Behind it is the novel. Part of what nineteenth-century novelists did so well was to explore the limits of social expectation through linguistic experiment. Sir Walter Scott, most famously, delved into the resources of the English language—old forms and regional dialects—to evoke long-ago and faraway worlds for his metropolitan reading public. Scott was, it might be said, a philologist of the fictional imagination (with the result that he is, after Shakespeare, the most cited author in the *Oxford English Dictionary*). One impact of his writing was to open verbal doors to later novelists: to come up with new words, or strange sounds, that for most readers seemed all too close to nonsense.[4]

Throughout Dickens's novels, too, the reader often stands close to the brink of nonsense. Twists in language are everywhere. Many of his characters have names evocative of creatures out of fairy tales: Pocket, Podsnap, Jaggers. Some speak in dialect or argot so strange as to seem nonsensical (witness Joe Gargery's garblings of English in *Great Expectations*, for example). Some are so mad as to make words themselves take wing (witness Mr. Dick in *David Copperfield*, who writes long letters to King Charles II and flies them up on kites). These are not simply oddballs or crazies; they are characters turned into caricature through the eyes of a child. Strange people or great cities all take on a fantastic quality when seen by Pip, or Nicholas Nickleby, or David Copperfield. How often all the world seems mirror-imaged, or upside down, as when Pip, at the opening of *Great Expectations*, finds himself held by his feet by that monstrous intruder in the churchyard. "What fat cheeks you ha' got," says the man. "Darn Me if I couldn't eat 'em," as if he were the big bad wolf talking to Little Red Riding Hood. Here is fairy tale turned into nightmare, much as, later in the novel, Miss Havisham will turn a card game into social hell.

Dickens reveals the all too blurry line between nonsense and terror, and his novels both reflect and later influence the ways in which writers for children toe that line. Nonsense and social satire also easily bleed into each other, not just in Dickens, but in his contemporary William Makepeace Thackeray. The opening of *Vanity Fair*, for example, offers patterns of exaggeration so great as to appear almost grotesque. Amelia Sedley's vocal concert concludes with a "ditty" that could come right out of Carroll, Lear, or, for that matter, Dr. Seuss:

> Ah! bleak and barren was the moor,
>> Ah! loud and piercing was the storm,
> The cottage roof was shelter'd sure,
>> The cottage hearth was bright and warm—
> An orphan boy the lattice pass'd,
>> And as he mark'd its cheerful glow,
> Felt doubly keen the midnight blast,
>> And doubly cold the fallen snow.[5]

And in Thackeray's cartoon illustrations to the novel, we can see the pictorial tradition of caricature running from William Hogarth to Edward Lear and even Shel Silverstein. Nonsense, then, offers more than play or foolishness. It bridges the discourses of adult and children's literature, and it crystallizes our social and aesthetic attitudes toward words and their relationship to worldly things, human intention, and the pictorial imagination.

So much has been written on this tradition, and on Lewis Carroll in particular, that it may seem almost nonsensical to think of saying something new.[6] The Alice books became classics within only a few years of their publication. Lear's nonsense verse was seen, even in his lifetime, as founding a genre. Most criticism of these writers has attended largely to their lives, as if the meaning of Wonderland or "The Owl and the Pussycat" could be discerned in the disappointments of these two eccentric, maladroit, and sexually challenging (or challenged) men. Biography has long been the venue for engaging with these writers, and while recent critics have sought to align their work with larger cultural conditions (U. C. Knoepflmacher's work on Carroll, for example, or Thomas Dilworth's work on Lear), answers to the conundrums of their craft still tend to be sought in the men themselves.[7] In many books and articles, they remain, in the words of Edward Lear's own poetic description of himself, "ill-tempered and queer." I cannot survey all the critical traditions behind these authors and of their nonsense and experience. But what I can do here is place their writings in the larger arc of children's literary history, and in the process ground their writings in the texture of English prose and poetry.

As a scholar of languages, I begin with the idea of linguistic meaning. Is there an essential meaning to an utterance? Do sounds have some unique reference in the minds of speakers? Are languages conventional and arbitrary systems of signification? Such were the questions being asked throughout the nineteenth century as the study of language moved from metaphysical speculation to historical science, from country-house amateurism to university discipline.[8] Carroll himself weighed in on these debates in the course of his textbook *Symbolic Logic*, published toward the end of his life in 1896. In this work, as well as a range of other logical and mathematical treatises, Carroll (or should we say Charles Lutwidge Dodgson?) set out to clarify the nature of his discipline by illustrating the confusions among academic logicians of his day. Scholars have long seen in these works a sensitive appreciation of the game-like nature of argument: the ways in which logical reasoning has the feel of rule-governed, yet arbitrary, behavior. Language is, in some sense, a game for Carroll (no wonder modern philosophers have found his work ripe for readings through the lens of Ludwig Wittgenstein, or Ferdinand de Saussure, or Freud, or Derrida). He concludes *Symbolic Logic* with an "Appendix Addressed to Teachers," in which he remarks that most authors of logic textbooks think of propositions as if they were real, almost living things.

> They speak of the Copula of a Proposition "with bated breath," almost as if it were a living, conscious Entity, capable of declaring for itself what it chose to mean and that we, poor human creatures, had nothing to do but to ascertain *what* was its sovereign will and pleasure, and submit to it. In opposition to this view, I maintain that any writer of a book is fully authorized in attaching any meaning he likes to any word or phrase he intends to use.[9]

Carroll noted elsewhere, "No word has a meaning inseparably attached to it; a word means what the speaker intends by it, and what the hearer understands by it, and that is all."[10]

It will be easy for us to appreciate this view of language behind nonsense literature. If writers may attach to words whatever meaning they like, then we can certainly see how a text such as, say, "Jabberwocky" stands as a prime example of the arbitrary and conventional nature of signifying.

> 'Twas brillig, and the slithy toves
> Did gyre and gimble in the wabe;
> All mimsy were the borogoves,
> And the mome raths outgrabe.

These lines are now so famous that it may be hard for modern readers to appreciate the novelty of their verbiage. When the poem's first stanza appeared in the little family magazine that Carroll put together for his siblings, *Misch-Masch*, in 1855, he called it a "Stanza of Anglo-Saxon Poetry" and printed it in letters imitating the Old English hands of early manuscripts. He then glossed each of the new words, in a fashion that aped brilliantly the pedantic dispassion of mid-nineteenth-century lexicographers.[11] In the same year, the new dean of Christ Church, Oxford, was named: Henry George Liddell, the man responsible (together with Robert Scott) for the most famous and important dictionary of ancient Greek. "Liddell and Scott" became the watchword for the academic life, to the point where they themselves could be the subject of Oxonian verse satire:

> Two men wrote a Lexicon, Liddell and Scott;
> One half was clever, one half was not.
> Give me the answer, boys, quick to the riddle,
> Which was by Scott, and which was by Liddell?[12]

And in the lexicography of nonsense, few have such exalted status as Humpty Dumpty, who in chapter 6 of *Through the Looking Glass* explicates the opening of "Jabberwocky," after having averred this belief in language use and meaning: "When I use a word it means just what I choose it to mean—neither more nor less" (p. 269). This view recalls, as readers have long noticed, Carroll's own position in *Symbolic Logic*—"that any writer of a book is fully authorized in attaching any meaning he likes to any word or phrase he intends to use."

There has been a lot of banter about "Jabberwocky," Humpty Dumpty, and the notions of linguistic representation, nonsense verse, and literary aesthetics they all represent. There is something about "Jabberwocky" that has made it not just memorable, but memorably subject to parody. Martin Gardner, the editor of *The Annotated Alice*, notes that there have been "endless" parodies, and translators from the 1870s on have taken it as something of a test case for their virtuosity (Robert Scott himself produced a brilliant version in German, wittily claiming it to be the original ballad on which Carroll based his English poem—and claiming, too, in good Victorian fashion, that the text was revealed to him in a séance).[13] The point of all the discourse around "Jabberwocky" is, it seems to me, precisely what Alice said about it first: "Somehow it seems to fill my head with ideas—only I don't exactly know what they are!" (p. 197).

That is what literature does. It fills our heads with ideas, even if we don't know what they are, and it is often left to pedagogues like Humpty Dumpty—or, for that matter, Henry George Liddell, or anybody up to and including me—to tell our students what it means. What is important about "Jabberwocky," and the larger strains of nonsense verse that it inspired, is not so much the details of its diction as the occasions of its reading and response. Carroll imagines something of a literary history here: an arc of texts and readings going back to the very origins of English literature. In this process, he shares with his contemporary philologists a fascination with the lineage of languages. Like Darwin, those philologists expressed a wonder at the great variety of tongues: the old words, the old sounds, the old texts.

Alice is full of wonder, too, but with a difference. For the Darwinian sense of wonder I noticed in my previous chapter is a marveling at order. All the strange creatures of the world fit into lineages and classifications. In Wonderland, however, the word that expresses Alice's amazement at the world is "queer." Humpty Dumpty is, to her eyes, a "queer creature," and when he attempts to do the arithmetic to discern just how many un-birthdays a person has in a year, he holds Alice's notebook upside down.

"That seems to be done right"—he began.

"You're holding it upside down," Alice interrupted.

"To be sure I was!" Humpty Dumpty said gaily, as she turned it round for him. "I thought it looked a little queer." (p. 268)

Everything looks a little queer in Wonderland. If Humpty Dumpty finds the numbers upside down, so, too, Alice had originally found the words of "Jabberwocky" written backward (only after she holds it up to the mirror does the poem make sense). We are in a queer world here, and the word (and its variants) appears more than twenty times in *Alice in Wonderland* and *Through the Looking Glass*.[14] It is the defining word for the Carrollian experience, and it will become the term not just for eccentricity, but for the whole aesthetic experience of children's literary fantasy.

*Queer* comes from a term that originally meant off-center, diagonal, or askew.[15] It appeared in the sixteenth century, denoting odd things or odd people, and by the nineteenth century it had become one of the most frequently deployed terms to define experience outside the strictures of Victorian propriety (the word does not connote homosexual experience or identity until the 1920s). "Queer Street" was the expression used to describe someplace awkward or where you would find yourself in trouble, debt, or illness (I find it fascinating, by the way, that Harry Potter's Diagon Alley—*diagonally*—is nothing less than a translation of "queer street").[16] The word is everywhere in Dickens, too—describing odd-shaped furniture, weird old houses, and bizarre expressions on strange people. How can we not hear the word in the name of Wackford Squeers, the head of the notorious school, Dotheboys Hall, in *Nicholas Nickleby*? And how can we not see the source of Carrollian or Lear-like caricature in a visitor's description of Ralph Nickleby from the same novel: "the longest-headed, queerest-tempered, old coiner of gold and silver there ever was" (chap. 10).

Life lived on the diagonal or the off-center, through the looking glass, or upside down is the world of the nonsense imagination, and it is the world that so appeals to childhood. "Dear, dear!" announces Alice as she picks up the White Rabbit's fan and gloves. "How queer everything is today!" (p. 37). Words are queer, songs are queer, dreams are queer. In *Through the Looking Glass*, there are "those queer Anglo-Saxon Messengers" that accompany the Lion and the Unicorn (p. 293)—a phrase that calls to mind the original publication of "Jabberwocky" as a mock Anglo-Saxon poem. And at the close of that book, when the Red Queen screamingly commands for all to drink to Alice's health, all the guests drink, though "very queerly they managed it" (p. 334).

Queer things are everywhere in Carroll's world, as they are also in Dodgson's. Go back to that quotation from *Symbolic Logic* now, not as a statement of linguistic theory but as a case of fantasy. Logicians, he complains, can think of logical phenomena as if they were "living, conscious" beings. Notions, things, or creatures are here animated into action. And once animated, they become not friends or playmates but superiors. We stand, in Carroll's words, subordinate, submissive, and in waiting to the "sovereign will and pleasure" of these creatures—a condition vivified to brilliant narrative throughout the Alice books. For there, the very life of Wonderland lies in the ways in which strange things not only come alive—playing cards or toys—but how they come alive to rule. "Off with their heads!" says the Queen of Hearts (p. 109), and the poor human creatures have nothing to do in this book but ascertain what is their sovereign's will and pleasure and submit to it. Even when Alice herself becomes a queen at the close of *Through the Looking Glass*, she has trouble with the sovereign's will and pleasure and submission. Her long exchanges with the Red and White Queens hinge on trying to ascertain what they want and mean, and by the time her subjects have drunk to her health (queerly, re-member), Alice is faced with a dilemma of decorum. "You must return thanks in a neat speech," says the Red Queen, and "Alice tried to submit to it with a good grace" (p. 334).

How can we submit to the will of imagined sovereigns? What hap-pens when inanimate objects or concepts come to life? Chess pieces we can see, but what of ideas such as the "copula of a proposition" as a living, conscious entity? Carroll's complaint reminds me of the end of Woody Allen's short story "The Kugelmass Episode," where a man has invented a machine to take him into books—to live with Madame Bovary or Alex Portnoy. But he's made an error, and he finds himself transported into *Remedial Spanish*, "running for his life over a barren, rocky terrain as the word *tener* ('to have')—a large and hairy irregular verb—raced after him on its spindly legs."[17]

And it reminds me, too, of things in Edward Lear. Lear populates his poetry with strange things come to life, with people from the ends of the earth with odd desires, and with plants and animals made up of things as queer as living propositions. His "Nonsense Botany," for ex-ample, imagines plants that bear unusual fruit: the *Guittara Pensilis* that bears guitars, the *Phattfacia Stupenda* with a big head for a flower. His poem "The Table and the Chair" imagines both these objects alive and speaking, going off on a walk into town, getting lost, and finding their way home to bed.[18] Lear's world is only superficially like that of Dr. Seuss. True, he imagines alphabets made up of oddities; true, his ani-mals and people have an almost surreal, overworked quality to them; true, there are situations of such absurdity that they have the feel of Seuss-like narrative:

> There was an Old Man whose despair
> Induced him to purchase a hare;
> Whereon one fine day, he rode wholly away,
> Which partly assuaged his despair.
>
> (p. 329)

But there is, throughout Lear, more Dickens than Dr. Seuss. His charac-ters could easily come from any of the novels. I see Wemmick from *Great Expectations*, with his "post-office box mouth," as something of a Lear-like creation, a blend of the human and the instrumental. Lear's charac-ters have pails for hats, trumpets for noses, lobsters in their hair, necks like cranes, and so on.

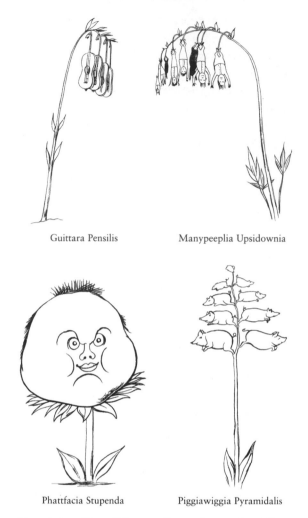

Guittara Pensilis          Manypeeplia Upsidownia

Phattfacia Stupenda          Piggiawiggia Pyramidalis

Fig. 9. Edward Lear, "Nonsense Botany." Reproduced from
Vivien Noakes, ed., *The Complete Verse and Other Nonsense*,
by Edward Lear (Harmondsworth, UK: Penguin Books, 2001), p. 252.

Lear's verse does many things, but it responds most pointedly to the social experience of childish vision and, in turn, to the ways in which the child's life seems—much like Pip's at the opening of *Great Expectations*—lived upside down. Scholars have long seen Lear as challenging the ideals of Victorian propriety and social status. There is, in the words of Thomas Dilworth, a kind of "subtle horror" to Lear's nonsense verse—as if he can all too easily cross that line that lies between Pip and Magwich or Miss Havisham.[19] But what Lear also does is to explore the terror that inheres in everyday experience: in names of towns, in words for common things, in bits and pieces of the body.

Every city or country in Lear's limericks becomes a place of brilliant weirdness. There once was a person from . . . fill in the blank. Then find a rhyme for that place, and in that rhyme lies the subversion of the civil order.

> There was an Old Person of Woking,
> Whose mind was perverse and provoking.

> There was an Old Person of Dover,
> Who rushed through a field of blue Clover.

> There was an Old Person of Cromer,
> Who stood on one leg to read Homer.

Again and again, familiar places populate themselves with eccentric inhabitants. And again and again, so many of these strange inhabitants are old. Lear imagines a geriatric world, an old folks' home of the bizarre. What he presents here is a vision of the old through childish eyes: as if what children see in their elders are patterns of behavior so unique or obsessive that it makes their own mischief small by comparison. Lear's achievement in these limericks is to make Victorian adulthood outré. Even the Old Person of Shoreham, "whose habits were marked by decorum," simply "bought an Umbrella, and sat in the cellar" hardly the behavior of the socially adept. Lear's people live on the borders of life:

> There was an Old Man on the Border,
> Who lived in the utmost disorder;
> He danced with the cat, and made tea in his hat,
> Which vexed all the folks on the Border.

This is a limerick version of Wonderland, where the animals dance and the Mad Hatter's tea party is distilled into tea in a hat. Lear's world, in short, is queer.

> There was an Old Man of Cashmere,
> Whose movements were scroobious and queer;
> Being slender and tall, he looked over a wall,
> And perceived two fat ducks of Cashmere.

Not even the *Oxford English Dictionary* defines "scroobious," a coinage worthy of "Jabberwocky"; and when Lear uses it again in "The Scroobious Pip," how can we not see his blend of Carrollian lexicography and Dickensian childhood?

Lear's is a queer world, but it is not just one that takes Dickensian characters to the border. It is a world beyond the borders, and throughout his writings, characters are always sailing to strange lands and distant islands. The Owl and the Pussycat go to sea in a beautiful pea-green boat—their version of Crusoe's canoe. For there is much of *Robinson Crusoe* in Lear. Islands are everywhere; boats fill his fantasies. In some sense, the collections of limericks may be read as voyages to the bizarre ends of the earth. Wherever Lear travels in these poems—from Troy, to New York, to Nepal—he finds eccentrics.

> There was an old man in a boat,
> Who complained of a pain in his throat:
> When they said, "Can you screech?" he replied, "I beseech
> You won't make any noise in my boat!"

These voyagers go nowhere. The man in the boat has trouble speaking, and he asks for silence in return. In "The Story of the Four Little Children Who Went round the World," written for the grandchildren of Lord Westbury in 1867, the travelers do get somewhere, but where they wind up is no land that can be found on maps. It is only Lear country: an island full of veal cutlets and chocolate drops; a landscape with no houses, but only large bottles without corks; horizons where creatures made out of vegetables can disappear "on the brink of the western sky in a crystal cloud of sudorific sand."[20]

Lear's own life was lived much among islands. In his travels through the Mediterranean, he often stopped on Greek isles to soak up sun and dally with the young men who were his adored (if fickle) companions. And when we come upon his enisled creatures, how can we not see in them a satire on the whole tradition of the English novel, a tradition stretching from Crusoe's adventures to those of Becky Sharp? Recall that ditty from *Vanity Fair* earlier in this chapter and set it against the opening stanza of "The Dong with the Luminous Nose":

> When awful darkness and silence reign
> Over the great Gromboolian plain,
>     Through the long, long wintry nights; —

When the angry breakers roar
As they beat against the shore; —
   When Storm-clouds brood on the towering heights
Of the Hills of the Chankly Bore . . .

                          (p. 422)

So much of this is similar to Thackeray: the dark, portentous landscape, the stormy night, the barrenness of distant place, and the lonely boy. In Lear, we are left always standing on the shore, trapped on islands of imagination, waiting for our ships to take us home.

And there is love throughout. I do not think there is a single romantic relationship in Dr. Seuss, but they fill Lear's fantasies. The Dong falls in love, tragically, with a Jumbly Girl, while the Owl and the Pussycat successfully unite themselves in marriage. In an early set of illustrations for the popular ballad "Kathleen O'Moore" (probably completed by 1841, when Lear was twenty-nine, and unpublished in his lifetime), he poignantly vivifies the love and death of the young girl. And in "The Courtship of the Yonghy-Bonghy-Bò," the title character asks Lady Jingly to marry him, only to get the response: "Your proposal comes too late. . . . For in England I've a mate."[21] Her betrothed is Mr. Handel Jones, Esquire—a name that could come right out of the Dickensian legal world, a name evocative of social standing and stability. Amid the nonsense and the repetitions of this poem (a poem that Lear himself set to music and was fond of performing in public) lies the lonely poignancy of Lear's own life. For even in escaping from a world of esquires, in traveling to coasts and islands, Lear's characters always come face to face with their own unassailable oddity. It is as if we see him constantly as some awkward child in an adult world. But unlike for Max of *Where the Wild Things Are*, his boat never returns him to his room and dinner.

Instead, Lear is always voyaging, and if there are reminiscences of Defoe or Dickens, there is also Darwin. Lear's illustrations of different-colored birds seem to be his nonsense version of the findings on the voyage of the *Beagle*. Even the turtle in "Yonghy-Bonghy-Bò" has a Darwinian precision about it. As we are informed by the modern annotator to Lear's *Complete Verse*, "The turtle on which the Yonghy-Bonghy-Bò escapes is the young *Chelonia Imbricata* for which Lear had made the lithograph for Thomas Bell's *A Monograph of Testudinata* (1836)" (p. 517). Both Lear and Darwin, in the 1830s, found themselves transported into nature and sought, in the beaks of finches or the backs of turtles, evidence for their place in the scope of creation. Both felt a sense of wonder at the observation of that scope, and there are passages throughout *The Voyage of the Beagle* that have all the feel of Lear or Carroll on the oddities of nature. The modern critic Jean-Jacques Lecercle singles one such moment out for delectation—Darwin on the guanacos: "That they are curious is certain; for if a person lies on the ground and plays strange antics, such as throwing up his feet in the air, they will almost always approach by degrees to reconnoiter him."[22] For Lecercle, this is the guanaco's "first encounter with British nonsense in act." Why should a natural scientist behave in this way? What role do strange antics have in the empirical cataloguing of nature? Lecercle goes on to note that "the reader of nonsense tales is an exploring naturalist," but there is more here. Darwin's language is the language not of science but of the novel. It has the feel of Dickens's early prose; it writes a story of a naturalist as one of Dickens's eccentrics—as if Mr. Dick from *David Copperfield* had shown up on the Patagonian coast to flip his feet up in the air. Curioser and curioser. It has the feel, too, of what would become Carroll's parody in *Alice in Wonderland*:

> "You are old, Father William," the young man said,
> "And your hair has become very white;
> And yet you incessantly stand on your head—
> Do you think, at your age, it is right?"
>
> (p. 70)

Darwin anticipates the edge of nonsense that the naturalist may reach in new worlds. Both Wonderland and Lear's verse take us over that edge. Lear himself had begun his career as a natural history illustrator; his first book to see print was *Illustrations of the Family of Psittacidae* (that is, parrots) of 1832, a project he described in a verse letter to his friend Harry Hinde:

> For all day I've been a-
> way at the West End,
> Painting the best end
> Of some vast Parrots
> As red as new carrots.
>
> (pp. 46–47)

Parrots and carrots. Lear's literary response to the naturalism of his day is something of an anti-evolution. Animals seem always to revert to their lower selves (here birds become, by simile association, plants);

people take on attributes of animals. Even the sounds Lear loves are something of a devolved language: names such as Dong and Yonghy-Bonghy-Bò and Pobble; words such as "scroobious"; objects such as bottles. These all evoke a kind of primitive, prelinguistic expressiveness, as if Lear seeks to travel back into a time before civilized speech. And there are occasions when meaning seems almost to disappear behind the euphony of certain words, where what he is describing is not something to be seen but heard: "All the Blue-bottle-Flies began to buzz at once in a sumptuous and sonorous manner, the melodious and mucilaginous sounds echoing all over the waters, and resounding across the tumultuous tops of the transitory Titmice upon the intervening and verdant mountains, with a serene and sickly suavity only known to the truly virtuous. The Moon was shining slobaciously from the star-bespringled sky …" (p. 227). Lear revels in the sounds of words used in new ways, and in a passage such as this one, words that have specific, dictionary meanings fracture into nonsense. He illustrates, here and throughout his work, the ways in which the language of the ordinary world can all too easily fracture into non-meaning; how the exiled or ill or socially excluded (for Lear was himself all these) see in the domestic, adult, secure, and healthy not decorum but division. And when we look up in the sky, how can we ever see the moon in the same way again? Unlike the "Jabberwocky" world of Carroll, Lear's is not a landscape of the completely fantastic. No playing cards come alive here. Instead, it is the world of everyday experience seen and heard in new ways, a world seen through the eyes of Mr. Lear.

> Some think him ill-tempered and queer,
> But a few think him pleasant enough.
>
> (p. 428)

The traditions of nonsense literature lived on beyond Carroll and Lear. There is babble, on occasion, in Kipling, Chesterton, and Walter De la Mare. Edmund Clerihew Bentley developed the verse form that bears his middle name: a stanza that insists upon a rhyme of the subject's name in order to bring out some absurd asset. Among the very first such verses, published in 1905, is this one:

> Sir Humphrey Davy
> Abominated gravy.
> He lived in the odium
> Of having discovered sodium.[23]

Hugh Lofting's Dr. Dolittle stories (1920, 1922) often trade on silly-sounding names and situations—witness, for example, the pushmi-pullyus, with a head at each end, one of which was always awake.[24] By the end of the Victorian era, nonsense seemed so ensconced in British and American literary life that Carolyn Wells could edit, in 1902, *A Nonsense Anthology* for Scribner's. Beginning with Carroll's "Jabberwocky," it runs through a whole range of poetry, from Lear's limericks through the patter songs of W. S. Gilbert to the precious menagerie of Hilaire Belloc and a whole host of anonymous (and largely forgettable) efforts. Some of this verse is clearly children's poetry, some clearly not. But Wells recognizes, at the opening of her introduction, just how nonsense takes us on a journey to the edges of experience; how it is less a state of mind or a condition of word usage than a place of the imagination. "On a topographical map of Literature Nonsense would be represented by a small and sparsely settled country, neglected by the average tourist, but affording keen delight to the few enlightened travelers who sojourn within its borders."[25] Emile Cammaerts, in his 1925 book *The Poetry of Nonsense*, recognizes, too, the genre's source in geography. For "if it had not been for this 'old man of Tobago'," the inspiration for Lear's geographical limericks, "mankind would have been deprived of thousands and thousands, . . . hailing from all corners of the earth."[26] It is as if nonsense repopulates the world, as if our reading were itself an act of traveling to places known only as names on a map. The sentiments of Wells and Cammaerts (and to some extent the sentiments of Lofting's Dr. Dolittle stories) are those of a post-imperial world. Names like Crimea and Khartoum, Mafeking and Mandalay evoke now not the heroics of conquest, but the eccentricities of those who cannot even conquer their own tics.

And in those eccentricities lie both political and aesthetic experience. The legacy of Carroll, Lear, and their inheritors lies in the anarchic ludistry of the Dadaists. The poets, painters, and performance artists of the first decades of the twentieth century made the absurd that century's defining aesthetic. Dada itself has long been seen as trading on the babble of the infant—the movement's very name conjures the nursery sounds, be they the repeated "da, da" of Russian or the French idiom for a rocking horse.[27] Could Tristan Tzara have composed his "Dada Manifesto" of 1918 without the poetry of nonsense?

> Every page must explode, either by profound heavy seriousness, the whirlwind, poetic frenzy, the new, the eternal, the crushing joke, enthusiasm for principles, or by the way in which it is printed. On the one hand a tot-

tering world in flight, betrothed to the glockenspiel of hell, on the other hand: new men. Rough, bouncing, riding on hiccups. Behind them a crippled world and literary quacks with a mania for improvement.

Or, as he aphorizes in a little Dada couplet:

> Knowledge, knowledge, knowledge,
> Boomboom, boomboom, boomboom.[28]

Tzara's Dada was not unique among the literary and aesthetic movements that sought inspiration in the nonsense of the child. The Russian avant-garde of the first decades of the twentieth century drew on infant babble to imagine a Futurist poetics. The language of the child challenged notions of linguistic convention. It was seen, to some extent, as the verbal equivalent of abstract art, in which conventions of representation were exploded into their small building blocks. Artists and theorists such as Aleksei Kruchenykh linked the childish and the primitive, the prattle of the nursery and the origins of language itself. Kruchenykh's contemporary, Sergei Tretyakov, characterized the poetry that was emerging from this movement as "strange books," with "tumbling, and often completely unpronounceable, letters and syllables." Two decades later, the Russian humorist Daniil Kharms found in the nonsense verse of childhood an insight into the absurdisms of life.[29]

Movements such as Dada, Futurism, and surrealism drew directly on the nonsense traditions of the nursery and schoolroom, while fostering forms of artistic performance that affected children's literature itself. Marcel Duchamp famously turned a urinal upside down and called it art. So, too, in childish play, any upside down thing becomes an object of imagination. As Emile Cammaerts put it in his 1925 book, in terms that must resonate with the Duchamp-like farcicality of his decade: "Every upturned table becomes a ship, every stick becomes an oar, chairs are harnessed like prancing horses. The spirit of Nonsense reigns supreme until the evil hour when, exhausted by his work, the child falls asleep and some grown-up restores order where chaos has prevailed."[30] This is a world askew, a world queer, if you will, in which the tilt and angle of existence leads to fantasy. It is a short step from this bedroom play to Antoine de Saint-Exupéry's Little Prince, who travels not just to new islands but new planets, and finds queer things there as well. He converses with a conceited man, who announces:

> "Ah! Ah! I am about to receive a visit from an admirer!" he exclaimed from afar, when he first saw the little prince coming. For, to conceited men, all other men are admirers.

"Good morning," said the little prince. "That is a queer hat you are wearing."

"It is a hat for salutes," the conceited man replied. "It is to raise in salute when people acclaim me. Unfortunately, nobody at all ever passes this way."[31]

But, of course, this is an English translation. The word "queer" here may well be conditioned by the queerness of the verse of Lear and Carroll and the language of the nonsense world. In French, the man is wearing "un drôle de chapeau," and the word "drôle" connotes not simply the modern English "droll," but something more complex: more childish, more theatrical, more jesting. The word as a noun originally meant a jester or a humorist; it would be used, both in French and in English, to mean something out of farce or even a puppet show. That "drôle de chapeau," then, is not merely queer. It is queer precisely in the ways in which the hats on Edward Lear's imagined drolleries are queer: as stage props in life's absurd theater.

The upside down, the messy, the nonsensical are everywhere in children's literature, but if there is one modern heir to their blend of the ill-tempered and queer, it is Shel Silverstein. Silverstein claimed never to have been influenced by his predecessors, but I find it hard not to see Carroll, Lear, and even Tristan Tzara in his books.[32] *Where the Sidewalk Ends* (1974), his major collection of children's verse, evokes a looking-glass world, as if, on opening the book, we cross over into nowhere.[33] "Homemade Boat" speaks to that tradition of post-Crusoe writing where the child sets off on a great journey—only here, it is a journey into absurd failure.

> This boat that we just built is just fine—
> And don't try to tell us it's not.
> The sides and the back are divine—
> It's the bottom I guess we forgot.

Silverstein's boat recalls the many loony crafts that sail the seas of Edward Lear. But it evokes, more generally, the upside-down world of nonsense literature—as if everything would be just fine were it not for the fact that the ship has no bottom.

Throughout Silverstein, as throughout Lear, there are people with clarinets for noses, characters who live in cups, a boy with hair so long it flaps him off into the sky. And if the Little Prince finds someone in a queer hat, so do we.

HAT
Teddy said it was a hat,
So I put it on.
Now Dad is saying,
"Where the heck's
   the toilet plunger gone?"

It is as if the little boy has found the Duchamp in himself; as if the act of taking something from the bathroom and putting it on his head becomes the ultimate in artistic expression. On planet Silverstein, much as on the planets the Little Prince visits, people are measured by their headgear.

Throughout *Where the Sidewalk Ends*, there is wit and brilliant linguistic inventiveness, but there is also a strain of sentiment that makes clear that nonsense is but the flip side of desire. Silverstein's poems have an achiness about them, as the speaker longs to be part of everyday society and yet is constantly aware that he can never fit in. We feel this throughout Edward Lear, and we feel this, too, in *Alice in Wonderland*. And so the poet looks for places where acceptance comes: places of fantasy and freedom. In such places there is beauty, and for all the craziness and cacophony of his lines, at times Silverstein seems remarkably old-fashioned. Here is the opening stanza of the title poem, "Where the Sidewalk Ends":

There is a place where the sidewalk ends
And before the street begins,
And there the grass grows soft and white,
And there the sun burns crimson bright,
And there the moon-bird rests from his flight
To cool in the peppermint wind.

Such lines prod us to travel back, not to old places but to old books: to the Edenic spots of ancient literature, to the Elysian fields, to the lyrics of Wordsworth, or to the hobo song, "The Big Rock Candy Mountain."

Oh the buzzin' of the bees
In the cigarette trees
Near the soda water fountain;
At the lemonade springs
Where the bluebird sings
On the big rock candy mountain.[34]

I still remember Burl Ives singing that song on a scratchy record of my childhood. And I still remember, too, the first German poem I was forced to memorize in college: Johann Wolfgang von Goethe's famous "Mignon."

> Kennst du das Land, wo die Zitronen blühn,
> Im dunkeln Laub die Gold-Orangen glühn,
> Ein sanfter Wind vom blauen Himmel weht,
> Die Myrte still und hoch der Lorbeer steht?
> Kennst du es wohl?
> > Dahin! Dahin
> Möcht ich mit dir, o mein Geliebter, ziehn.

> [Do you know the land where the lemon trees bloom,
> Where gold oranges gleam among the dark leaves' gloom,
> Where from blue heavens soft wind blows,
> Where the myrtle is silent, and the tall laurel grows?
> Do you know it well?
> > There it is! There
> Would I long to go with you, O my love!][35]

My memory of these texts takes me back to times when I was learning languages and lyrics. Childhood and freshman year are periods of change, and what the Russian Futurists or French Dadaists found so fascinating in the sounds of babble, or what we may see in writers as diverse as Silverstein and Goethe, is a deep nostalgia for a time almost before speech: a longing not just for a different place of fantasy, but for a place like Eden, where words simply are the things they claim to be, and where, like Eve and Adam, we may name the world anew.

I began at the edges of absurdity: with languages newly discovered; with strange creatures brought back from antipodes; with Dickens's oddballs and Thackeray's satire; with Wonderland, the looking-glass, and limericks; with Darwin and desire. Nonsense is more than play: it takes us to the limits of expression. At times, we hear it in the babble of the infant or the verses of the undergraduate. But at times, too, we may hear it on occasions that remind us that childhood remains a time of longing—when we find ourselves on queer streets or Diagon Alleys, when our boats take us not to where the wild things are, but to where the sidewalk ends.

· 10 ·

# Straw into Gold

## FAIRY-TALE PHILOLOGY

When I was four, my father would lull me to sleep with Rumpelstiltskin. Each night he would begin with the fair miller's daughter who could, so her father bragged, spin straw into gold. He would go on to tell me of the way in which the king heard about her gift, and about how he coerced her into spinning for him. One night, when she sat fearful of being found out, a little man appeared out of nowhere. He spun the straw into gold and, as repayment, asked for her necklace; the next night for her ring; the third night for her firstborn child. She agreed, and the king soon married her. Years later, when her son was born, the little man came to claim the child. This time he made another deal with the distraught queen: if she could guess his name, he would relent. She made guesses, and so did we. Each night we'd go through scores of names, from the familiar to the mad: Charles, James, John; and then names of friends and relatives—Sam, Sid, Norman, Sy; and then the Yiddish names, like incantations from a distant magic—Chaim, Lebbel, Mendel, Menasha, Velvel. The queen kept guessing, too, until one night she sent a messenger in search of the little man. This messenger came upon a campfire with a ring of little men. And in the middle, there was the imp, dancing in the fire and singing, "Rumpelstiltskin is my name!" So when the little man came back and asked, "What's my name?" she said, "Rumpelstiltskin." And he stamped his foot so hard he drove it into the ground, and then he picked himself up by his other leg and tore himself in half.

The end. Just why this was my favorite bedtime story is a mystery to me. And yet it stands as an exemplar of the fairy-tale tradition. All the familiar forms are there: the father and the daughter, the strange creature,

· 209 ·

the riddle, the forest. But there was more, of course. This is a story about artistry itself. Each night, we'd spin the straw of everyday existence into gold; each night, we'd tell a story, weaving names and details from the family into magic. This is a story, too, about naming: about guessing just who people really are, about living up to your own name, about cracking codes. There was a little Rumpelstiltskin everywhere in my childhood: the strange man on the street corner, the sad, disabled classmate, or the awkward uncle (my personalized version of the fairy tale was confirmed when I read a 2006 *New Yorker* interview with Maurice Sendak, who claimed that the characters in *Where the Wild Things Are* were all based on his Brooklyn relatives).[1] We lived with the fairy tale to make these frightening, unhappy people live as magic. We tried to imagine ourselves as a family of princes.

The fairy tale grew, as a literary genre, out of the folk stories of the European past. We like to believe that they have no real authors, that they have been orally transmitted, and that they remain flexible in their details and their telling. Like Aesop's fables, fairy tales come in famous groups with well-known characters: Beauty and the Beast, Hansel and Gretel, the Snow Queen, Rumpelstiltskin, the Little Mermaid, and the like. But fairy tales, as we know them now, are really the creation of literate collectors, editors, and authors working from the late seventeenth until the mid-nineteenth century. They appeared as literary texts during the age of Louis XIV, not so much as children's stories but as exemplary fables for the courtier adults. They taught ideal behavior. They became the fashion of aristocratic salons. They contributed to the mythology of courtliness and kingship. Indeed, our English term *fairy tale* is a translation of the French *conte de fées*, the genre that arose in the salon to narrate social criticism or offer moral instruction under the guise of fantasy.[2]

Charles Perrault emerged in the last decades of the seventeenth century as the best and most widely read of these tale-tellers. To him we owe what would become the Mother Goose stories, and his versions of "Cinderella," "Puss in Boots," "Little Red Riding Hood," and many other tales helped to establish these in the familiar canon of the children's library. In France, the vogue for *contes de fées* segued into a later, eighteenth-century fascination with the so-called oriental tale, reaching its apogee in Antoine Galland's 1704 translation of *The Thousand and One Nights*. As Walter Rex has put it, in his summary of these developments in *A New History of French Literature*, "Like a magic lamp or a secret cave, these tales opened up a whole range of literary possibilities: new forms, metaphors, characters, moralities; they promised to fulfill any author's or reader's desire."[3]

And so they did. The *contes* originally meant for literary salons and aristocratic audiences found later readerships in households and nurseries. French tales came into English (Perrault appeared in 1729; Jeanne-Marie Leprince de Beaumont's *Magasin des enfans* of 1757, containing such favorites as "Beauty and the Beast," was translated in 1761). Sarah Fielding's *The Governess* of 1749 incorporates a fairy tale of a dwarf and a giant as part of a larger, characteristically mid-eighteenth-century desire to teach "simplicity of Taste and Manners which it is my chief Study to inculcate." Fielding adds, "Giants, Magic, Fairies, and all Sorts of supernatural Assistances in a story, are only introduced to amuse and divert."[4] For Fielding and her readers, fairy tales are now like the Aesopica: moral allegories keyed to shaping social action.

By the late eighteenth and early nineteenth centuries, fairy tales had taken on other social purposes. The historical study of language (the discipline of philology) used fairy tales to ask questions about national origin, linguistic development, and personal and public psychology. Did languages and nations have a childhood? Many early philologists wrote as if they did, and it is no accident that some of the great tellers and retellers of the fairy tales—the Brothers Grimm, Montague Rhodes James, J. R. R. Tolkien, C. S. Lewis—were scholars of language and its history. As a philologist myself, I remain fascinated by their forays into fantasy. Why did my profession find the fairy tale so central to its life?

The brothers Jacob and Wilhelm Grimm are best known among my peers for their discovery of what has come to be called Grimm's law. They recognized, along with many other scholars in the late eighteenth and early nineteenth centuries, that languages from Europe, India, and Persia shared some common elements of word, sound, and grammar. From the modern, surviving tongues, an ancient "Indo-European" language was postulated, and the Grimms codified the set of relationships among the consonants in the different language branches descended from it. They showed that certain words could be traced back to Indo-European origins by comparing their sounds. For example, words that begin with *f* in the Germanic languages correspond to words that begin with *p* in the Romance languages (English *fish*, *father*, and *foot* correspond to Latin *pisces*, *pater*, and *pes*). Many other consonant associations could be found, and these correspondences made possible a new understanding of word origins and what those origins revealed about the social lives of early European peoples. For the Grimms and their contemporaries, there was a kind of metaphysics of the word. Words were, in some sense, fossil poems, embedded tales of a language and a people. The classicist Franz Passow, working in the wake of the Grimms' philology and lexicography, distilled their impact as follows: "A dictionary should offer the life history [*Lebensgeschichte*] of every individual word in precise and ordered overview." Herbert Coleridge, one of the founders of the *Oxford English Dictionary*, appealed to Passow's view to argue, "Every word should be made to tell its own story—the story of its birth and life."[5]

Philology was thus a form of storytelling, and it is no accident that the Grimms were as fascinated by folklore as they were by etymology. Word histories are like puzzles to solve, and indeed many of the Grimms' tales (notably "Rumpelstiltskin") hinge on knowing the name of the character (in this tale, his name means "the little cripple-legged one"). And if the world of the fairy tale was the world of the forest—with its darkness, its blind paths, and its organic undergrowth—so, too, was the world of philology. James A. H. Murray, the presiding editor of the *Oxford English Dictionary*, announced in 1884, describing the job of his editorial crew, "We are pioneers in an untrodden forest."[6]

The Grimms thought of their work precisely in these terms. Their *Kinder- und Hausmärchen* (nursery and household tales) appeared in two volumes (1812, 1815), and then in many subsequent editions.[7] Wilhelm Grimm noted that these were the "last echoes of pagan myths." He went on: "A world of magic is opened up before us, one which still exists among us in secret forests, in underground caves, and in the deepest sea, and it is still visible to children. [Fairy tales] belong to our national poetic heritage, since it can be proved that they have existed among the people for several centuries."[8] And what we find inside those secret forests, caves, and seas is not just a poetic heritage, but a personal one as well. For fairy tales are full of families, full of parents who bequeath a sense of self to children, full of ancestors and heirs whose lives play out, in little, the life of a nation from its childhood to maturity.

Many fairy tales begin with family history. "A poor woodcutter lived with his wife and two children" ("Hansel and Gretel"). "Once upon a time there was a miller who was poor" ("Rumpelstiltskin"). "Once upon a time there was a poor farmer" ("The Clever Farmer's Daughter"). "Once upon a time there was a fisherman" ("The Fisherman and His Wife"). Such men live by transforming the stuff of nature into goods: woodcutters go out into the forest, millers grind grain, farmers bring food from the soil, fishermen fish. They differ from, say, the merchant in "Beauty and the Beast"—a father who involves himself not in manufacture but in sales and transport, who is rich (or socially aspiring) enough to pay others to teach his children, keep his house, and cook his food.

But who, really, are the fathers? Paternity is everywhere—with real or surrogate parents, with fathers who remarry, with those who die or come anew. The Grimms recognized this, as they shaped their tales around a set of family themes that would reflect the changing nature of the European family in their time. The forests and the farms were losing people to the cities. An urban, literate middle class had been emerging that was paying for, rather than providing, goods and services. People were reading stories in addition to retelling them, and the book trade grew accordingly. But in addition to these demographic shifts, something had changed in the affect of family life. Affection was becoming the mark of successful parenting.[9]

Now throughout history, parents no doubt have had affection for their children. In the course of this book, I have explored ways in which the Greeks and Romans, medieval Europeans, and English and American Puritans loved and cared for offspring. But what has changed by the later eighteenth century is the idea of affection as a defining criterion for family goodness. Locke had argued, at the close of the seventeenth century, that "Fear and awe ought to give you the first power over [children's] minds, love and friendship in riper years to hold it."[10] Three-quarters of a century later, Rousseau could voice an ideal of affection that would displace "fear and awe" and push back, to the earliest years of child-rearing, love and friendship. In his magisterial study of the European family, Lawrence Stone makes clear how, by the later eighteenth century, the rising bourgeoisie had developed what he calls an "affectionate and permissive mode" of child-rearing.[11]

Scholars have long recognized the ways in which the Grimms calibrated their tales for these emerging middle-class audiences: they pared away some of the coarseness of the folk idiom, shaped particular motifs to literary expectations, and added layers of Christian morality or proverbial wisdom to enhance their practical didactic value. Whatever rusticity remains in their tellings is a highly stylized one.[12]

In such contexts of class and culture, fairy tales raised serious philosophical questions: was love something that you learned as a parent, or was it something inherent in giving birth? Could someone love a child that was not his or her own? The presence in society of stepparents or foster families addressed these questions pointedly, and one of the reasons that the Grimms were fascinated by stepfamilies was that they illustrated tensions in affection. "Hansel and Gretel" appears, in their first edition of the *Kinder- und Hausmärchen*, as a story with a father and a mother and their children; by the fourth edition, it becomes explicitly a tale of a father and his second wife. The evil stepmother—a figure we have now taken as emblematic of the fairy-tale bad family—evolves out of the mix of social changes affecting the raising of the European child.[13]

Family lives also stood behind stories of religious devotion, as well as social strife. When Rumpelstiltskin comes to the young queen to get his prize and asks her to guess his name, the first names she comes up with are Melchior, Caspar, and Balthasar. These are the names of the three wise men who attend the baby Jesus in the manger. What are they doing in this tale? Clearly, these are the first three names on the young woman's mind, and they reflect what the Grimms have done to the folktale behind their story. The story of a baby born in straw, the rough nativity of the manger, now stands behind the tale of a girl's child who was born out of the lie that she could turn straw into gold. That transformation now must resonate with a larger transformation: the straw of the manger made into the gold of incarnation; the message of Christian redemption, that our dross can become devotion. Now it is not a story of wise men who visit a boy, but a tale of a monster who would abduct a child. There is a kind of negative nativity to "Rumpelstiltskin" here—a feature of the story raised by these three names, spoken, it would seem, almost out of nowhere.

For the true redemption comes from God the Father. Religion is a family affair, and families in the Grimm tales are often broken versions of a holy household. Evil mothers and stepmothers abound; fathers are useless or fearful. Brothers and sisters bind together, as in "Hansel and Gretel," not just to find their way out of the forest, but to bring their family out of their domestic enforesting—to clear away the woody undergrowth of anger and suspicion.

All is not fantasy. If the Grimms' stories reflect changes in the family and society, they also reflect shifts in the economics of desire. What is "The Fisherman and His Wife" but a tale about economic aspiration gone mad? From hovel to cottage, castle, palace, imperium, papal see, and finally Godhood itself, the spaces of the wife's desires trace the architecture of power. It is not simply that the wife wants more; she wants to *be* more, wants to change her very essence in relationship to worldly goods.

The tale moves on an arc of ostentatious description. Each successive abode gets a progressively greater amount of descriptive verbiage, such that by the time the wife becomes the emperor, the passagework stands as an almost endless list of physical and bodily objects and ornaments. Such passages seem to me, too, ripe for the kind of participatory play so central to the fairy tale in its social telling: parent and child chime back and forth with names for Rumpelstiltskin; they enumerate the body parts and what they do for the wolf in "Little Red Riding Hood"; and here, they build together to create the verbal equivalent of the gold, stone, and marble magnificence. Don't want too much, the tale takes as its moral, or you will wind up back in a hovel. But what it also teaches is just how to make too much of something: how to build a castle or an empire out of words. The straw of language here becomes the gold of thrones.

And this is what makes so many of these tales truly philological. It is not simply that they reach back to an earlier, folk wisdom or folk narrative; it is not simply that they offer up tales from a Germanic or pan-European past. It is that the tales themselves—with their displays of verbal prowess, their elaborate lists, their technical vocabulary—could only have been composed by masters of the language. Indeed, "The Fisherman and His Wife" is in dialect, and reading its passages requires a level of philological awareness far beyond grammar and word.

> Dar wöör eens en Fischer un syne Fru, de waanden tosamen in'n Pißputt, dicht an der See . . .[14]

"Pißputt" not simply a "hovel," as the modern English translators have rendered it, but far more earthy: a pisspot. Both this tale and "The Juniper Tree" came to the Grimms by way of the artist Philipp Otto Runge, who had presented them in the Pomeranian dialect. But the Grimms augmented Runge's model.[15] In such a dialect world, the words for the riches of the castles and the thrones seem brilliantly out of place. As the fisherman's wife gets greater and greater power and more and more possessions, we see a veritable lexicon of luxuries. But what speaker of this dialect could have ever seen *Baronen, Graven,* and *Herzogen* (barons, earls, and dukes); could have ever held *Briljanten* and *Karfunkelsteen* (diamonds and garnets); could have felt the sway of *Zepter* or *Reichsappel* (scepter or imperial globe)? And when, in her ultimate transformation, this fisherman's wife says in her cacophonous dialect "Ja, ic bün Paabst" (for what would have to have been in high German "Ja, Ich bin Pabst"), we see the Grimms' philology pressed into the service of scathing satire.

This is a story of language gone wild, of people displaced not just from social setting but from verbal world. Families may leave the forests for the towns, and fishermen's wives may rise in the world; but as soon as they open their mouths, they show themselves.

Such dialect stories, too, are more than philological in the local sense. They take us to a time of language that the Grimms and their contemporaries imagined as recalling older verbal forms. This is, to some degree, the childhood of the German tongue. In his lecture "On the Origin of Language," delivered to the Berlin Academy of Sciences in 1851, Jacob Grimm makes clear these figurative associations between linguistic history and human development. The first stage of a language, he argues, is a "seedling phase." Its appearance "is simple, artless, full of life, like blood in a youthful body." He goes on:

> All words are short, monosyllabic, almost all formed with short vowels and simple consonants. The supply crowds thick and fast like blades of grass. All concepts result from a sensory outlook which itself was already a thought from which light and new thoughts arise on all sides. The relationships of the words and ideas are expressed naively and freshly but unadorned by subsequent, still unorganized words.[16]

There is, in these words, something of a childhood to language itself, and the language of fairy tales—especially the dialect tongue of such stories as "The Fisherman and His Wife"—was designed to evoke the child of speech and the child of the teller and reader. When, for example, Wilhelm Grimm sent one of his informant sources the published edition of the *Kinder- und Hausmärchen*, she replied by noting: "When I read these tales, I recalled some of the things that I had lost since my childhood."[17]

The Grimms' fairy tales are not written in the language of real children, nor do they seek to evoke the sounds of childish speech. Rather, the Grimms synthesized folk stories, personal remembrances, and an already rich tradition of literary fairy tales (from those of Charles Perrault in the 1690s to those of Clemens Brentano in the early 1800s) to create a literary language akin to their sense of early language itself. Compare Jacob Grimm's organic metaphors for language growth—seedling, blood, and blades of grass—with the imagery of his informant's letter: "It is to us all a reminder of ethereal youth, of the enlivening spirit of uniqueness that grows from the root and spreads into all of the most tender branches."[18]

Fairy tales take us back, then, not just to our own childhood imaginations, but to the childhood of language and society themselves. They may also take us back to the childhood of the teller, and in no fabulist is such a personal narrative as clear as in Hans Christian Andersen. Andersen was no philologist, but he was acutely conscious of living in a small European country with its own language, and acutely sensitive to his own provincial dialect. Many of his tales reflect a fascination with linguistic performance— with the ways in which a member of society comes to be measured by his or her mastery of speech and sound.[19]

Andersen's is less a life of facts than one of myths. Unlike the Grimm brothers, whose researches were shaped according to empirical philology and historical consciousness, Andersen made a fairy tale out of his own life. Awkward and gawky, constantly in need of attention, young Hans Christian grew up in a sad, provincial subsistence household. But there were always books. Andersen claims that his father sat by the birthbed and read aloud from Holberg's works the day he was born. Above his father's workbench was a shelf of books, and among his favorites were "plays and stories, . . . history and the Scriptures." When his father died and his mother remarried, Hans Christian sought out some kind of literary patronage. As he puts it in his autobiography, *The Fairy Tale of My Life*, "My passion for reading, the many dramatic scenes which I knew by heart, and my remarkably fine voice, had turned upon me in some sort the attention of several of the more influential families of Odense." Among them was a local army colonel who introduced Hans Christian to Prince Christian (who would later become king of Denmark). "If the prince should ask you what you have a liking for," said the colonel, "answer him that your highest desire is to enter the grammar school."[20] How like a fairy tale this story is: the young boy and the prince; the dead, beloved parent; and the need to act, to recite a life.

Such is the story of "The Nightingale," first published in Andersen's *Eventyr* (Tales) of 1843. The emperor of China learns about the marvelous nightingale from travelers who hear its song and write about it. "The books went through all the world, and a few of them once came to the Emperor. He sat in his golden chair, and read, and read." And when he asks his courtiers for the bird, they cannot find it. "Your Imperial Majesty cannot believe how much is written that is fiction, besides something that they call the black art." "But the book in which I read this," he replies, "was sent to me by the high and mighty Emperor of Japan, and therefore it cannot be a falsehood." It was not, and the bird is found, summoned to court, and commanded to sing. Soon, though, the emperor receives another gift, a parcel on which is written "The Nightingale." At first he thinks it is another book, but when he opens it, he sees it is an artificial bird. This mechanical toy sings just as well as the real nightingale and is more beautiful, and so the bird is banished. Unfortunately, the machine soon breaks down, and no one can fix it. In the end, the real bird returns to sing before the dying emperor, who is revived by his son and who permits the nightingale to come and go as she pleases.[21]

Readers have long seen this as one of the most autobiographical of Andersen's tales. It juxtaposes artifice and artistry, patronage and performance, to make a claim for the autonomy of genius. Like so many others of his stories—"The Ugly Duckling," "The Emperor's New Clothes," "The Little Mermaid"—"The Nightingale" argues that physical appearance does not always show artistic virtue. Great things may come in ugly packages, and beauty may be only skin deep. And yet, I see these stories not just as autobiographical but as philological tales: tales about literacy and social power, tales about understanding language and its roots, tales about looking for the authentic in public verbiage. Words were like ugly ducklings, for historical philology imagined them as rising out of dross into a well-formed beauty.

And as the nineteenth century progressed, the tales of nursery and household, forest and palace found themselves relocated in the ideals of the academy. Philologists became the arbiters of social life. Students of language and of lexicography ran universities and colleges, set literary taste, even advised governments. It is a telling circumstance that Alice Liddell, for whom Lewis Carroll wrote his famous stories, was the daughter of Henry George Liddell, the dean of Christ Church College, Oxford, and the coauthor of what still remains the most authoritative dictionary of ancient Greek. And Sir James A. H. Murray himself, general editor of the *Oxford English Dictionary*, set himself up as a kind of wizard of the word. With his ancient robes and antiquated academic cap, his long white beard and his almost biblical mannerisms, he was, even to his contemporaries, more a figure out of fairy tale than a familiar professor. As his granddaughter recalled, at Halloween, Murray would hide behind bushes "to jump out on the children as they rode round the house on a broomstick. Guests would be taken up to the nursery to throw dragon's blood on the fire. When they had been suitably scared by the vision of a spectral figure which, manipulated by strings, rose up from behind the rocking-horse, James would finish the evening with his famous ghost stories and recitations."[22]

Fig. 10. The philologist as wizard. Sir James A. H. Murray,
editor of the *Oxford English Dictionary* (c. 1910).

The spectral figures of this late Victorian nursery owe much to the
age's blending of the fairy tale with the fantastic. Forests and palaces—
the loci of the Grimms and Andersen—give way to haunts more freak-
ish. In part, the late Victorian investment in the fairy tale and the ghost
story reflects changes in social taste: a fascination with the paranormal,
a culture sharing in the seemingly perpetual mourning of Queen Victoria, and an investment in the aura of particular holidays (Christmas and
Halloween especially) and their rituals of storytelling and performance.[23]
Such fascinations will preoccupy me, in much greater detail, later in this
book; but what occupies me now is not so much their subject matter as
their performers. It is the vision of Murray—the bookman, the wizard of
words—tromping round the rocking horse, regaling relatives with tales,

that distills something new in nineteenth-century children's literature. Books, now, are everywhere; they are the portals to another world, not forest clearings or the eddies of the sea.

Part of the bookishness, too, comes from the ways in which the old tales were passed on. Perhaps the most influential of these intermediaries was Andrew Lang. In his twelve *Fairy Books* (each one called by a different color), published between 1889 and 1910, Lang domesticated the traditions of the Grimms and Andersen. Lang admitted that he made nothing up and did not draw on living folk traditions, but rather relied on published sources. As retold by Lang, and illustrated by Henry J. Ford, these fairy tales took on a distinctive late Victorian (one might say even Pre-Raphaelite) cast. They called attention to the mysteries of the past, evoked a pseudo-medieval world of millers, woodsmen, princes, and princesses. The Rumpelstiltskin, for example, who pokes his head into the miller's daughter's spinning room now looks for all the world like a familiar gnome, with his pointed cap and equally pointed beard.[24]

Lang's work, and Lang himself, had a great impact on many of the children's writers of the last decades of the nineteenth century, not the least of whom was Kenneth Grahame. Best known today for *The Wind in the Willows*, Grahame began his literary career in the circle formed around the publication of *The Yellow Book* (that marvel of 1890s decadence and beauty, famously illustrated by Aubrey Beardsley). Many of Grahame's earliest stories reflect the blend of aestheticism and fantasy shaped by that publication and by the reception of Lang's fairy books.[25] One of the best is "The Reluctant Dragon," originally published in 1898. For all its obvious appeal and adventure-story setup, this is fundamentally a story about language, from the dialect of the illiterate populace, through the book-learning of the boy, to the social eloquence of St. George and the literary aspirations of the dragon himself. This is a tale of reading rather than of action—a story for the grammar school rather than the playing field.

The boy spends "much of his time buried in big volumes." His book-learning helps, eventually, when his father finds a dragon just outside of town. The boy knows his dragons, having read in "natural history and fairy tales"; as his mother puts it, "He's wonderful knowing about book-beasts." And this, too, is a dragon out of books—not the fairy-tale adventures of the past, but the book-learning of the present. This is a poetic dragon, one who lolls about to make up verse and prose. He offers up a "sonnet-thing" to the young boy (the boy declines to listen). He corrects

Fig. 11. Rumpelstiltskin. From Andrew Lang, *The Blue Fairy Book*
(London: Longmans Green, 1889). Stanford University Library.

grammar. He works out a sham fight with St. George. This is a schoolmas-
terly dragon, one whose conception of violence has more to do with the
solecism than the sword:

> "Don't be *violent*, Boy," he said without looking round. "Sit down and get
> your breath, and try and remember that the noun governs the verb, and
> then perhaps you'll be good enough to tell me *who's* coming."

The real battles here are wars of eloquence: St. George with his public
oratory, and the dragon with his "ramping performance for the benefit of
the crowd." And when one of that crowd turns to St. George and asks if
he will finally dispatch the dragon, we see the real mastery of the saint—
not with the weapon, but with the word:

"'Bai't you goin' to cut 'is 'ed orf, master?" asked one of the applauding crowd....

"Well, not *to-day*, I think," replied St. George, pleasantly. "You see, that can be done at *any* time. There's no hurry at all. I think we'll all go down to the village first, and have some refreshment, and then I'll give him a good talking-to, and you'll find he'll be a very different dragon."

At that magic word *refreshment* the whole crowd formed up in procession and silently awaited the signal to start.[26]

The magic of this story lies with the magic of a word, as if that single noun could conjure people into action. And for St. George, what makes the monster socially malleable is not the deeds of a hero but the "good talking-to" of a schoolmaster.

In the end, this is a tale of speeches and performances, of books and songs. It is a story for the generation of book-learned youth—a generation whose desires were anticipated by Hans Christian Andersen when he recalls the opportunity to tell the prince he wants to go to grammar school above all else. It is a tale, too, for a generation that sees beasts not in the forests but in folios.

That generation would have found the beasts in E. Nesbit's "The Book of Beasts," a little story that appeared as part of her *Book of Dragons* of 1900. Little Lionel is taken from his nursery when he inherits the royal throne, and when he finds himself ensconced in the palace—after tea, and cake, and toast, and jam—he turns to his old nurse: "I think I should like a book." He runs off to the royal library, marveling at all the books and wanting to read them all. But he should not, advises the Prime Minister. For the old king was something of a wizard, and his books were magical. So when Lionel impatiently opens "The Book of Beasts," he finds the animals miraculously come alive. The painted butterfly flies off the page. The bird of paradise flutters away. That night, surreptitiously, Lionel returns to the library to open up the book to "Dragon." And sure enough, the dragon flies away to haunt the woods. In trouble now with nurse and minister, Lionel makes a law "forbidding people to open books in schools or elsewhere." But he must disobey, and the rest of the story hinges on the other beasts—a manticore, a hippogriff—that escape, chase the dragon, and eventually (with Lionel's help) return it to its proper page within the book. In the end, Lionel asks the hippogriff where he would like to live, and he begs to be returned to his page. "I do not care for public life," he states.[27]

Tales such as Grahame's and Nesbit's reflect a growing late Victorian concern with scholarship and reading as a way of life. The mysteries of the book must not escape, for books themselves, much like forests, may stand as environs for the eerie or the exotic. The book becomes that bearer of the fairy-tale world, and each opening is like a door into the dark. How can we not see, in the image of *The Monster Book of Monsters* from the Harry Potter stories, the legacy of Nesbit's book? How can we not see, in the contests with the dragons, bits of Grahame? How can we not see, in Albus Dumbledore, a wizard of the word akin to James A. H. Murray? The legacy of fairy-tale philology lies in the ways in which we may imagine dialect and desire, personal growth and linguistic change, schoolmasters pushing students and amanuenses through untrodden forests.

For J. R. R. Tolkien, long before Middle Earth beckoned, he had cleared away the forests of philology and made its study safe for students.[28] As a young professor at Leeds University, he aspired to return to Oxford to take up the chair in Anglo-Saxon studies, and so, when he applied for the position in 1925, he characterized his time at the provincial school thus: "I began with five hesitant pioneers out of a School . . . of about sixty members." Tolkien writes that he added to the numbers of his students, augmenting medieval teaching with courses in Old and Middle English, medieval Welsh, and Icelandic. "Philology, indeed, appears to have lost for these students its connotations of terror if not of mystery."[29] Like James A. H. Murray, Tolkien imagines philologists as pioneers. And if the lexicographer had cut a trail through a forest, the professor dispelled a classroom terror.

Tolkien has long stood as something of an emblem of a fairy-tale philology. His elvish idioms of *The Lord of the Rings* recall Old Norse runes and Old English charms. His literary criticism, especially his field-defining essay of 1936, "*Beowulf*: The Monsters and the Critics," set a tone for Anglo-Saxon studies as invested in the monstrous—as if *Beowulf* had come to apotheosize fairy-tale imagination. Tolkien himself had claimed, in his essay "On Fairy Stories," that it was philology that prompted his initial forays into the field. "Of course, I do not deny, for I feel strongly, the fascination of the desire to unravel the intricately knotted and ramified history of the branches on the Tree of Tales. It is closely connected with the philologists' study of the tangled skein of Language, of which I know some small pieces."[30] The imagery recalls a range of idioms from nineteenth-century linguistics, science, and desire: the tree of language, like the tree of biological development; the "web of words" in which

James A. H. Murray found himself caught. The quest for knowledge here becomes a kind of fairy tale in miniature: a story of the Gordian knot that could only be untied by the master of the riddle; or, for that matter, the linguistic origin of Tolkien's treelike Ents in *The Lord of the Rings*, whose knots and branches (Latin *ramus*, "branch") can support the little Hobbits on their journey from the forest to the battlefield.

At moments such as this one, Tolkien's essay seems what it has long been taken to be: a manifesto for writers, something of a guide to the aesthetics of *The Hobbit* and *The Lord of the Rings*. But it is more. "On Fairy Stories" appears less a program for a writer than a record of a reader. It reviews the canons and the history of the fairy tale, from Perrault and the Grimms through Tolkien's own time. It quarrels with the *Oxford English Dictionary*'s definition of *fairy tale* itself, as Tolkien shows how the editors misquoted one of their key medieval sources (a line from the poetry of John Gower) and how their conception of the fairies offers a far too narrow literary history for any reader of the tales.

But Tolkien's essay, too, speaks to the arc of fairy-tale philology that I have sought to trace here: the concern with words themselves as having marvelous histories of their own; the need for a literate engagement with the world; the sense that language itself has something of a childhood; and the image of the scholar as a kind of wizard.

One of the most revealing moments in the essay is Tolkien's encounter with the Grimms' tale "The Juniper Tree."

> For one thing, they [i.e., fairy stories] are now *old*, and antiquity has an appeal in itself. The beauty and horror of *The Juniper Tree* (*Von dem Machandelboom*), with its exquisite and tragic beginning, the abominable cannibal stew, the gruesome bones, the gay and vengeful bird-spirit coming out of a mist that rose from the tree, has remained with me since childhood; and yet always the chief flavour of that tale lingering in the memory was not beauty or horror, but distance and a great abyss of time, not measurable even by *twe tusend Johr*.[31]

I find this a remarkable account, for it is less a survey of the tale itself than of its impact on the young Tolkien. It returns him to his own childhood (much as the tales themselves, as I noted earlier, returned the Grimms' informants to theirs). It recalls what anyone who returns to the original Grimms after their modern saccharinization sees: the deep horror in the tales, the gruesomeness, the tragedy, the dark beliefs and practices. Here is a story about a boy who is beheaded by his stepmother—who then tries to cover up her mishap and pass off responsibility to his sister. The stepmother cuts up the boy's body and feeds it to the father, and the sister buries the bones by the tree. A little bird sitting in the juniper tree sings out a poem announcing the deed, and finally—after the bird picks up a range of objects, each of which will have an impact on the story and its characters—the stepmother is killed, the boy comes back to life, and the old family of father, son, and daughter reunites for dinner.

What Tolkien clearly found so fascinating in the story is not just the terror but the tree, a tree of magical and almost animated power: "The branches separated and came together again as though they were clapping their hands in joy."[32] How can we not see the great ents embodied here? How can we not see, too, the great tree Yggdrasil of Old Norse mythology—the tree that spans the range from hell to Middle Earth, the tree that Tolkien himself illustrated in a line drawing in a textbook by his colleague E. V. Gordon, *An Introduction to Old Norse*?[33] How can we not recall the image of the Tree of Tales itself, where history is "ramified," where life branches off?

What Tolkien must also have found fascinating in this story is its dialect. "The Juniper Tree" is one of the two tales the Grimms published in the Pomeranian dialect (the other one, as I have already discussed, was "The Fisherman and His Wife"). Tolkien quotes from the German in his brief account and clearly knows that the phrase "twe tusend Johr" is not standard, High German for "two thousand years" (in which it would be "zwei tausend Jahre"). The status of "The Juniper Tree" as a dialect tale makes this a perfect subject for the philologist, especially one with the kind of dialect imagination of a Tolkien, whose own writings would develop words and phrases, images and idioms that drew on the old dialects of Saxon, Norse, and Celtic speakers. Antiquity, as Tolkien put it, has an appeal in itself, and part of that appeal lies in the recognition that the histories of words are like a great tree; the job of the tale-teller, like that of the lexicographer, is to go back to deep roots buried in the past and, in the process, tell a story rich with wonder and delight.

If Tolkien looks back two millennia, to the origins of the vernaculars and to the deep past of an arboreal imagination, he also looks ahead to more modern and familiar figures of dark practices. In *Harry Potter*'s Snape, we may see something of the legacy of these desires: fascination with the dark arts not so much of magic, but of literature. Tolkien's claims for the fairy story are aesthetic: they assess the beauty and the power of a tale; they call attention to the ways in which most fairy stories teach

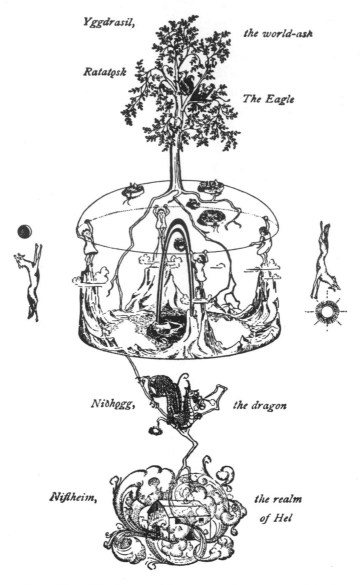

Fig. 12. The world ash tree and the cosmography of Norse mythology.
Attributed to J. R. R. Tolkien. E. V. Gordon, *An Introduction to
Old Norse*, 2nd ed. (Oxford: Oxford University Press, 1957), p. 197.
By permission of Oxford University Press.

not so much moral lessons, but appreciations of aesthetic value (clearly, that's what he had gotten from "The Juniper Tree"). Such are Snape's claims for his potions. What he announces, on the first day of his class, to the young wizards at Hogwarts is nothing less than a program of aesthetic appreciation: "I don't expect you will really understand the beauty of the softly simmering cauldron with its shimmering fumes, the delicate power of liquids that creep through human veins, bewitching the mind, ensnaring the senses. . . . I can teach you how to bottle fame, brew glory, even stopper death."[34] Snape's goal is an instruction in the arts of beauty and the recognition that the true powers behind public fame and fortune are the wizards. In later Harry Potter books, we will see Snape bottling his own fame as he pores over the Pensieve, pulling skeins of thought out of his mind much as Tolkien and his peers would unravel the tangled skeins of language. As we read on in *Harry Potter*, we may see, too, items of fairy-tale philology brought back to vivid life: the Whomping Willow as a Tolkien-like Tree of Tales; the dragons bearing legacies of Grahame and Nesbit; the forest creatures greeting Harry like inhabitants of some Grimm zoo; the strangely knowing birds that come out of "The Juniper Tree" or "The Nightingale." And in Dumbledore himself, we see a figure redolent of Murray and, indeed, of the *Oxford English Dictionary* itself— for there, the word appears as an old dialect term for a bumblebee. In one of Tolkien's poems, "Errantry," a "merry passenger . . . battled with the Dumbledores."[35]

The Harry Potter books have come under close criticism for their seemingly clichéd tone and their all too common turns and tropes. And yet it is precisely in these commonalities that I find the straw of old philologists, spun into new gold, not just by the author, but by all her characters. And behind it all, as behind "Rumpelstiltskin," lies a question of the name and origin: who am I?

# *Theaters of Girlhood*

DOMESTICITY, DESIRE, AND
PERFORMANCE IN FEMALE FICTION

At the close of *Harry Potter and the Prisoner of Azkaban*, Sirius Black mounts Harry's hippogriff to fly away to freedom. Escaped from prison, captured, misunderstood, and eventually rescued and revealed, Black spends the book largely as the beneficiary of Hermione's skill. She is the one, as in all the Harry Potter stories, who figures things out, who uses ingenuity and knowledge to crack codes or subvert subjection. And yet, at the novel's close, when Black wheels the hippogriff, Buckbeak, around to face the open sky, he turns to Harry and says: "We'll see each other again. You are—truly your father's son, Harry."[1] Viewers of the movie version of this book, however, will hear something very different at this moment. There, Black turns to Hermione, not Harry, and affirms: "You really are the cleverest witch of your age."

The movie of *The Prisoner of Azkaban* transforms a moment of male bonding into one of female affirmation. It displaces Black's avowal of paternal influence—you are your father's son—into a benediction of female accomplishment. In this revision, the movie takes as its telos the authority of girlhood. It makes Hermione the real performer of the story: the stage manager of magic; the director of its time shifts, costume, and control. The film becomes a girls' film, one in which the female audience can find their affirmation. Yet the book remains, in spite of Hermione's obvious centrality, a story about men and boys: about Harry's search for his relationship to his dead father; about his need to find surrogates in Black, or Dumbledore.

But by refiguring the final focus of the story from the boy to the girl, the movie also affirms one of the controlling themes of female fiction, almost from its origin: that girls are always on the stage; that being female is a show; that there is always, as the girl grows up, a tension between staging one's behavior for the delectation of others and finding inner virtue in devotion to the family or to learning. Throughout the Harry Potter tales, Hermione emerges as the beneficiary of three centuries of girls'-book identity. At times the plucky youth, at times the serious student, at times the foolish lover, at times the tomboy, at times the blossoming maiden—taken together, all these aspects of her personality make her the heir to everyone from Jenny Peace in Sarah Fielding's *The Governess*, to Jo in Alcott's *Little Women*, to Alice in Carroll's *Wonderland*, to all the girl guides, or "new women," or adventuresome or studious females who fill the range of popular writing well into the later twentieth century. Hermione owes as much to *The Girl's Own Paper* as to Girton College, as much to Goody Two-Shoes as to Nancy Drew.

Scholars of children's literature have traced this inheritance in great detail.[2] They have identified the ways in which writers have shaped the social vision of female identity. They have explored the ways in which the female body takes on a unique identity in schoolroom stories and in fairy tales. They have detailed the audiences for the popular journals and magazines that provided entertainment for upper-, middle-, and working-class young women from the mid-nineteenth century on. They have shown, too, how books originally not written for younger readers became, in their abridged versions, fodder for the girl's imagination. Samuel Richardson's *Pamela*, for example, came out in a cut-down, children's version in 1756. Much like the chapbooks of Defoe's *Robinson Crusoe*, the abridgments of *Pamela* created narratives of social fantasy and moral guidance for a gendered generation.

From this large legacy of literature and scholarship, I want to focus on the problem of performance. Girls always seem to be put up on stages. How they look and sound is, in a way, far more important than how boys do. True, I have made much of the boy's performing life: the cutting up at school, the diction and the dress of adventure, the care for the body that marks the counsel of advisers from Chesterfield to Baden-Powell. But there is something different about girls and girlhood. There seems to be, more pointedly than with boys, a tension between what I would call (appropriating the vocabulary of the art historian Michael Fried) absorption and theatricality.[3] Absorption, in this case, means how someone ignores the audience. Reading alone, nursing a child, caring for a parent, holding a lover's hand—all these, and many other kinds of actions, may be thought of as absorptive. In pictorial representations of such actions, we do not see faces meeting our gaze; eyes are turned down rather than out. By contrast, theatricality means how someone plays to the viewer. Standing in full-face portrait, enacting great rhetorical gestures, playing out the battle scenes of history or the histrionics of the theater itself—these are activities far from absorption.

I use this pair of terms as axes for the study of girls' books. For in these terms lie the questions that inhere in many female fictions. Should the girl pursue a life in public or in private? Should she place desire over duty? How can she avoid the temptations of applause to find true fulfillment in good works or small devotions? At different moments in the history of literature for young women, there may be emphases on one side or the other. At different moments, too, the canon of approved or valued books and authors may be set according to those emphases. What has emerged today as something of that historical canon—Fielding, Alcott, Burnett, L. M. Montgomery—may be approached as a story, too, not only of girls' books but of female authorship itself. What does it mean to be a woman writer? Does it mean, primarily, to be an author for a female readership? And is the aspiration to be a writer or an artist a capitulation to theatricality—a setting oneself up on stages keyed to public view and publication? Such questions will not go away. Hermione in *Harry Potter* prods us into asking them. So, too, does E. B. White, and I conclude this chapter with a view of *Charlotte's Web* and of its spider heroine as a figure who, like many of the girls I read here, finds herself both absorbed in writing and set up to stage the triumphs of her all too piggish friend.

Girls lived in social history, but they also lived in fairy tale and fable. In the Aesopica, girls often appear as objects of sexual desire or derision. There are the fables of parents and daughters, all of them with the smoke of illicit sexuality about them. In one, a father falls in love with his own daughter (Perry 379).[4] In another, a father has two children, an ugly girl and a handsome boy (Perry 499). The girl, tired of her brother's preening, falsely accuses him of "touching something that was only for women." And there is the fable of the mother and her daughter in which the girl, told she is "senseless" by the mother, finds a farmer having sex with one of his donkeys (Perry 386). Asked what he is doing, he replies, "I'm trying to put some sense into her." Well, she says, maybe you could put some sense into me? What follows, of course, is farcical. There are few, if any, young women in Aesop who develop moral virtue or the social prowess of their male peers. Boys learn lessons in the fables; girls seem to learn nothing.

Such stories, and their later transformations, mark the girl as either dangerous or in danger: sexually predatory, or sexually vulnerable. The body of the girl becomes the subject of the fable and the fairy tale. In the Grimm brothers' *Märchen*, girls are often marked as creatures physically different from the boys, and they have a different relationship to nature and society than males. "Little Red Riding Hood" is very much a story of the girl's vulnerable body—indeed, in its early, pre-Grimm versions, it reveals itself to be a tale about hygiene and boundaries. Folklorists have recovered one form of the tale in which the girl gets into bed with a were-wolf, who has already killed the grandmother. The girl complains that she has to "go badly," and the werewolf impatiently replies, "Do it in bed, my child!" Refusing to soil the bed, the girl gets to go outside, but only with a rope tied to her leg. Nonetheless, she escapes. In this version, basic sanitary needs give rise to social decorum. What distinguishes the girl from the beast is the recognition that you don't shit in the bed. And in the later transformations of "Red Riding Hood," we see bodily boundaries crossed: the wolf's eating of the grandmother; the woodsman's cutting open of the wolf; Red Riding Hood's own possible association with menstrual blood. This is a story rich with innuendo, with the fears of violation and the careful balancing of decorum and desire.[5]

Fairy-tale girls are often in the forest, and they differ from the boys. Boys are explorers, woodcutters, path-makers, or controllers. Girls remain lost or threatened. One great exception, of course, is Gretel, who masterminds her and her brother's salvation after the birds eat up Hansel's bread-crumb pathway and the witch locks him up. Gretel takes the initiative to close the oven door on the witch and help the two of them cross the river on a duck's back. But even here, Gretel imagines, in a moment of despondency, a death much like Red Riding Hood's: "If only the wild beasts had eaten us in the forest," she says to Hansel, "then we could have at least died together!"[6]

It is as if the girl's body is itself a kind of forest for the fairy-tale imagination: something dark and inexplicable, something in need of management, of clearing, of cleansing. Woodsmen come in and cut down trees. Who clears away the darkness of the female form? It may be little wonder that, centuries after myths and fairy tales had shaped girls' origins, Sigmund Freud could still exclaim in exasperation, "We know less about the sexual life of little girls than of boys. We need not feel ashamed of this distinction. After all, the sexual life of adult women is a 'dark continent' for psychology."[7] Freud synthesizes here the legacies of exploration and mythology. He returns us to the nineteenth-century fantasies of boyhood conquest: the encounters of H. Rider Haggard's Africa and the imagery of Sheba's Breasts. But he returns us, too, to the world of the Grimms and their folk forebears: to the transformation of the sexual life of little girls into figure and fantasy.

Historians of the family have done much since Freud to reveal pre-adult female sexual and social life. Much recent research has shown that girls had greater status in the family than was previously imagined. In Greece and Rome, they could receive an education. In medieval and Renaissance Europe, they could come into land and wealth. The very idea of "girlhood" in pre-modern and early modern Europe is a questionable one, as daughters often would be married by their middle teens and be mothers by their twenties. Only in the mid-eighteenth century did girls begin to go away to school and have, at least in literature, a life apart from parents or their future husbands. By the nineteenth century, the girl's social status and her body, too, were changing.[8] Social historians record a lowering of the age of onset of menstruation, most likely due to better food and hygiene. By contrast, the age of marriage was rising (by the beginning of the twentieth century, it was twenty-five in Britain).[9] Young women were going to school, entering the workforce, traveling, reading, and writing. They were, as almost everyone had recognized by the end of the Victorian age, different beings from their earlier counterparts.

Such changes led to a new social category of girlhood itself. While the word *girl* had been used in English since the Middle Ages, and while distinctions had long been made among the various stages of female development, the idea of girlhood as a special category of identity is something that emerges in the mid-Victorian period (the *Oxford English Dictionary* lists 1785 for the first appearance of "girlhood," and the word does not appear again until 1831). Sally Mitchell, in her study of the New Girl in late nineteenth- and early twentieth-century Britain, finds a shift in categories of advice books: "Advice books that in the 1860s had titles such as *Hints on Self Help: A Book for Young Women* (Jessie Boucherett, 1863) were—though directed to much the same group of readers—more likely two decades later to use the new term: *English Girls: Their Place and Power* (Isabel Reany, 1879), *What Girls Can Do* (Phillis Browne, 1880), or *What to Do with our Girls* (Arthur Talbot Vanderbilt, 1884)."[10] I do agree with Mitchell that the terms *girl* and *girlhood* signify as much a state of mind as a "chronological or legal concept," but I would place their origins somewhat earlier than she claims and in a different venue. It seems to me that the first work of literature (not simply of advice) designed for readers in their girlhood was Mary Cowden Clarke's *The Girlhood of Shakespeare's Heroines*, first published in 1851 and 1852 and frequently reprinted throughout the nineteenth and early twentieth centuries.[11]

Clarke, a Shakespearean of note in her own day and the wife of a literary scholar, set out to offer both the "juvenile" and the "older reader" prequels, as it were, to Shakespeare's plays. Tracing the early (and, of course, completely imagined) lives of figures such as Rosalind, Ophelia, Juliet, and a dozen other female characters, Clarke sought to explain their motives and their actions in the plays as the culmination of their growth. In the process, she wrote what really are a series of Victorian novellas, synthesizing the taste for adventure and advice that had governed young people's literature for decades. Her heroines take on, at times, a life apart from Shakespeare's. Some of them suffer at the hands of fathers or friends; some develop imaginative lives of their own.

And yet, because her subjects are dramatic characters, Clarke scripts the girls' lives as dramatic. Her heroines constantly need to find a middle way between the demands of private life and the temptations of public life. *The Girlhood of Shakespeare's Heroines* offers essays in absorption and theatricality. In the process, Clarke's novellas show a vision of mid-Victorian girlhood as a place of performance and control.

Perhaps the most effectively performative of these tales is "Ophelia: The Rose of Elsinore." It opens with a *tableau vivant*—a careful description of Ophelia's nursery, seen through the newborn's eyes, as if it were a stage set.

> The babe lay on the nurse's knee. Could any impression have been received through those wide-stretched eyes, that stared as wonderingly as if they were in fact beholding amazed the new existence upon which they had so lately opened, the child would have seen that it lay in a spacious apartment, furnished with all the tokens of wealth and magnificence, which those ruder ages could command. There were thick hangings of costly stuff to exclude the keen outer air and chill mists of that north climate. The furniture of the room was constructed of the rarer kind of woods, and fashioned with the utmost skill and taste in design then attained. The dogs that sustained the fir clumps blazing on the hearth, were of classical form and device; and the andirons on either side, were of a no less precious material than silver. (p. 161)

The infant Ophelia is constantly looking, constantly shifting her eyes around to take in the scenery of court life. It is in her nature to observe. "She was none of those fretful children, who, the very first thing they uniformly do upon waking up from sleep, is to roar; on the contrary, she lay silent and still for a moment or two, then raising herself softly against the side of the cot, rubbed her eyes, and looked over. It was a strange scene she beheld" (pp. 167–68). She is, in youth, a creature of absorption, taking in the world in all its detail, ensconced in a bassinet, or on a knee, or in adult arms. As she ages, she becomes a listener as well as a looker. Her foster sister, Jutha, tells her "quaint tales, and sing[s] her old ballads" (p. 175). Jutha recounts a "strange legend of a princess who was shut up by the king her father in a high strong tower," and another story of a "wicked steward" who betrayed his king (p. 177). Ophelia is enraptured. And it goes on. She sees the horrible "idiot-boy" Ulf, whose hideousness shows more horribly than ever in her eyes. He seems to her some fiendlike creature as he crouches there, "drawing the flaps of his ears over till the tops reach beneath his chin; pulling his nether lip down, and turning it inside out, till it lies stretched, and spread, displaying his cankered gums and his yellow and black teeth,—some flat, like tombstones,—some long, narrow, and sharp, like the fangs of a dog" (p. 191).

Ulf comes off here less as some creature out of fairy tale than as a kind of kiddie Caliban, a monster shaped according to costume and performance practices of mid-Victorian Shakespeareana. At the story's close, when Ophelia sickens with a fever, she imagines other stagy horrors: dreams of the dead king Hamlet; ghostly apparitions of her now-dead foster sister Jutha; other ethereal beings. "Then I saw one approach, whose face I could not see, and whose figure I knew not. She was clothed in white, all hung about with weeds and wild flowers; and from among them stuck ends of straw, that the shadowy hands seemed to pluck and spurn at" (p. 224). Is this a vision of the girl grown up, mad, spurned by Hamlet, self-drowned? "I saw her glide on, floating upon [the water's] surface; I saw her dimly, among the silver-leaved branches of the drooping willow, as they waved around and above her, up-buoyed by her spreading white garments." This may well be an odd anticipation of her own death later in the play. But as it stands here, it looks more like a distinctively Victorian vision of that death: a kind of weird blend of the Lady of Shalott and Shakespeare's own Ophelia, mediated by an almost Pre-Raphaelite pictorial sensibility (John Millais had painted his *Ophelia* in 1851, and I find its vision strikingly in tune with Clarke's verbal portrait).

Fig. 13. John Millais, *Ophelia*, 1851. © Tate, London 2007.

Strange fare, perhaps, for young girls; but Clarke's lessons are clear. Girls grow up in the eyes of others. They are always on the stage. In the recesses of home or forest may lurk creatures who scare or threaten. But far scarier are the imaginations of the child. Ophelia's feverish hallucinations are the stuff of art and drama: visions shaped by the aesthetics of Clarke's day, awful futures for the girl who would grow up to choose the wrong man and the wrong life. And madness, whether it be Hamlet's or Ophelia's, is a histrionic thing.

There is much in Clarke's Ophelia that is classically Victorian. This blend of Pre-Raphaelite pictorialism and Tennysonian mythmaking had its impact throughout nineteenth-century literature—perhaps nowhere in children's books as fully articulated as in L. M. Montgomery's *Anne of Green Gables*.[12] Though first published in 1908, the book really stands as testimony to earlier literary history. It ripples with allusions to Shakespeare and Tennyson, Walter Scott and the Romantics. And it is rife, too, with scenes of theatrical performance. Anne always seems the object of others' eyes, always the focus of attention, whether it be on the first day of her new school or on the rooftop, walking along on a dare. At one point, she even has the idea to act out part of Tennyson's *Lancelot and Elaine*, whose dramaturgy recalls the heated visions of Clarke's Ophelia and their pictorial afterlife. Her idea is to find a little boat (called a flat) and lay the figure of the dead Elaine in it.

> The black shawl having been procured, Anne spread it over the flat and then lay down on the bottom, with closed eyes and hands folded over her breast.
>
> "Oh, she does look really dead," whispered Ruby Gillis nervously, watching the still, white little face under the flickering shadows of the birches. "It makes me feel frightened, girls. Do you suppose it's really right to act like this? Mrs. Lynde says that all play-acting is abominably wicked." (p. 255)

Is all play-acting wicked? Is the girl expected to behave domestically and sincerely, rather than in public spectacle? This moment in the novel crystallizes its controlling tensions between absorption and theatricality. *Anne of Green Gables* is, in many ways, a lesson in the ways a pictorial and dramatic imagination shapes the lives of female children.

From the start, Anne is miscast. The old Prince Edward Island brother and sister, Matthew and Marilla Cuthbert, are expecting to adopt a boy from an orphanage. But the child that shows up at the station is a girl. "You don't want me," Anne cries, and she launches into nothing less than a soliloquy of self-remorse. "You don't want me because I'm not a boy? I might have expected it! Nobody ever did want me. I might have known it was all too beautiful to last. I might have known nobody really did want me. Oh, what shall I do? I'm going to burst into tears!" (p. 74). Burst into tears she does, flinging out her arms, then burying her face in her hands, then crying "stormily." The old couple, staggered by this display, are at a loss, until Marilla tells Anne that there is no need to cry. "Yes, there *is* need," replies Anne, and the reader almost hears the italics (the reader, too, may hear something of the Shakespearean in Anne's retort: King Lear's "O, reason not the need"; 2.4.263). "Oh," Anne concludes her speech, "this is the most *tragical* thing that has ever happened to me!" (p. 76).

Anne enters the Cuthberts' absorptive, untheatrical, provincial house like a displaced actress. She is all exclamation points and italics, all flailing body, a pint-sized tragedian playing before an audience of rubes. And, as if to remind us that she really is imagining herself in a Shakespearean world, she asks the couple to call her "Cordelia." Part disregarded child, part Lear himself, Anne answers as a character, claiming that her own name, Anne Shirley, is too "unromantic." Marilla replies, "Anne is a real good plain sensible name." In this exchange, we see what we will see

Fig. 14. "They looked at her." From L. M. Montgomery,
*Anne of Green Gables* (Boston: L. C. Page, 1908).

throughout the novel: the theatrical impulses of the girl shut down by
claims for good, plain, sensible behavior. It is as if Anne had gotten a little too much Mary Cowden Clarke into her, as if she imagined herself as
living in the girlhood of Shakespeare's heroines.

Scenes much like this one fill the novel. Anne measures herself against
Shakespearean women. "Well, I don't know," she replies at one point. "I
read in a book once that a rose by any other name would smell as sweet"
(p. 89). Is Anne now Juliet? Hamlet's "sweets to the sweet" shows up in a
conversation (p. 200). And there are other figures out of literature against
whom Anne assesses her experience: Tennyson's Lady of Shalott, Scott's
Lady of the Lake, Robert Browning's Pippa. Anne's is a costumed world—

Fig. 15. "She balanced herself uprightly." From L. M. Montgomery, *Anne of Green Gables* (Boston: L. C. Page, 1908).

as when, on the first day of Sunday school, she grudgingly accepts the "good, sensible, serviceable" gingham dresses that Marilla makes for her. "I did hope," Anne notes, "there would be a white one with puffed sleeves" (p. 125). And so, secretly, on the way to church, she decks out her plain straw hat with a "heavy wreath" of flowers found upon the way: "a golden frenzy of wind-stirred butter-cups and a glory of wild roses" (p. 126). Is this Ophelia, again, strewing flowers in her hair? Walking down the aisle in Sunday school, Anne finds herself the object of derision, and the illustration to the novel's first edition captures this theatricalized moment perfectly. There is Anne, center stage, in her flowered hat, and there the audience of other girls, hooting and whispering at her performance.

And later in the novel, when the girls are playing games of dare, Anne steps onto a roof to walk along the ridgepole line. "Anne climbed the ladder amid breathless silence, gained the ridge-pole, balanced herself uprightly on that precarious footing, and started to walk along it, dizzily conscious that she was uncomfortably high up in the world and that walking ridge-poles was not a thing in which your imagination helped you out much" (pp. 220–22). She falls and nearly breaks her neck, but wrestles herself up with only a bad ankle. Like so many moments in the novel, this is not just a story of theatrical performance, but a warning against pride. Don't get too high up in the world, the passage seems to say, for your imagination cannot help you there. But still, for all those who would wish her to fall down, we wish her to stay up. Performance tempts, whether it be the high-roof act of an imaginative girl or the virtuoso writing of a woman novelist. Such scenes reflect on Montgomery's own lessons to female readers: that there is a place for the female imagination, that artistry is not merely artifice, but a gift for the drama and the dare.

In the first edition of the novel, this scene (like many of the others I have noted here) comes with a picture. We see Anne poised like a gymnast on the roof ridge, much as we will see her, later in the book, hanging on for dear life to a bridge piling. Her attempt to portray Tennyson's Elaine in her boat has gone awry, and she finds herself trapped in the river. Anne needs a rescuer, and this picture shows us one.

These are *tableaux vivants*, less illustrations of the action of the novel than images from the dramatic impulses behind it. It is no accident that *Anne of Green Gables* soon became one of the most theatricalized of children's books.[13] Plays, films, adaptations, illustrations—all have come together to enhance, in the book's afterlife, its underlying fascination with the theater of girlhood. And it is no accident, as well, that L. M. Montgomery's own home has become something of a site of pilgrimage for generations of the novel's readers. Green Gables is a shrine, and the surrounding acreage has been transformed into a public Eden. One of the earliest reviews of the novel even makes the point: "No better advertisement of the charm of its landscape could be devised than the admirable descriptions of its sylvan glories which lend decorative relief to the narrative. . . . [Montgomery] makes us fall in love with the surroundings."[14] Even Montgomery herself drew on these visions of performance and scenery. Her own photographs, though taken in the first decades of the twentieth century, look back in their feel and form to Lewis Carroll and Julia Margaret Cameron, with their programmatic staginess, their costumes

Fig. 16. John Water-
house, *The Lady of
Shalott*, 1888. © Tate,
London 2007.

Fig. 17. "He pulled close
to the pile." From L. M.
Montgomery, *Anne of
Green Gable*s (Boston:
L. C. Page, 1908).

and personae, and their sentimental placement of the child in the land-scape. Montgomery herself posed as a sea nymph in a 1904 photo taken by her friend Nora Lefurgey, and here, too, we may see the visual conventions of half a century before: the arc of the rocks, the crashing sea, the bend of her body.[15]

What strikes me in this constellation of verbal and pictorial imagery is a sense that, even in the twentieth century, the conventions of the girl's imagination remain those of mid-Victorian sentimentality. Tennyson, Scott, the Pre-Raphaelites—they all provided the vocabulary for under-standing drama and desire; they all filtered the inheritance of medieval adventure and Shakespearean tragedy; and they helped foster a narra-tive form that made novels into strings of set pieces, *tableaux vivants*, into which the reader could imagine herself. If, as I have argued earlier, the boys' book made young men tell the stories of their lives as color com-mentary on the playing field or on martial exploits, telegraphed to news-papers, then the girls' book made young women see themselves as posing in the dioramas of desire.

Louisa May Alcott saw this feature, too. Throughout her life, the the-ater held her. As a child, she dreamed of becoming another Sarah Sid-dons (the most famous actress of the late eighteenth and early nineteenth centuries).[16] And she grew up not only with the aspirations of an actress, but with the awe of an audience. As the child of one of America's most visible preachers and social reformers, Alcott lived with the theatrics of the spirit. Her father, Bronson, was perhaps the most charismatic (and controversial) teacher of his day. His life vacillated between great pub-lic moments of display—as in his famous "conversations" with divinity-school students and his successful tour of Midwestern American towns—and equally great moments of despair and withdrawal. His family was audience to the pageantry of his aspirations, as well as to the farces of his failures (as when he dragged his wife and children off to Fruitlands, the agricultural commune of 1843).[17]

Outside the Alcott family, too, theater was everywhere. The moral stage had emerged, in the early nineteenth century, as the place of social reform. Plays such as *The Drunkard* of 1844 (still considered the longest-running play in American history) drove home ideals of ethical behav-ior, and Mark Twain was heard to say that nine-tenths of the American population got its morality from theaters rather than from churches.[18] And what most of those Americans would have seen—the genre that shaped both morality and spectacle—was melodrama. By the middle of the nineteenth century, this form had come to dominate the popular stage. With its exaggerated gestures, its romantic plotlines, and its portentous language, melodrama was as much maligned as loved. Dickens has Mr. Crummles in *Nicholas Nickleby* speak "in the highest style of melodrama," while Ralph Waldo Emerson, writing in 1854, could avow: "My idea of heaven is that there is no melodrama in it at all."[19]

This is as strong a statement of the old Puritan anti-theatrical inheritance as one could wish. For most people still thought of the playhouse as the place of sin. The theater and the prostitute were still indelibly associated in most minds. Some even came to see Abraham Lincoln's assassination as, in the words of one clergyman, "a warning from God about the dangers of the theater."[20] Puritan suspicion did not go away, and I find *Little Women*—with not just its own ambivalence about the theater, but its emphases on absorption in reading and its cataloguing of the books and things of cultural experience—a profoundly Puritan work.[21] Introspection and reflection, writing down one's life in a diary or journal, reading as a child—these are the hallmarks of the Puritan literary experience. *Pilgrim's Progress* provided a template for the sacral life. "Playing Pilgrims" is the title of chapter 1, and these words signal both the actions of the four March sisters and the motives of their lives. It is a Christmas without Father, and the mother and her daughters reminisce about how, when they were little, they used to "play Pilgrim's Progress." They would dress up as characters from Bunyan's novel, and Mrs. March would fashion bundles for them out of cloth and paper for their "burdens." As each of the sisters recalls what she liked the best, Mrs. March explains: "We are never too old for this, my dear, because it is a play we are playing all the time in one way or another. Our burdens are here, our road is before us, and the longing for goodness and happiness is the guide that leads us through many troubles and mistakes to the peace which is a true Celestial City" (p. 53). Life is a theater of the pilgrimage. This is a different kind of play-acting than that of Anne Shirley. Models of behavior come not from the scenes of Shakespeare or the medieval fantasies of Tennyson or Scott, but from the moral allegory of John Bunyan.

Even when the girls put on the Christmas play in chapter 2, there is the sense that theater is a passing fancy: something to grow out of, something for children. As the girls grow, books replace plays, and reading displaces performance. Thy life to mend, the book attend. So counseled *The New England Primer*, and the March girls take this lesson to heart in their own individual ways.

Jo, in particular, lives in the book. Early on, she remembers old Uncle March's library, in whose comfortable chairs she could "curl . . . herself up . . . like a regular book-worm." By contrast, Beth, we are told, "was too bashful to go to school . . . and she did her lessons at home, with her father." And Amy, cursed with a nose she does not care for, spends her leisure time drawing "whole sheets of handsome ones to console herself" (pp. 77–79). Each girl grows up defined by forms of literacy. Writing, drawing, reading, reciting—all come together to create an absorptive, rather than a theatrical, world for the family. Books mark social relations, perhaps no more terrifyingly than when Jo and Amy fight over a book.

Chapter 8 begins as Jo and Meg prepare to leave for something of a special outing. Amy asks where they are going; they refuse to tell her. Then she knows: "You're going to the theater to see the 'Seven Castles'." Amy is not invited, and she vows revenge. And this vow sticks in Jo's mind, for in spite of the "comical red imps, sparkling elves, and gorgeous princes and princesses, Jo's pleasure had a drop of bitterness in it." What would Amy do to make her sorry? When the girls return, Amy is reading, never looking up, absorbed in her book. But the next day, Jo finds out just what Amy had done: she took Jo's manuscript of her story and burned it. "You wicked, wicked girl!" Jo screams. "I can never write it again, and I'll never forgive you as long as I live" (pp. 108–10).

This episode dramatically encapsulates the tensions between books and theater governing the novel. It makes Jo pay for going to the play, takes her own book and burns it up. True, this manuscript was just "half a dozen little fairy tales," but Jo had "put her whole heart into her work, hoping to make something good enough to print" (p. 111). Thy book and heart shall never part. So counseled *The New England Primer*, too, and Alcott's words evoke the idioms of that great Puritan tradition that saw introspection, journal writing, personal anthologies, and diaries as central to the shaping of the moral self. And so the March girls continue to put their hearts into their texts. They form a private version of Charles Dickens's Pickwick Club and publish their own paper (which the novel reproduces in the typeface of the time). Later on, Dickens's *Martin Chuzzlewit* and Susan Warner's *Wide, Wide World* show up as markers of Jo's life. Soon Jo is back to writing, and she works up in the garret: "Quite absorbed in her work, Jo scribbled away till the last page was filled" (p. 177). And when there eventually comes word of Mr. March's illness, it comes by way of the telegram. Letters then go back and forth. The girls write to their mother. Amy, at Aunt March's, has such a rough time of things that she composes her "last will and testiment" (notice the mis-spelling). Notes and letters, bits of writing, pieces of signed paper—all fill the novel as we see not just a world of women readers, but a lesson for the novel's readership as well. To read *Little Women* is to be, as Jo is, "quite absorbed"—to find in its texts and "testiments" the models for a life.

How jarring, then, that at the close of the first volume of the novel, Al-cott returns to the theatrical imagery of the beginning. "So grouped the curtain falls upon Meg, Jo, Beth, and Amy. Whether it ever rises again, depends upon the reception given to the first act of the domestic drama, called 'LITTLE WOMEN'" (p. 255). It is as if, for all the claims of reading and absorption, Alcott cannot let go of her fascination with the drama. It is as if the novel's voice here is the voice not of the mature woman but of the young girl of decades before, dreaming of becoming Sarah Siddons. It is as if the novel's first part ends where Alcott's life began: in the domes-tic drama of a family that lived its life in public. And if Alcott herself had to grow up as a writer and reader, so, too, must the March girls—and so, too, must the novel's audience. Readers of *Little Women*, reared on senti-ment and melodrama, may come to expect high style and histrionics, but they must turn away (as do the March girls) from the spectacles of emo-tion to the textbooks of the heart. As Benjamin Franklin had put it, syn-thesizing the traditions of a Puritan poetics from Bunyan to Isaac Watts, "you must spread all upon Paper." This is precisely what Alcott herself sets out to do. And so, when volume 2 begins, we find the family not en-amored of the stage plays of the holiday or the theatrics of the tantrum but "quiet," with the war over and "Mr. March safely at home, busy with his books" (p. 263).

Would that we all were safely home, busy with our books. Books take us far away, but in the end they always leave us secure in our chair. From Bishop Ælfric's time until our own, books have been the keys that un-lock the imagination. They provide, as medieval and Renaissance teachers knew, the seeds of knowledge: *seminary* is a word that comes from the Latin for "seedbed." Cultivation is the art of raising children and teaching them, and compilations for instruction came to be called *florilegia*—a Latin word modeled on the Greek *anthologos*, meaning "bouquet of flowers."

Books and gardens, keys and stages, places of absorption and theatricality—all come together in Frances Hodgson Burnett's *Secret Garden*.[22] Much like *Anne of Green Gables*, this book begins with a dis-placed child: Mary Lennox, taken from India after her parents died, has been shipped off to Misselthwaite Manor in Yorkshire. Alone, sad, and underfed, Mary finds herself quarrelling with the Yorkshire Martha, maid to those at Misselthwaite. Their conversation cannot but recall, for me, Ælfric's old colloquies with his Anglo-Saxon students.

> "If I had a raven or a fox cub I could play with it," said Mary. "But I have nothing."
> Martha looked perplexed.
> "Can tha' knit?" she asked.
> "No," answered Mary.
> "Can tha' sew?"
> "No."
> "Can tha' read?"
> "Yes."
> "Then why doesn't tha' read somethin', or learn a bit o' spellin'? Tha'st old enough to be learnin' thy book a good bit now."
> "I haven't any books," said Mary. "Those I had were left in India."
> "That's a pity," said Martha. "If Mrs. Medlock'd let thee go into th' library, there's thousands o' books there." (p. 32)

As in *Little Women*, the library is the place of self-discovery. But here it is not the welcome room of Uncle March, but the closed-off purview of Mrs. Medlock (a name redolent of locked-off rooms, and gates, and hearts). And so, the place that Mary enters is not the room of a house but the abandoned garden, and the key she finds gives her access not to the words of others, but to the stylings of herself.

If Jo March gives voice to her inner life through writing, Mary inscribes her desires on the landscape. She digs up, replants, orders, organizes, and reshapes the garden, and the curling vines and flowers that eventually emerge come off as forms of letters. Mary writes on nature itself, and if the grounds of the garden stand as something of a page for Mary's implements, then the garden is, too, a stage for her performance. And yet Mary's greatest achievement lies in the resurrection of the boy, Colin, the invalid son of Misselthwaite's master. Coming upon him in the house, Mary finds a whining, sickly child. His mother, dead in childbirth, haunts the household's memories, and Colin seems to be afflicted with a host of physical disorders. Supposedly hunchbacked, he cannot leave his bed.

Mary befriends, encourages, and cajoles. She recognizes that his deformity is imaginary. She gets him out of bed, eventually having him wheeled into the newfound yet still secret garden. She gets him to act the little rajah, giving orders to the servants, gaining confidence, absorbing nature and its beauty. "They drew the chair under the plum-tree, which was snow-white with blossoms and musical with bees. It was like a king's canopy, a fairy king's. There were flowering cherry-trees near and apple-trees whose buds were pink and white, and here and there one had burst open wide. Between the blossoming branches of the canopy bits of blue sky looked down like wonderful eyes" (p. 125). Nature becomes a stage set, managed by Mary's dramaturgy, and Colin becomes a kind of noble audience. These garden scenes come off as masques of wonder, as Mary and the local boy Dickon bring Colin buds and feathers, eggshells and flowers. "It was like being taken in state round the country of a magic king and queen and shown all the mysterious riches it contained" (p. 125). Colin soon takes over the garden, as if he were royalty itself. "This is my garden," he announces to the gamekeeper Ben Weatherstaff (p. 131), and in his affirmation of his ownership, Colin rises out of his wheelchair.

> Colin was standing upright—upright—as straight as an arrow and looking strangely tall—his head thrown back and his strange eyes flashing lightning.
> "Look at me!" he flung up at Ben Weatherstaff. "Just look at me—you! Just look at me!" (p. 130)

This is as wildly theatrical a moment as any in the literatures of childhood: the boy standing up, his prowess signaled by Burnett's rhetorical repetitions and interruptions. Look at me, he cries, three times (much as, half a century later, Dr. Seuss's Cat in the Hat will cry, at a moment of juggling theatrics, "Look at me, look at me, look at me now!").

Mary is the director of this drama. She prods Colin into action, gives him cues for his lines, and pulls away the curtains of self-pity to reveal the real boy. Colin gains in confidence, takes on new roles. "When he held up his head and fixed his strange eyes on you it seemed as if you believed him almost in spite of yourself though he was only ten years old—going on eleven. At this moment he was especially convincing because he suddenly felt the fascination of actually making a sort of speech like a grown-up person" (p. 139). He plans a set of scientific experiments, but also considers the garden as a place of magic. He takes on different personae: at one point, he speaks "in a High Priest tone" (p. 141); at another, he plays rajah to his country court (p. 142). Each visit to the garden is a "ceremony" (p. 149), and the theater of the young boy's growth soon shapes his confrontation with the memory of his mother. Wandering among the many rooms of Misselthwaite Manor, Mary and Colin come upon the portrait room, filled with pictures of Colin's ancestors. When Mary returns to Colin's room, she finds it changed. There was a picture over the mantel, and she finally sees what it is: "She could look at it because the curtain had been drawn aside" (p. 155). This is the picture of his mother, a picture he finally can stand to look at. The curtains of illness and memory have been cast aside; the old role of the invalid has been abandoned. And finally, when Colin's father returns to the manor, he is dumbstruck at the young man his sick boy has become. There is the father, at the garden of his dead wife's desire, and there comes the son: "The feet ran faster and faster—they were nearing the garden door—there was quick strong young breathing and a wild outbreak of laughing shouts which could not be contained—and the door in the wall was flung wide open, the sheet of ivy swinging back, and a boy burst through it at full speed" (p. 171). Just as the fabric curtain had been pulled away to reveal Colin's mother, so the ivy curtain swings back, and the new Colin makes his dramatic entrance.

There is a powerful theatricality to Burnett's *Secret Garden*, but it lies in the growth of a boy, not in the showing off of girlhood. Mary stands as a figure of the theater, not because she is the actress, but because she is the stage director. And in this role, she offers another vision of the female author for the female reader. The literary fictions I have explored here all figure forth ideals of a creative life. The girl may grow up as Jo March, absorbed and writing, chronicling the stories of her family, putting away the old hunger for the stage in favor of the pleasures of the book. She may, by contrast, grow into Anne Shirley, learning to master her theatrical impulses, bringing a bit of floral drama to the otherwise dull, simple lives of her adoptive family. Or she may grow up into Mary Lennox, a stage manager of human growth, playwright and director of men.

There is, as well, a powerful absorptive quality to Burnett's novel. For it is in the very image of the garden that the book emerges. Florilegia, anthologies—these are not simply my own scholarly associations. Nineteenth-century writers for children had long thought of books as gardens. Robert Louis Stevenson published *A Child's Garden of Verses* in 1885, and to read through this assembly is to pick and choose among the flowers of its stanzas. Birds and beasts, haylofts and farmsteads fill these poems. There is the "Land of Story Books," and there are "Garden Days," "Nest Eggs," and "Flowers." Stevenson's book stands as something of a secret garden of the child's poetic fancy. Reading and writing verse become forms of cultivation. The gardener in the poem of that title is as much verse-maker as planter; his rows of plants are like the lines of words. "And when he puts his tools away, / He locks the door and takes the key." Stevenson closes this book with a poem "To Any Reader," inviting the child to look "through the windows of this book" to see another child, playing in another garden.[23]

Gardens are spaces of both theater and repose in children's literature, and Kenneth Grahame picked up on this imagery in the preface to his *Cambridge Book of Poetry for Children* of 1915.

> In compiling a selection of Poetry for Children, a conscientious Editor is bound to find himself confronted with limitations so numerous as to be almost disheartening. For he has to remember that his task is, not to provide simple examples of the whole range of English poetry, but to set up a wicket-gate giving attractive admission to that wide domain, with its woodland glades, its pasture lands arable, its walled and scented gardens here and there, and so too its sunlit, and sometimes misty, mountain-tops— all to be more fully explored later by those who are tempted on by the first glimpse.[24]

Much like the forest of the fairy tale, the garden is a space that defines boys and girls as different. Each one enters this place of the imagination and shapes himself or herself uniquely. The scented gardens and the misty mountaintops become the wide domain of literature.

And so does the farm. For Dorothy in L. Frank Baum's *Wonderful Wizard of Oz*, the farm is an empty stage.[25] "Not a tree nor a house broke the broad sweep of flat country that reached the edge of the sky in all directions" (p. 2). When the cyclone comes and lifts Dorothy off to Oz, she lands in a place shaped not by agriculture but by theater. The Munchkins are costumed players, and when they greet her, Dorothy comes off as a kind of bad-dream player who has forgotten her lines. And when the travelers arrive at the Emerald City, they find the Great Oz dressed up as nothing less than a circus entrepreneur—indeed, by the time of *The Patchwork Girl of Oz* of 1913, the wizard is explicitly modeled on P. T. Barnum.[26]

The inherent theatricality of *Oz* gave it a stage and screen life almost as soon as the book appeared. Stage musicals and silent films proliferated in the first three decades of the twentieth century, culminating, of course, in the great 1939 MGM film.[27] As Salman Rushdie recognizes in his evocative study of that movie, the MGM screenwriters and directors brought out the spectacle behind the book and its theatrical tradition. At the very moment when Dorothy is swept off in her little house by the cyclone, she sees characters float by her window—now a kind of "cinema-screen" in which, frame by frame, she sees the black-and-white figures of her Kansas life flit by. In the books, as Rushdie points out, "there is no question that Oz is real." In the film, there is no question that it is but a space of the imagination: another screen on which to project fears and fantasies, desires and despairs.[28]

*Oz*, much like *Anne of Green Gables*, opens with a little girl displaced into a family not her own. There is the pet dog, Toto, who in the book makes Dorothy laugh and saves her "from growing as gray as her other surroundings." Of course, Toto has morphed, in the 1939 film, into a threatened beloved, subject to the threats of Agnes Gulch. This constellation of images and anxieties governs the opening of another tale of girlhood theatrics. For at the start of E. B. White's *Charlotte's Web*, the farmer, Mr. Arable, is out to kill the runt of the pig's litter.[29] His daughter Fern pleads with him, saves the little piglet, christens him Wilbur, and nurtures him into growth. Fern's very name evokes the forest and the garden: the wild plant that can be cultivated, the ground cover that becomes, in human hands, an ornamental (Dorothy Gale's last name, too, evokes the phenomenon that will sweep her away to Oz). How arable (recall the "arable" of Grahame here) is her imaginative landscape? What takes root and grows in her little pasture?

Fern is not the heroine of *Charlotte's Web*. Charlotte the spider brings together all the strains of female fiction I have traced here: the young girl as author and performer; as stage manager of others; as theatrical, creative presence in a world of dullness. Like Anne Shirley, Charlotte is something of an actress. "Greetings and salutations," she announces to the pig. "It's just my fancy way of saying hello or good morning" (p. 35). Fancy, yes, but a bit theatrical as well. Charlotte displays her artistry in her great web. For, like all women of the literary imagination—from Homer's Penelope on—Charlotte is a weaver, and her web weaves words designed to catch the eyes of others (is it significant that the farm's owner is Homer L. Zuckerman?). "Some Pig," she weaves in her web, in a ruse to convince the Arables not to slaughter Wilbur. And later on, as she weaves again, we see her as artist of the world and word: "Far into the night, while the other creatures slept, Charlotte worked on her web. First she ripped out a few of the orb lines near the center. She left the radial lines alone, as they were needed for support. As she worked, her eight legs were a great help to her. So were her teeth. She loved to weave and she was an expert at it" (p. 92). She plans to write the word "terrific" in her web, and she "got so interested in her work, she began to talk to herself, as though to cheer herself on" (p. 94). This is a moment of literary absorption, a scene of creativity akin to that of Jo March writing in her garret (like Jo, too, Charlotte writes in the upper corners of her building).

But writing single words will not suffice. One night, as Wilbur lies ready for sleep, he asks her, "Tell me a story!" (p. 101). And that's just what Charlotte does, telling a tale about a cousin spider who catches fish in her web. Another story, calls out Wilbur, and she obliges. And now, "sing something," he asks. And so she sings a lullaby.

> Sleep, sleep, my love, my only,
> Deep, deep, in the dung and the dark;
> Be not afraid and be not lonely!
> This is the hour when frogs and thrushes
> Praise the world from the woods and the rushes.
> Rest from care, my one and only,
> Deep in the dung and the dark!

Like the great lullabies of past traditions—the medieval songs, the Mother Goose rhymes, Isaac Watts—Charlotte's song iterates us into dreams. Be not afraid and be not lonely. How like Watts's "Cradle Hymn" this is: a sublime moment of peace with creation.

Charlotte embodies female creativity. As heir to the girls who teach and write, who sing and show—Jenny Peace, Anne Shirley, Jo March, Mary Lennox—she reshapes the natural world into comforting artifice. But like Mary Lennox in particular, she puts her man on stage. For, much as Mary would save Colin from a death-in-life of bedridden invalidism, Charlotte saves Wilbur from slaughter. She makes him famous, gets him on the stage at the county fair. "Zuckerman's famous pig," reads the sign above him. And famous he is, garnering a special prize. "The fame of this unique animal," says the speaker at the fair, "has spread to the far corners of the earth" (p. 157). Charlotte has made him famous, and as the Zuckermans and Arables climb into the award ring, the crowd cheers, and "a photographer took Wilbur's picture." The narrative continues: "A great feeling of happiness swept over the Zuckermans and the Arables. This was the greatest moment in Mr. Zuckerman's life. It is deeply satisfying to win a prize in front of a lot of people" (p. 160). It always is, and throughout children's literature, boys and girls win their prizes in the face of obstacles and envy. Running the race, winning the spelling bee, claiming the crown of beauty, finishing the Triwizards Tournament—it is deeply satisfying to win a prize in front of a lot of people. *Charlotte's Web* calls its climax at this moment of familiar children's theater; only here, the true prizewinner remains in the shadows. Charlotte, we know, is the real force behind Wilbur's success and, in turn, the adult humans' happiness. And as she fades and dies, Wilbur cares for her unhatched eggs. Soon Charlotte's children will spin webs of their own, greet and salute friends, and continue their mother's artistry. If there is a vision of literary history here, it is this vision of the mother and the child. No father of poetry now, Charlotte is the mother of creation, and the book's last lines say it all: "It is not often that someone comes along who is a true friend and a good writer. Charlotte was both" (p. 184). For E. B. White, his Charlotte must have been his wife, Katharine Angell. Novelist, editor at the *New Yorker*, memoirist of their Maine garden, she remains behind White's work, as true friend and good writer.

The story of the girls' book is the story of the writer and the friend. Such books teach many things (social decorum, personal care, moral virtue); but what they teach most of all is cultivation of the imagination. Gardens, like books, may stand as places of absorption, places where the girl may lose herself in reading, in writing, or in reminiscence. Or they may be places of the theater, stage sets to be prepared for the entrance of the winning actress or actor. Hermione straddles both places, learning from the library but also directing the theater of her boys. Whether inspiring Harry to seek a new plan to win a contest or cheering him on at Quidditch, she is the mistress of the house. At times, Harry seems as much Hermione's creation as Rowling's; and whatever the books tell us, we know—along with the movie's Sirius Black—that she is the cleverest witch of her age.

Fig. 18. Children's tea party, c. 1900. From Peter Hunt, ed., *Children's Literature: An Illustrated History* (Oxford: Oxford University Press, 1995).

# Pan in the Garden

## THE EDWARDIAN TURN
## IN CHILDREN'S LITERATURE

Readers of the lushly produced *Children's Literature: An Illustrated History*, published by Oxford University Press in 1995, will come across a wonderfully illuminating photograph in Julia Briggs's chapter, "Transitions (1890–1914)." Three little girls sit at their tea party under an arbor. Perhaps sisters, perhaps models, the girls range in age from probably two to ten. As the middle girl carefully pours cream into a teacup, the oldest and youngest stare into the camera. The caption to the photograph calls attention to the ways in which "imaginative games," such as playing at tea parties, took hold at the end of the nineteenth century, and how the imitation of "adult behavior" provided the larger social context for the fictions of such writers as Robert Louis Stevenson, Richard Jefferies, E. Nesbit, and Kenneth Grahame.[1]

What we have here, however, is not simply a case of imaginative or imitative play. What we have is the emblem of the Edwardian age, the great tea party that, for the first decade of the twentieth century, exemplified what the literary historian Samuel Hynes has called the "turn of mind" of that age. His description of many of the official "garden party" portraits of the royals resonates strikingly with this picture of the three children. He writes of "a present, dominated by King and Queen, symbols of the established order—rich, punctilious, and unoccupied—and behind them the past, a corridor of peace, sunlit and pastoral."[2] In the *Children's Literature* photograph, too, we see an ordered, ritualized world; a corridor of peace, sunlit and pastoral.

In many ways, modern children's literature remains an Edwardian phenomenon. This period defined the ways in which we still think of children's books and of the child's imagination. During its few years, the age produced a canon of authors and works that are still powerfully influential in the field. It provided an imaginative landscape that still controls much contemporary writing. It filtered earlier works through that landscape in order to produce a modern canon. Our default mode of childhood, if you like, remains that decade or so before the First World War: the time between the death of Queen Victoria in 1901 and the assassination at Sarajevo in 1914, the time when writers looked back over loss and could only barely anticipate the end of the old order. Edwardian England—and its counterpart, Rooseveltian America—live in our memories as gilt-edged times of childhood taste.[3]

These years, in both Britain and America, were ruled by men who were widely perceived never to have grown up. Edward VII, the perpetual Prince of Wales, did not ascend the throne until he was nearly sixty, and yet he was often portrayed as boyishly arrested in his willfulness, his appetites, and his adventurism. He loved the costume of the military, loved to shoot, loved the tea party. His American counterpart, Theodore Roosevelt, the youngest man ever to become a U.S. president, had always been seen as willful, almost manic, and his White House was filled with the childhood buddies of his youngest son, Quentin (who was nine when his father became president). "You must remember," wrote one diplomat to another about Roosevelt, "that the President is really six years old."[4] In fact, when Roosevelt visited England in May 1910 to deliver the Romanes lecture at Oxford, he explicitly requested to meet Rudyard Kipling, Andrew Lang, and Kenneth Grahame (*The Wind in the Willows* had become a favorite of the president).[5] It was little wonder, for Roosevelt's own vast published corpus was filled with stories of adventure and survival, especially his tales of his own youthful treks and travails in Montana and the Dakotas.

The years before the First World War in Britain and America were also years that socially and politically redefined childhood. There was, as many writers of the time would recognize, a new playfulness to life: a sense not just of living under a boyish king or president, but of living in the toyhood of the future. The airplane and the motorcar were technological advances seen as playthings of the wealthy and the curious. There was an "infancy" to such technologies, much as there was an infancy to other sciences and modes of inquiry. For sociology and psychology, disciplines just beginning to gain traction in the period, laughter and play were often the subject of scholarly inquiry (not just in Britain and America: Henri

Bergson's *Laughter* appeared in France in 1900; Freud's *On Jokes* in Austria in 1906). There was, as well, a new concern, on both sides of the Atlantic, with child welfare. London and New York in particular were seen as dungeons for the child: places of ill health, poor hygiene, and horrid work conditions. Jacob Riis's *How the Other Half Lives* of 1890 provoked decades of social reform in America. In Britain, government inquiries exposed the malnutrition and disease that possessed urban children. Free school meals were instituted in 1906, school medical inspections in 1907. Child labor and child welfare were (as much as temperance and woman suffrage) the social concerns of the age.[6]

In addition to these social and political movements, there were a range of literary and aesthetic developments that would contribute to the Edwardian period's fascination with children and children's books. One of these changes was a new preoccupation with the occult, the fantastic, and the spiritual. After decades of Victorian social realism, readers and writers at the end of the nineteenth century and the beginning of the twentieth began to turn toward more speculative modes of fiction. Edwardian science, in the words of Samuel Hynes, sought in part to "restore metaphysics to the human world," and this scientific impulse led to what we might today call pseudoscientific fascinations with the spirit world, the psyche, and the supernatural.[7] This was the great age of the séance, and a range of writers from the 1890s through the 1910s explored the literary implications of these fascinations. H. G. Wells, Ford Madox Hueffer, Henry James, and G. K. Chesterton are but the best-known writers who turned their attentions to various forms of supernaturalism, science fiction, and ghost stories.[8] Whatever the intended audiences for such fictions, children were often at their heart. The little charges of the governess in James's *Turn of the Screw* may be the best known of such fictional children. And what is clear from many of the ghost and horror tales of the time is that, even in the absence of young characters, fear often reduces grown men to whimpering babies. Take, for example, Perceval Landon's "Thurnley Abbey," published in 1908, in which the main character, Mr. Broughton, is so terrified of a bit of skull thrown at him "that he screamed and screamed till Mrs. Broughton . . . held on to him and coaxed him like a child to be quiet."[9]

These social and literary developments had an impact on the Edwardian theater. Instead of the old high melodramas of the nineteenth century, the London stage began to mount plays of political and social (and even sexual) commentary. Family life—its failures and its tensions, its expectations and its traumas—came to dominate the stage. Chekhov and Ibsen had great influence on the English problem plays of the early twentieth century. Shaw's social satires reshaped visions of the family in the areas of work and class. There was a new didacticism in the theater, a new attention to religion, sex, and labor that would challenge, in Hynes's words, the "extravagantly genteel standard of decorum . . . [of] Edwardian audiences."[10]

Shakespeare was not immune to these changes. The visual effects on the Edwardian stage were broader than those of the Victorians—perhaps in response to the experimentalism of the Ibsen generation; perhaps, too, in response to the expectations raised by the new medium of film (Shakespeare's plays began to be filmed almost as soon as cinema began).[11] The costumes and makeup were more fantastic. The drawing of the great

Fig. 19. Sir Herbert Beerbohm Tree as Caliban. Charcoal drawing by
Charles A. Buchel, 1904. By permission of the Folger Shakespeare Library.

Herbert Beerbohm Tree as Caliban in 1904 limns a Shakespeare for the fearful fantasy of childhood.[12] This is a face that could be out of Stevenson, or Wells, or H. P. Lovecraft (*The Tempest*, along with *A Midsummer Night's Dream*, was one of the favorite Shakespeare plays of late Victorians, as they were seen to conjure magic worlds and spirits in ways that would feed the later flowering of Edwardian fantasy).[13] And finally, there was the music hall—what came to be called, by the 1890s, the "theater of variety." The high point of the music hall was the last decade of the nineteenth century and the first decade of the twentieth, as theaters came to be constructed with a grandeur previously reserved for "legitimate" theater. London's Coliseum rose up in 1904, the Palladium in 1910. Their very names evoke an old Roman imperial idiom, now grafted onto popular performance.

Much has been made of the changes these social and aesthetic moves worked on the children's literature of the first decade of the twentieth century. For one thing, critics have long noticed the explosion of authors, novels, plays, and poems. Many of our most familiar works of children's literature were written in this period: *Peter Rabbit, Peter Pan, The Wind in the Willows, The Secret Garden, Anne of Green Gables, The Railway Children.* The look of the modern children's book took shape at this time: the rich embossed covers of adventure books, the evocative line drawings that adorned the texts, the etchings and photographs that brought far-off places and events into the child's room. The technologies of book and newspaper production dovetailed with a sensibility reared on the Pre-Raphaelites, the Arts and Crafts movement, and Art Nouveau. It is as if the great aesthetic movements of the later nineteenth century would find their afterlife in children's books; as if John Millais, William Morris, and Aubrey Beardsley would find themselves morphed into children's book illustrators Ernest H. Shepard and Arthur Rackham.[14]

The impact of this age would be felt, too, on later writers. P. L. Travers published *Mary Poppins* in 1934, but set it in Edward's decade. C. S. Lewis, J. R. R. Tolkien, and A. A. Milne had Edwardian childhoods, and it is no accident that the feel of so much of their fantasy (the Professor's study at the opening of *The Lion, the Witch, and the Wardrobe*, the greensward of Middle Earth's Shire, Owl's grand home in the beech tree in *Winnie-the-Pooh*) takes us back to a time before the First World War shattered everything. To look upon the maps of Middle Earth, or of the Willows, or of the Hundred Acre Wood, is now, after decades of war rooms and map rooms, to see the cartographies of nostalgia.

If there is, then, an Edwardian turn to children's literature, what are its specific byways? One takes us to the forest. As Hynes puts it:

> From the *Yellow Book* to the Pan-ridden stories of E. M. Forster one finds the same fascination with pagan deities, under the hill or behind a hedge, with witches and wood nymphs, with supernatural visitors from above or below. Barrie's *Peter Pan* was the most successful play of 1904, and not, as is now happily the case, for audiences of children only (Rupert Brooke came down from Cambridge to see it and thought it was the best play he had ever seen). Pan is particularly omnipresent of the period.[15]

Pan is everywhere, not just in the *Yellow Book* but in the children's book. Grahame's *Wind in the Willows* offers, at the moment of its most sublime climax, the vision of the Piper at the Gates of Dawn—the vision of the forest deity himself, as Mole feels "a great Awe upon him" and sees what Grahame calls "the Friend and Helper": "the backward sweep of the curved horns, gleaming in the growing daylight; . . . the stern, hooked nose between the kindly eyes, . . . the long supple hand still holding the pan-pipes."[16] In *The Secret Garden*, Mary Lennox comes upon the country boy, Dickon, much as Mole comes upon his god. She hears "a low, peculiar whistling sound" and seeks it out.

> A boy was sitting under a tree, with his back against it, playing on a rough wooden pipe. He was a funny looking boy about twelve. He looked very clean and his nose turned up and his cheeks were as red as poppies and never had Mistress Mary seen such round and such blue eyes in any boy's face. And on the trunk of the tree he leaned against, a brown squirrel was clinging and watching him, and from behind a bush nearby a cock pheasant was delicately stretching his neck to peep out, and quite near him were two rabbits sitting up and sniffing with tremulous noses—and actually it appeared as if they were all drawing near to watch him and listen to the strange low little call his pipe seemed to make. (p. 57)

Mole's Pan and Mary's Dickon both lie at the nexus of the natural and supernatural worlds. Each one brings the creatures into harmony, like a little local Orpheus, taming the animals into an audience. They stand as figures of inspired, yet untutored, artistry—figures who may inspire, too, the writers of these novels. For in both Grahame and Burnett, the writing here rises to a high level of preciousness. The sentences are long and running on (notice the string of *and*s in *The Secret Garden*). Both writers offer long lists of exotica, a powerful engagement with the senses, and a sustained set of literary allusions going back to Shakespeare. Indeed, Rat in *The Wind in the Willows* sounds very much like Ferdinand in Shakespeare's *Tempest* as he enters Pan's domain.

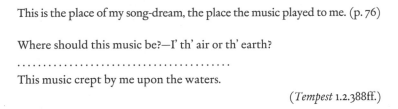

This is the place of my song-dream, the place the music played to me. (p. 76)

Where should this music be?—I' th' air or th' earth?
..........................................
This music crept by me upon the waters.

(Tempest 1.2.388ff.)

If Barrie's *Peter Pan* was the most successful play of 1904, a good deal of its success came, no doubt, from its evocative recall of such woodland fantasy, its blend of *The Tempest* and the tom-tom, its filtering of high Victorian school and domestic culture through the scrim of Edwardian nostalgia. *Peter Pan* is a play that looks back to a lost age of Victorian security. It seeks a meaning in fantastic rather than empirical or scientific life. It sees life as theatrical and peformative, rather than as authentic and sincere. It exposes the conventions of social life as conventions, and in the process calls attention to the gap between morality and propriety.[17]

*Peter Pan* opens in a house of words. The nursery looks out over Bloomsbury, a section of London chosen, as the play's directions state, because "Mr. Roget once lived there." The stage directions go on: "So did we in days when his *Thesaurus* was our only companion in London; and we whom he has helped to wend our way through life have always wanted to pay him a little compliment" (pp. 1309–10). The play's opening space is that of the Victorian verbal imagination. Roget's *Thesaurus* stands here as an emblem of nineteenth-century erudition, of the kinds of massive projects, such as the *Oxford English Dictionary* or Darwin's *Origin of Species*, that help us to "wend our way through life," that change the ways in which we see the world. *Peter Pan* opens in this nostalgic Victorian world: the house, the room, the clock, the toys—all evoke that comfortable clutter that scores of surviving photographs have revealed as the safe space of domestic childhood.

And yet, from the start, something is different. The children are not so much acting as themselves as acting as others. There is a theater to the nursery here. Young John (whom a stage direction parenthetically instructs to speak "histrionically") announces to his mother, "We are doing an act; we are playing at being you and father" (p. 1311). "Stand you for my father," commands Prince Hal to Falstaff in Shakespeare's *Henry IV: Part I*, in one of the great moments of theatrical play-acting. Playing at being father is one of the first moves in the repertoire of the child—indeed, how can we not compare this moment with the opening of Alcott's *Little Women*, when the girls are playing roles designed to fill the space left by their absent father, and their mother recalls when they used to play scenes out of Bunyan's *Pilgrim's Progress*? There is a self-conscious theatricality in both works at their opening—a hearkening back to earlier, literary templates for performance. But while *Little Women* shows the sisters moving beyond theater into writing, service, and domestic responsibility, *Peter Pan* only heightens the histrionic qualities of childhood. Peter himself enters not so much as a figure out of fantasy as a figure out of a child's fantasy of the Shakespearean imagination. If little John's words recall Prince Hal, Peter's entry recalls images of *A Midsummer Night's Dream*: "In so far as he is dressed at all it is in autumn leaves and cobwebs." Like one of Oberon's fairies (remember, one of them was "Cobweb"), Peter comes to transport the moral out of everydayness.

Act I is an essay in the fairy tale. Barrie has taken bits and pieces out of Grimm, Mother Goose, and Andersen and animated them. There is the shadow that Peter cannot stick on; the strange but powerfully significant kiss that Wendy would plant on Peter; the so-called fairy language; the lost boys. And then there are the stories that Wendy would tell: she recalls explicitly the tale of Cinderella, and she uses this brief taste of fairy tale to get Peter to take her off to Neverland. "I know lots of stories," she announces. "The stories I could tell to the boys!" (p. 1320).

What does it mean to live your life in stories? What does it mean, Barrie asks throughout the play, to have your life determined by the word, the book, the tale? If Roget's *Thesaurus* was a guide to life, then so are *Märchen* or *Eventyr* or *contes de fées*. So, too, is *Robinson Crusoe*, and there is something undeniably Robinsonian about the island Neverland of Act II. In the stage directions, Barrie describes the pirate boys and Captain Hook with a degree of physiognomic detail worthy of Defoe describing Friday. Here is Hook: "cadaverous and black-avised, his hair dressed in long curls which look like black candles about to melt, his eyes blue as the forget-me-not and of a profound insensibility, save when he claws, at which time a red spot appears in them." He is a creature of a Robinsonade; but he is also an inhabitant of the old Victorian schoolroom, with his elegant diction, an impressive courtliness, a "public school" nickname, and a dress that, we are told, "apes the dandiacal" (p. 1324).

Hook comes off here as something of a cross between the aesthete of the age of Oscar Wilde and the wild man of Stevenson's *Treasure Island*.

A schoolmaster manqué, he embodies the theatricality that inheres in all pedagogues. I see him standing behind Harry Potter's Snape (the hair, in particular, seems similar in both); like Snape, he assaults the student with a relentless questioning. Snape is, in many of his scenes, merely a bully, but Hook is far more complex. Look at his interplay with Peter in Act III:

> HOOK. If you are Hook, come tell me, who am I?
> PETER. A codfish, only a codfish.
> HOOK (aghast). A codfish?
> SMEE (drawing back from him). Have we been captained all this time by a codfish?
> STARKEY. It's lowering to our pride.
> HOOK (feeling that his ego is slipping from him). Don't desert me, bullies.
> PETER (top-heavy). Paw, fish, paw!
> . . . . . . . . . . . . . . . . . . . . . . . .
> HOOK. Have you another name?
> PETER (falling to the lure). Ay, ay.
> HOOK (thirstily). Vegetable?
> PETER. No.
> HOOK. Animal?
> PETER (after a hurried consultation with Tootles). Yes.
> HOOK. Man?
> PETER (with scorn). No.
> HOOK. Boy?
> PETER. Yes.
> HOOK. Ordinary Boy?
> PETER. No!
> HOOK. Wonderful boy?
> PETER (to Wendy's distress). Yes!
> HOOK. Are you in England?
> PETER. No.
> HOOK. Are you here?
> PETER. Yes.

(pp. 1333–34)

Again, this has a curiously Shakespearean feel. Moments here recall Hamlet questioning Polonius about the shape of clouds; others recall the double-entendre wordplay of Romeo and his buddies (the word *codfish* has, throughout Shakespeare, the dirty overtones of *codpiece* that would have transported a student into laughter, then or now). Moments, too, have the feel of Lear: Who are you? "Well, then, I am Peter Pan!" an announcement that has all the drama of Lear himself announcing to the blind Gloucester, "Ay, every inch a king." And there is certainly Roget among the models here. Hook's questions—vegetable, animal, boy, ordinary boy, wonderful boy?—evoke the categories of Roget's organization of the world, a system of progressive specificity. It is as if we see Hook poring through the pages of the *Thesaurus*, finding the precise terms for boy, ordinary boy, wonderful boy, until we hit upon the final definition: Peter Pan.

And we see, too, Hook through the pages of the classroom. Listen to the mad soliloquy he offers at the start of Act V: "How still the night is; nothing sounds alive. Now is the hour when children in their homes are a-bed; their lips bright-browned with the good-night chocolate, and their tongues drowsily searching for belated crumbs housed insecurely on their shining cheeks. Compare with them the children on this boat about to walk the plank. Split my infinitives, but 'tis my hour of triumph!" (p. 1345). Read this as an Edwardian gloss on the Victorian imagination. Nothing is whole here. Even the opening stage direction, "communing with his ego," could not have been conjured up in English much before the opening of the twentieth century (the *Oxford English Dictionary* offers an 1894 citation for "ego" as the first use in this sense, and the first specifically Freudian use in English came only in 1910). Hook is an ego-driven Hamlet here, a figure of the stage splintered into sad allusion. His opening words recall that moment from Shakespeare's play when the prince meditates upon his deed:

> 'Tis now the very witching time of night,
> When churchyards yawn and hell itself breathes out
> Contagion to this world: now could I drink hot blood,
> And do such bitter business as the day
> Would quake to look on.
>
> (*Hamlet* 3.2.280–84)

But this is a children's *Hamlet*, as we move from churchyards to bedrooms. No one is drinking hot blood here; children drink, instead, their good-night chocolate. "Split my infinitives." This should, of course, be "shiver my timbers" (a phrase probably originating in the novels of Frederick Marryat and gaining currency, most famously, in the mouth of Long John Silver in *Treasure Island*). Things become words; the ship becomes the book. And when Hook dies, he gives himself up to the crocodile, mur-

muring (as the stage directions have it) "Floreat Etona"—long live Eton College (p. 1351).

Hook dies an old Etonian to the last, and with his words he evokes the Victorian ideals of public-school life. Indeed, it is as if Hook's Etonianism stands as a riposte to Tom Brown's Rugby: the great rival school and, as much as Eton, the source of the ideals of good sportsmanship and civic responsibility. "The battle of Waterloo was won on the playing fields of Eton": this famous quotation, attributed to the Duke of Wellington but first attested only in the 1850s, takes us back to the adventurism of the age of the boys' book. What dies with Hook is that adventurist ideal, and certainly for Barrie—who revised the play extensively for publication in 1928—that ideal must have rung even more hollow after the death of an entire generation of young men in the First World War. "To die," says Peter Pan, "would be an awfully great adventure" (p. 1336). How can we not hear such words on the lips of men such as Rupert Brooke, who saw the play on opening night in 1904 and, a decade later, would enlist? How can we not hear Peter's fancies turned to ash in the mouths of the soldiers who would die? *Dulce et decorum est pro patria mori.* These are the last lines of Wilfred Owen's poem of that title, perhaps the most famous poem of the war. These are the lines that, as the poem states, would not be told "with such high zest / To children ardent for some desperate glory."[18]

It is a cliché to aver that the First World War ended the childhood of the Edwardian era. But it is no cliché, I think, to find in *Peter Pan* a prescient recognition of that end. I won't grow up: Peter's refusal offers not just the denial of maturity; it denies history itself. It opens up a door to the Neverland that never was (what is nostalgia, really, but a longing for a past that never happened?). And in the words of Owen's poem we may see, too, the obituary for the Edwardian turn of mind: *dulce et decorum,* sweet and decorous. Horace's Latin lines adapt themselves here to the memory of the garden party, with its sweets and social rituals.

For *The Wind in the Willows*, sweetness and decorum are the two poles of its nostalgia.[19] And yet, here the vision of Edwardian England lies less in garden-party photographs than in the technological inventions that would captivate the fancies of the rich: new playthings such as motorcars, new challenges to nature, new threats to country sweetness and social decorum. Toad lives at the epicenter of Edwardian anxiety in the book. His fascination with the motorcar, his appetites, his mania, all descend into theater. Toad stands as something of a figure for Edwardianism itself in the book, and to appreciate the full bore of his foolishness and foppery, we must begin with the book's very Victorian beginning.

> The Mole had been working very hard all the morning, spring-cleaning his little home. First with brooms, then with dusters; then on ladders and steps and chairs, with a brush and a pail of whitewash; till he had dust in his throat and eyes, and splashes of whitewash all over his black fur, and an aching back and weary arms. Spring was moving in the air above and in the earth below and around him, penetrating even his dark and lowly little house with its spirit of divine discontent and longing. It was small wonder, then, that he suddenly flung down his brush on the floor, said 'Bother!' ... and bolted out of the house. (p. 1)

Grahame opens with a lexicon of Victorian domesticity. "Spring-cleaning" is a phrase that emerges, in fact, only in the second half of the nineteenth century (the earliest example from the *OED* is from 1857). Part of this phrase's origin, of course, lies in the rise of cleanliness as a social ideal: the concern, in both England and America, with personal and domestic hygiene. But the symbolic resonances are also obvious. Spring is the time of renewal, of clearing out the past. The *OED* offers this quotation from *The Pall Mall Gazette* of 1889 that, I think, beautifully captures the late Victorian association of domestic ordering and literary form that Grahame evokes here: "There are few points of mutual sympathy between the poet and the spring-cleaner." The *OED* also quotes from Harriet Martineau's *Autobiography* (from a letter from 1873): "This will be a busy month, with the spring cleaning and whitewashing."

*The Wind in the Willows* begins with the words of late Victorian ordering. This is a fresh start, but it is a fresh start in a world of comfortable familiarity: the world of Grahame's own childhood. The whole first chapter expands on this idiom. Mole leaves his little house, and when he comes upon the rabbit calling for a toll, he bowls the rabbit over, "chaffing" the other rabbits and calling out "onion-sauce, onion-sauce" (these expressions are firmly grounded in Victorian colloquialism: *chaff*, meaning to rail at, seems to disappear from use after the 1880s; *onion-sauce*, meaning something like "hogwash," is a post-Dickens expression). And there is more. Just before Mole meets up with Water Rat, he dreams of a "bijou riverside residence" (a perfect, and well-attested, Victorianism); and in what is perhaps the most famous expression of the whole book, Rat soon advises Mole that "there is nothing half so much worth doing as simply messing about in boats" ("messing about" emerged only in the 1880s as a way of talking about pleasant time-wasting; the *OED*, in fact, quotes this passage from *The Wind in the Willows* to illustrate the usage).

If the book opens in the verbal world of Victorian banter, it opens, too, in the most recognizable literary world of any age: a river journey. Like all great adventures (from the *Odyssey* to *Huckleberry Finn*), *The Wind in the Willows* sets its heroes on the water. But, for any reader of the novel's age, the boat story most familiarly evoked here would have been Jerome K. Jerome's *Three Men in a Boat*.[20] First published in 1889 and frequently reprinted, this novel chronicled the humorous, but often trivial, misadventures of three young men on the Thames. By the late 1880s, the river had become something of a middle-class playground, and the fashion for rowing—stopping off for picnics, pub excursions, and the like—fueled the popularity of Jerome's work. By offering an adventure story set not in the far reaches of the empire but close to home, by writing in a chatty, colloquial style, and by focusing on the foibles of his heroes, Jerome set the pattern for a generation of popular writers, and the animals of Grahame's tale replay this story.

Watch Rat and Mole pack their picnic basket; watch them navigate the river, inattentively, until they hit the bank "full tilt"; watch them try to recover the basket of food from the river; watch them retreat to Rat's place, relaxing in dressing gowns and slippers. So much of this journey has the feel of *Three Men in a Boat* that it is hard not to imagine Grahame's having had it in mind. Take, for example, this description of the journey's plan in Jerome's novel:

> Then we run our little boat into some quiet nook, and the tent is pitched, and the frugal supper cooked and eaten. Then the big pipes are filled and lighted, and the pleasant chat goes round in musical undertone; while, in the pauses of our talk, the river playing round the boat, prattles strange old tales and secrets, sings low the old child's song that it has sung so many thousand years. (p. 21)

Jerome's evocation of this riverine and boyhood Eden shapes the arc of Grahame's sentences. So, too, Jerome's witty evocations of the failures of these poor young men look forward to the foolishness of Rat and Mole:

> Then Harris tried to open the tin with a pocket-knife, and broke the knife and cut himself badly; and George tried a pair of scissors, and the scissors flew up, and nearly put his eye out. While they were dressing their wounds, I tried to make a hole in the thing with the spiky end of the

hitcher, and the hitcher slipped and jerked me out between the boat and the bank into two feet of muddy water, and the tin rolled over, uninjured, and broke a tea-cup. (p. 170)

The misadventures of the three men and of Rat and Mole resonate not just with each other, but with something of a broader late Victorian and Edwardian sense of infelicitous travel. The image of the bumbling college student and the blithe twittiness of boys of a certain social class come through brilliantly in the words of Basil Boothroyd, the early twentieth-century editor of *Punch*, who, when asked whether he had had a good holiday, could respond, "Awful. Nothing went wrong at all."[21]

This is the pleasant, muddle-headed ease of *The Wind in the Willows*. Nostalgia falls upon the animals like a light snow, and Grahame's writing—much like Jerome's in the passage I quoted—is often filled with evocations of an earlier, Romantic sensibility. The "Dulce Domum" chapter, in particular, assembles all the emotional responses of a world of reading: there are echoes of Wordsworth and Shelley, resonances to Charles Dickens. The little field mice knock on Mole's door, caroling away, and Rat offers to send them off in search of food at any cost at this time of the night:

> "Here, you with the lantern! Come over this way. I want to talk to you. Now, tell me, are there any shops open at this hour of the night?"
>
> "Why, certainly, sir," replied the field-mouse respectfully. "At this time of the year our shops keep open to all sorts of hours."
>
> "Then look here!" said the Rat. "You go off at once, you and your lantern, and you get me—"
>
> (p. 56)

Such an exchange recalls the end of Dickens's *Christmas Carol*, when Scrooge, groggy from his dreams, calls to the young boy in the street to buy the turkey. And when Mole explains to Rat that these mice are actors, too, and that they "make [their plays] up all by themselves," he imagines a world of Stevenson and Barrie, pirates and Peter Pan. Mole explains: "They gave us a capital one last year, about a field-mouse who was captured at sea by a Barbary corsair, and made to row in a galley; and when he escaped and got home again, his lady-love had gone into a convent. Here, you! You were in it, I remember. Get up and recite a bit" (p. 57). Alas, the little mouse is tongue-tied, and in spite of all the coaxing, he cannot perform. Only when another mouse knocks on the door and comes in with the food do we feel that he has been rescued (as have we, to some extent). Then, "there was no more talk of play-acting." Grahame raises the specter of a *Peter Pan*-like performance, only to shut it down. The novel recognizes the temptations of the theater, understands the rich temptations of playing pirates, but it has no place for such histrionics in its quiet, Victorian domestic fantasy of "savoury comforts." We are, here, not in Captain Hook's parody of schoolroom recitation, but instead in the candlelit remembered world of household reading.

This is the world of Wordsworth and Shelley; the world of the Shakespearean song; the world of poetry and drama filtered for the childish reader.[22] Compare the selections from Grahame's own *Cambridge Book of Poetry for Children*, and you get a gloss on Rat and Mole, the river and the room.[23]

> My soul is an enchanted boat,
>     Which, like a sleeping swan, doth float
> Upon the silver waves of thy sweet singing.
>                     (pt. 1, p. 78)

So begins Shelley's "To a Singer," and so it stands in the *Cambridge Book* as a counterpoint to Rat's messing about in boats. Such a poem provided the late nineteenth and early twentieth-century reader with a deep, Romantic vision of the music of the waters, the sweet fantasy of the imagination as a river journey. You can hear its chords in Jerome's imagination of the river's "strange old tales and secrets," and if his river tells of an "old child's song," so does the range of Romantic poetry adapted, in the late Victorian and Edwardian periods, for children. Turn, in Grahame's *Cambridge Book*, to Wordsworth's "Recollections of Early Childhood," to see the source of his lush sublimity:

> There was a time when meadow, grove, and stream,
>     The earth, and every common sight,
>         To me did seem
>     Apparell'd in celestial light,
> The glory and the freshness of a dream.

"Ye blessed creatures," Wordsworth goes on later in the poem, "I have heard the call / Ye to each other make" (pt. 2, p. 4). So, too, has Grahame heard the call, and much like Burnett's *Secret Garden*, his *Wind in the Willows* builds an evocative language out of such a vision. Such is the heart of Grahame's vision of the "Piper at the Gates of Dawn." One can open that chapter almost at random and find passagework of a Wordsworthian purple: "A wide half-circle of foam and glinting lights and shining shoulders of green water, the great weir closed the backwater from bank to bank, troubled all the quiet surface with twirling eddies and floating foam-streaks, and deadened all other sounds with its solemn and soothing rumble" (p. 75). This is what the Victorians had done to the Romantic poets: found in forest glade or childhood reminiscence visions of a rhetorical sublime. The solemn and soothing rumble of this passage comes not only from the evocation of eddying water, but from the very sounds of the vowels and consonants that make up these descriptive words.

And into this Victorian rumble Edwardian modernity had already crashed. Long before Mole returned to his sweet home, he and Rat had gone to visit Toad. They come upon him in all his country-house distractedness. Toad has moved beyond boating, he announces: "Silly boyish amusement." Now he is possessed by caravanning, and he shows the two visitors his "gipsy caravan, shining with newness, painted a canary-yellow picked out with green and red wheels" (p. 15). For Toad, this is the height of travel, and the colors and the glitter of this caravan have all the feel of late Victorian decadence (it is as if the vehicle had come straight from the *Yellow Book*, limned by someone like Aubrey Beardsley). But this is 1908 now, and pretty horse-drawn wagons soon must cede the way. No soothing rumble now: they hear a "faint warning hum." They see "a small cloud of dust, with a dark centre of energy, advancing on them at incredible speed, while from out of the dust a faint 'Poop-poop!' wailed like an uneasy animal in pain." The car rushes past them, knocking them over and driving the caravan into a ditch. But, for a moment, they get a "glimpse of an interior of glittering plate-glass and rich morocco, passionate, while its pilot, tense and hugging his wheel, possessed all earth and air for the fraction of a second, flung an enveloping cloud of dust that blinded and enwrapped them utterly, and then dwindled to a speck in the far distance, changed back into a droning bee once more" (p. 19). This is the other side of the Edwardians: not the world of static tea parties, but one of active, power-driven engines; a fascination with the newfangledness of fast technologies, but also with the need to dress those fast technologies in cloaks of artifice. This may be a motorcar, but it is one that glitters with glass and leather. This may be a machine, but it seems to possess an animal vigor all its own. This is what we might call the technological sublime, a glimpse into a gas-fueled future that possesses the beholder. The car becomes an object of desire—not simply because Toad wants one, but because, in its very description, we see passion at its center.

If Mole and Rat wish to retreat into the memories of earlier domestic bliss, Toad leaps ahead into the all too fast future. His adventures take him to all the byways of familiar England: the public house, the jail, the laundry room, the railroad. His tale dominates the final sections of *The Wind in the Willows*, and each exploit takes the traditions of adventure, social commentary, and fantasy and transforms them into farce. It is as if Toad takes us through the history of all the books that any child would know. There is *Gulliver's Travels*, for example, in that brilliant moment when Toad, "to his horror, . . . recollected that he had left both coat and waistcoat behind him in his cell, and with them his pocket-book, money, keys, watch, matches, pencil-case—all that makes life worth living, all that distinguishes the many-pocketed or no-pocketed productions that hop or trip about permissively, unequipped for the real contest" (p. 87). A man is the sum of what he pockets, and Toad finds himself stripped of the accoutrements of civilization. Compare Gulliver, placing the Lilliputians in his pockets so that they may see his watch, his purse, his comb, his guns, and his razor.

If there is the world of Gulliver, there is also the world of Tom Brown. Recall how the school story had transformed boys' lives into present-tense narrative—how the tales of sportsmanship made it possible to offer color commentary on the everyday. Here is Toad in a particularly self-narrating moment: "My enemies shut me up in prison, encircled by sentries, watched night and day by warders; I walk out through them all, by sheer ability coupled with courage. They pursue me with engines, and policemen, and revolvers. I snap my fingers at them, and vanish, laughing, into space" (p. 117). His is the rhetoric of the sporting match melded with the idiom of the adventure story. It is as if not simply Grahame, but Toad himself has written the novel of his life—a novel of gung-ho and cutting up, of heroism and hilarity.

And let us not forget the most enduring of the late Victorian and Edwardian fictions: Anthony Hope's *Prisoner of Zenda* (first published in 1894, adapted for the stage in 1895, and filmed as early as 1913); Stevenson's *Dr. Jekyll and Mr. Hyde* (published in 1886, staged in 1887, and first filmed in 1912); and Sir Arthur Conan Doyle's Sherlock Holmes stories (first appearing in 1887 and continuing for forty years). What readers, and soon playgoers, found so enduring in these works was their concern with costume and impersonation. They make adventure inseparable from dress-up, and Toad's tale chimes with their details. When he comes home from his exploits, he finds Rat and recognizes that "he could lay aside a disguise that was unworthy of his position" (p. 123). Such a decision lies at the heart of these late Victorian and Edwardian works, for it asks the questions central to the age: What is the nature of the self? How do we dress to reveal, or conceal, our inner being? Will the dark inside come out, regardless of our costume? Recall now King Edward's own obsessions with proper dress, with the love of the uniform, with his controlling sense of correctness in wearing the right spurs. Toad's escapades had been ones of "escapes," "disguises," and "subterfuges."[24] And when Rat finally gets Toad to calm down, he implores him to "go off upstairs at once, and take off that old cotton rag that looks as if it might formerly have belonged to some washerwoman, and clean yourself thoroughly, and put on some of my clothes, and try and come down looking like a gentleman, if you *can*" (p. 123). For Rat, impersonation is a vice. The true gentleman is not a creature of the theater, but a man of the house.

Like Captain Hook—or even, for that matter, like the prisoner of Zenda, or Dr. Jekyll, or Holmes himself—Toad is a creature of theatricality. His histrionics, his rants, his costume changes, even his obsession with the look and show of motorcars all mark him as a self that lives only for performance. Little wonder that after Toad Hall has been cleared of its invading stoats and weasels, its master can reassert his ownership through a command performance. The book's final chapter may be called "The Return of Odysseus," but it is a music-hall Odysseus who comes back. Toad imagines a play of his adventures, and he fantasizes about writing up a "programme of entertainment for the evening" (p. 145). He even makes up a great song with which to entertain his guests. But when the time comes and the guests have arrived, the food has been eaten, and the wine has been drunk, his fellows call upon him for a speech.

> But Toad only shook his head gently, raised one paw in mild protest, and, by pressing delicacies on his guests, by topical small-talk, and by earnest inquiries after members of their families not yet old enough to appear at social functions, managed to convey to them that this dinner was being run on strictly conventional lines.
>     He was indeed an altered Toad!
>
> (p. 149)

He is still a Toad of his time, but now not an appetitive, performing creature; he is instead a strict, conventional host, displaying all the Edwardian social ideals of small talk and little delicacies.

*The Wind in the Willows*, as I have reviewed it here, traces a tension between Victorian domesticity and Edwardian change. It absorbs many of the literary fascinations of the period: the heightened Romantic vocabulary, the precious figuring of Pan, the everyday adventurism of young men in a boat. But it also apposes them to technological and social change, to theater and to costume, to passion. What seems to win out, in the end, is decorum.

Edwardian culture lived on the cusp of innovation and nostalgia, social change and comfortable domesticity. From *Peter Pan* and *The Wind in the Willows* we may conjure patterns for the stories of their age and ever after. There is a kind of technological supernaturalism, for example, to the train in Nesbit's *Railway Children* (1906), a blend of the power of mechanical life and Pan himself.[25] Witness the way in which the children come upon the train in rural Yorkshire, after they have been removed from London (their father has been falsely accused of selling state secrets to the Russians and is imprisoned for five years).

> The way to the railway was all down hill over smooth, short turf with here and there furze bushes and gray and yellow rocks sticking out like candied peel out of the top of a cake.
>
> The way ended in a steep run and a wooden fence,—and there was the railway with the shining metals and the telegraph wires and posts and signals.
>
> They all climbed on to the top of the fence, and then suddenly there was a rumbling sound that made them look along the line to the right, where the dark mouth of a tunnel opened itself in the face of a rocky cliff; next moment a train had rushed out of the tunnel with a shriek and a snort, and had slid noisily past them. They felt the rush of its passing, and the pebbles on the line jumped and rattled under it as it went by.
>
> "Oh!" said Roberta, drawing a long breath; "it was like a great dragon tearing by. Did you feel it fan us with its hot wings?"
>
> "I suppose a dragon's lair might look very like that tunnel from the outside," said Phyllis.
>
> But Peter said:—
>
> "I never thought we should ever get as near to a train as this. It's the most ripping sport!"
>
> "Better than toy-engines, isn't it?" said Roberta.
>
> (I am tired of calling Roberta by her name. I don't see why I should. No one else did. Every one else called her Bobbie, and I don't see why I shouldn't.)

"I don't know; it's different," said Peter. "It seems so odd to see *all* of a train. It's awfully tall, isn't it?"

The children imbue the train with a monstrous, fantastic energy. It comes round like a dragon, shattering the still complacency of a landscape that comes off as little more than decorated cake. That great Edwardian tea party—a social life coated in candied peel, in essence—breaks up before the rich imagination that the train provides. This scene strikingly resonates with Toad's first vision of the motorcar, for both evoke the ways in which technology can inflame the passions. The glade here holds no Pan, but instead harbors an equally erotic creature. It is a rush, a ripping sport.

Writers of the Edwardian age transformed vehicular machines into live creatures. Animated, playful, at times threatening, always awe-inspiring, trains, automobiles, and airplanes burst upon the childhood imagination in ways that had to be governed. What seems to me characteristically Edwardian about, for example, the Thomas the Tank Engine stories of the Reverend W. Audry (first appearing in 1946) is the way in which they blend the animated animal tale with the mechanical. They make technology benign; they fantasize about a time before trains ferried soldiers off to war, a time before they carried city children off to country retreats to avoid the Blitz.

Such is the train that opens C. S. Lewis's *The Lion, the Witch, and the Wardrobe*.[26] "Sent away from London during the war because of the air-raids," the Pevensie children find themselves in the house of an old professor, "ten miles from the nearest railway station and two miles from the nearest post office" (p. 111). This is a journey not just over space but back in time, a trip back to the age of the Edwardian country house, a landscape where technology is only barely there. It is a place, too, of the children's literary imagination. What will the children find in the Professor's woods? they ask themselves. Owls, hawks, stags, badgers, foxes, rabbits? Their fantasy of nature is a fantasy of books, as if they hoped to find *The Wind in the Willows* just outside their door. And when they walk through the magic wardrobe, they are taken not just to a place, but to a time of the imagination: a time of Barrie, Grahame, Nesbit; a literary time of Edwardian fiction.

Lewis makes such literary time travel explicit at the opening of the first novel in the Narnia series, *The Magician's Nephew*. Though it was first published in 1955 (five years after *The Lion, the Witch, and the Wardrobe*),

Lewis later made it clear that he intended this to be the first installment in the broader Narnia narrative, and it begins in the grandfatherly voice of the old Professor himself: "This is a story about something that happened long ago when your grandfather was a child." Lewis was born in 1898, and so that childhood would have been an Edwardian one. He goes on: "In those days Mr. Sherlock Holmes was still living in Baker Street and the Bastables were looking for treasure in the Lewisham Road" (p. 11). This is the heyday of Conan Doyle and Nesbit (whose *Treasure Seekers* of 1898 and *Wouldbegoods* of 1899 featured the Bastable children). This is, too, the age of Burnett, whose *Secret Garden* must be what is evoked in the opening discussion between Polly and Digory in their London backyard. What would it be like to live in the country, asks Digory, rather than in London? "And if your father was away in India—and you had to come and live with an Aunt and an Uncle who's mad (who would like that?)—and if the reason was that they were looking after your Mother—and if your Mother was ill and was going to—going to—die." Digory offers up a garbled summary of the plot of *The Secret Garden*, as if to illustrate just how he views the world through the experience of books. And when he tells Polly of noises he hears in the Ketterleys' house, he imagines that there is a pirate shut up in a top-floor room, "like the man at the beginning of *Treasure Island*" (p. 12).

Whatever magic lies in Lewis's tales, it is the magic of books, and in particular the books of his childhood. But more than simply looking for allusions or trying to locate Edwardian identities in later tales, we might see, in the end, that the Edwardian embodies something about childhood itself. All children live on such a cusp: between the memories of their comfortable youth and the fears of the future; between machines that work as playful toys and those that morph into weapons; between a natural world through which they romp and the demarcation of that world by the fences, walls, rails, roads, and bridges of adult administration. Life may be one great garden party, but when you step away from candied peels and cakes, or when you leave the comforts of your little river cottage, or jump out the window of the nursery, you may find yourself beached on an island Neverland, hosting a party run on far from strictly conventional lines.

## · 13 ·

# Good Feeling

PRIZES, LIBRARIES, AND THE INSTITUTIONS
OF AMERICAN CHILDREN'S LITERATURE

"It is deeply satisfying," noted the narrator of E. B. White's *Charlotte's Web*, "to win a prize in front of a lot of people." Prize culture has informed literary publishing for more than a century, and in America it has helped shape the canon of children's books since the 1920s. The American Library Association began awarding the Newbery Medal for the best children's book of the year in 1922, and it inaugurated the Caldecott Medal for outstanding illustration in 1938.[1] Prizes such as these, together with a raft of other markers of distinction, approval, and praise, have come to condition children's literature in modern America. Beverly Lyon Clark, in her study of the institutions of American children's literature, *Kiddie Lit*, notes that the imprimatur of such awards can lead to sales reaching to the scores of thousands, making certain books mainstays of publishers' backlists, public-library lending, and school instruction.[2]

If the libraries and classrooms, bookstores and bedrooms were filled with prize-winning books, so, too, the books themselves were filled with prizes. Contests, races, and competitions came to shape the arc of storytelling. Biographies of past politicians, soldiers, inventors, and explorers focused on their triumph over doubt and their rewarding achievements. Winning the prize became both the internal and the external criterion for literary canonicity, and what emerged in the course of the American twentieth century was nothing less than a literature of winners.[3]

Readers had created canons and criteria for children's reading long before these prizes. The fifteenth-century advisory poem *The Book of Curtesye* set out a syllabus of study for the child: the poets Chaucer, Lydgate, and Hoccleve were to be commended for their mastery of English style, their moral content, and their entertaining quality. Roger Ascham, in his *Scholemaster* of 1570, condemned the medieval romances and adventure tales as "papist" in ideology and sinful in influence. John Locke, at the close of the seventeenth century, had his best books for the child (Aesop, recall, prominent among them), as did Sarah Trimmer at the close of the eighteenth. John Newbery's own choice of books in the middle of the eighteenth century gave rise to a publisher's canon of texts, while the schoolrooms of Britain and America fed the vogue for both stories of instruction and chapbook versions of the great adventure classics.

But what seems distinctive about the American experience, beginning in the late nineteenth century, is not simply a culture of recommendation, but a culture of what Beverly Lyon Clark calls "guardianship." The rise of American children's literature is, to a large degree, inseparable from the rise of the public lending library, and by the 1870s librarians had become the guardians of children's reading.[4] The fact that it is the American Library Association that gives the major children's book awards makes clear that in this country, there is a unique relationship between the worlds of children's reading and the structures of the library. What does it mean to enter into libraries in late nineteenth- and early twentieth-century America? How do children's books present these entries, and how do they imagine libraries or library-like settings? How did America create, in short, a cultural imagination of the library as the space of imaginative exploration?

This chapter's double focus lies in libraries and prizes, and we need to understand the intertwining growth of both in the past century. Though libraries existed throughout Britain and its colonies during the eighteenth century, it is with Benjamin Franklin that we find the origin of the distinctively American lending library. Franklin came up with the idea of sharing books among his own debating society's membership, and the earliest form of this system was a subscription service, where each member invested in the collection. By the end of the eighteenth century, societies and social clubs began establishing their own collections. Cities and towns began to sponsor, in the nineteenth century, collections (supported by taxation) to be used by local citizens, and by 1876—the year the American Library Association was founded—there were nearly two hundred such public libraries (not to mention the hundreds of subscription, club, and social ones). As many historians of the public library have noted, this particular institution came of age in the decades of Progressive reform. The impulses of social work, the attentions to the city poor, the revulsion at child labor—all contributed to the mission of the public library. Most librarians at this time were women, motivated in large part to serve communities out of the so-called settlement house movement, and they came to serve, figuratively speaking, as the mothers of reading for countless children.[5]

The first children's room in any public library opened in Brookline, Massachusetts, in 1890, and women such as Mary Bean (Brookline's librarian), Anne Carroll Moore (the children's librarian at the New York Public Library), and Effie Louise Power (the children's librarian in Cleveland) established what is the now-familiar feel of the children's room and its books. Not only did these women, and their many contemporaries throughout America, govern the kinds of books children should be reading, but they made the library a place of the imagination. Anne Carroll Moore invented Children's Book Week, for example, and she and her peers set aside space for exhibitions and times for storytelling.[6]

By the end of the First World War, the public library rivaled the schoolroom as a place of American socialization. In the words of many early twentieth-century librarians and critics, libraries made *citizens*. They offered amenities designed to teach children how to read and how to behave: to be quiet, respectful, thoughtful, and literate. The fact that many of the children of the urban library were new immigrants only enhanced the importance of this social function. Many libraries insisted that children wash their hands before opening books. Many developed, too, a system of overdue fines designed not merely to pay for library upkeep, but to instill a sense of discipline and economic responsibility in the young citizen.[7]

Librarians were guardians of literacy and culture for the young, and into this culture of guardianship came another, central feature of early twentieth-century life. By the time the American Library Association established the Newbery Medal, prizes had been established as the currency of social value in Europe and America. True, there had been prizes for all forms of literature ever since the ancient Athenians set up the dramatic competitions in the sixth century BC. But by the early twentieth century, things were different. The Nobel Prizes, first awarded in 1901, served to codify achievement in the disciplines of research, service, and imagination—indeed, the Nobels helped not only to reward achievement but to define the disciplines themselves, as if what was physics, chemistry, or literature was now to be determined by the possibility of being judged prizeworthy. The critic James English has chronicled the rise of this modern prize culture, and he argues that the Nobels, in particular, cata-lyzed a process building in the late nineteenth and early twentieth cen-turies: a process of value-making for the great industrialist fortunes of the time. Prizes became essential, English argues, to "the cultural economy as a whole." They validated artistic or scientific achievement; but they also validated the prize-givers. They fed into a view of "the essentially competitive character of cultural life" that was the consequence of in-dustrial entrepreneurship. Competition was the way of the world. It was no coincidence, either, that the Olympic Games were revived at this time (1896), and that the criteria for "amateur" and "professional" emerged along economic lines. The public library and the prize thus emerge as in-stitutions of approval and reward, ways of confirming individual achieve-ment while at the same time validating the social mission of the volunteer and the philanthropist who make both possible.[8]

And so, in 1921, the bookseller and editor of *Publishers' Weekly*, Frederic G. Melcher, proposed to the American Library Association that a prize be given for the best children's book of the year.[9] Rather than naming it after a living donor or bequeathing an award through a will, Melcher suggested naming the award after John Newbery. His choice says some-thing about the world of children's books in the early twentieth century: by naming the prize after a bookseller and publisher, Melcher made clear that the presiding aegis over children's literature was economic. The busi-ness of America was business (in Calvin Coolidge's bon mot of 1925), and the Newbery Medal signaled that books were a business, too.

Still, Melcher's plan was not to reward popularity or sales, but rather "literature." Again and again, in the description of the medal and the lay-ing out of the criteria of assessment, "literature" and "literary quality" crop up as the key terms. But what did these terms mean in America in the early 1920s? Did they connote a social purpose or reformist goal, as in the work of the most widely read writers of the age: H. G. Wells, Sinclair Lewis, Sherwood Anderson, and H. L. Mencken? Or did they connote an adventurism in language use, as in the modernism of Yeats, Pound, Woolf, Joyce, Eliot, and Wallace Stevens? Neither. The literary qualities sought by the Newbery committee were largely concerned with theme and plot, character and style, setting, and clarity of organization. These are the committee's criteria for "good writing," and one of the central purposes of the award, in Melcher's original phrasing, was "to give those librarians, who make it their life work to serve children's reading inter-ests, an opportunity to encourage good writing in this field."

The Newbery Medal remains a paradox. A prize named for a book-seller, established by a publisher, fostered in an age of capital and commerce, the Newbery comes up with an ideal of the "literary" keyed to the ideals of the public library. "Accuracy, clarity, and organization": these are the governing terms of the award criteria, and these, too, are the ideals of librarianship.

Given these guidelines, it is no surprise that the first winner of the Newbery Medal in 1922 was Hendrik Willem Van Loon's *Story of Mankind*.[10] It is, by any reading, a delightful book: rich with engaging anecdotes, clear judgments, and precise chronology. It gives us history that is accurate, clear, and organized. The very theme of the book is organization: how do we sort out all the details of the world; how do we find our place in history and experience? "I want you to learn something more from this history than a mere succession of facts," Van Loon writes, interrupting his account of the Holy Alliance of 1815. "I want you to approach all historical events in a frame of mind that will take nothing for granted. . . . Try to discover the hidden motives behind every action and then you will understand the world around you much better and you will have a greater chance to help others, which (when all is said and done) is the only truly satisfactory way of living" (p. 370). This is history as social lesson; history that speaks to the motives of the reformist librarians who, throughout the late nineteenth and early twentieth centuries, were helping children to understand the world around them and help others. And toward the close of *The Story of Mankind*, Van Loon waxes eloquent about the progress of science and medicine. "Today the rich people who in past ages donated their wealth for the building of a cathedral, construct vast laboratories where silent men do battle upon the hidden enemies of mankind and often sacrifice their lives that coming generations may enjoy greater happiness and health" (p. 431).

Van Loon's idealism was not lost on the librarians who awarded him their prize. Anne Carroll Moore, who reviewed the book for *The Bookman* in November 1921 and who developed her responses in her influential collection of reviews, *Roads to Childhood*, called it "the most invigorating and, I venture to predict, the most influential children's book for many years to come." The book will, she goes on, "revolutionize" history writing for the young. Its maps are "animated." It has "liberated" ideas. Notice the power of her judgments here—the words of politics and power. This is a new book for "this generation and the next," a book that will change lives, so it seems, as much as wars and revolutions will.[11]

But there is something about Van Loon's book, and about all the early winners of the Newbery Medal, that goes beyond clarity of argument or "literary quality," or even vividness of writing. This is a book of adventure. *The Story of Mankind* records exploits of imaginative heroes. It sets sail on the ocean of history, and if my figurative phrasing seems a little overdone, it is exactly what the book itself offers. Look at the short excerpt published in *Horn Book Magazine*'s collection *Newbery Medal Books: 1922–1955.*

> The engineer and the scientist and the chemist, within a single generation, filled Europe and America and Asia with their vast machines, their telegraphs, their flying machines, their coal-tar products. They created a new world in which time and space were reduced to complete insignificance. They invented new products and they made these so cheap that almost every one could buy them.
>
> First one part, then another of the old ship of state was changed. Her dimensions were increased. The sails were discarded for steam. . . . But the captain and the mates remained the same. They were appointed or elected in the same way as a hundred years before. They were taught the same system of navigation which had served the mariners of the fifteenth century. . . . In short, they were (through no fault of their own) completely incompetent . . .
>
> And the moral of the story is a simple one. The world is in dreadful need of men who will have the courage of their own visions and who will recognize clearly that we are only at the beginning of the voyage, and have to learn an entirely new system of seamanship.
>
> They will have to serve for years as mere apprentices. They will have to fight their way to the top against every possible form of opposition. When they reach the bridge, mutiny of an envious crew may cause their death. But some day, a man will arise who will bring the vessel safely to port, and he shall be the hero of the ages.[12]

The story of mankind remains a story of the ship. It takes us back to the canoes and cannibals of Crusoe, to the island fantasies of Stevenson, to the heroic technological exploits of Jules Verne. These are tales not just of exploit, but of reward: Robinson comes home to find himself a wealthy man; there is a treasure on the South Sea island; Verne's explorers win out, always, in the end.

And so did Van Loon. His son's biography recounts the hardships that beset the author in the early 1920s. Penurious, holding a Ph.D. and in need of a job, the elder Van Loon accepted a teaching position at Antioch

THE SCENE OF OUR HISTORY IS LAID UPON A LITTLE PLANET, LOST IN THE VASTNESS
OF THE UNIVERSE.

Fig. 20. Frontispiece to Hendrik Willem Van Loon, *The Story of Mankind*
(New York: Boni and Liveright, 1921).

College in the fall of 1921. At the same time, the publisher Horace Liveright asked him to write something in response to H. G. Wells's *Outline of History*, published in 1920 to great acclaim. Van Loon typed away (so the son tells us), producing a one-volume, personally illustrated book, which the firm of Boni and Liveright highlighted in their catalogue. Positive reviews started coming in—not just from Anne Carroll Moore in *The Bookman*, but from prominent professors in such publications as *The Nation* and the *New York Times* and, perhaps most stunning of all, from the great historian Charles A. Beard. In the end, writes the son, *The Story of Mankind* "netted Hendrik Willem well over half a million dollars." In June of 1922, the book won the Newbery Medal, and Van Loon sailed back to his native Holland to show off his success. Even though the trip was a disappointment ("He saw his native land as the personification of his father, the killjoy out to humble him and make him look ridiculous"), he returned to great éclat—summarized by the telegram his wife sent him: "YOU ARE FAMOUS."[13]

*The Story of Mankind* has its own story, and the telling recapitulates the ideals of the storybook success for a prize-winning world. And as the Newbery Medals progressed, they reinforced this narrative of travel and adventure, personal triumph and public reward. Nineteen twenty-three saw the award go to Hugh Lofting's *Voyages of Dr. Dolittle* (the sequel to *The Story of Dr. Dolittle*, published in 1920). Here, the doctor travels with ten-year-old Tommy Stubbins, and they sail to shores and islands far away. Animals and aboriginal people fill their adventures, and the two wind up on Spider Monkey Island, where the doctor's exploits, knowledge, and bravery manage to get him appointed king. In acts of social reform not far from Van Loon's vision of the role of idealized leaders, the doctor

> showed them what town-sewers were, and how garbage should be collected each day and burnt. High up in the hills he made a large lake by damming a stream. This was the water-supply for the town. None of these things had the Indians ever seen; and many of the sicknesses which they had suffered from before were now entirely prevented by proper drainage and pure drinking-water.
>
> Peoples who don't use fire do not of course have metals either; because without fire it is almost impossible to shape iron and steel. One of the first things that John Dolittle did was to search the mountains till he found iron and copper mines. Then he set to work to teach the Indians how

these metals could be melted and made into knives and plows and water-pipes and all manner of things.

In his kingdom the Doctor tried his hardest to do away with most of the old-fashioned pomp and grandeur of a royal court. As he said to Bumpo and me, if he must be a king he meant to be a thoroughly democratic one, that is a king who is chummy and friendly with his subjects and doesn't put on airs. And when he drew up the plans for the City of New Popsipetel he had no palace shown of any kind. A little cottage in a back street was all that he had provided for himself.[14]

Dr. Dolittle comes off as the embodiment of Van Loon's vision of the engineer, the hero who arises with a new kind of social seamanship. Tales of adventure, yes, but always with the goal of bettering society.

To read through the list of the first Newbery Medal winners is to attend to voyages and visions of this kind. The winner for 1924 was Charles Boardman Hawes's *Dark Frigate*—a sea-adventure tale set in the days of King Charles II. Nineteen twenty-five had Charles Finger's *Tales from Silver Lands*, set in "the Far South near Cape Horn, . . . a place of many islands." The award of 1926 went to Arthur Bowie Chrisman's *Shen of the Sea*; and for the next two decades, just about every book takes its reader to a foreign land or a distant time. These were books to transport the imagination of the child into the faraway or long ago. Heroes and villains abound. Boys and girls sail in ships, ride horses, travel in covered wagons or coaches. Elizabeth Gray's *Adam of the Road* won in 1943, and it sets its adventure at the end of the thirteenth century as the young boy and his father, a famous minstrel, ride the highways of old England. The fact that this boy is named Adam Quartermain speaks volumes, of course: volumes looking back to H. Rider Haggard's tales of Allan Quatermain (notice the slight difference in spelling), as if the evocation of this hero placed the book in line with expectations of adventure.[15]

Many of these Newbery books are now neglected or forgotten, but the 1944 winner, Esther Forbes's *Johnny Tremain*, remains a staple of the schoolroom and a classic of American children's literature (by one recent count, it is the sixteenth best selling children's book of all time).[16] What sets it apart from its peers? For one thing, it is a story of both personal and national coming of age. The revolutionary break with Britain mirrors Johnny's break with parental authority. And the vision of the young boy, and the young country, overcoming trauma and travail spoke directly to a readership of wartime. The reviewer for the *Springfield Sunday Union and Republican* could write in November 1943 that Forbes had the "ability to make an event of 1½ centuries ago read like a war communiqué from Italy."[17]

What compels the reader of the book is Johnny's accident. Apprenticed to a silversmith, Johnny aspires to a mastery of his craft. One Sunday (working on the Sabbath, of all times), as the silver melts in the crucible, Johnny gets ready to pour.

> He moved forward delicately, his right hand outstretched. The crucible began to settle—collapse, the silver was running over the top of the furnace like spilled milk. Johnny jumped toward it, his right hand still outstretched. Something happened, he never knew exactly what. His feet went out from under him. His hand came down on the top of the furnace.
>
> The burn was so terrible he at first felt no pain, but stood stupidly looking at his hand. For one second, before the metal cooled, the inside of his right hand, from wrist to fingertips, was coated with solid silver. He looked at the back of his hand. It was as always. Then he smelled burned flesh. The room blackened and tipped around him. He heard a roaring in his ears.
>
> (p. 33)

Pride goeth before a fall. But there is more to Johnny's story than the canned moral tale of humbling and then recovery that leads him out of his despondency after the accident and into printing, revolutionary action, and eventually the confidence that will permit him, at the novel's end, to show his injured hand to Doctor Warren and make plans for an operation. This is a story of the work of hands: of silversmithing, printing, writing. It is a story of the ways in which artistic and political activity go, truly, hand in hand; a story of just how the plastic or prose products of the hand can change a life. Johnny's hand is the emblem of the novel's artistry, and in this emblem *Johnny Tremain* aspires to be not just a tale well told, but a self-conscious work of literature that takes aesthetic value, and its social implications, as its theme.

Such a theme has long motivated the literature of war, and *Johnny Tremain* remains a war book both in the subject matter of its telling and the time of its writing. As noteworthy as the book's story is its style. The 1930s and early 1940s had seen the emergence of a new kind of public reportage. Edward R. Murrow spoke to his radio audience during the London Blitz "from atop a city in flames." William L. Shirer published his *Berlin Diary* as an eyewitness account of Hitler's rise. Daily dispatches for the newspapers telegraphed battle. Some of this reportage, of course, looks back to the traditions of war journalism that had taken shape in the mid-nineteenth century, and dispatches from Crimea and South Africa, as I have illustrated, had a lasting impact on the idiom of books for young people. What is different about the reportage of the mid-twentieth century, however, is its voice: the focus on eyewitness experience; the staccato telegraphy of description; the violence and brutality of the events. Readers of the age would have found such forms in novels as well as journalism, and Norman Mailer's *The Naked and the Dead* (1948) captures this flavor.

> Nobody could sleep. When morning came, assault craft would be lowered and a first wave of troops would ride through the surf and charge ashore on the beach at Anopopei. All over the ship, all through the convoy, there was a knowledge that in a few hours some of them were going to be dead.[18]

Compare the opening of Mailer's book with Forbes's closing gestures.

> Everywhere else in the village was silence. The music, small as the chirping of a cricket, filled that silence. Down the road came twenty or thirty tired and ragged men. Some were blood-stained. No uniforms. A curious arsenal of weapons. The long horizontal light of the sinking sun struck into their faces and made them seem much alike. Thin-faced in the manner of Yankee men. High cheek-boned. Unalterably determined. The tired men marched unevenly, but Johnny noticed the swing of the lithe, independent bodies. The set of chin and shoulders. Rab had been like that.
>
> (pp. 255–56)

The flow of these phrases has the unmistakable cadence of wartime fiction. Sentences simply lay out subject, verb, and object. Often, they will fracture into fragments. Everywhere, death hangs—whether it be in anticipation of the soldier's death, as in Mailer, or in the recollection of Rab's death, as in Forbes. It must have been writing such as this that provoked the reviewer to see *Johnny Tremain* as akin to war communiqués from Italy.

War wrecks the bodies of its soldiers, and throughout the accounts of Murrow and Shirer, and in the fiction of Mailer, we see wounded and maimed men. *Johnny Tremain* has none of the gore of battlefield or hospital, but it does have, in Johnny's damaged hand, an image of deformity. Forbes has displaced the war wound onto Johnny's hand: as if he must live his life as someone mutilated, much like a soldier coming home. He looks for work after the accident, but fails. "He would take [his hand] out of the pocket where he always kept it, with a flourish, display it to the sickening curiosity of the master, apprentices, journeymen, lady customers" (p. 44). I cannot get the image out of my mind of the young sailor coming home in the film *The Best Years of Our Lives* (1946), his hands replaced by metal claws. Johnny, too, for one shining yet horrific moment, seems to have a metal hand, as the silver flows over his palm. But here, this is an image rather than a fact—the human hand, damaged perhaps beyond repair, burned yet gleamingly metallic.

It is, of course, Johnny's right hand. What can he do without it? He finds a new life with the Lorne family. He learns to ride a horse. And he reads—not just perusing books, but loving them, in "an orgy of reading."

> Mr. Lorne had a fine library. It was as if Johnny had been starved before and never known it. He read anything—everything. Bound back copies of the Observer, Paradise Lost, Robinson Crusoe—once more, for that was one of the books Rab had brought him to read in jail—Tom Jones and Locke's Essays on Human Understanding, Hutchinson's History of Massachusetts Bay, Chemical Essays, Spectator Papers, books on midwifery, and manners for young ladies, Pope's Iliad. It was a world of which he never had guessed while living with the Laphams, and now he remembered with gratitude how his mother had struggled to teach him so that this world might not have been forever closed to him. How she had made him read to her, when he would rather have been playing.... So he sat for hours in the Lornes' sunny parlor, the books about him stretching to the ceiling.
>
> (p. 96)

Like any child, Johnny would find himself anew in the library, and literary celebrations such as this one (together with the vividness of the political and social writing of the novel) must have appealed especially to the librarian judges of the Newbery Medal. The books Johnny read are the foundational books for the eighteenth century; and the foundational books, too, for the history of children's literature I have been writing here. Adventure, romance, knowledge, history: all come together in this canon of his reading. And soon, too, Johnny learns to write with his left hand.

I grew up, like so many children, writing with my right, and when I was no more than five, my parents took me to the Brooklyn branch of the New York Public Library. At that time, all you needed for a library card was the ability to sign your own name, and I remember on that day in October, as the autumn sun came through the vast windows and the books seemed to stretch to the ceiling, carefully writing my name in ink on the little white library card. My right hand ached from the exertion (it must have been the first time I had ever written my full name), and my mother brought me to the children's section, where I picked out the first book I think I ever truly read: Robert McCloskey's *Make Way for Ducklings*.

Published in 1941, *Make Way for Ducklings* was the story of the Mallards, looking for a place to live and raise their family. When they find a nice place on an island in the Charles River, in Boston, Mr. Mallard announces that he has to go away for a week, but that he will rejoin his wife and what will be their eight hatched ducklings in the Public Garden. Mrs. Mallard, raising her children, leads them along in time to make the rendezvous. She literally stops traffic, as a policeman holds up the flow of cars to let her and her children pass. And sure enough, there is the father, right where and when he said he would be.

I loved that book. Many others must have, too, for it won a Caldecott Medal in 1942 for best illustrated book.[19] When Robert McCloskey rose to accept the award, he told the story about how, when he had been an art student in Boston, there really was a family of ducks that lived in the Boston Public Garden. Inspired by his observation, he began to draw ducks left and right, at one point buying a bunch of mallards and sketching them as they swam in his bathtub. McCloskey reflected on the process of drawing: "If you ever see an artist draw a horse, or a lion, or a duck, the lines flowing from his brush or crayon in just the right place so that all of the horse's feet touch the ground, the lion couldn't be mistaken for a pin cushion, and the duck is a duck, and you think, 'My, how easily and quickly he does that, it must be a talent he was born with'—well think it if you must but don't say it!" Being an artist takes hard work, not just talent, and McCloskey concludes: "It shows that no effort is too great to find out as much as possible about the things you are drawing. It's a good feeling to be able to put down a line and know that it is right."[20]

It's a good feeling to put down a line, whether it be the outline of a duck or the letters of your name. Johnny Tremain must learn to put down lines left-handed (and eventually to set type in the print shop). *The Story of Mankind*, in Van Loon's telling, is a story of people making an effort, of hard work and struggle, and in the end, a good feeling of success. It's a good feeling, too, to raise your children, to put down a line of ducks, as Mrs. Mallard does across the road—a straight line, "right into the Public Garden." And "there was Mr. Mallard waiting for them, just as he had promised."[21]

How many fathers returned, just as they had promised? For anyone among this book's contemporary, wartime audience, this question must have hung over the story. *Make Way for Ducklings* is as much a war book as *Johnny Tremain*. Its lesson is that mothers can raise children on their own. Its fantasy is that fathers, even though they leave, always come back. Its social vision is that, whatever chaos reigns abroad, policemen still make way for families, and public gardens can be places of repose.

It *is* a good feeling. Artistic creativity comes with rewards, and we may recall, after McCloskey's judgment, the reflection by E. B. White that opened this chapter: "It is deeply satisfying to win a prize in front of a lot of people." Both *Make Way for Ducklings* and *Charlotte's Web* are books of artistry, for Charlotte herself is an artist of the farmyard imagination—writing her words in her web, weaving the plots that will bring Wilbur the pig his rewards. Johnny Tremain must give up his career as a craftsman in silver, but by the novel's end, he can stand up to take his place in battle. "A man can stand up": these are the last words of the book, and they must resonate, I think, with all the men—and women—who stood up for literacy, virtue, artistry, and social reform in the first decades of the twentieth century. Even Wilbur stands up. Reading through Van Loon's biography, I cannot but recall the capital letters of Charlotte's "SOME PIG" in Mrs. Van Loon's telegram, "YOU ARE FAMOUS"—as if it would always be the job of women to remind their men of their accomplishments.

And Van Loon, Esther Forbes, Robert McCloskey, and now more than one hundred authors and illustrators have stood up to accept their prizes. What many of their books share is this sense of accomplishment: the sense that standing up, or traveling, or even reading books, gives you a good feeling. The pain of wartime, the disruptions of the 1920s and 1930s, the fears of homecoming (will they recognize me? what can I do, wounded, once again?)—all these lead us into places where we can feel good or deeply satisfied. The men and women who established the American public library sought to make reading rooms the places of such feeling. Books can transport us far away; but they can also make us feel at home. And in the end, so many of these books ask deeper questions. What are the prizes for domestic life? What medals will we win for simply living well?

# Keeping Things Straight

STYLE ·AND THE CHILD

Throughout the history of children's literature, boys and girls have been taught style. From the Roman and late antique instructions in social behavior with the family and the slave; through medieval and Renaissance handbooks of dress, speech, and table manners; to the Puritans' concerns with proper conduct and the eighteenth- and nineteenth-century concerns with proper "cutting up," or the anxiousness about theatricality and play—throughout all these periods and genres, children have learned ways of being in the world. Style marks the child as male or female, rich or poor, educated or illiterate. "Le style," said the Comte de Buffon famously, "c'est l'homme même"—the style is the man himself.[1] But it is also the child.

The word *style* comes from the Latin *stylus*, originally meaning the pointed object poets and schoolchildren used to mark their letters on wax tablets. To write in a certain style, for antique authors, was to compose in a language or an idiom befitting certain subject matters. There were levels of style, according to the gravity of the subject. And when a writer wrote in a particular and individual style, it was a way of adapting the words to personal expression. "Style" yoked together hand and thought, expression and imagination. Early on in the history of English, the word came to connote any manner of public behavior, but it was only in the late eighteenth and early nineteenth centuries that *style* could mean a valued form of that behavior in the social sense. Having not just *a* style but style itself seems to emerge as a category of identity keyed to fashion and education, wit and bearing—valued qualities emerging in the age of Fanny Burney, Jane Austen, and Benjamin Disraeli, that is, the age of social novelists and chroniclers of habit. The *Oxford English Dictionary* offers Jane Austen's *Sense and Sensibility* (1797) as the earliest source for the literary use of the word *stylish* to describe fashionable or socially ideal appearance: "A smart, stilish girl, they say, but not handsome." The *OED* adduces Disraeli's novel *Vivian Grey* (1826) with the phrase, "Most amusing, delightful girl, great style!" Harriet Martineau, writing in 1833, could note, "His daughters look very well in their better style of dress."

By the first third of the nineteenth century, girls could be seen as stylish, and by the mid-Victorian period boys, too, could have a certain style about them. The Rugby education that Tom Brown gets from peers, as well as teachers, is an education in a style of life. The sense of "cutting up" in *Tom Brown's Schooldays* is a sense of style; the very verb here signals shape in fashion (as in the cut of one's clothes or, more figuratively, the cut of one's jib—an idiom that emerges in the 1820s). Style connotes aesthetic value: it is a marker not just of a social class or gender role, but of an artistic sensibility. What does it mean to be a stylish child, and how are the ideals of such a style in keeping with the ideals of a writing style for children's books and literary expression?

There are many ways of charting out the history of the stylish child. The school, the playground, and the home have long served as the places where a style is taught and learned, and to a large extent much of my previous analysis has centered on the shape of children's style in all these venues. What happens, though, to style and childhood in an age of social conformity? Mid-twentieth-century America produced some of the best known of our children's books. E. B. White's *Stuart Little*, Dr. Seuss's *The Cat in the Hat*, and stories by Robert McCloskey and George Selden all seek, in their various ways, to understand the place of the stylish or aesthetically creative child in a community. What is the place of role-playing in social development? How can one grow up as an individual and serve an organization? What are the dangers of nonconformity? Such questions, as historians have known for decades, shaped the culture and the politics of mid-twentieth-century America. What are the answers for the children's book?

Some of these answers look back to earlier literary forms, and some draw our eyes not to the stylish but to the awful. Ugliness, filth, and bad behavior had filled children's books from their beginning, though few such examples have had the staying power of the German Struwwelpeter. Slovenly Peter, or Shock-headed Peter, as he became known in English translation, was the boy without hygiene: his hair went wild without washing; his fingernails grew into tentacles. In the range of illustrations to his story, running from his first appearance in Heinrich Hoffmann's *Lustige Geschichten und drollige Bilder* of 1845, through the English and American editions of the nineteenth and twentieth centuries (one of which was translated by Mark Twain), he comes off as part bad boy and part monster.[2]

The Struwwelpeter tradition has provoked a range of literary and artistic forms, stories of little boys whose deceits distort their physical appearance. Pinocchio is certainly the best known, and perhaps now the most iconic, of such bad boys. He originally appeared in Carlo Collodi's contributions to the *Giornale per i bambini* between 1881 and 1883, and the stories of the puppet (the *burattino* of the original Italian title) were collected in book form shortly after the final installment appeared in the winter of 1883.[3] *Le avventure di Pinocchio* is many things, but it is first and foremost a tale of metamorphosis: a story of a puppet who becomes a real boy; a story about artifice that apes the artistry of life. Theatricality is everywhere in the novel, and styles of life are everywhere in evidence. Early on in the novel, Pinocchio sells his spelling book to buy admission to a puppet show.[4] In a moment worthy of St. Augustine's *Confessions*, he leaves literacy aside for spectacle (the young Augustine had been captivated by the theater, and, as he reports, "Many and many a time I lied to my tutor, my masters, and my parents, and deceived them because I wanted to play games or watch some futile show or was impatient to imitate what I saw on the stage").[5] Pinocchio becomes part of the show, as the stage puppets recognize him as their "brother," and in the novel—as well as in the famous Disney film of 1940—this episode stands as a terrifying critique of theatricality itself.

Throughout *Le Avventure*, Pinocchio seesaws from home to wilderness, from welcoming domestic figures to theatrical abductors. Even Pinocchio's later transformation into a jackass is a kind of theatrical metamorphosis. Recall St. Augustine again: "Rapiebant me spectacula theatrica"; the spectacle of the theater, he wrote in the *Confessions*, ravished him.[6] Pinocchio, too, has been abducted, enwrapped, and enraptured through the machinations of the theater manager. And when he finally appears on stage, as a donkey, his attire and his bearing captivate the audience. "Era insomma un ciuchino da innamorare!" "In short," we are told, "he was a donkey to steal your heart away."

There remains something uneasy about performance and pretense in children's literature, and the style of the child often must be controlled,

Fig. 21. Struwwelpeter. From Heinrich Hoffmann, *Lustige Geschichten und drollige Bilder*, 1845.

lest it transmute into affectation. The Disney version of Pinocchio makes these anxieties explicit. Indeed, this is a film about performance itself; an animated cartoon about animation; a lesson about what it means to live without strings. The movie's villains are stylish ones. "An actor's life for me," the Fox croons, as he lures the puppet boy away from school. "You wear your hair in a pompadour." Such a style would have been the very emblem of affectation—the *Oxford English Dictionary* notes that *pompadour*, used for a man's hairstyle, is restricted to the United States, and its quotations indicate that, for the mid-twentieth century, it was often associated with a form of costume, stage dress, or performative pose (notice, for example, this quotation from 1955, from the novelist William Gaddis: "His hair, a shiny black pompadour which he wore like a hat"). In the movie, Stromboli the puppeteer is not simply a coarse monster; he is the stage manager from hell. The island of lost boys is filled with play and play-acting, and Pinocchio's transformation into a donkey has about it all the flavor of a costume change.

"A real boy." A real boy is no creature of the theater, but a child of school and home. Disney's *Pinocchio*, for all its brilliance as a work of animation, is a profoundly anti-theatrical tale: one that consistently presents performance as seductive, dangerous, duplicitous, and vile. For mid-twentieth-century America, the movie illustrated a central problem in the social education of the child: How can you have an individual identity without playing a role? How can you have a style without losing substance?

Two major works of American children's literature answer these questions in different ways: E. B. White's *Stuart Little* (1945) and Dr. Seuss's *The Cat in the Hat* (1957). Both present highly stylish central characters who challenge the expectations of middle-class family life. But while Stuart is always a model of sartorial decorum and verbal precision, the Cat is a travesty of dress and speech. Stuart comes off as master of the house; the Cat comes off as a master of street theater. But both offer ideals of the imagination for the child: ways of adjudicating between the desire to cross boundaries and the need to find a home.[7]

Before looking at *Stuart Little*, however, I turn to another work by E. B. White that had as lasting an impact on young readers as any of his stories: *The Elements of Style*, the little manual originally written by William Strunk, Jr., before the First World War and revised by White for republication in 1957.[8] *The Elements of Style* is a handbook of English composition, but it is, as well, a guide to life, and the advice it offers for the placement of a word or on the arc of a sentence is advice for living in the world. It is, as I take it here, a kind of gloss on the ideals of social style embodied in the fiction of White's *Stuart Little*.

Like many manuals of speech and writing, *The Elements of Style* begins with basics such as grammar and punctuation. Learn how to form the possessive; learn the proper uses of the comma; learn how to deploy participles. The book then moves to composition. Clarity and brevity are the ideals. Colloquialisms and slang should be avoided. These are the elements of writing, but they also are the elements of life. "Vigorous writing is concise." Make "every word tell." Such advice takes us back to Lord Chesterfield, who counseled his son: "One must be extremely exact, clear, and perspicuous, in every thing one says; otherwise, instead of entertaining or informing others, one only tires and puzzles them."[9] Writing and speech are social arts, and style reveals the inner character of the performer. White notes that "every writer, by the way he uses the language, reveals something of his spirit, his habits, his capacities, his bias." Style is "the Self escaping into the open" (pp. 59–60).

Too often, childhood selves escape into the open without regulation. White's own voice clearly emerges as that of the parent and the teacher. "Young writers often suppose that style is a garnish for the meat of prose, a sauce by which a dull dish is made palatable. Style has no such separate entity.... The beginner ... should begin by turning resolutely away from all devices that are popularly believed to indicate style—all mannerisms, tricks, adornments. The approach to style is by way of plainness, simplicity, orderliness, sincerity" (p. 62). This is, it seems to me, as much a lesson in the Puritan as it is a lesson for the publishing ideal, and White's aesthetic remains very much an old, American praise of simplicity. Write naturally, place yourself in the background, do not overwrite, do not overstate. These are the injunctions of his subheadings, and each brings us back to the life lessons ranged from *The New England Primer* to *Little Women*. The self should not intrude. Theatrical attention-getting—whether it be in the form of Pinocchio's prancing or Anne Shirley's gallivanting on a rooftop—is a vice. White writes, "Avoid the elaborate, the pretentious, the coy, and the cute.... Anglo-Saxon is a livelier tongue than Latin, so use Anglo-Saxon words" (p. 69). Whatever the validity of White's philology (this is an argument that has been made since Milton's teacher Alexander Gil condemned the inrush of new Latinate words in the early seventeenth century), his is a claim for linguistic and social belonging. Like Lord Chesterfield, like Dr. Arnold of Rugby, like the innumerable schoolmasters of children's fiction, White emerges from these pages as a taskmaster of directness, a teacher of the arts of Englishness.

And in the midst of his advice, much like John Locke digressing in *Some Thoughts concerning Education*, White can offer up vignettes of startling brilliance: "Muddiness is not merely a disturber of prose, it is also a destroyer of life, of hope: death on the highway caused by a badly worded road sign, heartbreak among lovers caused by a misplaced phrase in a well-intentioned letter, anguish of a traveler expecting to be met at a railroad station and not being met because of a slipshod telegram. . . . Think of the tragedies that are rooted in ambiguity" (p. 72). Embedded in this exhortation is a theory not just of good writing, but of literature itself. For it is literature that lies in ambiguity. The misreading and misapprehension of the signs and symbols of our everyday existence generate the drama and the plot of fiction. "Try to keep things straight" (p. 73). But, try as we might, things go astray, the highway is a death trap, and the words we think we write and say escape into the open, taking on a selfhood we cannot control.

Here lies the essence of White's *Stuart Little*, the novel that seeks a clarity of vision in the muddiness of life. Stuart lives as a little traveler, constantly in danger of wrecking lives and loves. He is, from his first appearance, a creature of style, and it is style that gets him through the day. Even at birth, Stuart is stylish; at just a few days old, he is already "wearing a gray hat and carrying a small cane" (p. 1). His page-one portrait shows a model of sartorial simplicity, circa 1945: all except for that tail that loops like some unanswerable question mark from behind his smart jacket.

Stuart's adventures are adventures in decorum and control. How can he wash up after falling down the drain? How can he keep himself clean and fit in a mouse's form? The opening chapters read like an allegory of hygiene or, perhaps, like a riposte to the world of Struwwelpeter. Middle-class city life, for Stuart, is a life of ritualized action: a pattern of transforming threats and challenges into controlled behavior. Robinson Crusoe may have his shipwreck; Stuart has his model yacht. The sailboat-race chapter takes the traditions of the Robinsonian adventure story and domesticates them into toy-scale Central Park. His little boat, the *Wasp*, goes prow to prow with the *Lillian B. Womrath*, owned by a fat, sulky boy of twelve. Soon we are in the world of boys' books once again: the present-tense narrative, the lists of all the mechanics of boat craft. Small ripples become giant waves; a paper bag becomes a monstrous drag on jib and spar. And when Stuart finally wins, when he surmounts the "dirty weather" of the park, the flotsam of the lake, and the duplicity of the *Lillian B. Womrath*'s owner, he springs to the wheel. The other boat "had gone off in a wild direction and was yawing all over the pond." But "straight and true sailed the Wasp, with Stuart at the helm" (p. 45). Notice the language here: the contrast between wild direction and true, straight control. The race is now not just a race between two sailors, but between two forms of the imagination, two forms of a style. "Try to keep things straight": Stuart does, and in doing so he learns the elements of style.

And after he falls in love with the bird Margalo (what heartbreak here), after he secures the little car with the invisibility button, accidentally causing it to crash (death on the highway avoided by a hair's breadth), Stuart becomes the teacher. Driving through upstate New York, he comes upon a sad man sitting on the curb. The man is the superintendent of schools, upset because he cannot find a substitute teacher for the day. Stuart volunteers. He changes clothes, into what White calls his "pepper and salt" jacket, old striped trousers, Windsor tie, and spectacles. "Do you think you can maintain discipline?" the superintendent asks. "Of course I can," Stuart replies. "I'll make the work interesting and the discipline will take care of itself." And when he shows up, White reports, "everyone's eyes lit up with excitement to see such a small and good-looking teacher, so appropriately dressed" (pp. 87–88).

Stuart recognizes that the subject matter of the classroom must take second place to social habit. Indeed, his lesson may be seen as putting into practice the advice of White's contemporary Dr. Benjamin Spock, the well-known adviser on child-rearing. In his great *Baby and Child Care* (first published in 1946), Dr. Spock has a chapter titled "What a School Is For," which opens with claims strikingly akin to Stuart's. "The main lesson in school is how to get along in the world. Different subjects are merely a means to this end. . . . You learn only when things mean something to you. One job of a school is to make subjects so interesting and real that children want to learn and remember."[10] As Stuart said, make the work interesting, and the discipline will take care of itself. And so, jettisoning lessons based on rote and reason, he asks what is really important. Henry Rackmeyer answers: "A shaft of sunlight at the end of a dark afternoon, a note in music, and the way the back of a baby's neck smells if its mother keeps it tidy." "Correct," says Stuart; "you forgot one thing, though. Mary Bendix, what did Henry Rackmeyer forget?" "He forgot ice cream with chocolate sauce on it," the girl answers. "Exactly. . . . Ice cream is important" (pp. 92–93). Schooling lies not in affirming facts or espousing an ideology. It lies in the poetry of everyday life. What matters is to find that shaft of sunlight, that little bit of the sublime in ordinary days. There is a music to experience, a beauty in the memories of ordinary domesticity. Such knowledge far exceeds what is testable.

Would that Stuart himself could put these lessons into practice. Later on in his journey, when he stops at Ames's Crossing, he finds himself attracted to a little girl, no bigger than himself. He tries to set up a little date: there is the picnic, the canoe, the flowers, and the river. All is elaborately prepared, and yet all comes to nothing. Someone has damaged his canoe: the pillow is missing; the backrest is gone; the seams are split. "It was just a mess. It looked just the way a birchbark canoe looks after some big boys are finished playing with it" (p. 121). Now all the strands of *Stuart Little* come together; now they recall not just the hero's mastery of the boat in Central Park, but a whole history of boating. "My soul is an enchanted boat," wrote Shelley in the poem Kenneth Grahame reprinted in his *Cambridge Book of Poetry for Children.* And Grahame's own animals, messing about in boats, show us the nexus of leisure and pleasure. Shipwreck threatens everywhere, and what the history of such shipwrecks shows—from *Robinson Crusoe* to *Treasure Island,* from *The Wind in the Willows* to *Stuart Little*—is that one must face failure with style. Here, at this moment of great challenge, Stuart fails. Emotion overwhelms him. Alone, "with his broken dreams and damaged canoe" (p. 124), he sleeps out in the rain.

Language, wrote White in *The Elements of Style,* "is perpetually in flux." He goes on:

> It is a living stream, shifting, changing, receiving new strength from a thousand tributaries, losing old forms in the backwaters of time. To suggest that a young writer not swim in the main stream of this turbulence would be foolish indeed, and such is not the intent of these cautionary remarks. The intent is to suggest that . . . the beginner err on the side of conservatism, on the side of established usage. No idiom is taboo, no accent forbidden; there is simply a better chance of doing well if the writer holds a steady course, enters the stream of English quietly, and does not thrash about.
>
> (p. 76)

And so, Stuart continues on his journey. His forays into turbulence— whether they land him on a garbage scow or underneath a damaged canoe—may teach him to err on the side of established usage. But there may be poetry, still, in the everyday. At last he comes upon a telephone lineman, and when Stuart notes that his travels will continue to take him north, the lineman replies:

> Following a broken telephone line north, I have come upon some wonderful places. . . . My business has taken me into spruce woods on winter nights where snow lay deep and soft, a perfect place for a carnival of rabbits. I have sat at peace on the freight platforms of railroad junctions in the north, in the warm hours and with the warm smells. I know fresh lakes in the north, undisturbed except by fish and hawk and, of course, by the Telephone Company, which has to follow its nose. I know all these places well. They are a long way from here—don't forget that. And a person who is looking for something doesn't travel very fast.

All teachers, all parents, are telephone workers. We work the lines of communication, make sure that voices get through, assist in the placing of that call to the imagination. In the end, *Stuart Little* and *The Elements of Style* take us to an imaginative space of beauty: a Puritan sublime, a place of natural simplicity, marked by the straight lines of effective English. The lesson of the novel, like that of the handbook, is for a regulated imagination—a way of learning how to shape the self and its experiences into "established usage." In this sense, the close of the novel compares to the close of *The Wind in the Willows*. There, after adventures histrionic and hysterical, Toad comes home to his hall and presides over a dinner "run on strictly conventional lines." White shows us, as if in response to Grahame's image, where the conventional lines of life lie—whether they be strung across telephone poles or written out on paper.

*Stuart Little* appeared in 1945, and White's revision of *The Elements of Style* came out in 1959. But both look back to a prewar vision of a pastoral America. I called the ideals of *The Elements of Style* Puritan, and I think there is a profoundly Puritan streak to *Stuart Little*. For as the hero travels away from the city's bustle, he returns to the heart of an old America: upstate New York, the little towns and rivers that inspired Washington Irving and James Fenimore Cooper. This is a return to the childhood of America itself, and if White's work (not only *Stuart Little*, but *Charlotte's Web* too) stands as "classic" in the canons of children's literature, it may well be because it makes all of its readers long for a collective, national childhood.

That longing filled the social and literary visions of America after the Second World War. It is, of course, a commonplace to note that the nation emerged from the war militarily supreme, yet culturally insecure. "Red scares" arose almost as soon as the troops returned, and the classroom was often a site of deep suspicion. Teachers at all levels faced scrutiny; children were taught the evils of communism. Popular film reflected the fears, from science fiction such as *Invasion of the Body Snatchers* (1956), which thinly veiled the communist threat as an alien attack, to schlock such as the 1953 *Runaway Daughter*, which was, its poster claimed, "a startling story of the Red Menace at work in our schools . . . planting seeds of treason among the men and women of tomorrow." Justice William O. Douglas, who served on the Supreme Court from 1939 to 1975, recalled in his autobiography the legal tenor of the age: "The radical has never fared well in American life. . . . America has long been and remains a conservative nation."[11]

Justice Douglas may have been right about the political climate of the postwar era, but the literary climate was more volatile. Norman Mailer's *The Naked and the Dead* (1948) challenged the proprieties of novelistic realism. Arthur Miller's *The Crucible* (1953) looked back to Puritan colonialism to interrogate the politics of the McCarthy witch hunts. Leslie Fiedler's 1948 essay "Come Back to the Raft Ag'in, Huck Honey!" dazzlingly sought to reassess the canons of the nineteenth-century "boys' book" by bringing out what he called the "homoerotic aspects" of *Huckleberry Finn* and *Moby Dick*. Fiedler's essay, radical when it appeared in the *Partisan Review*, saw in America a "nostalgia for the infantile." "The mythic America is boyhood," he argued, and he classed Twain and Melville, James Fenimore Cooper and Richard Henry Dana, as writers of "books found, illustrated, on the shelves of the children's library."[12]

Fiedler's criticism came as a shock to readers raised on decades of complacent celebration of American fiction. After all, as Justice Douglas observed, "America has long been and remains a conservative nation," especially when it came to its families and children. To imagine "children's books" as being as frank with race and sexual desire as Fiedler did was to challenge the academic, the librarian, and the parent. It was to challenge, too, the rising climate of what William H. Whyte was to label, in his 1956 book, "the organization man." On the basis of researches he conducted for *Fortune* magazine, Whyte painted a portrait of aspirant America—the America of young parents and young workers. Whyte's theme was that individualism remains possible in organized life. He argued for a "social ethic" that "rationalizes the organization's demands for fealty and gives those who offer it wholeheartedly a sense of dedication in doing so." He made clear just what it means to work: "When a young man says that to make a living these days you must do what somebody else wants you to do, he states it not only as a fact of life that must be accepted but as an inherently good proposition."[13]

Into this world waltzed the Cat in the Hat. He emphatically does not do what somebody else wants him to do—and that resistance is his own inherently good proposition. A performance artist in an age of organization men, the Cat embodies the transgressive side of 1950s culture—the spirit that provoked not only Fiedler's criticism, but the poetry of Allen Ginsberg and the riffs of Elvis Presley (Seuss's book, Ginsberg's poem *Howl*, and Elvis's first televised performances all appeared within the short span from 1955 to 1957).[14] All of these literary and artistic debuts forced readers and audiences to see common things in new ways—*Howl*, with its catalogue of crazed detritus; or Presley's "Hound Dog," which "ain't never caught a rabbit." So, too, Seuss's Cat takes everyday things and piles them up in creative, though dangerous, ways. He puts the cake on his head, the toy ship on his finger, the fish on his umbrella, the milk on his foot, and on and on. And when everything comes crashing down, the Cat brings in his helpers, Thing One and Thing Two, to have even more destructive fun.

*The Cat in the Hat* is many things, and critics have long noted its subversive quality. Louis Menand, in a brilliant *New Yorker* essay of 2002, considered it a "Cold War invention" and located the book in its climate of 1950s politics, book publishing, and public-school education. The book, in his words, "transformed the nature of primary education and the nature of children's books."[15] It showed how a limited vocabulary could generate nearly endless verbal play. It showed how illustrated storybooks could be far more effective than primers and textbooks for teaching reading. And it showed, too, how the children's book was, in Menand's formulation, something of a self-referential story: a story, here, about how with a limited set of words and things, the author could juggle us into amazement.

But what the Cat has, in addition to all of these qualities and contexts, is style. He wears, like so many of Seuss's creatures, exaggerated forms of everyday clothing. The bow tie and the hat morph into a circus-sized costume. He constantly seeks attention: "Look at me, look at me," he cries. He brings color into the children's monochrome world (in the illustrations, the boy and the girl are garbed in black and white—except for her red bow—and their toys are but line drawings). This is a red house with a blue tree, but all of that is outside. The Cat brings color to the world of things. In *The Cat in the Hat Comes Back*, color is, in fact, precisely the problem. The pink stain in the bathtub, left by the Cat's bath, infests the whole house. All the little cats, named by letters of the alphabet, cannot erase it—until the tiniest one, armed with the secret weapon, Voom, blows it all away.

It may be easy to see this story as political allegory (the Cat as ultimate "pinko"), but it is also a story about being colorful. Compare this tale with Seuss's *Bartholomew and the Oobleck*. In the black-and-white world of the kingdom, the king wishes for something new to arrive, and what he gets is a green, gooey, snot-like precipitation that smothers everyone. *Green Eggs and Ham* takes its governing conceit from the very weirdness of its title: why are certain colors appetizing and others not? Or recall *One Fish, Two Fish, Red Fish, Blue Fish*. Here, the world is organized by number and by color. Indeed, part of the remarkable impact that Seuss's books had on the children's book industry lay not only in the use of illustration, but in the thematics of color. Seuss shows how certain hues can carry emotional impact; how our range of colors is socially shaped; how turning one ordinary item into an extraordinary shade can make it odd, or strange.[16]

Or poetic. It seems to me that, at his best, Seuss speaks directly to the heightened traditions of colorwriting found in Grahame, Burnett, Kipling, and Barrie. But instead of using colorful words, instead of investing in a rich language drawn from the Romantics, Shakespeare, and the Victorians, Seuss limits the vocabulary and makes each book an essay in single tinctures. What his books teach, I think, is that the child can have a colorful life; that style is something we put on or invite into the house; and that as long as mother is away, we all can be as pink as possible.

Seuss's books share with many others of the 1950s and early 1960s an argument for the aesthetic life amid the everyday. In Robert McCloskey's *Burt Dow, Deep-Water Man* (1963), for example, the down-easter Burt goes out fishing one day and gets caught in a storm. In a bizarre take on both the Book of Job and *Pinocchio*, he takes shelter in the belly of a whale, but when the storm is over, he cannot get out. Realizing that he has cans of paint left over in his boat, he splashes them artistically on the inside of the whale's belly, and the animal ejects him. But in the process, Burt sees (and we see) something else. Here is the heart of postwar abstract art. Burt's splashings, illustrated in vivid color in the book, look for all the world like Jackson Pollock. And when Burt steps back to admire his handiwork, we are told: "He had found himself in paint."[17]

How many children found themselves in paint? How could the baby-boom boys and girls—children, now, of the organization men of Whyte's decade—express their individuality, or find a style? Seuss and McCloskey ask this question, as did George Selden in his 1960 book *The Cricket in Times Square*.[18] Little Chester Cricket finds himself far away from his Connecticut home, having been inadvertently brought to the city by picnicking New Yorkers. He meets up with the train station's denizens: the cat and the mouse, who take him around the city and help him settle into a newsstand run by an Italian immigrant family. Soon, people start to hear the cricket making music—not just chirps, but versions of the classical themes playing on the radio. The music teacher Mr. Smedley hears about the cricket and visits the newsstand (run by the operatically named Mr. Bellini). Mr. Smedley writes a letter to the *New York Times*, and Chester soon becomes a performing sensation. But such a life of performance brings Chester little joy, and he decides to offer one last concert to the city. All Times Square quiets to hear him, and at the end, Chester departs for home.

This, too, is a story about self-expression, but now in a special social sense. The city, here, is not the place of loss or social congestion (as it remains in *Stuart Little*) but the hub of artistry. It offers one great audience for a performer, and Chester reveals the bright and dark sides of a theatrical life. Like Pinocchio, he seems to have no strings—but unlike the puppet, he knows when to say farewell, step off the stage, and return to the country life. Style and performance are, for the child, glorious things in these books, but they must be regulated. We must know when to sing and when to stop, when to fish for a living and when to paint. Struwwelpeter's hair and nails grow endlessly. Pinocchio's nose stretches with each lie. By the mid-twentieth century, children's literature was addressing the need for expression in the face of social expectation, and the individual emerged not unbridled or unkempt, but always controlled. We can welcome the Cat into our house, but we must clean up and go in time for dinner. Burt Dow may find himself in paint, but his gallery lies in the inside of the beast, not on the walls of his home.

Robert McCloskey's books illuminate the ways in which style is shaped and governed by the love of family. *Make Way for Ducklings* illustrates the ideals of domestic life as matters of aesthetic choice—where is the nicest place to live? (It seems to me that the idea of *choosing* a nice place to live is something that emerges distinctively in mid-twentieth-century America.) *Blueberries for Sal* shows how we select the sweetness in the world and how adventure—little Sal confronted with a baby bear—can resolve itself through taste. In *One Morning in Maine*, Sal has grown to an age when she can lose a tooth—and lose it she does, as she and her family go clam-digging. There is a pearl in every shell, whether it be in the rough covering of a mollusk or the awkward adolescence of a girl. These stories show us children who can pick and choose among the ripest things of life; the mother who orchestrates a kitchen like a work of art; and the father who is himself the artist, fixing his family forever on the page.[19]

Unlike McCloskey, Roald Dahl illustrates the dangers of imagination unbridled. In *Charlie and the Chocolate Factory*, performance takes on a dark edge (the book appeared first in America, in 1964, and was not published in England until 1967).[20] Willy Wonka—a blend of Captain Hook, circus ringmaster, puppeteer, and mad scientist—shows what happens when aesthetic pleasure becomes a destructive end unto itself. The book is rife with caricature and sharp parody. The children who win access to the chocolate factory are (except Charlie) creatures out of some medieval book of sin: gluttony, envy, pride, wrath. Only Charlie survives the tour; in the process, he wins the right to succeed Wonka as the master of the factory.

Willy Wonka, much like the Cat or Burt Dow or Chester Cricket or Stuart Little, stands as a figure for the children's book author. He has rewards to give, and his factory is filled with machines that transform the ordinary things of this world into wondrous goodies. But there is something dark about it all in Dahl's vision (the Oompa-Loompas who man the machinery seem little more than pygmy slaves). Dark, too, are his other assays in style. Take, for example, *The Fantastic Mr. Fox*, with a creature whose sly abilities, whose cool, whose taste for good food gets the better of the farmers on whose land he lives—leaving them robbed, wet, angry, and ill.[21] Or take, too, Dahl's screenplay for the James Bond film of 1967, *You Only Live Twice*, where Blofeld's underground space station comes off as a weirdly, worldly chocolate factory and where the Japan of the setting remains a place of highly stylized food, furniture, and sex. What brilliance to turn Bond over to a children's author—a move that reveals just how childish the Bond fantasy really is.

And in this film, as in all the stories of the stylish, there are *styli*—figurations of that old meaning of the word, the writing instrument, the pointer, or the stick. The science fiction fiend points with his laser, while the Cat has an umbrella that points out the world (little wonder that Hagrid, in *Harry Potter*, carries not a wand but a garish pink umbrella as his magical stylus). Burt Dow has his paintbrush, Wonka his walking stick, and even Chester Cricket has his legs, tuned like a bow across the strings of his imagination. Stuart Little, from the first, stands with his cane. He, of all the stylish heroes of this chapter, has the greatest range of instruments that scribe his life into the world: the ice skates made of paper clips, the oar for his canoe, the bow and arrow that he aims at the great cat.

So many characters in modern children's literature are armed with pointers, pencils, pens, and pokers of the readable imagination that I cannot name them all. I close by looking back to the gift of a stylus in an earlier tale of children and their animals. *Winnie-the-Pooh* is full of writing. There are the badly spelled injunctions at the house of Owl: PLES RING IF AN RN-SER IS REQUIRD and PLEZ CNOKE IF AN RNSR IS NOT REQUID; the word HUNNY written on the honey jar; the birthday message Owl will write out for Piglet, HIPY PAPY BTHUTHDTH THUTHDA BTHUTHDY; the sign that Pooh has found the North Pole (NORTH POLE / DISCOVERED BY POOH / POOH FOUND IT); and finally, Piglet's distress message as his house is swept away in the flood, HELP! PIGLET (ME). And so, it is no accident that when the book is done and everyone is ready for a party (ostensibly in honor of Pooh's heroism), the gifts given are the tools of writing.

> It was a Special Pencil Case. There were pencils in it marked "B" for Bear, and pencils marked "HB" for Helping Bear, and pencils marked "BB" for Brave Bear. There was a knife for sharpening the pencils, and india-rubber for rubbing out anything which you had spelt wrong, and a ruler for ruling lines for the words to walk on, and inches marked on the ruler in case you wanted to know how many inches anything was, and Blue Pencils and Red Pencils and Green Pencils for saying special things in blue and red and green.[22]

Inscriptions that meant something in another world are here transformed into the symbols of self-reference. Instead of B, HB, and BB standing for the hardness of the pencil lead, they stand for Pooh in his heroic incarnations. And if we had any thought that this was a world of simply black and white, the colored pencils offer the chance to say those special things in blue and red and green.

Dr. Seuss tells us special things in blue and red and green. So do all children's writers. For in the end, Pooh's gift is the gift of style, the instruments to write the story of your life. Christopher Robin, reentering the story at its very end, has the last word on writing. "Was Pooh's pencil case any better than mine?" he asks, and the father-narrator replies, "It was just about the same." That is the concluding exchange of the book: the real measure of a man lies in the quality of his pencil case. And whether we write our life out on the pages of a book or in the snow of winter fears, we will do so with a style that becomes uniquely our own.

# Tap Your Pencil on the Paper

CHILDREN'S LITERATURE IN AN IRONIC AGE

At the close of Jon Scieszka's Time Warp Trio book *Summer Reading Is Killing Me!* (1998), there is a "Summer Reading List" designed, it would appear, for schoolroom use. "Each student," it begins, "must read four books during the summer and fill out the attached study guide for two of them." The books are classified for Early Readers, Middle Readers, and Older Readers. Each category runs through the familiar texts in alphabetical title order. Many of these books are ones I have discussed here, from Aesop's fables and *Alice in Wonderland* to *The Wind in the Willows* and *Johnny Tremain*. All the familiar authors appear, from Dr. Seuss, the Grimms, and Robert McCloskey to Tolkien and Verne. But by the end of the list, something odd has begun to happen. There is the category "Be-Extremely-Careful-When-You-Readers," and under it, one heading: "Anything with Teddy Bears in It, by Anyone." And following this one, there is the final category: "Perfect-for-Knocking-Out-Parrots-and-Saving-the-Day-Readers." At the end, there is the Study Guide itself. It begins straightforwardly enough: "Write the title and author of the book." It then enjoins the student to identify major characters and imagine who would play them in a movie version. But then something odd happens:

> Tap your pencil on the paper.
> Stare out the window and daydream.
> Put the study guide away and don't look at it again until the night before the first day of school.[1]

What's going on here? Is Scieszka glibly subverting the very principles and canons of instruction and delight that children's literature has sought to promulgate? Is he reflecting the life of the modern child—disaffected, procrastinating, daydreamy? Or is he showing us something far more profound: that in an age of books, with so many things to read, nothing comes without irony? Throughout this book, as throughout all the Time Warp Trio stories, smart yet somewhat lazy urban kids find themselves trapped in moments of high culture. Everything is already said; everything has been quoted. Life in such a world is life in the already-uttered, where no statement can be taken at face value and where success comes not just through strength or knowledge but through a streetwise, bullshitty wit.

This is the condition of late twentieth- and early twenty-first-century children's literature: the condition of the overwhelming reading list, of libraries where books stand nearly to the ceiling, where everything seems already to have been said and done, and where life can be measured by the actions of our fictive friends. It's hard to see the difference between fact and fiction, and Scieszka's boys find themselves trapped in history. The premise of the Time Warp Trio books is that an uncle of one of the boys had given him THE BOOK, a magical volume that enables the boys to travel into historical times. Each journey, however, comes at a price, for even though THE BOOK travels with them, it invariably becomes lost or stolen. The boys need to recover it, survive the trials of history, and make it back to the comforting safety of late twentieth-century Upper West Side New York City.

Throughout the history of children's literature, we have seen books serve as magic things, as vehicles of transport and travail. "There is no Frigate like a Book," wrote Emily Dickinson, and children from Robinson Crusoe's days onward have seen their books as ships of imagination. The early twentieth-century Newbery Medal committees saw tales of travel and adventure as central to their award criteria. The record of those medals, and the now nearly countless lists of prizewinners, course readers, and recommended volumes—all these form the canons of our children's literary consciousness.

What Scieszka recognizes is that in an age of streetwise snarkiness, no canons can be taken at face value. His Time Warp boys exemplify what I see as the late twentieth-century child in books. No longer are we traveling the seas, exploring continents, or staking out our homesteads on the prairie. Much recent children's literature locates its boys and girls on city streets, in high apartments, in schoolyards that abut boulevards and highways. Laura Ingalls Wilder's little house on the prairie has been replaced by Eloise's Plaza Hotel. L. M. Montgomery's Green Gables has been passed over in favor of Francesca Lia Block's Los Angeles (called, in her Weetzie Bat books, Shangri-LA). The subway car and the convertible are the new frigates of our fantasy.

I use the word "irony" to characterize this mix of urban disaffection, snarky wisdom, and "been there, done that" distance that the modern child affects. It is in many ways the state of the contemporary child, and educators and psychologists have recognized this feature as much as writers have. It used to be said that children had no sense of irony, that what distinguished children from adults was their sincerity, their acceptance, their openness. Not for the child was the jaded weariness of grown-up life, the disappointments in friends, family, and leadership. But children have been coming into their ironic own for decades.[2] Contemporary children live in communities of false belief and mistrust. They learn that other people lie. They learn, too, that their own beliefs may not be shared by others. Appearance and reality are no longer clearly demarcated, and many children come to cultivate a kind of knowing distance from experience: a sense of humor, a witty detachment, a blasé unflappability in the face of deceit or disappointment. This is the idiom of life critiqued at the close of the twentieth century by Jedediah Purdy, a young, home-schooled Harvard graduate who lamented what he saw as the end of personal sincerity and common naïveté. The ironist, Purdy complained, "subtly protests the inadequacy of the things he says, the gestures he makes, the acts he performs. . . . His wariness becomes a mistrust of language itself." Nothing is new in Purdy's purview. "Everything we encounter is a remark, a re-release, a ripoff, or a rerun." Irony is the condition of urban anomie, of kids who have grown up too fast, of situation comedies where nobody takes anything, or anybody, seriously.[3]

This is the world of "whatever"—a blowing off of the impediments to life. The *Oxford English Dictionary* notes that this word emerged in the 1970s to connote indifference, skepticism, impatience, or passive acceptance of other people's failures. The *OED* offers this citation from an essay in *The Village Voice* of July 21, 1998, that, to my mind, perfectly captures the tone of late twentieth-century American life: "If someone came running to say he'd just seen Jesus preaching on the steps of the 72nd Street subway stop, most New Yorkers would reply, 'Whatever'."

Beginning in the 1960s, children's literature came to reflect this growing sense of the ironic. Louise Fitzhugh's *Harriet, the Spy* of 1964 seemed to break all the old rules of sincerity and sentiment when it appeared.[4]

Instead of participating in the life around her, eleven-year-old Harriet would rather spy on others: note their actions and write them down in her book. Her classmates and her family are not immune to her observations, and one day her secret thoughts are opened to them all. The kids are playing tag, and suddenly Harriet realizes that in the excitement of the game, her books were knocked out of her arms and the notebook is missing. There's Janie Gibbs, reading to the other children from the notebook. All of them hear the criticism and the snide asides. All of them read of Harriet's odd ambition: "When I grow up I'm going to find out everything about everybody and put it all in a book. The book is going to be called *Secrets* by Harriet M. Welsch. I will also have photographs in it and maybe some medical charts if I can get them" (p. 187). And so the kids get back at Harriet in her own way: they write things themselves. They pass notes back and forth. "Harriet M. Welsch smells. Don't you think so?" and "There's nothing that makes me sicker than watching Harriet M. Welsch eat a tomato sandwich" (pp. 190–91).

Harriet may be a spy, but she is, of course, a writer, and in her observational and literary ambitions she comes off as a kind of Upper East Side Jo March. Girls find themselves in books, but unlike boys—who would seek stories of adventure taking them to unknown places and strange peoples— the girls behind Harriet's literary genealogy are readers of the local. Like Jo, Harriet wants to be an author, and the title of her book gives voice to the profound need to define the self through writing. But if there is a strain of Jo March in Harriet, there is also Anne Shirley of Green Gables: on stage in school, seemingly better than her peers, passing a judgment phrased in the language of allusion and invention.

There is a wonderful moment early in the novel when Harriet's teacher, Miss Elson, sets out to plan the Christmas pageant with her students. They are an unruly lot, passing notes back and forth, ignoring her calls for order (p. 143). Some students suggest a pirate theme, some vote for the Trojan War, others want to be soldiers. One student proposes that they do a dance "about the Curies discovering radium." Another suggests that they all dress up as things you eat at Christmas. Soon this suggestion gains ground, and, much to Harriet's dismay, it is accepted. Her friend Simon objects, but in vain: "I would a whole lot rather be a soldier than some carrots and peas" (p. 146).

I know I'd rather be a soldier than a carrot, and at this moment *Harriet, the Spy* takes stock of all the scenes of pageantry and play-acting that fill the heritage of children's literature; it reflects humorously on the range of school tales and their teachers (how can we not find, in this scene, something of an ironic take on Stuart Little's commanding performance as a substitute teacher?). Imagination can make us soldiers or carrots, and what Harriet realizes is that she often remains the lone reconnaissance scout amid a troop of vegetables. Now, her responses recall the tradition of G. A. Henty and Robert Baden-Powell—indeed, Harriet may well be seen as living out a manual of "scouting for girls." Compare her authorial plans with the advice that Baden-Powell gave in *Scouting for Boys*:

> When you are travelling by train or tram always notice every little thing about your fellow-travellers; notice their faces, dress, way of talking, and so on, so that you could describe them each pretty accurately afterwards; and also try and make out from their appearance and behaviour whether they are rich or poor (which you can generally tell from their boots), and what is their probable business, whether they are happy, or ill, or in want of help.[5]

Scouting becomes, in Baden-Powell's terms, not just a condition of experience, but a response to reading. It teaches recognition and makes every scout a little social novelist.

Harriet is a little social novelist, but what distinguishes her from her bookish forebears is the lesson that truth may not always be the best course. Never lie, the boys' books always enjoined; and the girls' books, similarly, sought to teach that the theatrical performances of social life were often ruses, lies, or masks that should be jettisoned in favor of sincere absorption in the life of home and family. Parents and nursemaids, throughout the books I have studied, always give advice, and so does Harriet's nurse, Ole Golly. Having been dismissed by the Welsch family, she marries and moves to Quebec, but toward the novel's end she writes to Harriet and offers lessons on both life and literature.

> Dear Harriet,
>
> I have been thinking about you and I have decided that if you are ever going to be a writer it is time you got cracking. You are eleven years old and haven't written a thing but notes. Make a story out of some of those notes and send it to me.
>
> > "'Beauty is truth, truth beauty,'—that is all
> > Ye know on earth, and all ye need to know."
> > John Keats. And don't you ever forget it.
>
> Now in case you ever run into the following problem, I want to tell you about it. Naturally, you put down the truth in your notebooks. And what

would be the point if you didn't? And naturally those notebooks should not be read by anyone else, but if they are, then, Harriet, you are going to have to do two things, and you don't like either of them:

1) You have to apologize.
2) You have to lie.

Otherwise you are going to lose a friend. Little lies that make people feel better are not bad, like thanking someone for a meal they made even if you hated it, or telling a sick person they look better when they don't, or someone with a hideous new hat that it's lovely. Remember that writing is to put love in the world, not to use against your friends. But to yourself you must always tell the truth.

Another thing. If you're missing me I want you to know I'm not missing you. Gone is gone. I never miss anything or anyone because it all becomes a lovely memory. I guard my memories and love them, but I don't get in them and lie down. You can even make stories from yours, but remember, they don't come back. Just think how awful it would be if they did. You don't need me now. You're eleven years old which is old enough to get busy at growing up to be the person you want to be.

No more nonsense.
Ole Golly Waldenstein
(pp. 275–76)

This letter reads like an ironic assemblage of old, familiar literary moments: a little bit of John Keats, an echo of Shakespeare's Polonius ("to thine own self be true"), a hint of E. B. White's *Elements of Style*. Like White, she asks, implicitly, what makes a young writer. Be true to yourself, yes; but you may need to lie to others. The difference between notes and literature, it seems, is the difference between mere reportage and the arc of fabrication. In some sense, Golly may agree with White: both make clear that the job of writing is to put love in the world (and few books of children's literature are as full of love, requited and unrequited, as *Charlotte's Web* and *Stuart Little*). But she takes issue with the memorializing sentimentality that books such as his provoke: "I never miss anything or anyone." This is hard-nosed advice for a little girl, and it is advice not just for her but for the reader, too. Irony distances us from our past. It makes us recognize that what is gone is gone. Golly's advice chimes perfectly with the researches of the psychologist Ellen Winner and those working in her wake. As one recent literary critic puts it, paraphrasing Winner's work, "Children must be able to reflect upon beliefs and recognize them as subjective states that are different from objective truth. In addition, children must be able to attribute false beliefs to others and must know when to attribute a false belief to another person."[6] Mastering these beliefs and reflections leads to mastery of irony, and in this context it seems to me that in the end, Golly's advice is "Be ironic."

Ironic, too, is Golly's use of literature here. Keats's closing lines to the "Ode on a Grecian Urn" have been invoked as something of an aesthetic manifesto almost since the time he wrote them. For any reader of the twentieth century, however, lines such as these have fossilized into cliché. How can we quote, this passage from Ole Golly's letter seems to ask, and still have our quotations matter? The answer is to call attention to the status of the quotation as cliché; to ironize the relationship among the text, the speaker, and the audience; and finally, to signal that ironic relationship with another cliché. "And don't you ever forget it" has, of course, the flavor of the hackneyed phrase. But in this context, it becomes part of a more complex communication. It is as if Golly's letter now becomes a statement of aesthetic belief, a meditation on truth and experience, life and memory. "No more nonsense." She teaches Harriet to live in a world without self-indulgent sentiment; to recognize not simply that on occasion one must lie, but also that all stories told have something of a lie about them.

At the book's close, when Harriet realizes that sometimes you have to lie, she writes her final entry in the notebook, slams it shut, and stands up. The ruses of fiction sometimes must take second place to the realities of living. And we, as readers, must realize that when we have finished books we love, we have to close them, put them aside, cherish their memory but not wallow in them, and—much like Johnny Tremain at the close of his novel—stand up.

So many children's books end with the main character standing up that it must have come as a shock to readers in 1970 to find Judy Blume's Margaret end her novel sitting down. *Are You There God? It's Me, Margaret* challenged the decorum of girls' fiction when it first appeared.[7] Its schoolroom story of the misfit sixth-grader focused less on lessons of community or friendship and more on the rites of maturity: buying the first bra, feeling attraction to boys, getting the first period. The novel traces Margaret's progress through the girl's imaginary conversations with God (each one signaled by the call of the title). Her prayers are not so much expressions of religious doubt or need as they are letters to her best reader: expressions to an ideal audience for the inner life. They stand, much like Harriet's entries in her notebook, as attempts to find a feeling voice. And like Harriet—in fact, like all young women who become the writers of their own books—Margaret looks for signs. This is a book about how children can find meaning in the body: how we take control of life and, in the process, put our mark on the world.

*Are You There God?* begins and ends with blood. Early on, when the family moves from New York to the New Jersey suburbs, Margaret's father thinks that he should mow his own lawn. Forgetting to turn off the mower when he reaches inside to check the level of the grass, he cuts himself badly on the blades. "Barbara," he yells to his wife. "I've had an accident." He wraps his hand in a towel, but the blood soaks through. "'Oh my God!' my mother said when the blood seeped through the towel. 'Did you cut it off?'" (p. 15). Mother and daughter scout the area, but find nothing. A visit to the hospital reveals no mortal wound, and only a few stitches are needed to fix up the father's finger.

Margaret's father deals with his failure to cut his own lawn, eventually, by hiring a boy and burying himself in magazines when the boy comes over to perform the chore. Her father has attempted to put his mark on his land, to cut his own lawn with his own hands. What gets cut, however, is his hand, and the blood marks his failure as maker of his own life. For Margaret, however, blood comes at the novel's end, when she sits down on the toilet and sees the red spots that mark her first period. Moose—the boy her father hired and on whom Margaret has a crush—has been cutting the grass. "I went back into the house. I had to go to the bathroom. I was thinking about Moose and about how I liked to stand close to him. I was thinking that I was glad he wasn't a liar and I was happy that he cut our grass. Then I looked down at my underpants and I couldn't believe it. There was blood on them. Not a lot—but enough. I really hollered, 'Mom—hey Mom—come quick'" (p. 147). This final scene brilliantly recapitulates the moment of her father's accident. There is the lawn, the mowing, the blood, and the yell. And just as when the father calls to the mother, so when Margaret calls to her she answers with the same "My God!" Now, it is not a question of whether "you cut it off." Now it is a matter of "you've really got it." Margaret comes of age, not just as a woman but as a writer. She marks her world, and the blood spots on her underwear are signs of growth as much as letters on a page.

At such a moment, *Are You There God?* rises to the level of the literary. It illustrates how moments of great understanding come not just on the prairies or the oceans, but in bathrooms of the suburbs. Everyday experience is in itself a wonder; and throughout many of Blume's books the point is not to shock with unremitting naturalism, but to show how, at our most physically natural, we can make our mark on the world.

Is the close of *Are You There God?* ironic? Irony depends on a knowing repetition. It requires an awareness of what happened, once, as being straight, sincere, or humorless, so that its repetition can be funny, strange, or oddly meaningful. There's something ironic, in a limited sense, in the man's moving to the suburbs and hurting himself on his own lawn mower. But there's no humor in his bloody hand. There's something ironic, in a different sense, about having the great moment of self-recognition read in menstrual blood. "I started to laugh and cry at the same time," Margaret says (p. 147). Such is what Jedediah Purdy recognizes as the irony of "unexpected significance": "It uncovers, in what is ordinarily imagined to be unimportant or banal, something that elicits surprise, delight, and reverence.... This irony is ecstatic." I doubt that Purdy had this moment in *Are You There God?* in mind, and I doubt, too, that Judy Blume's uncompromising social realism would appeal to Purdy's faith in what he calls "the meaningfulness of things" as being traceable to Plato and Aristotle.[8] But what I do not doubt is that Purdy has captured a sense of the ironic that moves us to surprise and joy. Laughing and crying at the same time, her nose running, Margaret is nothing less than ecstatic.

Ecstasy comes in strange ways in late twentieth-century children's literature, and part of that strangeness has led many critics, teachers, and librarians to classify Blume's books as outside children's literature itself. "Young adult fiction" is the form often applied to Blume's books, for the characters are often on the cusp of adult life. Young adult is the category for the novels of Francesca Lia Block as well, whose Weetzie Bat books present a high school girl of style and spiky wit, seeking ecstasy amid the boredom of high school and the ordinariness of urban days.[9]

> The reason Weetzie Bat hated high school was because no one understood. They didn't even realize where they were living. They didn't care that Marilyn's prints were practically in their backyard at Graumann's; that you could buy tomahawks and plastic palm tree wallets at Farmer's Market, and the wildest, cheapest cheese and bean and hot dog and pastrami burritos at Oki Dogs; that the waitresses wore skates at the Jetson-style Tiny Naylor's; that there was a fountain that turned tropical soda-pop colors, and a canyon where Jim Morrison and Houdini used to live, and all-night potato knishes at Canter's, and not too far away was Venice, with columns, and canals, even, like the real Venice, but maybe cooler because of the surfers.
>
> (pp. 1–2)

With this virtuoso sentence, Block defines her special version of the urban ironic. Everyday places have a sanctity to them, but our modern saints are Marilyn and Morrison and Houdini. We take communion in this world at shrines of hot dog stands, and our memories are moved not by madeleines dipped in tea but by potato knishes. Block's opening returns us to the lists that have governed so much of children's literature: from the Greek catalogues of gods and heroes through the *nominalia* of hornbooks, the arrangements of particulars in Puritan and Lockean assemblies, the double-entry bookkeeping of Scrooge's London, and the oddities that tumble out of Wonderland.

Here, in this picture of young adult Los Angeles, Block illustrates how Weetzie Bat's ironic vision makes all things into representations of other things; how it turns everything into a simulacrum or a reminiscence; how California's fake Venice can be even cooler than the real one. Weetzie dresses in secondhand garb. She goes to old movies; she looks for her "Mr. Right," now called "My Secret Agent Lover Man" (a name that recalls 1960s television and 1950s jazz). She and her friends make a movie called Shangri-L.A., a remake of the classic *Lost Horizon*. As in the Tibetan fantasy of the old film, no one really grows old in Hollywood. Marilyn, Elvis, James Dean, Charlie Chaplin, Harpo, Bogart, Garbo—everyone is fixed, forever, in celluloid.

To read through *Weetzie Bat* and other books by Block, or to read through the many other works of ironizing young adult fiction of the past two decades, is to see childhood as something like Christmas in southern California. Santas and mangers among palm trees seem not simply out of place; they stand as an ironic commentary on the fantasy of Christmas itself as a child's happy holiday, as if snow, sleigh bells, and the tinsel-covered tree were some vague memory of a past life, or lived only in literature and film. Young Jedediah Purdy, I think, really couldn't get that— that the modern (or should I say postmodern?) world, even in West Virginia or New England, lives its rituals as unbelieved and ironized.

Of course, Purdy may refuse to get it, and a good deal of the children's literature of the late twentieth century refused as well, presenting tales of found sincerity and healing faith. Chris Van Allsburg's *Polar Express*, a brilliant, beautiful book (winner of the Caldecott Medal for 1986), presents a journey into authenticity. It is as if Van Allsburg takes the old tropes of the railway journey—the tales of E. Nesbit, or the trips of London children in the Second World War behind Lewis's *Narnia*—and tries to imbue them, one last time, with real meaning.

Van Allsburg's work has an exquisite power to it, and his illustrations often show us young boys lifted out of lassitude and shown the ecstasy of faith. These are, I think, boys' books, and they may represent, as well, a response to the ironies of stories such as those I have reviewed here. For what is clear with Harriet, Margaret, and Weetzie Bat is that the gifted masters of ironic detachment are girls. They are the true performance artists: writing, costuming themselves, speaking lines on a stage set of their own imagination. In their books, the men appear as hopeless (Harriet's sad schoolboy with the purple socks), impotent (Margaret's self-mutilated father), or gay (Weetzie's beloved friend, Dirk). How can the boy find his place in a world of ruling girls? Must he retreat into sincerity, or can he one-up ironists of the imagination?

One solution is bullshit. The boys of much contemporary literature are artists of the game, and bullshit remains very much a boy's game. Scieszka's Time Warp boys (no older, really, than Margaret or Harriet) are masters of the art, as are so many others: the glib little detective Nate the Great; the brilliant thirteen-year-old Artemis Fowl; the boys at Camp Green Lake in Louis Sachar's *Holes*. It is in this book, in particular, that the ability to bullshit becomes a survival strategy.[10] Sent to a camp for juvenile delinquents, Stanley Yelnats finds himself forced to dig holes in the deep Texas desert. Such digging supposedly builds character, but the boys (and we) learn soon enough that they have been set upon a particular task by the imperious camp warden—a woman convinced that an old family treasure lies buried somewhere beneath the sand. Of course, the boys eventually find the treasure; Stanley realizes that it in fact belongs to his family and not the warden's, the camp is closed; and all the bad adults pay for their cruelty.

Childhood is, here, a hole from which we dig ourselves out. And sometimes, as Ole Golly had advised Harriet, we need to lie. Stanley's first letter to his mother is not so much a lie as it is bullshit:

> Dear Mom,
>     Today was my first day at camp, and I've already made some friends. We've been out on the lake all day, so I'm pretty tired. Once I pass the swimming test, I'll get to learn how to water-ski.
>
> (p. 46)

What makes this bullshit, and not merely lying, is its artifice, its imagination, and its writer's knowledge that the letter may not be taken as factual. As Stanley explains to a bunkmate, who is watching him write over his shoulder, "I don't want her to worry about me." It is not that he wishes to convince his mother of the truth of the letter; he simply wants her to know he is all right. The bullshit lies precisely at the moment when the letter makes the leap from passing the swimming test to learning how to water-ski. That leap reveals the bullshitter's imagination—there are many things that children do after they learn to swim, but immediately learning how to water-ski is probably not one of them. There is a vast gap in ability between passing a swimming test and water-skiing. In that gap lies fiction.

Bullshit, according to Harry Frankfurt, differs from lying in that it is not false but phony.[11]

> In order to appreciate this distinction, one must recognize that a fake or a phony need not be in any respect (apart from authenticity itself) inferior to the real thing. What is not genuine need not also be defective in some other way. It may be, after all, an exact copy. What is wrong with a counterfeit is not what it is like, but how it was made. This points to a similar and fundamental aspect of the essential nature of bullshit: although it is produced without concern with the truth, it need not be false. The bullshitter is faking things. But this does not mean that he necessarily gets them wrong.
>
> (pp. 47–48)

Frankfurt's analysis first appeared as an essay in the journal *Raritan* in 1986 and was republished as a little book by Princeton University Press in 2005. It has sold hundreds of thousands of copies, turning the reticent septuagenarian philosopher into a cultural arbiter for the early twenty-first century. *On Bullshit* is a Baedeker to its time: a definition of a social idiom, a way of being, that seems to pervade our lives. "One of the most salient features of our culture," Frankfurt opens, "is that there is so much bullshit" (p. 1). Bullshit, he claims, is far more dangerous than lying, because it seems so much more seductive, so much more exciting. There is a vertiginous quality to bullshit, a thrill that the bullshitter gets of making up the details, forming a persona, raising expectations. Bullshit is the artistic fiction of our age.

And, as with all arts, it is learned. Frankfurt develops his analysis by looking at a novel by Eric Ambler, *Dirty Story*, in which the main character receives advice from his father. Frankfurt quotes: "Although I was only seven when my father was killed, I still remember him very well and some of the things he used to say. . . . One of the first things he taught me was, '*Never tell a lie when you can bullshit your way through*'" (p. 48). Bullshit, Frankfurt goes on, is "panoramic rather than particular" (p. 51).

It requires a certain creativity, "more expansive and independent" than mere lying, "with more spacious opportunities for improvisation, color and imaginative play. This is less a matter of craft than of art" (p. 52). The art of the storyteller is a kind of bullshit, and Frankfurt's choice of literary text is telling. Does bullshit mark the difference between child and adult? Is the art something that fathers pass down to their sons, much as they would pass down a family tradition or a cottage industry? For Stanley Yelnats, for the Time Warp Trio boys, for the nearly countless wise kids on the pages of our fictions, bullshit is the creative option. Like irony, it necessitates a knowing detachment from experience, a kind of above-it-all imagination of a world in which you would rather live.

It is, like irony, a way of coping with the simulacra of experience: the already-quoted, already-used quality of words and things; the suspicion, in Jedediah Purdy's words, "that everything is derivative" (p. xi). Bullshit remains the space for creativity in such a derivative world. True, Weetzie Bat and Harriet and Margaret have spaces for creative life that are not bullshit, but these are the spaces of performance, imitation, pastiche, and parody. Bullshit is a boy's game—and at moments of great fakery, when we can actually imagine ourselves water-skiing in the Texas desert, we can feel almost an ecstasy at our imagination. In the presence of a bullshit artist at his best, we may feel what Purdy would want us to feel in ecstatic irony: "something that elicits surprise, delight, and reverence."

What is the place of children's literature in an ironic and bullshitting world? One answer might be found in the history I have traced in this book. Beginning with the Greek and Roman schoolroom recitations, children have been taught to take on other voices. Whether recalling scenes from Homer, Virgil, or the dramatists, or going through the words of household colloquies, the student puts on a persona—becomes god, or hero, or master. Aesop's fables, in their classical, medieval, and modern forms, argue for *ingenium* over brute strength. John Newbery's Goody Two-Shoes shows her cleverness in understanding weather patterns and crop plantings. Robinson Crusoe and Lemuel Gulliver use their wits to survive in hostile territories and present themselves to others. Alice finds herself, in Wonderland, amid a crowd of fantasists and fiction-makers, all masters of an art of self-imagination that we might today call bullshit. Young Charles Darwin, recall, was chastised for reporting on the marvelous, though somewhat made-up, creatures he would see on his walks; Dr. Seuss, too, seemed to take up the challenge of filling up a landscape with created oddities. What better bullshitter in children's literature could there be than Peter T. Hooper, who begins his tales of ovuline adventure in *Scrambled Eggs Super* with "I don't like to brag, and I don't like to boast"? Even Eric Ambler's fiction, on which Frankfurt draws, looks back to those boys' books of fatherly advice in which writers such as Henty, Kipling, or Baden-Powell would take aside a character and offer up aphorisms beginning "My boy . . ." We may, at the opening of the twenty-first century, live in a time when irony and bullshit are defining modes of culture and expression, but that is not to say that they are new.

For if I have said anything here, it is that the story of the child is a story of literature itself: of finding characters that fit your mold; of telling tales about yourself to audiences skeptical or censoring; of dealing with parental stricture, pedagogic task, and social expectation in ways that preserve the inner self while at the same time keeping on the mask of conformity. Girls and boys do it differently, but what their stories always tell us is that childhood is an age of the imagination, and that every time we enter into fiction, we step back into a childhood of "what if" or "once upon a time."

What their stories tell us, too, is that the child's life is a tapping of the pencil on the paper. The media of writing have been part of children's literature since Greek antiquity. Schoolchildren copied out their masters' texts in awkward letters. Aesop tells the fable of the boy who stole a writing tablet. Medieval and Renaissance children filled their books with scribbles and responses, while throughout the literary history of childhood, fictive characters find ways of reading, writing, and expressing themselves. As Benjamin Franklin put it, in his Silence Dogood essay on the making of a New England funeral elegy: "You must spread all upon Paper." In *Through the Looking Glass*, the White King struggles furiously to turn experience into a text, but as he writes, he stumbles—the pencil is too thick for him. "I can't manage this one bit," he pants out. "It writes all manner of things that I don't intend." And at the close of *Winnie-the-Pooh*, the party gifts for Pooh include a pencil case and pencils, erasers and a ruler, and pencils in blue and red and green for "saying special things in blue and red and green." The children in the stories I have closed with here are also writers: Harriet, with her imagined novel coming out of her spy book; Stanley, who writes his letter home. Scieszka may have captured the ironic wittiness of current children and their homework. But he also gives voice to older verities: our children often daydream with a pencil in their hand.

I watch my own son daydreaming with pencil and paper, putting his study guides away. And while reading to him all his life, I would see the preparations for his dreams. When he was little, he would curl up, his head under the covers, and listen to the board books and simple stories: *Goodnight Moon*, *Pat the Bunny*, and the illustrated tales about the dog Carl, whose words we would provide. As he grew older, we moved to books of greater narrative complexity: *Make Way for Ducklings*, *The Cat in the Hat*, *James and the Giant Peach*. We passed through the phases of a young boy's fascinations: stories about trucks and cranes; histories of dinosaurs; science fiction fantasies; tales of chemists and chemical reactions. There was *Redwall*, *Harry Potter*, *Artemis Fowl*. As I finish this book, our bedtime reading now is Richard Dawkins's *The Ancestor's Tale*, a narrative history of evolution.

Looking back, could I see my son evolve? Are each of his books way stations on the path to young adulthood? And if they are, what will he become? Like many children of his time and place, he is an ironist of the imagination. Sometimes he comes home sulking, wounded in his pride or prowess, and we will get out our equivalent of Harry Potter's *Monster Book of Monsters*: books of historical, chemical, and living, livid tales. Thy life to mend, this book attend. The real wizardry of *Harry Potter*, as of all these books, lies in literacy, and my son claims—somewhat disingenuously, I believe—to have outgrown them. We still read as the ritual, yet most of his time these days is spent not over volumes, but hunched in the garage over an electric arc. Among his hobbies now is welding. Shielded by his helmet, he takes scraps of metal and joins them into new shapes. This is his wizardry, his wand, his will. It is his pencil, too, for he will tap the hot electric tip on metal sheets and scraps as if to write a story of his life in flux. His most recent project has been to weld a set of rods into an open cube. And so, one recent evening, I tried to explain to him how I felt about all of this. I told him how I marveled at his skill, and how I thought that welding really was a way of bringing things together. The red-hot metal heals over the seams and cracks; small fragments mend into new wholes. He's actually making things, building out of the shards of life holders for his imagination (for what else could an open-sided cube contain?). I finished my speech and he looked up, smiled briefly, and then caught himself—remembering that he was, in fact, a teenager—and said, "Dad, you read too much."

# Epilogue

## CHILDREN'S LITERATURE AND
## THE HISTORY OF THE BOOK

From the beginning, children read their books with pictures. The little fragment of papyrus from Byzantine Egypt that recounts the labors of Hercules survives with an illustration of the hero and the lion just barely intact.[1] Other illustrated texts survive from early periods. Manuscripts of Terence's plays (one of the mainstays of the classical and medieval schoolroom) appeared throughout the Middle Ages with pictures of characters and scenes.[2] The Psalter, the collection of psalms from which Christian children learned to read for a millennium, often featured highly wrought initial letters, depicting the psalmist David or the subject matter of his poems.[3] Two English manuscripts of the early sixteenth century, probably made for purposes of teaching aristocratic children, present illustrated beasts and flowers with such vividness and color that they seem to transcend the old medieval categories of the bestiary and the herbal and rise to the level of pedagogic art.[4]

Among the first books printed in Europe were Aesop's fables, which were often graced with elaborate frontispieces illustrating Aesop himself and the animal inhabitants of his stories. The early printed volumes of the Puritans, from James Janeway's *Token for Children* to *The New England Primer*, offered illustrations, as did John Bunyan's *Pilgrim's Progress* (recall that Benjamin Franklin praised the edition "with copper cuts" that he purchased as a teenager). John Locke made clear that teaching worked best when text came with pictures, and he put this principle into practice in his fully illustrated edition of Aesop. Indeed, for many modern readers, the phrase "children's literature," and especially "children's books," connotes a volume in which pictures take precedence over text.

The history of the children's book is often thought of as a history of illustration—a natural association behind the collaborative volume *Children's Literature: An Illustrated History*.[5]

Recent studies of children's reading habits have made much of the pictorial imagination.[6] For Ellen Handler Spitz, learning to read has been inseparable from learning to see. Texts and pictures are both objects of interpretation, and the classic picture books of the twentieth century "expand a child's inner world by means of images and words that affix themselves to the walls of a museum of the mind."[7] For the editors of the *Norton Anthology of Children's Literature*, the look of books is as important as their words, and this volume includes not only reproductions of the black-and-white pictures gracing the texts reprinted, but also a full section, ranging from Hoffmann's *Struwwelpeter* to Scieszka's *The Stinky Cheese Man*, in full color and on glossy stock.[8] The importance of illustration has been lauded, too, by the book industry, most notably in the establishment of the Caldecott Medal by the American Library Association in 1938, awarded to "the most distinguished American picture book for children." In the words of the citation for the 2007 Caldecott winner, David Wisner for his book *Flotsam*, "Telling tales through imagery is what storytellers have done through the ages."[9]

My history of children's literature has largely been a story of fiction and poetry: tales that evoke imaginative worlds in words but that stress, too, the power of the literary imagination to create spaces of adventure, ease, acceptance, excitement, growth, and understanding. Some of the most vivid of the works I have discussed need, it would seem, no illustration: how can we not see, in our mind's eye, Friday's face in *Robinson Crusoe*, or the landscape of *The Secret Garden*, or the ship in *Treasure Island*? Words alone create the vision. Some books, however, have become part of the children's literary canon with programs of illustration that are now inseparable from the books. How can we recall *Alice in Wonderland* without John Tenniel's iconic pictures? And some books that were not originally illustrated have become intimately associated with their later pictures. How can we think of *The Wind in the Willows*, for example, without Ernest Shepard's line drawings, or Arthur Rackham's brilliant color paintings—even though both were prepared decades after the book's publication? How can we recall our earliest encounters with the classics, be it Homer's *Odyssey*, or Swift's *Gulliver's Travels*, or Mark Twain's *Huckleberry Finn*, without their pictures in a "children's edition"?

The history of children's literature is a history of image as well as word. It is a history, too, of artifacts: of books as valued things, crafted and held, lived with and loved. The historical study of the children's book thus dovetails beautifully with the discipline of book history, what French scholars have dubbed *l'histoire du livre*.[10] Emerging in the last third of the twentieth century, this discipline has brought together the traditions of descriptive bibliography, library science, paleography, and sociology to recover the material cultures of reading. How a book looks, how it feels, even how it smells can affect the experience of reading as much as what it says. Meaning embraces media, and for the study of children's literature, that meaning goes beyond mere illustration to embrace the volumetrics of the child's grasp.[11]

Pictures graced children's books for centuries, often in the form of woodcuts or metal-plate etchings. John Newbery's *Pretty Book of Pictures for Little Masters and Misses* (1752) may be one of the first where the image takes precedence over the text. Newbery here, and elsewhere, took particular care to bring the picture in line with the word, but many other early publishers were not so attentive. Often, children's books were built up out of woodcuts lying around in the shop or borrowed from other works. This is particularly true of books of natural history or alphabets, where pictures may be traced back to much older works (in fact, even Newbery's *Pretty Book* bases some of its pictures on animal illustrations going back to Edward Topsell's *History of Four-Footed Beasts*, published in 1608 and for a century one of the most popular textbooks of fauna). In Germany, Johann Comenius's *Orbis Sensualium Pictus* (1658) influenced two centuries of pedagogic book-making, leading up to the twenty-four-volume encyclopedic work of F. J. Bertuch in his *Bilderbuch für Kinder* (first appearing in 1790).[12]

John Harris was among the first English publishers to offer higher-quality illustration for children's books than simple woodcuts.[13] His *Comic Adventures of Old Mother Hubbard and Her Dog* (1805), by Sarah Catherine Martin, had copperplate etchings throughout, and in successive volumes such etchings were hand-colored by artists (or perhaps even by readers) after printing. Harris began his career in the house of Newbery, and by 1801 he was running the firm. But soon his publications diverged from the Lockean instructional principles of his predecessor. Harris's books were often pure entertainments, and the colors of his prints were decried for their gaudiness. Still, Harris's productions were immensely popular throughout the early nineteenth century, and their pictorialism set a standard for later illustration.

By the middle of the nineteenth century, new technologies of lithography made possible a wider range of illustration in the children's book trade than before and, more importantly, provoked a reconception of the children's book as fundamentally an illustrated object. Chromolithography—the technique of using different stones for different colors in the same picture and then printing successively—first showed up in the late 1830s. The German *Struwwelpeter* was one of the first illustrated children's books to be manufactured with the chromolithographic process (in 1845), and in the hands of the British illustrator Walter Crane, the technique produced volumes of remarkable aesthetic power.[14]

Crane is one of the first great illustrators of the children's book, and scholars and collectors have long valued his vivid lines, his fantastic images, and his almost Pre-Raphaelite precision.[15] Like many of his contemporaries, he was influenced by Tennyson's medievalism, by the aesthetics of John Ruskin and Dante Gabriel Rossetti, and by the vogue for Japanese woodblock prints. There is something in his imagery that I, as a medievalist, find uniquely compelling. In *The Frog Prince* of 1874, for example, the image of the Frog asking leave to enter the castle has all the richness of a manuscript illumination. Here is the stark perspective, as the tessellated flooring rushes back to a deep vanishing point. Here is the iconography of artifice and artistry, as the potted citrus tree evokes the Edenic fruit trees that fill medieval illustrations of the courtly garden. The picture is all squares and rectangles, clean lines and perpendiculars, and yet the folds of the woman's dress break all this regularity with flowing curves and diagonals. In such a picture, we can see not just the story of the Frog asking for entry, but the reader herself or himself: we stand at the doorways to imagination, wishing to be let in, and the world we live in—regulated by straight lines and clear perspectives—bends before a guardian of the imagination, with flowing clothes and hair that beckon to a fantastic world in which no angles are right.

Crane's visions join with those of his contemporaries Kate Greenaway and Randolph Caldecott to contribute to most modern readers' sense of children's book illustration. Greenaway is, however, more domestic in her attentions than Crane. Her pictures are often of the insides of the house: the kitchen, the bedroom, the parlor.[16] In a wonderful set of illustrations for *A Apple Pie* (1886), Greenaway takes the tradition of the alphabetic primer and transforms it into an ideal of home life. This is a world of pinafores and pantaloons, a fantasy of home life keyed not to the social worlds of late nineteenth-century England, but instead to

Greenaway's imagination of an earlier, perhaps even late eighteenth-century ideal. It is as if she is channeling the mind's eye of a Sarah Fielding or a Sarah Trimmer, and the pie itself, in her sequence, becomes an object of desire never really eaten but always slightly out of reach. The apple pie is, perhaps, childhood itself: fought over, longed for, peeped into, sang for; and finally (in the indefinable string UVWXYZ), one has "a large slice" and goes "off to bed." Greenaway's books give us a large slice of an imaginary childhood, comforting and sweet as apple pie before bedtime.

Fig. 22. Walter Crane, *The Frog Prince* (London: George Routledge, 1874).

# UVWXYZ

ALL HAD A LARGE SLICE
AND WENT OFF TO
BED

Fig. 23. Kate Greenaway, "uvwxyz." From *A Apple Pie* (London: Frederick Warne, 1886).

In Britain, there has been a Kate Greenaway Medal for excellence in children's book illustration since 1955, and in America there is a prize, too—the famous Caldecott Medal. Much like Crane and Greenaway, Randolph Caldecott remains iconic in the history of children's book illustration.[17] Through his training and experience in academic watercolor (he exhibited at the Royal Academy of Art), Caldecott was able to bridge the sensibilities of public taste and publishers' needs. Among his best-known works are the picture books he published with Edmund Evans for the firm of Routledge, and these illustrated volumes, much like those of Greenaway, imagine an idealized English past of late eighteenth- and early nineteenth-century order. *The House That Jack Built* appeared in 1878, and its vividness of line and color (especially in its depiction of animals) influenced author-illustrators from Beatrix Potter to Maurice Sendak. The cat in this book, modeled on life drawing and the anatomical study of the feline skeleton, crouches among fallen apples—returning us to the Edens of the early primers, as this little creature clears away the rats that may infest our sacred spaces. A had always been for apple.

What is remarkable about Caldecott, however, is not only the conspectus of his oeuvre but the fact that he produced so much before an early death at forty; and the fact, too, that his passing stimulated a level of public literary and artistic mourning hardly, if ever, seen for someone associated with children's literature. Just about everyone who mattered in the worlds of English taste opined on Caldecott's importance, from Lord Leighton, the president of the Royal Academy, to George Du Maurier, the author of *Trilby* (one of the best-selling books of the late nineteenth century). In reading through these testimonies, we are struck by their attention to the brightness of his vision: his work has grace, charm, beauty, humor, character, refinement, happiness, and innocence; it is spare, clean, sparkling. These are the words that appear throughout his critical reception, as if there is nothing dark or sinister behind him. Austin Dobson wrote, in 1887 (the year after Caldecott's death), that "no taint clings to [his pictures] of morbid affectation or sickly sentiment; they are genuine utterances of a manly, happy nature."[18]

Behind these comments is a larger and more complex question about the relationship of text and picture in the children's book. Do pictures truly illustrate their texts? That is, do they present the world of the imaginative fiction or the poem genuinely, giving line and form to fantasy? The novelist G. K. Chesterton, in an inscription in one of Caldecott's books that became widely quoted in the testimonies, put it thus: "Don't believe in anything / That can't be told in coloured pictures."[19] It is as if the purpose of the illustration is to create believable worlds; as if the virtues of the illustrator are the virtues of real feeling.

Part of the impulse of much later, twentieth-century children's book illustration has been to challenge the verities of charm and sparkle—indeed, to challenge the idea that the picture illustrates reality at all. Part of the wit and irony of Maurice Sendak, for example, lies in his ability to create visual narratives that undermine our expectations of mimetic illustration. Part of the power of Robert McCloskey's *Burt Dow, Deep-Water Man* (as I have already suggested) is to show how finding oneself in paint may be finding oneself in abstraction, rather than figuration. The cutouts of Eric Carle evoke the segmentation of the insect world (brilliantly in *The Very Hungry Caterpillar*); but they also evoke the segmentation of pictorial representation itself. In Lane Smith's illustrations to Jon Scieszka's *The Stinky Cheese Man and Other Fairly Stupid Tales* (1992), we see something of a modern (even postmodern) Hieronymus Bosch—in the words of the *Norton Anthology of Children's Literature*, this is a "collage medium" that is "deliberately ironic" and "assumes intertextual skills," where the characters "try to break the bounds of the book."[20] Ironic distance, rather than emotional mimesis, may well be the mark of the most recent illustrated children's books. And yet, throughout the history of children's publishing, there have been other places where the characters break the bounds of the book itself.

Perhaps the most obvious of such places is the pop-up book. Now, books had been popping off their pages almost since their origin.[21] Medieval manuscripts and early printed texts sometimes attached revolving discs or pasted on bits of folded, geometric shapes to illustrate mathematics, anatomy, and mystical codes. In the late eighteenth century, the publisher Robert Sayer developed what he called metamorphoses books. Each book was really a single sheet, folded into four sections. By means of hinges, cuts, and flaps, the sheets could be manipulated to reveal hidden pictures in the course of reading. By the early nineteenth century, flaps were appearing, and by the mid-nineteenth century, "movable books" were showing up that had their pictures pop up with each turned page.

Collectors and bibliographers love these books: each a rarity, each one a testimony to the craft that made them. I loved them, too, especially the ones that offered towers and dragons leaping out of the page. What is amazing about pop-up books is that they are, in themselves, the very thing they hope to represent. They tell a story, but they also embody the story. They make acts of reading acts of interactive manipulation—but they never let the child forget that they are books. They never let the child forget, as well, that life is full of artifice: that all the things you think are real may just be paper cutouts, colored boards, or strips hinged with bits of metal. Reading a pop-up book is like riding through a Western movie set—all fronts, no backs—or through what was once called a Potemkin village: the mock settlements set up to impress the Empress Catherine II of Russia.

The pop-up book has an aesthetic but also a social and political lesson to teach, and it is no accident that the most imaginative examples of the genre came out of Eastern Europe in the period after the Second World War.[22] Under the aegis of the Czech government agency Artia, the artist Voitech Kubasta produced some of the most vivid examples of the movable book. His brilliant color schemes fill landscapes of distant places: Marco Polo's China, or nineteenth-century India, or Noah's ark, or even outer space. Kubasta's little adventurers, such as Tip and Top and Moko and Koko, seem to go everywhere, in every form of transportation. Marketed to the English-language reader (through Artia's arrangement with the London firm of Bancroft and Company), the books reached a wide audience in the West. But there is something more in these books than fantasy. They vivify the Eastern European desires of the 1950s and 1960s: the imagination of a travel outside the rigors of command economies. During this period, and even after the repression of the 1968 Prague Spring, Czechoslovakia had one of the highest standards of living in Eastern Europe—certainly when measured by the ownership of automobiles and televisions. Still, the memories of repression and the disappointments of the present would not go away. In April 1956, after Khrushchev's famous de-Stalinization speech, the Czech writer Jaroslav Seifert remarked at a meeting of the writers' congress: "Again and again, we hear it said at this Congress that it is necessary for writers to tell the truth. This means that in recent years they did not write the truth . . . All that is now over. The nightmare has been exorcised."[23]

It has long been the role of children's literature to exorcise nightmares. The bustle of Kubasta's pop-ups seem to be the dreamscapes for a gray post-Stalinist world. They play into the needs of consumer culture. But they also play into the realities of life. Their vivid spaces are but paper thin. Depth is but an illusion. Who would not wish to set sail on Kubasta's Noah's ark, with its smiling animals and happy child adventurers? The pop-up books coming out of Czechoslovakia speak also to a larger history of children's literature in Eastern Europe and, in particular, the unique schools of animation and illustration that grew up in Prague during the mid-twentieth century. During this time there was, as many of its chroniclers and participants recognized, a distinctive Czech aesthetic sensibility: an approach to stylization and humor based in part on traditional fairy tales and stories of village life, but also calibrated to critiques of the political regime. The artists, in the words of the great animator Zdenka Deitch, "were always finding ways around [censorship], showing things that the officials didn't see."[24] What better way to show the things that the officials didn't see than through stop-motion animation? This form was developed into a high art in postwar Czechoslovakia. Much like the pop-up book, stop-motion animation makes the viewer shape a narrative out of disparate bits and pieces. It segments life into quanta of experience. We read between the lines, or, in this case, between the frames.

There is a remarkable Eastern European aesthetic for the children's book in the mid-twentieth century: a fascination with the ways in which color and line stand in stark contrast to the monochrome city; an attention to plenitude in a time of want; a need to tell the truth in careful yet compelling ways. The work of Jan Pieńkowski (who was born in Poland in 1938, spent the war unsettled with his family, and eventually settled in England in 1946) has, for all its delight, darker memories in it.[25] His sharply cut, black silhouettes make such books as his *Fairy Tales* (2005) strangely terrifying—as if the flesh and blood of his characters had been drained away. His *Haunted House* of 1980, which won the Kate Greenaway Medal in Britain, is a surreal take on the surveillance culture of his Eastern European childhood. A black cat watches everything, and monstrous things pop out of the bathroom and the kitchen. There is always a ghoul in the cupboard.

The modern pop-up book has been powerfully influenced by these Eastern European artistic traditions. Even though the English or American child would have had little, if any, experience with the political and economic deprivations of midcentury Eastern Europe, the books do go beyond mere entertainment to illustrate just how our worst nightmares can come out of nowhere. But these books teach, as well, that they are only paper thin, that they can be conjured up, or closed, by the controlling child.

There is a politics to children's book-making, and if the physical forms of the pop-up could be pressed into the service of critiquing mid twentieth-century totalitarianism, then other forms could express their own political and social moments. Perhaps the kind of book that comes closest to making something tactile out of board and paper, other than the pop-up, is the great nineteenth-century adventure book. Covered in gold letters, with colored pictures set into, or raised out of, leather covers, these books embody the ideals of exploration and conquest of the late Victorian period. But they also embody the mechanization of artistic reproduction in the nineteenth century. Machines stamped the bindings, put on the pictures, inked and gilded the letters.[26] Such volumes are, in a fundamental way, about their own mechanical production. They yoke together art and technology and, in many cases, stand as marvels of production on a par with the marvelous tales told between their covers. As adventure books took on the detailed description of instruments of war and measurement, so, too, did the books themselves become the products of the instruments of the publishing company. In Britain, the firm of Blackie and Son of Glasgow, for example, helped to foster a synthesis of industrial design with the emerging Art Nouveau movement. Designers such as Talwyn Morris (who was Blackie's art director from 1893 until his death in 1911) gave to the publishing house a clearly defined look that set its products apart. The artist Charles Rennie Mackintosh also designed for Blackie, giving a spare and geometric shape to books that had previously been larded with gold and great embossing.[28]

In France, the firm of P.-J. Hetzel put the books of Jules Verne in elaborate covers, each calling attention to the global range of Verne's *Voyages Extraordinaires*. These covers became maps to the unknown, rich with the images of global circularity and with representations of fantastic animals and plants.[28] The firm of Lefèvre and Guèrin in Paris, similarly, shaped its great embossed covers to reflect the journeys of its books. In many reprintings of two works of the Crusoe tradition—Wyss's *Le Robinson suisse* and Catherine Woillez's *Robinson des demoiselles*—the covers show dramatic scenes from the book, each presented in a kind of medallion, with the title of the book arched over the picture. These images remind me of nothing so much as great war medals: their gilded imagery surrounded by elaborate decorations drawn from plant and animal motifs; their pictures framed in a circular or oval shape; their forms topped by a fleur-de-lys or bud-shaped adornment. These are more than just books. They are the medals of accomplishment, the objects that reward the child for the heroics of the read adventure.[29]

These books are treasures, and they make the bookshelf into an assembled treasury. Even in children's books far less elaborate than these nineteenth-century volumes, the covers and the pictures invite readers to hold them dear. Literacy becomes its own reward, as books become objects of value and desire. So many of these kinds of books are now available as images on Web sites that we may lose touch with them as tactile objects. One may sit down and scan through hundreds of them in an afternoon. And yet, we are but looking at a screen. Their depth is flattened out; their colors only digital imaginings; their heft lighter than paper.

As a historian of books and reading, I return in closing to my opening claims: that the book as object offers a unique point of communion and communication with the child. Reading involves all of the senses, for all of us can remember the smell of a page, the crackle of the binding glue, the pebbled surface of a cover. The history of children's literature remains a history of the senses, and the goal of many of the works I have surveyed here has been to evoke the sights and smells and sounds and tastes and feel of distant lands. "Eat me" and "drink me" are the commands given to Alice as she enters Wonderland. We sit with Crusoe at his table and ingest the delicacies of his island. We shiver with Anne Shirley as she sinks into the water, and we hear the pipes of Dickon in *The Secret Garden*. All of these scenes, and so many more, teach lessons in describing sense impressions. Little wonder, then, that Edward Lear or Carlo Collodi should figure forth their characters with larger-than-normal hands, ears, or, in particular, noses. Lear's Dong with the Luminous Nose and Collodi's Pinocchio share an extended organ of sensation. At stake is not just whether my nose grows if I tell lies. What matters is that all forms of fiction need our attentive organs. My nose grows as I find an old book in a library, rich with the musk of damp page or cold leather. The wolf in "Little Red Riding Hood" stands, in this context, as a frightful mutation of the reader: we need big eyes to read, big hands to turn the page, big ears to hear the call coming from where the wild things are.

Perhaps this explains the feature that contemporary Japanese anime artists find so compelling: children with overly large eyes, yet little button noses. Such images recast the Western iconography of sight and smell. They illustrate how, in a world of graphic illustration and fantastic line and color, we come to the world with our eyes wide open.[30] Their work interprets the aesthetic of the book for a new generation of world readers—as if life itself were now some great pop-up book or comic strip, as if there were no feeling and no flash unsuitable for children's sight, and for children's literature.

# Acknowledgments

I have no memory of learning how to read, but my suspicion is that it was with my mother. I dedicate this book to her in recognition of her lifetime love of words and pictures. My son, Aaron, has taught me to see the world anew; my wife, Nancy, has helped me understand what I have seen; my brother, Mark, has shown me how to illustrate experience in unexpected ways.

My editor at the University of Chicago Press, Randy Petilos, welcomed this book when it was a proposal and continued to have faith in its completion. The readers for the Press offered insightful, detailed, and immensely helpful reports that compelled me to enhance and expand my original submission. During the years in which I have worked on this study, I have benefited from the rich resources of the Stanford University Library, the Huntington Library, and the libraries of the University of California, the University of Oxford, the University of Cambridge, and Princeton University. I am grateful to the librarians and staffs of these institutions for their assistance and support. When I began work on this project, there was little available online or in electronic form. At the time of its completion, there is a growing body of texts, pictures, and critical material in electronic formats on all aspects of the history of children's literature. I have relied on some of this material, and I hope that my readers will find in this book a provocation to research their own interests, both online and in traditional archives.

I thank the colleagues who have read portions of this book and the institutions where I have delivered sections of it. These include the faculties in the departments of English and Comparative Literature at Stanford and audiences at the University of California at Berkeley, the University of Chicago, Concordia University, the University of Toronto, Harvard University, the University of Wisconsin, and the Huntington Library. Among those who have read and responded to my work, I single out Lisa H. Cooper, Joseph A. Dane, Mary F. Godfrey, Shirley Brice Heath, Nicholas Jenkins, Stephen Orgel, Leah Price, Jennifer Summit, Kathryn Temple, and Deanne Williams. I commend those undergraduates at Stanford who completed honors theses on children's literature under my supervision and whose work helped hone my own: Hannah Asrat, Joanna Dionis, Asta So, and Beth Wilkins. I thank my graduate students Sara Pankenier and Jessica Straley for the invitation to serve as a reader of their dissertations on children's literature. The opportunity to teach courses in this field at Stanford has also helped me frame my arguments for the widest possible audiences, and I am grateful to my students and my graduate teaching assistants, Harris Feinsod and Jillian Hess. Anna North, my student and later my administrator in the Stanford Humanities Fellows Program, has always been a terrific interlocutor on all things critical and literary. Finally, I want to acknowledge U. C. Knoepflmacher, my former Princeton colleague, who provided me with an exacting model of historical scholarship on children's literature long before I ever thought of writing on the subject.

No portion of this book reprints, verbatim and complete, any previously published article or essay. I have, however, drawn on some sentences and paragraphs from some of my publications in developing the book: "Children's Literature and the Stories of the List," *Yale Review* 89 (2001): 25–40; "Children's Literature and the Art of Forgetting," *Yale Review* 92 (2004): 33–49; "Chaucer's Sons," *University of Toronto Quarterly* 73 (2004): 906–15; "'Thy life to mend, this book attend': Reading and Healing in the Arc of Children's Literature," *New Literary History* 37 (2006): 631–42; and "Aesop, Authorship, and the Aesthetic Imagination," *Journal of Medieval and Early Modern Studies* 37 (2007): 579–94.

For permission to reprint illustrations, I am grateful to the following institutions and copyright holders:

The Bodleian Library, Oxford University, for permission to print the illustration from *Le roman d'Alexandre*, MS Bodley 264, fol. 56r.

Random House, for permission to print the illustration from Dr. Seuss, *If I Ran the Zoo*, 1950.

Oxford University Press, for permission to print the illustration of the world ash tree from E. V. Gordon, *An Introduction to Old Norse*, 2nd ed., 1957, p. 197.

The Tate Gallery, London, for permission to print reproductions of John Millais, *Ophelia* (1851) and John Waterhouse, *The Lady of Shalott* (1888).

The Folger Shakespeare Library, for permission to print the reproduction of Sir Herbert Beerbohm Tree as Caliban, charcoal drawing by Charles A. Buchel, 1904.

# Notes

INTRODUCTION: *Toward a New History of Children's Literature*

1. Francis Spufford, *The Child That Books Built: A Life in Reading* (London: Faber, 2002), p. 9.

2. On the rise of what I have elsewhere called biblio-autobiography (that is, the chronicle of life told in terms of books read), see my "Epilogue: Falling Asleep over the History of the Book," *PMLA* 121 (2006): 229–34. Besides Spufford's memoir, another brilliant version of this kind of narrative is Alberto Manguel, *A History of Reading* (New York: Knopf, 1999), and also his *A Reading Diary* (New York: Farrar, Straus and Giroux, 2004).

3. Philippe Ariès, *Centuries of Childhood: A Social History of Family Life*, trans. Robert Baldick (New York: Knopf, 1962); originally *L'Enfant et la vie familiale sous l'ancien régime* (Paris: Plon, 1960). For an important reassessment of Ariès's achievement, and its implications for the scholarly study of the history of childhood, see Margaret L. King, "Concepts of Childhood: What We Know and Where We Might Go," *Renaissance Quarterly* 60 (2007): 371–407.

4. Among the many studies that have sought to recover a history of childhood in the pre-modern period, see in particular Mark Golden, *Children and Childhood in Classical Athens* (Baltimore: Johns Hopkins University Press, 1990); Beryl Rawson, *Children and Childhood in Roman Italy* (Oxford: Oxford University Press, 2003); Steven Ozment, *Ancestors: The Loving Family in Old Europe* (Cambridge, MA: Harvard University Press, 2001); Nicholas Orme, *Medieval Children* (New Haven, CT: Yale University Press, 2001); C. John Sommerville, *The Discovery of Childhood in Puritan England* (Athens: University of Georgia Press, 1992); and the two-volume *History of the European Family*, edited by David I. Kertzer and Marzio Barbagli: *Family Life in Early Modern Times, 1500–1789*, and *Family Life in the Long Nineteenth Century, 1789–1913* (New Haven, CT: Yale University Press, 2001, 2002). For a full bibliography on the historical study of childhood, see the material in King, "Concepts of Childhood," pp. 398–407.

5. Marx Wartofsky, "The Child's Construction of the World and the World's Construction of the Child: From Historical Epistemology to Historical Psychology," in *The*

*Child and Other Cultural Inventions*, ed. F. S. Kessel and A. W. Sigel (New York: Praeger, 1983), p. 190.

6. Antoine de Saint-Exupéry, *The Little Prince*, trans. Katherine Woods (New York: Harcourt, Brace and World, 1943), pp. 1–3.

7. For the critical traditions centering on reader response theory and the history of literary reception, see Hans Robert Jauss, *Toward an Aesthetic of Reception*, trans. Timothy Bahti (Minneapolis: University of Minnesota Press, 1981); Susan R. Suleiman and Inge Crosman, eds., *The Reader in the Text* (Princeton, NJ: Princeton University Press, 1980); Seth Lerer, *Chaucer and His Readers: Imagining the Author in Late-Medieval England* (Princeton, NJ: Princeton University Press, 1993); and James L. Machor and Philip Goldstein, eds., *Reception Study: From Literary Theory to Cultural Studies* (New York: Routledge, 2001).

8. Victoria A. Kahn, "The Figure of the Reader in Petrarch's *Secretum*," *PMLA* 100 (1985): 154.

9. Hayden White, "The Value of Narrativity in the Representation of Reality," *Critical Inquiry* 7 (1980): 5–27; this quotation from p. 23.

10. See Seth Lerer, "Children's Literature and the Stories of the List," *Yale Review* 89, no. 1 (2001): 25–40.

11. Denis Hollier, ed., *A New History of French Literature* (Cambridge, MA: Harvard University Press, 1989); David E. Wellbery, ed., *A New History of German Literature* (Cambridge, MA: Harvard University Press, 2004).

12. Denis Hollier, "On Writing Literary History," in *New History of French Literature*, p. xxv.

13. Recent studies that still imagine a golden age of children's literature (invariably, Britain from the 1860s to the 1920s) include Humphrey Carpenter, *Secret Gardens: A Study of the Golden Age of Children's Literature* (London: Allen and Unwin, 1985); and Peter Hunt, *An Introduction to Children's Literature* (Oxford: Oxford University Press, 1994). But note, too, the application of this phrase to the postwar period in Peter Hollindale and Zena Sutherland, "Internationalism, Fantasy, and Realism, 1945–1970," in *Children's Literature: An Illustrated History*, ed. Peter Hunt (Oxford: Oxford University Press, 1995), pp. 256–60.

14. I appropriate this formulation from John Guillory, which he set out in his "Canonical and Non-canonical: A Critique of the Current Debate," *ELH: A Journal of English Literary History* 54 (1987): 483–527, and developed in his *Cultural Capital: The Problem of Literary Canon Formation* (Chicago: University of Chicago Press, 1993).

15. See Michel Manson, "Continuités et ruptures dans l'édition du livre pour la jeunesse à Rouen, de 1700 à 1900," *Revue française d'histoire du livre* 82 (1994): 93–126; Francis Marcoin, "La fiction pour enfants au XIXe siècle," *Revue française d'histoire du livre* 82 (1994): 127–44; and, more generally, Christian Robin, ed., *Un éditeur et son siècle: Pierre-Jules Hetzel (1814–1886)* (Saint-Sébastien: Société Crocus, 1988).

16. See Beverly Lyon Clark, *Kiddie Lit: The Cultural Construction of Children's Literature in America* (Baltimore: Johns Hopkins University Press, 2003), especially her bibliographical survey of the teaching, study, and criticism of the discipline (pp. 239–46).

17. See, for example, Lynn Hunt, *The Family Romance of the French Revolution* (Berkeley and Los Angeles: University of California Press, 1992).

18. Notice, for example, the scholarly and critical recovery of Maria Edgeworth, whose bibliography has burgeoned in the last two decades. See in particular Caroline Gonda, *Reading Daughters' Fictions, 1709–1834: Novels and Society from Manley to Edgeworth* (Cambridge: Cambridge University Press, 1996); and Elizabeth Kowaleski-Wallace, *Their Fathers' Daughters: Hannah Moore, Maria Edgeworth, and Patriarchal Complicity* (New York: Oxford University Press, 1991).

19. The spur to a good deal of late twentieth-century work in family history came from Lawrence Stone, especially his groundbreaking *The Family, Sex and Marriage in England, 1500–1800* (London: Weidenfeld and Nicolson, 1977), and the many studies written in its wake. Works that have sought to relocate the role of mother and child in the family and in literature include Ellen Seiter, *Sold Separately: Children and Parents in Consumer Culture* (New Brunswick, NJ: Rutgers University Press, 1993); Anne Higonnet, *Pictures of Innocence: The History and Crisis of Ideal Childhood* (London: Thames and Hudson, 1998); and Eve Bannet, *The Domestic Revolution: Enlightenment Feminisms and the Novel* (Baltimore: Johns Hopkins University Press, 2000).

20. Jack Zipes, "Taking Political Stock: New Theoretical and Critical Approaches to Anglo-American Children's Literature in the 1980s," *The Lion and the Unicorn* 14 (1990): 7–22; this quotation from p. 9.

21. For many, "children's literature" largely means English-language literature. Peter Hunt's *Introduction* and his edited *Illustrated History* attend almost exclusively to British, American, and Commonwealth traditions. *The Norton Anthology of Children's Literature*, edited by Jack Zipes, Lissa Paul, Lynne Vallone, Peter Hunt, and Gillian Avery (New York: Norton, 2005), is subtitled *The Traditions in English*, and most of the contributions to the journals *Children's Literature* and *The Lion and the Unicorn* focus on English-language texts.

22. See Jay Fliegelman, *Prodigals and Pilgrims: The American Revolution against Patriarchal Authority, 1750–1800* (Cambridge: Cambridge University Press, 1982).

23. See Joseph Bristow, *Empire Boys: Adventures in a Man's World* (London: Harper Collins, 1991).

24. Even before the Grimms, German-language interests in books for children were served by Joachim Campe's *Robinson der Jüngere* (Hamburg: Bohn, 1779) and by F. J. Bertuch's *Bilderbuch für Kinder* (whose twenty-four volumes began to appear in 1790). Heinrich Hoffmann's *Struwwelpeter* appeared in 1845, and Wilhelm Busch's *Max und Moritz* in 1865; and by 1866 Adalbert Merget could publish his *Geschichte der deutschen Jugendliteratur*. For the early history, see Horst J. Kunze, "German Children's Literature from Its Beginnings to the Nineteenth Century: A Historical Perspective," in *The Arbuthnot Lectures, 1980–1989* (Chicago: American Library Association, 1990), pp. 1–12; Sabine Knopf, "Kinderlesegesellschaften des 18. Jahrhunderts," *Aus dem Antiquariat*, 1993, pp. A16–A18. The great historian of German children's literature is Klaus Doderer. See in particular his *Literarische Jugendkultur: Kulturelle und gesellschaftliche Aspekte der Kinder- und Jugendliteratur in Deutschland* (Weinheim: Juventa, 1992); *Das Bilderbuch: Geschichte und Entwicklung des Bilderbuchs in Deutschland von den Anfängen bis zur Gegenwart* (Weinheim: Beltz, 1973); and *Fabeln: Formen, Figuren, Lehren* (Zurich: Atlantis, 1970).

25. See, for example, the special issue of *Revue française d'histoire du livre*, "Le livre d'enfance et de jeunesse en France," 82 (1994), and the special issue of *Études françaises*, "Robinson, la robinsonnade et le monde des choses," 35, no. 1 (1999).

26. Paul Hazard, *Books, Children, and Men* (Boston: Horn Book, 1947).

27. For the current, critical sense of "world literature," see David Damrosch, *What Is World Literature?* (Princeton, NJ: Princeton University Press, 2003), in particular his argument that "world literature is not an infinite, ungraspable canon of works but rather a mode of circulation and of reading, a mode that is as applicable to individual works as to bodies of material, available for reading established classics and new discoveries alike" (p. 6). See, too, the treatment by Pascale Casanova, *The World Republic of Letters*, trans. M. B. DeBevoise (Cambridge, MA: Harvard University Press, 2004).

28. Quoted and translated in Raffaella Cribiore, *Gymnastics of the Mind: Greek Education in Hellenistic and Roman Egypt* (Princeton, NJ: Princeton University Press, 2001), pp. 39–40.

29. Frederick Douglass, *The Life and Times of Frederick Douglass* (New York: Bonanza Books, 1962), p. 93.

30. Future work on the history of children's literature might include, for example, fuller engagement with the French and Italian traditions of the fairy tale; more work with Wilhelm Busch and his impact on comic books and visual culture; mid-Victorian so-called street Arab novels and their relationship to Dickens; Nancy Drew and the Hardy Boys; and the growing impact of Japanese anime and manga on the graphic novel.

31. F. J. Harvey Darnton, *Children's Books in England: Five Centuries of Social Life* (originally published in 1932), 3rd ed., rev. Brian Alderson (Cambridge: Cambridge University Press, 1992); Perry Nodelman, *The Pleasures of Children's Literature*, 3rd ed. (White Plains, NY: Allyn and Bacon, 2002); Hunt, *Children's Literature: An Illustrated History*. Other studies that have sought to survey various traditions of children's literature beyond single periods include John Rowe Townsend, *Written for Children: An Outline of English Children's Literature* (London: Miller, 1965), revised as *Written for Children: An Outline of English-Language Children's Literature* (New York: Lippincott, 1983); Alec Ellis, *A History of Children's Reading and Literature* (Oxford: Oxford University Press, 1968); Cornelia Meigs, *A Critical History of Children's Literature: A Survey of Books in English* (London: Macmillan, 1969); Gillian Avery, *Childhood's Pattern: A Study of the Heroes and Heroines of Children's Fiction* (London: Hodder and Stoughton, 1975); Fred Inglis, *The Promise of Happiness: Value and Meaning in Children's Fiction* (Cambridge: Cambridge University Press, 1981); Alison Lurie, *Don't Tell the Grown-Ups: Subversive Children's Literature* (Boston: Little, Brown, 1990); Roderick McGillis, *The Nimble Reader: Literary Theory and Children's Literature* (New York: Twayne, 1996); and Gail Schmunk Murray, *American Children's Literature and the Construction of Childhood* (New York: Twayne, 1998). Encyclopedias and reference works include Humphrey Carpenter and Mari Prichard, *The Oxford Companion to Children's Literature* (Oxford: Oxford University Press, 1984); and Peter Hunt, ed., *Children's Literature* (London: Routledge, 2006). Guides to children's literature outside of the English-language traditions include Klaus Doderer, ed., *Lexicon der Kinder- und Jugendliteratur* (Basel: Beltz, 1975–82); and

François Caradec, *Histoire de la littérature enfantine en France* (Paris: Albin Michel, 1977). Recent anthologies include John W. Griffith and Charles H. Frey, eds., *Classics of Children's Literature*, 4th ed. (Upper Saddle River, NJ: Prentice Hall, 1996); J. D. Stahl, Tina L. Hanlon, and Elizabeth Lennox Keyser, eds., *Crosscurrents of Children's Literature: An Anthology of Texts and Criticism* (New York: Oxford University Press, 2007); and Zipes et al., *Norton Anthology of Children's Literature*. All of these collections offer bibliographies and guides to scholarship and teaching.

32. I discuss many of these traditions and critical approaches in my *Chaucer and His Readers*.

33. Mark Twain, *A Connecticut Yankee in King Arthur's Court*, ed. Bernard L. Stein (Berkeley and Los Angeles: University of California Press, 1994), p. 67.

34. Shelby Wolfe and Shirley Brice Heath, *The Braid of Literature: Children's Worlds of Reading* (Cambridge, MA: Harvard University Press, 1992), p. 4.

35. Marcel Proust, *Remembrance of Things Past*, trans. C. K. Scott Moncrieff (New York: Random House, 1934), vol. 1, p. 32.

36. Leonard Marcus, *Margaret Wise Brown: Awakened by the Moon* (Boston: Beacon Press, 1992), p. 187.

37. For reading in bed in the twelfth century, see the episode in Guibert of Nogent's *De vita sua* where he describes his love of learning as a student: "How often they thought I was asleep and resting my little body under the coverlet when my mind was really concentrated on composition, or I was reading under a blanket, fearful of the rebuke of others" (bk. 1, chap. 15; translated by John F. Benton as *Self and Society in Medieval France: The Memoirs of Guibert of Nogent* [Cambridge, MA: Medieval Academy of America, 1984], p. 78). Compare the opening of J. K. Rowling's *Harry Potter and the Prisoner of Azkaban*: "It was nearly midnight and he was lying on his front in bed, the blankets drawn right over his head like a tent, a torch in one hand and a large leather-bound book propped open against the pillow" (London: Bloomsbury, 1999; p. 7).

38. Wolfe and Heath, *Braid of Literature*, p. 53.

39. Roger Chartier, *The Order of Books. Readers, Authors, and Libraries in Europe between the Fourteenth and the Eighteenth Centuries*, trans. Lydia Cochrane (Stanford, CA: Stanford University Press, 1994), p. 20.

CHAPTER ONE: *Speak, Child*

1. H. I. Marrou, *A History of Education in Antiquity*, trans. George Lamb (Madison: University of Wisconsin Press, 1982); S. F. Bonner, *Education in Ancient Rome* (Berkeley and Los Angeles: University of California Press, 1977); George Kennedy, *A New History of Classical Rhetoric* (Princeton, NJ: Princeton University Press, 1994); Y. L. Too, ed., *Education in Greek and Roman Antiquity* (Leiden: Brill, 2002).

2. Mark Golden, *Children and Childhood in Classical Athens* (Baltimore: Johns Hopkins University Press, 1990).

3. Beryl Rawson, *Children and Childhood in Roman Italy* (Oxford: Oxford University Press, 2003). See also Paul Veyne, ed., *A History of Private Life*, vol. 1, *From Pagan Rome to Byzantium*, trans. Arthur Goldhammer (Cambridge, MA: Harvard University Press, 1987).

4. Rawson, *Children and Childhood in Roman Italy*, p. 32.

5. Martin Bloomer, "Schooling in Persona: Imagination and Subordination in Roman Education," *Classical Antiquity* 16 (1997): 57–78.

6. See Raffaella Cribiore, *Writing, Teachers, and Students in Graeco-Roman Egypt*, American Studies in Papyrology, no. 36 (Atlanta: Scholars Press, 1996); and Cribiore, *Gymnastics of the Mind: Greek Education in Hellenistic and Roman Egypt* (Princeton, NJ: Princeton University Press, 2001). See also her "A Homeric Writing Exercise and Reading Homer in School," *Tyche* 9 (1994): 1–8.

7. Of course, Aesop was himself illiterate, and his fables were not written down and codified until centuries after his death.

8. See A. D. Booth, "Elementary and Secondary Education in the Roman Empire," *Florilegium* 1 (1979): 1–14; and Booth, "The Schooling of Slaves in First-Century Rome," *Transactions of the American Philological Association* 109 (1979): 11–19.

9. Quintilian, *Institutio Oratoria*, ed. and trans. H. E. Butler, Loeb Classical Library (Cambridge, MA: Harvard University Press, 1920), 1.1.21. Book, chapter, and paragraph numbers are hereafter given in my text.

10. For the Greek text, see Homer, *Iliad*, ed. and trans. A. T. Murray, Loeb Classical Library (Cambridge, MA: Harvard University Press, 1924), 9.434–43. I prefer here the translation of Richmond Lattimore, *The Iliad of Homer* (Chicago: University of Chicago Press, 1954).

11. Rawson, *Children and Childhood in Roman Italy*, p. 169.

12. Ibid., pp. 327–28.

13. Cribiore, *Gymnastics*, p. 138. For the text and facsimile reproduction, see E. Lobel and C. H. Roberts, eds., *The Oxyrhynchus Papyri*, pt. 22 (London: Egypt Exploration Society, 1954), pp. 84–88.

14. Lobel and Roberts, *The Oxyrhynchus Papyri*, p. 88.

15. J. J. O'Donnell, *Augustine: Confessions*, 3 vols. (Oxford: Clarendon Press, 1992); R. S. Pine-Coffin, trans., *Augustine: The Confessions* (Harmondsworth, UK: Penguin, 1962); Peter Brown, *Augustine of Hippo* (London: Faber, 1967).

16. Pine-Coffin, *Augustine*, 1.16, p. 34; hereafter cited in my text.

17. O'Donnell, *Augustine*, p. 89.

18. Material in the following discussion is taken from the editions and translations in Cribiore, *Writing, Teachers, and Students*. When she does not provide translations of Greek texts, I have relied on modern ones, cited in notes below.

19. *Iliad*, ed. Murray, 2.134–36; translation modified by me.

20. Ibid., 2.147–48; translation modified by me.

21. O. Guérard and P. Jouguet, *Un livre d'écolier du IIIe siècle avant J. C.* (Cairo, 1938). In quoting and translating from its literary excerpts, I rely on modern editions, cited in notes below.

22. Euripides, *Phoinissai*, ed. and trans. Arthur S. Way, Loeb Classical Library (Cambridge, MA: Harvard University Press, 1912), lines 529–34; translation modified by me.

23. Homer, *Odyssey*, ed. and trans. A. T. Murray, Loeb Classical Library (London: William Heinemann, 1924), 5.116–24; translation modified by me.

24. The text is edited and translated in D. L. Page, *Greek Literary Papyri*, vol. 1, Loeb Classical Library (Cambridge, MA: Harvard University Press, 1942), pp. 260–69. This

quotation is from lines 45–50; in revising Page's translation, I have benefited from the advice of my colleague Susan Stephens.

25. For a brilliant survey and analysis of these traditions, see Robert Kaster, *Guardians of Language: The Grammarian and Society in Late Antiquity* (Berkeley and Los Angeles: University of California Press, 1988).

26. Virgil, *Aeneid*, trans. Allen Mandelbaum (New York: Bantam Books, 1971), 6.679–81.

27. See Stephen V. Tracy, "The Marcellus Passage (*Aeneid* 6.860–886)," *Classical Journal* 70 (1974–75): 37–42.

28. *Vita Donatiana* [Donatus's *Life of Virgil*], in *Vitae Vergilianae Antiquae*, ed. G. Brugnoli and F. Stok (Rome: Typis Officinae Polygraphicae, 1997); this quotation from p. 32.

29. Servius, ad loc. 6.859, in G. Thilo and H. Hagen, eds., *Servii Grammatici qui fervntvr in Vergilii carmina commentarii* (Hildesheim, Germany: G. Olms, 1961), 2:120–21.

30. *Cicero: De Oratore*, ed. and trans. E. W. Sutton and H. Rackham, Loeb Classical Library (Cambridge, MA: Harvard University Press, 1942). Book, section, and line numbers are given in my text. See also Bonner, *Education in Ancient Rome*, pp. 223–24.

31. Bonner, *Education in Ancient Rome*, p. 224.

32. See A. C. Dionisotti, "From Ausonius' Schooldays? A Schoolbook and Its Relations," *Journal of Roman Studies* 72 (1982): 83–125. Translations are my own.

33. Ibid.

34. *The Republic of Plato*, trans. F. M. Cornford (New York: Oxford University Press, 1945), 431C, p. 125.

35. Golden, *Children and Childhood in Classical Athens*, p. 7.

36. See the discussions in Golden, *Children and Childhood in Classical Athens*; Rawson, *Children and Childhood in Roman Italy*; and Bloomer, "Schooling in Persona." For general surveys, see Keith Hopkins, *Conquerors and Slaves* (Cambridge: Cambridge University Press, 1978); and Keith Bradley, *Slavery and Society at Rome* (Cambridge: Cambridge University Press, 1994).

37. For Aesop's fables and their versions in the later Babrius and Phaedrus, see Ben Edwin Perry, *Aesopica* (Urbana: University of Illinois Press, 1952); and Perry, *Babrius and Phaedrus*, Loeb Classical Library (Cambridge, MA: Harvard University Press, 1965).

38. Perry, *Babrius and Phaedrus*, p. 17; translation modified by me. Page numbers are hereafter given in my text.

39. Rawson, *Children and Childhood in Roman Italy*, pp. 176–77.

40. Quoted in Bradley, *Slavery and Society at Rome*, p. 143.

41. Perry, *Babrius and Phaedrus*, pp. 247–49.

42. Rawson, *Children and Childhood in Roman Italy*, p. 20.

CHAPTER TWO: *Ingenuity and Authority*

1. There are many versions of Aesop's fables available in English, and many ways of accessing their traditions. Scholars traditionally refer to each fable by its Perry number, that is, the number assigned to it in Ben Edwin Perry's thematic catalogue. See Ben Edwin

Perry, *Aesopica* (Urbana: University of Illinois Press, 1952). These numbers are also used to refer to later versions of the fables that translate or recast Aesopic originals. See Ben Edwin Perry, *Babrius and Phaedrus*, Loeb Classical Library (Cambridge, MA: Harvard University Press, 1965). Unless otherwise noted, all references to the fables and all editions and translations of them in my text come from Perry's *Babrius and Phaedrus*. The so-called *Life of Aesop*, a Greek prose text probably compiled in the second century AD, is available in a modern English translation in Lloyd W. Daly, *Aesop without Morals* (New York: Thomas Yoseloff, 1961). A more recent English translation of the fables, keyed to Perry numbers, is Laura Gibbs, *Aesop's Fables* (Oxford: Oxford University Press, 2002). Gibbs also maintains a Web site containing her translations, versions in Latin and in selected earlier English translations, and a table of Perry numbers and fable topics: http://www.mythfolklore.net/aesopica/.

2. Quintilian, *Institutio Oratoria*, ed. and trans. H. E. Butler, Loeb Classical Library (London: William Heinemann, 1921), 1.9.2.

3. Quoted in Jan Ziolkowski, *Talking Animals* (Philadelphia: University of Pennsylvania Press, 1993), p. 92.

4. See the discussions in Perry, *Babrius and Phaedrus*; Daly, *Aesop without Morals*; Gibbs, *Aesop's Fables*; Klaus Grubmüller, *Meister Esopus: Untersuchungen zu Geschichte und Funktion der Fabel im Mittelalter* (Zurich: Artemis, 1977); John Winkler, *Auctor and Actor: A Narratological Reading of Apuleius's "Golden Ass"* (Berkeley and Los Angeles: University of California Press, 1985); and Annabel Patterson, *Fables of Power: Aesopian Writing and Political History* (Durham, NC: Duke University Press, 1991).

5. See the discussion in Grubmüller, *Meister Esopus*, pp. 87–88; this quotation from p. 88 (my translation from the German).

6. Ibid., p. 88 (my translation from the German).

7. Quoted and discussed in Patterson, *Fables of Power*, pp. 6–7.

8. Daly, *Aesop without Morals*, p. 273.

9. Raffaella Cribiore, *Gymnastics of the Mind: Greek Education in Hellenistic and Roman Egypt* (Princeton, NJ: Princeton University Press, 2001), p. 180.

10. This translation (with modifications by me) is from Edward Wheatley, *Mastering Aesop: Medieval Education, Chaucer, and His Followers* (Gainesville: University of Florida Press, 2000), p. 39.

11. Ibid., p. 38; translation modified by me.

12. Perry, *Babrius and Phaedrus*, pp. 190–91.

13. Ibid., pp. 4–5.

14. Ibid., pp. 190–91. Catullus's first poem opens "Cui dono lepidum nouum libellum / arido modo pumice expolitum?" For the contexts behind these lines, see William Batstone, "Dry Pumice and the Programmatic Language of Catullus 1," *Classical Philology* 93 (1998): 126–35.

15. Ibid., pp. 4–5. For the resonances to earlier Hellenistic poetry here, see Perry's note on these pages.

16. For the medieval Aesopica, see Grubmüller, *Meister Esopus*; Wheatley, *Mastering Aesop*; and the studies of A. E. Wright: '*Hie lert uns der meister': Latin Commentary and*

*the German Fable, 1350–1500* (Tempe: Arizona Center for Medieval and Renaissance Studies, 2001), and *The Fables of "Walter of England"* (Toronto: Pontifical Institute of Mediaeval Studies, 1997).

17. Wright, "Hie lert uns der meister," p. 28.

18. Ibid., p. 36.

19. Ibid., p. 42.

20. Ibid., p. 43.

21. Ibid., p. 37.

22. Perry 540. The text and translation of the earliest form is in Perry, *Babrius and Phaedrus*, pp. 388–89.

23. Wright, *Fables of "Walter of England,"* p. 133.

24. Martial, *Epigrams*, ed. and trans. D. R. Shackleton Bailey, Loeb Classical Library (Cambridge, MA: Harvard University Press, 1993), 4.86.10–12.

25. Perry, *Babrius and Phaedrus*, pp. 254–55; my translation.

26. Quotations from the *Canterbury Tales* are from Larry D. Benson, ed., *The Riverside Chaucer*, 3rd ed. (Boston: Houghton Mifflin, 1987).

27. *Marie de France, Fables*, ed. and trans. Harriet Spiegel (Toronto: University of Toronto Press, 1987). Fable numbers and line numbers are hereafter given in my text. For critical guidance, see R. Howard Bloch, *The Anonymous Marie de France* (Chicago: University of Chicago Press, 2003).

28. Perry, *Babrius and Phaedrus*, p. 585.

29. Quoted in Ziolkowski, *Talking Animals*, p. 207.

30. Quoted in Wright, "Hie lert uns der meister," p. 241.

31. Phaedrus 1.7, in Perry, *Babrius and Phaedrus*, p. 201. I have modified Perry's translation here.

32. Wright, *Fables of "Walter of England,"* p. 92.

33. Kenneth McKenzie and William A. Oldfather, *Ysopet-Avionnet: The Latin and French Texts*, University of Illinois Studies in Language and Literature, vol. 5, no. 4 (Urbana: University of Illinois, 1921).

34. William Shakespeare, *Hamlet*, 5.1.172ff., in *The Complete Pelican Shakespeare*, ed. Stephen Orgel and A. R. Braunmuller (Harmondsworth, UK: Penguin, 2002). All quotations and citations from Shakespeare's works will be from this edition.

35. George D. Gopen, ed., *The Moral Fables of Aesop by Robert Henryson* (Notre Dame, IN: University of Notre Dame Press, 1987), lines 1356–58 (this translation mine). Line numbers are hereafter given in my text.

36. Wright, "Hie lert uns der meister," p. 167.

37. Ibid., p. 252.

38. R. T. Lenaghan, *Caxton's Aesop* (Cambridge, MA: Harvard University Press, 1967), p. 10.

39. Ibid., pp. 173–74. For Macho's Aesop, see Pierre Ruelle, *L'Esope de Julien Macho* (Paris: Société des anciens textes français: A. et J. Picard, 1982).

40. Lenaghan, *Caxton's Aesop*, pp. 113–14.

41. Mary Macleod Banks, ed., *An Alphabet of Tales*, Early English Text Society, Original Series, nos. 126, 127 (London: K. Paul, Trench, Trubner, 1904–5), pp. 236–37.

42. The quotations from *The Clerk's Tale* are from Benson, *The Riverside Chaucer*, lines 385, 383. The story of Griselda, it is worth noting, has had an important afterlife in the popular literatures of Europe. Charles Perrault, who would be best known for his collections of fairy tales, published a version in 1694 as *Griseldis, nouvelle. Avec le conte de Peau d'Ane et celui des Souhaits ridicules.* In England, Maria Edgeworth published her *Modern Griselda* in 1805, a didactic novel that some have seen as anticipating the social fictions of Jane Austen.

43. Babrius 2.107, in Perry, *Babrius and Phaedrus*, pp. 140–41.

44. Wright, *Fables of "Walter of England,"* pp. 92–93.

CHAPTER THREE: *Court, Commerce, and Cloister*

1. See Daniel T. Kline, ed., *Medieval Literature for Children* (New York: Routledge, 2003); Gillian Adams, "Medieval Children's Literature: Its Possibility and Actuality," *Children's Literature* 26 (1998): 1–24; Susan S. Morrison, "Medieval Children's Literature," *Children's Literature Association Quarterly* 23 (1998): 2–28; Bennett A. Brockman, "Children and Literature in Late Medieval England," *Children's Literature* 4 (1975): 58–63; and Meredith McMunn, "Children and Literature in Medieval France," *Children's Literature* 4 (1975): 51–58. The work of Nicholas Orme in medieval children's education has had a broad impact on studies of children and literature. See his *From Childhood to Chivalry* (London: Methuen, 1984); *Medieval Children* (New Haven, CT: Yale University Press, 2001); and "Children and Literature in Medieval England," *Medium Aevum* 68 (1999): 218–46.

2. Miri Rubin, *Corpus Christi* (Cambridge: Cambridge University Press, 1991), p. 138.

3. Ibid., pp. 136–37.

4. Quoted in Brian Tierney, *The Middle Ages*, 4th ed. (New York: Knopf, 1983), p. 247.

5. See Seth Lerer, *Chaucer and His Readers: Imagining the Author in Late-Medieval England* (Princeton, NJ: Princeton University Press, 1993), p. 15.

6. See Orme, *Medieval Children*, pp. 313–15.

7. Ibid., p. 312; Barbara Hanawalt, *Growing Up in Medieval London* (Oxford: Oxford University Press, 1993), p. 144.

8. Quoted in Orme, *Medieval Children*, p. 255.

9. Those children came from noble and aristocratic families, merchant and artisan homes, urban and rural lives. While I generalize about the forms and idioms of "medieval children's literature," I specify in the course of this chapter just what kinds of works fit what kinds of children.

10. British Library, MS Harley 208, discussed in Orme, *Medieval Children*, p. 247.

11. Martha Rust, "The ABC of Aristotle," in Kline, *Medieval Literature for Children*, pp. 62–78, esp. p. 65.

12. On the worlds of Anglo-Saxon manuscripts, learning, and literature, see C. R. Dodwell, *Anglo-Saxon Art: A New Perspective* (Manchester: Manchester University Press, 1982); Janet Backhouse, D. H. Turner, and Leslie Webster, eds., *The Golden Age of Anglo-Saxon Art, 966–1066* (London: British Museum, 1984); Martin Irvine, *The Making of Textual Culture: Grammatica and Literary Theory, 350–1100* (Cambridge: Cambridge Univer-

sity Press, 1994); Simon Keynes and Michael Lapidge, trans. and eds., *Alfred the Great* (Baltimore: Penguin, 1983); Nicholas Brooks, ed., *Latin and the Vernacular Languages in Early Medieval Britain* (Leicester: Leicester University Press, 1982); and D. A. Bullough, "The Educational Tradition in England from Alfred to Aelfric: Teaching *Utriusque Linguae*," *Settimane di studio del Centro italiano di studi sull'alto medioevo* 19 (172): 453–94.

13. On the Old English riddles, see Craig R. Williamson, *The Old English Riddles of the Exeter Book* (Chapel Hill: University of North Carolina Press, 1977); his translation of the riddles is in *A Feast of Creatures* (Philadelphia: University of Pennsylvania Press, 1992). For the literary and institutional backgrounds to material in this paragraph, see my *Literacy and Power in Anglo-Saxon England* (Lincoln: University of Nebraska Press, 1991), esp. pp. 97–125.

14. See G. N. Garmonsway, *Aelfric's Colloquy*, rev. ed. (Exeter: University of Exeter Press, 1991). All translations from the *Colloquy* are mine.

15. The quotations below are from the text and translation in David Bevington, *Medieval Drama* (Boston: Houghton Mifflin, 1975).

16. The quotations below are from the text in Bevington, *Medieval Drama*.

17. See Orme, "Children and Literature in Medieval England," p. 238.

18. Ibid.

19. See H. N. Hillebrand, *The Child Actors*, University of Illinois Studies in Language and Literature, vol. 11, nos. 1–2 (Urbana: University of Illinois Press, 1926), p. 11.

20. Ibid., pp. 324–25; Suzanne Westfall, *Patrons and Performance: Early Tudor Household Revels* (Oxford: Clarendon Press, 1990), p. 41.

21. Quoted and discussed in Orme, "Children and Literature in Medieval England," p. 236.

22. Quoted in Orme, "Children and Literature in Medieval England," p. 219. For other examples of the lullaby in Middle English, see Maxwell S. Luria and Richard L. Hoffman, *Middle English Lyrics* (New York: Norton, 1974), pp. 194, 195, 221.

23. See the remarks by Bartholomaeus Anglicus as translated into Middle English by John of Trevisa in M. C. Seymour et al., eds., *On the Properties of Things; John Trevisa's Translation of Bartholomaeus Anglicus "De proprietatibus rerum": A Critical Text* (Oxford: Clarendon Press, 1975).

24. See Orme, *Medieval Children*, p. 141.

25. See Helen Cooper, *Great Grandmother Goose* (New York: Greenwillow, 1978); and Iona and Peter Opie, *The Lore and Language of Schoolchildren* (Oxford: Clarendon Press, 1967).

26. This material has been edited and discussed in Eleanor Relle, "Some New Marginalia and Poems of Gabriel Harvey," *Review of English Studies*, new series, 23 (1972): 401–26.

27. Rossell Hope Robbins, *Secular Lyrics of the XIVth and XVth Centuries*, 2nd ed. (Oxford: Clarendon Press, 1955), p. 105; modernized by me.

28. British Library, MS Royal 18.A.17, printed in Robbins, *Secular Lyrics*, p. 85.

29. Ibid., pp. 105, 265.

30. These verses are quoted and discussed in Orme, *Medieval Children*, pp. 146, 148, 151.

31. Michael Camille, *Image on the Edge* (Cambridge, MA: Harvard University Press, 1992).

32. Ibid., pp. 99–128.

33. Orme, *Medieval Children*, p. 183.

34. For more examples of late medieval and early Modern English verse for children and its various contexts, see L. G. Black, "Some Renaissance Children's Verse," *Review of English Studies*, new series, 24 (1973): 1–16. Black calls such verse a "poetry of social gesture" (p. 16).

35. *The Treatise on the Astrolabe* is printed in Larry D. Benson, ed., *The Riverside Chaucer*, 3rd ed. (Boston: Houghton Mifflin, 1987), pp. 662–83. I have discussed this work at length in the context of Chaucer's figurations as the "father of English poetry" and the critical reception of that image in my "Chaucer's Sons," *University of Toronto Quarterly* 73 (2004): 906–15.

36. I have discussed material in this paragraph in the larger context of late medieval English advisory and paternalistic writing in my *Chaucer and His Readers*.

37. I have discussed this material in my *Chaucer and His Readers*, pp. 85–116, detailing the bibliographical, historical, and social contexts of the poetry of Huntington Library MS HM 140. Quotations from this manuscript are from my editions in *Chaucer and His Readers*.

38. F. Harth, "Carpaccio's Meditation on the Passion," *Art Bulletin* 22 (1940): 28, quoted and discussed in my *Chaucer and His Readers*, pp. 110–11.

39. F. J. Furnivall, ed., *Caxton's Book of Curtesye*, Early English Text Society, Extra Series 3 (London: Oxford University Press, 1868), line 309. Line numbers are hereafter given in my text. For discussion, see my *Chaucer and His Readers*, pp. 249–50.

40. Orme, *Medieval Children*, p. 297.

41. William Tyndale, *The Obedience of a Christen Man and How Christen Rulers Ought to Governe . . .* (Antwerp: J. Hoochstraten, 1528). For a review of early modern condemnations of medieval romance, poetry, and writings generally as being childish or corrupting, see the discussions in Brockman, "Children and Literature in Late Medieval England"; and Bennett A. Brockman, "Robin Hood and the Invention of Children's Literature," *Children's Literature* 10 (1982): 225–34.

42. *Statutes of the Realm* (London: Dawson's, 1810–28), 34 Henry VIII c. 1.

43. Roger Ascham, *The Schoolmaster*, ed. Lawrence V. Ryan (Ithaca, NY: Cornell University Press, 1967), p. 68.

44. I adapt the following discussion from my "Medieval Literature and Early Modern Readers," *Papers of the Bibliographical Society of America* 97 (2003): 311–32.


CHAPTER FOUR: *From Alphabet to Elegy*

1. See C. John Sommerville, *The Discovery of Childhood in Puritan England* (Athens: University of Georgia Press, 1992). See also the discussions in Mary V. Jackson, *Engines of Instruction, Mischief, and Magic: Children's Literature in England from Its Beginnings to 1839* (Lincoln: University of Nebraska Press, 1989); Patricia Demers, *Heaven upon Earth: The Form of Moral and Religious Children's Literature, to 1850* (Knoxville: University of Tennessee Press, 1993); and Patricia Crain, *The Story of A: The Alphabetization of America from "The New England Primer" to "The Scarlet Letter"* (Stanford, CA: Stanford

University Press, 2000). See, too, the following contributions to Gillian Avery and Julia Briggs, eds., *Children and Their Books* (Oxford: Clarendon Press, 1989): Keith Thomas, "Children in Early Modern England," pp. 43–78; Nigel Smith, "A Child Prophet: Martha Hatfield as *The Wise Virgin*," pp. 79–94; and Gillian Avery, "The Puritans and Their Heirs," pp. 95–118.

2. James Janeway, *A Token for Children: Being an Exact Account of the Conversion, Holy and Exemplary Lives and Joyful Deaths of several Young Children* (London, 1671). Quotations in my text are from this edition.

3. See Sommerville, *Discovery of Childhood*, pp. 21–22; and the material assembled in Charles W. Bardsley, *Curiosities of Puritan Nomenclature* (London, 1897).

4. Quoted in Bardsley, *Curiosities*, p. 44.

5. On the relationship between Bunyan's allegorical personae and the names of historical Puritans, see Bardsley, *Curiosities*, pp. 198–201. For the details of Puritan naming that I summarize in this paragraph, see also pp. 39, 44, 118–19, 125.

6. See Sacvan Bercovitch, *The Puritan Origins of the American Self* (New Haven, CT: Yale University Press, 1975); and his introduction to Bercovitch, ed., *The American Puritan Imagination: Essays in Revaluation* (Cambridge: Cambridge University Press, 1974), p. 13.

7. Jay Fliegelman, *Prodigals and Pilgrims: The American Revolution against Patriarchal Authority, 1750–1800* (Cambridge: Cambridge University Press, 1982), p. 94.

8. Cotton Mather, *Perswasions from the Terror of the Lord* (Boston, 1711), p. 35; quoted in David Stannard, *The Puritan Way of Death* (New York: Oxford University Press, 1977), p. 66.

9. Ian Watt, *The Rise of the Novel* (Berkeley and Los Angeles: University of California Press, 1957), p. 217.

10. All quotations from *The New England Primer* are from the earliest surviving edition (Boston: S. Kneeland and T. Green, 1727), reproduced in facsimile in Paul Leicester Ford, *The New-England Primer* (New York: Dodd, Mead and Co., 1899).

11. See Crain, *The Story of A*, pp. 26–37.

12. Ibid., p. 33.

13. See the discussions in Lisa Jardine, *Erasmus, Man of Letters: The Construction of Charisma in Print* (Princeton, NJ: Princeton University Press, 1993); and Jonathan Goldberg, *Writing Matter: From the Hands of the English Renaissance* (Stanford, CA: Stanford University Press, 1990), esp. p. 65.

14. John Earle, *Micro-cosmographie: or, A Piece of the World discovered; in Essays and Characters* (London: Edward Blount, 1628). See Bruce McIver, "John Earle: The Unwillingly Willing Author of *Microcosmography*," *English Studies* 72 (1991): 219–29. See also the brief discussion in Stannard, *Puritan Way of Death*, p. 48.

15. Elisha Coles, *Nolens Volens: or, You Shall make Latin whether you will or no . . .* (London: T. Basset and H. Brome, 1675).

16. See Noel Malcolm, "The Publications of John Pell, F. R. S. (1611–1685): Some New Light and Some Old Confusions," *Records of the Royal Society of London* 54 (2000): 275–92, esp. pp. 278–80 for discussion of *The English Schoole*.

17. Tobias Ellis, *The English School* (London: John Darby, 1680). On Pell's influence on Ellis, see Malcolm, "Publications," p. 279. For a brief discussion of Ellis, see Demers, *Heaven upon Earth*, pp. 79–81.

18. See David H. Watters, "'I spake as a child': Authority, Metaphor, and *The New England Primer*," *Early American Literature* 20 (1985–86): 193–213; Crain, *The Story of A*, pp. 38–54; and the material in the facsimile edition of Ford, *The New-England Primer*.

19. *Oxford English Dictionary*, s.v. "lay," v., def. 60, "lay up," def. k. All quotations and citations from the *Oxford English Dictionary* are from the online *OED*, at http://dictionary.oed.com.

20. Watters, "'I spake as a child'," p. 196.

21. Janeway, *Token*, pp. 113–31.

22. All quotations from Bunyan's *Pilgrim's Progress* are from the edition of James Blanton Wharey and Roger Sharrock (Oxford: Clarendon Press, 1960), cited by page number in my text. Among the vast and growing bibliography on Bunyan, I single out for special reference those studies keyed to his reception in the Puritan tradition and as a children's author in particular. See N. H. Keeble, "'Of him thousands daily Sing and talk': Bunyan and His Reputation," in *John Bunyan, Conventicle and Parnassus*, ed. N. H. Keeble, pp. 241–64 (Oxford: Clarendon Press, 1988); Kathleen M. Swaim, *Pilgrim's Progress, Puritan Progress* (Urbana: University of Illinois Press, 1993); and Richard L. Greaves, *Glimpses of Glory: John Bunyan and English Dissent* (Stanford, CA: Stanford University Press, 2002). In addition to these books, there are discussions throughout Jackson, *Engines*; Sommerville, *Discovery of Childhood*; and Fliegelman, *Prodigals and Pilgrims*, as well as the classic arguments in Watt, *Rise of the Novel*.

23. Christopher Ness, *A Spiritual Legacy* (London, 1684), pp. 114–15. My attention was called to this book by Sommerville, *Discovery of Childhood*, p. 123.

24. Unless otherwise noted, all quotations from Franklin's works are from *Benjamin Franklin: Writings*, ed. Leo Lemay (New York: Library of America, 1987), cited by page number in my text.

25. John Bunyan, *Grace Abounding*, ed. Roger Sharrock (Oxford: Clarendon Press, 1962), p. 98; quoted in Swaim, *Pilgrim's Progress, Puritan Progress*, p. 170.

26. Mark Twain, *Huckleberry Finn*, ed. Sculley Bradley et al. (New York: Norton, 1977), chap. 17, p. 83.

27. Ager Scolae, *Pilgrim's Progress in Poesie* (London, 1697), A2. For a brief review of early adaptations, see Keeble, "Of him thousands daily Sing and talk," pp. 245–46; and Greaves, *Glimpses of Glory*, pp. 612–13.

28. See Fliegelman, *Prodigals and Pilgrims*.

29. There are discussions of Watts's children's verse and its impact throughout Jackson, *Engines of Instruction*; and Samuel Pickering, *John Locke and Children's Books in Eighteenth-Century England* (Knoxville: University of Tennessee Press, 1981). For a survey of the *Divine Songs* and their sources, their printing history, and their impact, see Watts, *Divine Songs, Facsimile Reproductions of the First Edition of 1715 and an Illustrated Edition of circa 1840*, ed. J. H. P. Pafford (London: Oxford University Press, 1971), pp. 1–124.

30. Quoted, without source, in Donald Davie, *The Eighteenth-Century Hymn in England* (Cambridge: Cambridge University Press, 1993), p. 30.

31. All quotations from the *Divine Songs* are from the first edition (London: M. Lawrence, 1715).

32. The first edition (1715) reads "brighter."

33. Isaac Watts, *The Art of Reading and Writing English*, 2nd ed. (London: John Clark, 1727), pp. 75, 82.

34. Isaac Watts, *Divine Songs*, 8th ed. (London: Richard Ford, 1727), p. 47. Quotations from "A Cradle Hymn" are from this edition, pp. 47–50.

35. *Silence Dogood, No. 7*, in Franklin, *Writings*, pp. 19–23.

36. See Bardsley, *Curiosities*, pp. 146–47. Bardsley finds "Silence" as a popular girl's name throughout the period, probably from the injunction of St. Paul: "Let the woman learn silence with all subjection" (I.Timothy, ii.11). "Dogood" is less common but still in the records (*Curiosities*, p. 165). Both names appear, too, as characters in *Pilgrim's Progress*.

37. Franklin, *Writings*, p. 23.

CHAPTER FIVE: *Playthings of the Mind*

1. John Clarke, *An Essay upon the Education of Youth in Grammer-Schools* (London, 1720), pp. 4, 8–9; quoted in Samuel Pickering, *John Locke and Children's Books in Eighteenth-Century England* (Knoxville: University of Tennessee Press, 1981), p. 10.

2. John Locke, *Some Thoughts concerning Education* (London, 1693). All quotations from this work are from the edition of James L. Axtell, *The Educational Writings of John Locke* (Cambridge: Cambridge University Press, 1968). Axtell reviews the origins and early reception of this work. Pickering, *John Locke and Children's Books*, remains the only sustained study of Locke's impact on the children's book industry of the eighteenth century. But many later studies have reviewed in detail Locke's impact on the reception of the Aesopica, on educational theory and practice, and on the rise of the English novel. See in particular Geoffrey Summerfield, *Fantasy and Reason: Children's Literature in the Eighteenth Century* (London: Methuen, 1984); Michael McKeon, *The Origins of the English Novel, 1600–1740* (Baltimore: Johns Hopkins University Press, 1987); Peter Schouls, *John Locke and Enlightenment* (Ithaca, NY: Cornell University Press, 1992); Jayne Lewis, *The English Fable: Aesop and Literary Culture, 1651–1740* (Cambridge: Cambridge University Press, 1996); Richard A. Barney, *Plots of Enlightenment: Education and the Novel in Eighteenth-Century England* (Stanford, CA: Stanford University Press, 1999); and Patricia Crain, *The Story of A: The Alphabetization of America from "The New England Primer" to "The Scarlet Letter"* (Stanford, CA: Stanford University Press, 2000). After this chapter was completed, I became aware of the late Gillian Brown's work on Locke, print culture, and children's literature. A portion of this work appeared posthumously as "The Metamorphic Book: Children's Print Culture in the Eighteenth Century," *Eighteenth-Century Studies* 39 (2006): 351–62.

3. Sarah Trimmer, *The Guardian of Education*, vol. 1 (1802), p. 62, quoted in Sylvia Kasey Marks, *Writing for the Rising Generation: British Fiction for Young People, 1672–1839* (Victoria, BC: University of Victoria, 2003), p. 18.

4. *A History of Little Goody Two-Shoes; Otherwise called Mrs. Margery Two-Shoes* (London: Newbery, 1772), p. 122. Page numbers are hereafter given in my text.

5. The classic statement of this development remains Ian Watt, *The Rise of the Novel* (Berkeley and Los Angeles: University of California Press, 1957); see in particular p. 64.

6. Ibid., p. 15.

7. John Locke, *An Essay concerning Human Understanding*, 5th ed. (London, 1706), bk. 4, para. 11.

8. See *Oxford English Dictionary*, s.v. "plaything."

9. On Newbery and his sales, see Mary V. Jackson, *Engines of Instruction, Mischief, and Magic: Children's Literature in England from Its Beginnings to 1839* (Lincoln: University of Nebraska Press, 1989), pp. 80–99.

10. Ibid., p. 86.

11. Sarah Fielding, *The Governess; Or, The Little Female Academy* (London, 1749), pp. x–xi. All quotations are from the facsimile edition, prepared with introduction and notes, by Jill E. Grey (London: Oxford University Press, 1968).

12. See Pickering, *John Locke and Children's Books*; and Christopher Flint, "Speaking Objects: The Circulation of Stories in Eighteenth-Century Prose Fiction," *PMLA* 113 (1998): 212–26.

13. Samuel Pickering and Mary V. Jackson, in particular, have done so, as had Gillian Brown.

14. Thomas Bridges, *The Adventures of a Bank-Note* (London, 1770–71), p. 1. Page numbers are hereafter given in my text.

15. See Pickering, *John Locke and Children's Books*; and Jackson, *Engines*, passim.

16. Quoted in Pickering, *John Locke and Children's Books*, p. 235, n. 24.

17. [John Locke], *Aesop's Fables in English and Latin, Interlineary . . .* (London: A. and J. Churchill, 1703).

18. Ibid., fable 20, p. 42.

19. Ibid., fable 201, pp. 297–98.

20. See Locke, *Essay concerning Human Understanding*, bk. 1, para. 15; bk. 2, para. 3.

21. Schouls, *John Locke and Enlightenment*, p. 3.

22. Quoted in Schouls, *John Locke and Enlightenment*, p. 105.

23. *A Little Pretty Pocket-Book*, 10th ed. (London: J. Newbery, 1760), p. 6.

24. Abraham Aesop, Esq., *Fables in Verse, for the Improvement of the Young and the Old* (London: [Newbery], 1783), p. vi. Page numbers are hereafter given in my text.

25. Charles Johnstone, *Chrysal: or, the Adventures of a Guinea . . . by an Adept* (Dublin: Dillon Chamberlaine, 1760), vol. 1, p. 9.

26. Francis Coventry, *History of Pompey the Little, or The Life and Adventures of a Lap-Dog* (Dublin: George Faulkner, 1751), p. 38.

27. Ibid., pp. 39–40.

28. See Flint, "Speaking Objects," p. 225, n. 9.

29. Though I write about *The Governess*'s thematic attention to childhood development generally, I should make clear that this was a book originally intended for girls of the upper class. Much recent criticism of Fielding has called attention to the book's gender- and class-specific audience, and I do not slight the contributions of these scholars to recovering the social context of the work's original dissemination. My concern

here is to locate the book in the larger environment of Locke's theories of education and, more pointedly, to see its attentions as perhaps more universal than others have to this point. See, for example, Arlene Fish Wilner, "Education and Ideology in Sarah Fielding's *The Governess*," *Studies in Eighteenth-Century Culture* 24 (1995): 210–18; and Linda Bree, *Sarah Fielding* (New York: Twayne, 1996).

CHAPTER SIX: *Canoes and Cannibals*

1. The classic account of *Robinson Crusoe*'s status in the history of the English novel, its debts to the Puritans and to Locke, and its impact on later fiction remains Ian Watt, *The Rise of the Novel* (Berkeley and Los Angeles: University of California Press, 1957), pp. 60–92. Watt's version of that history has been qualified and challenged by a range of recent scholarship. See in particular Michael McKeon, *The Origins of the English Novel, 1600–1740* (Baltimore: Johns Hopkins University Press, 1987), esp. pp. 315–37; and Richard A. Barney, *Plots of Enlightenment: Education and the Novel in Eighteenth-Century England* (Stanford, CA: Stanford University Press, 1999), esp. pp. 206–54. On *Crusoe*'s impact on children's literature, see Mary V. Jackson, *Engines of Instruction, Mischief, and Magic: Children's Literature in England from Its Beginnings to 1839* (Lincoln: University of Nebraska Press, 1989), esp. pp. 118, 154–55, 239–40, 250; and Samuel Pickering, *Moral Instruction and Fiction for Children, 1749–1820* (Athens: University of Georgia Press, 1993), pp. 58–80. On the tradition of the Robinsonade not just in English but in European literature of the eighteenth and nineteenth centuries, see the collection of essays in *Études françaises*, special issue, "Robinson, la robinsonnade et le monde des choses," 35, no. 1 (1999). On the impact of *Robinson Crusoe* on early American literature and on the shaping of the Revolutionary American consciousness, see Jay Fliegelman, *Prodigals and Pilgrims: The American Revolution against Patriarchal Authority, 1750–1800* (Cambridge: Cambridge University Press, 1982), esp. pp. 67–83.

2. Daniel Defoe, *Robinson Crusoe*, ed. Michael Shinagel, 2nd ed. (New York: Norton, 1994), p. 113. All quotations from the novel are from this edition, cited by page number in my text.

3. *La vie et les aventures surprenantes de Robinson Crusoé.* . . . See the discussion in François Caradec, *Histoire de la littérature enfantine en France* (Paris: Albin Michel, 1977), pp. 97–101.

4. See Martin Green, *The Robinson Crusoe Story* (University Park: Penn State University Press, 1990), p. 26.

5. Jean-Jacques Rousseau, *Emile, or On Education*, trans. Allan Bloom (New York: Basic Books, 1979), p. 188. Page numbers are hereafter given in my text. For a discussion of Rousseau's view of *Crusoe*, and the larger context for the novel's place in Rousseau's theories of education and society, see Bloom's introduction, pp. 3–28.

6. Fliegelman, *Prodigals and Pilgrims*, p. 77.

7. *Crusoe*, of course, provoked more than just children's literature. For a survey running from Joachim Campe's German *Robinson der Jüngere* of 1779 to Michel Tournier's *Vendredi: ou Les limbes du Pacifique* of 1967, see Green, *The Robinson Crusoe Story*. Not included in Green's survey is J. M. Coetzee's *Foe* (1986).

8. The following discussion of these words' origin is based on the etymology given in the *Oxford English Dictionary*, s.v. "canoe" and "cannibal."

9. See John Clement Ball, "Max's Colonial Fantasy: Rereading Sendak's 'Where the Wild Things are'," *ARIEL: A Review of International English Literature* 28 (1997): 167–79.

10. See Margaret Spufford, *Small Books and Pleasant Histories: Popular Fiction and Its Readership in Seventeenth-Century England* (London: Methuen, 1981); Cathy Lynn Preston and Michael J. Preston, eds., *The Other Print Tradition: Essays on Chapbooks, Broadsides, and Related Ephemera* (New York: Garland, 1993); and Andrew O'Malley, *The Making of a Modern Child: Children's Literature and Childhood in the Late Eighteenth Century* (New York: Routledge, 2003).

11. See Michael J. Preston, "Rethinking Folklore, Rethinking Literature: Looking at *Robinson Crusoe* and *Gulliver's Travels* as Folktales; A Chapbook-Inspired Inquiry," in Preston and Preston, *The Other Print Tradition*, pp. 19–73. See also Fliegelman, *Prodigals and Pilgrims*, pp. 67–83, on the American abridgments and adaptations of Crusoe.

12. Quoted in Pickering, *Moral Instruction*, p. 59.

13. Quoted in Pickering, *Moral Instruction*, p. 68.

14. Quoted in Pickering, *Moral Instruction*, pp. 64–65.

15. Jack Zipes, Lissa Paul, Lynne Vallone, Peter Hunt, and Gillian Avery, eds., *The Norton Anthology of Children's Literature: The Traditions in English* (New York: Norton, 2005), pp. 1633–43. Page numbers are hereafter given in my text.

16. Preston, "Rethinking Folklore, Rethinking Literature." Page numbers are given in my text.

17. *Treasure Island* was originally published in 1883. I quote from the edition in John W. Griffith and Charles H. Frey, eds., *Classics of Children's Literature*, 4th ed. (Upper Saddle River, NJ: Prentice Hall, 1996), pp. 647–765.

18. A. A. Milne, *Winnie-the-Pooh* (originally published 1926; New York: Dutton, 1954). Page numbers are given in my text.

19. For material on Wyss and *The Swiss Family Robinson*, I am indebted to J. Hillis Miller, "Reading *The Swiss Family Robinson* as Virtual Reality," in *Children's Literature: New Approaches*, ed. Karin Lesnik-Oberstein, pp. 78–92 (London: Palgrave Macmillan, 2004). For an account of *The Swiss Family Robinson*'s publishing history in France, together with the publication history of the remarkable *Le Robinson des demoiselles*, see Pierre Amandry, "La libraire Lefèvre et Guérin, 1860–1920," *Revue française d'histoire du livre* 82 (1994): 219–24.

20. *The Swiss Family Robinson* (New York: George H. Doran Co., n.d.). Page numbers are given in my text.

21. *The Swiss Family Robinson, in Words of One Syllable*, abridged and adapted from the original story by I. F. M. (New York: McLoughlin, n.d.).

22. See Andrew Martin, *The Mask of the Prophet: The Extraordinary Fictions of Jules Verne* (Oxford: Clarendon Press, 1990). For further discussion of the impact of *Robinson Crusoe* on Verne's career and on his publishing relationship to the firm of Pierre-Jules Hetzel, see Caradec, *Histoire de la littérature enfantine en France*, pp. 158–78.

23. Herbert R. Lottman, *Jules Verne: An Exploratory Biography* (New York: St. Martin's Press, 1996), p. 167.

24. Jules Verne, *The Mysterious Island*, trans. Jordan Stump (New York: The Modern Library, 2001). For a detailed review of the novel's debts to Robinson Crusoe, see Daniel Compère, "Les déclinaisons de *Robinson Crusoe* dans *L'Île mystérieuse* de Jules Verne," *Études françaises*, special issue, "Robinson, la robinsonnade et le monde des choses," 35, no. 1 (1999): 43–54.

CHAPTER SEVEN: *From Islands to Empires*

1. W. E. Henley, review of *Treasure Island*, *Saturday Review*, 8 December 1883, 737–38, quoted in Joseph Bristow, *Empire Boys: Adventures in a Man's World* (London: HarperCollins, 1991), p. 110. Bristow's book remains the most comprehensive and provocative account of the relationships among imperial ideology, boys' books, and the cultures of adventure in the nineteenth and early twentieth centuries.

2. Quoted in Bristow, *Empire Boys*, p. 111.

3. See Lise Andries, "Les images et les choses dans *Robinson* et les robinsonnades," *Études françaises*, special issue, "Robinson, la robinsonnade et le monde des choses," 35, no. 1 (1999): 95–122.

4. In addition to Bristow, *Empire Boys*, my account has been influenced by the following studies: Patrick Brantlinger, *Rule of Darkness: British Literature and Imperialism, 1830–1914* (Ithaca, NY: Cornell University Press, 1988); Hugh Brogan, *Mowgli's Sons: Kipling and Baden Powell's Scouts* (London: Jonathan Cape, 1987); Jeffrey Richards, ed., *Imperialism and Juvenile Literature* (Manchester: Manchester University Press, 1989); and Jane Hotchkiss, "The Jungle of Eden: Kipling, Wolf Boys, and the Colonial Imagination," *Victorian Literature and Culture* 29 (2001): 435–49. For the stimulus of working on this and the following two chapters, I am grateful to my student Jessica Straley and the example of her dissertation, "How the Child Lost Its Tail: Evolutionary Theory, Victorian Pedagogy, and the Development of Children's Literature, 1860–1920" (Ph.D. diss., Stanford University, 2005). There are many general surveys of the British colonial experience that bear on my study. Still useful for its overarching narrative and assembly of primary source materials is Paul Knaplund, *The British Empire, 1815–1939* (New York: Harper and Brothers, 1941). A more recent account of the colonial experience, from the point of view of cultural criticism and literary theory, is Albert Memmi, *Portrait du colonisé, précédé du portrait du colonisateur*, originally published in 1965 and expanded as *The Colonizer and the Colonized*, trans. Howard Greenfield (Boston: Beacon Press, 1991). It is almost impossible now to write about the colonial experience and literary history in any context without reference to Edward Said, *Culture and Imperialism* (New York: Knopf, 1991).

5. The work now known as *Lord Chesterfield's Advice to His Son* was originally published as *Letters written by the Late Right Honourable Philip Dormer Stanhope, Earl of Chesterfield, to his son, Philip Stanhope . . .* (London: J. Dodsley, 1774). These letters of advice were subsequently republished, abridged, edited, and incorporated into a range of advisory books for the next century—for example, in such forms as *The Young Gentleman's Parental Monitor* (London: Hartford, 1792) and *The American Chesterfield* (Philadelphia: J. Grigg, 1827). The letters have been frequently anthologized. I quote from

the selection in Jack Zipes, Lissa Paul, Lynne Vallone, Peter Hunt, and Gillian Avery, eds., *The Norton Anthology of Children's Literature: The Traditions in English* (New York: Norton, 2005), pp. 1430–32.

6. Samuel Johnson, *A Dictionary of the English Language* (London, 1755), s.v. "propriety."

7. Fanny Burney, *Cecilia* (London, 1782), vol. 2, chap. 5, p. xiii.

8. Thomas Hughes, *Tom Brown's Schooldays, by an Old Boy* (London, 1857). I quote from the selection in Zipes et al., *Norton Anthology of Children's Literature*; page numbers are given in my text.

9. *Oxford English Dictionary*, s.v. "cut," v., def. 60 m, n, o.

10. See Carolyn Marvin, *When Old Technologies Were New* (New York: Oxford University Press, 1988).

11. Edison was dubbed "the Wizard of Menlo Park" in an article in the *New York Daily Graphic*, 10 April 1878. Early biographies of Edison that have taken on an exemplary force for younger readers include W. K. L. Dickson and Antonia Dickson, *The Life and Inventions of Thomas Alva Edison* (New York: Crowell, 1894); and Francis Trevelyan Miller, *Thomas A. Edison, Benefactor of Mankind* (n.p., 1931).

12. See my extensive discussion in "Hello, Dude: Philology, Performance, and Technology in Mark Twain's *Connecticut Yankee*," *American Literary History* 15 (2003): 471–503.

13. Hans Christian Andersen, *The Fairy Tale of My Life* (New York: Cooper Square Press, 2000), p. 410; this is a facsimile reprinting of the English translation of 1871 (London: Paddington Press).

14. Quoted in Marvin, *Old Technologies*, p. 196.

15. See Richard Klein, *Cigarettes Are Sublime* (Durham, NC: Duke University Press, 1993), pp. 11, 56, 135.

16. So-called penny journals and dime novels proliferated in the United States at the end of the nineteenth century, and their fascination with inventors, scientists, and explorers contributed to the rise of the science fiction genre at that time. Studies that address the place of this material in science fiction as a form of children's literature include, in particular, H. Bruce Franklin, *Future Perfect: American Science Fiction of the Nineteenth Century* (New York: Oxford University Press, 1966); Margaret Esmonde, "Children's Science Fiction," in *Signposts to Criticism of Children's Literature*, ed. Robert Bator (Chicago: American Library Association, 1983); and Paul Alkon, *Science Fiction before 1900: Imagination Discovers Technology* (New York: Maxwell Macmillan International, 1994).

17. H. Rider Haggard, *King Solomon's Mines* (London, 1885). I quote from the text available online at Project Gutenberg.

18. Bristow, *Empire Boys*, pp. 127–40; these quotations from pp. 128, 133.

19. For a review of Henty's work, see Bristow, *Empire Boys*, pp. 146–54. Earlier studies I have found useful include Guy Arnold, *Hold Fast for England: G. A. Henty, Imperialist Boys' Writer* (London: Hamish Hamilton, 1980); and the magnificently dated biography by George Manville Fenn, *George Alfred Henty: The Story of an Active Life* (London: Blackie, 1907). The most comprehensive bibliographical study of Henty's publishing career is Peter Newbolt, *G. A. Henty, 1832–1902: A Bibliographical Study of His British Editions* (Brookfield, VT: Scolar Press, 1996).

20. G. A. Henty, *With Buller in Natal, or A Born Leader* (London, 1901). I quote from the text available online at Project Gutenberg.

21. "Milliner's Dream," August 2, 2005, http://millinersdream.blogspot.com/2005/08/treasured-volume.html.

22. *Oxford English Dictionary*, s.v. "treasure," v., def. 4. The quotation from Longfellow, "Day Is Done," is from the text in F. O. Matthiessen, ed., *The Oxford Book of American Verse* (Oxford: Oxford University Press, 1950), p. 115.

23. Máire ní Fhlathúin, ed., *Kim*, by Rudyard Kipling (London: Broadview, 2005) offers a complete bibliography, critical discussion, and a selection of early reviews, discussions, and drafts of the novel. Further references to the novel in this edition are by page number in my text. Among the vast bibliography on Kipling, I single out Zohreh T. Sullivan, *Narratives of Empire: The Fictions of Rudyard Kipling* (Cambridge: Cambridge University Press, 1993).

24. J. H. Millar, "Recent Fiction," *Blackwood's Edinburgh Magazine* 170 (December 1901): 793–95, reprinted in Fhlathúin, *Kim*, pp. 335–37.

25. Robert Baden-Powell, *Scouting for Boys*, quoted from the 1910 edition (London: Pearson), in Fhlathúin, *Kim*, pp. 345–48.

26. See Brogan, *Mowgli's Sons*; and Tim Jeal, *Baden-Powell* (London: Hutchinson, 1989).

27. Baden-Powell, *Scouting for Boys* (London: Pearson, 1908), p. 17, quoted in Bristow, *Empire Boys*, p. 179.

28. *Oxford English Dictionary*, s.v. "smart," def. 12a.

29. Baden-Powell, *Scouting for Boys* (1909), p. 121, quoted in Bristow, *Empire Boys*, p. 191.

30. Robert Baden-Powell, *Rovering to Success* (1922), selections reprinted in Zipes et al., *Norton Anthology of Children's Literature*, pp. 1460–79; this quotation from p. 1470.

CHAPTER EIGHT: *On beyond Darwin*

1. Robert Baden-Powell, *Rovering to Success* (1922), selections reprinted in Jack Zipes, Lissa Paul, Lynne Vallone, Peter Hunt, and Gillian Avery, eds., *The Norton Anthology of Children's Literature: The Traditions in English* (New York: Norton, 2005), pp. 1460–79; this quotation from p. 1472.

2. Gillian Beer, *Darwin's Plots: Evolutionary Narrative in Darwin, George Eliot and Nineteenth-Century Fiction* (London: Routledge and Kegan Paul, 1983), p. 119.

3. Peter Hunt, *An Introduction to Children's Literature* (Oxford: Oxford University Press, 1994), p. 59. Darwin's impact on English fiction has received many important treatments. In addition to Beer, *Darwin's Plots*, see Leo J. Henkin, *Darwinism and the English Novel, 1860–1910* (New York: Russell and Russell, 1940); George Levine, *Darwin and the Novelists: Patterns of Science in Victorian Fiction* (Cambridge, MA: Harvard University Press, 1988); and Lisa Hopkins, *Giants of the Past: Popular Fictions and the Idea of Evolution* (Lewisburg, PA: Bucknell University Press, 2004). Many specific studies of Darwin's impact on individual authors or traditions have also appeared. Among the most productive for the study of children's literature is R. P. S. Jack, "Peter Pan as

Darwinian Creation Myth," *Literature and Theology* 8 (1994): 157-73. For a general review of Darwin's work in the popular mind, see Alvar Ellegård, *Darwin and the General Reader: The Reception of Darwin's Theory of Evolution in the British Periodical Press, 1859-1872* (Göteburg: Acta Universitatis Gothenburgensis, 1958). As in previous chapters, I am indebted to Jessica Straley, "How the Child Lost Its Tail: Evolutionary Theory, Victorian Pedagogy, and the Development of Children's Literature, 1860-1920" (Ph.D. diss., Stanford University, 2005).

4. Beer, *Darwin's Plots*, p. 29.

5. For a review of Erasmus Darwin's work in the larger context of late eighteenth-century Britain, the Darwin and Wedgwood family intertwinings, and natural science before the rise of evolution, see Jenny Uglow, *The Lunar Men: The Friends Who Made the Future, 1730-1810* (London: Faber, 2002).

6. John Bowlby, *Charles Darwin: A New Life* (New York: Norton, 1990), p. 30.

7. Quoted in Uglow, *Lunar Men*, p. 429.

8. William Diller Matthew, *Outline and General Principles of the History of Life* (Berkeley and Los Angeles: University of California Press, 1928), p. 6, quoted in (and providing the title for) Peter Bowler, *Life's Splendid Drama: Evolutionary Biology and the Reconstruction of Life's Ancestry, 1860-1940* (Chicago: University of Chicago Press, 1996), p. 3.

9. Paul H. Barrett, Donald J. Weinshank, and Timothy T. Gottleber, eds., *A Concordance to Darwin's "Origin of Species," First Edition* (Ithaca, NY: Cornell University Press, 1981).

10. Charles Darwin, *The Voyage of the Beagle*, http://charles-darwin.classic-literature.co.uk/the-voyage-of-the-beagle/ebook-page-13.asp.

11. See Guy Kendall, *Charles Kingsley and His Ideas* (1947; reprint, New York: Haskell House, 1973); and Susan Chitty, *The Beast and the Monk: A Life of Charles Kingsley* (London: Hodder and Stoughton, 1974). For critical assessments and contexts of *The Water-Babies* in particular, see Gillian Avery, "Fantasy and Nonsense," in *The Victorians*, ed. Arthur Pollard, pp. 287-306 (London: Sphere, 1970); Humphrey Carpenter, *Secret Gardens: A Study of the Golden Age of Children's Literature* (London: Allen and Unwin, 1985), pp. 23-43; Hunt, *Introduction to Children's Literature*, pp. 77-78; and Brian Alderson, ed., *The Water-Babies*, by Charles Kingsley (Oxford: Oxford University Press, 1995), with its important introduction, pp. ix-xxix. All quotations from *The Water-Babies* are from this edition, cited by page number in my text.

12. See Kendall, *Charles Kingsley*, pp. 135-36.

13. Richard Darwin Keynes, ed., *The Beagle Record* (Cambridge: Cambridge University Press, 1979), p. 345; diary entry for 18 January 1836.

14. Quoted in Beer, *Darwin's Plots*, p. 81.

15. Charles Darwin, *On the Origin of Species*, first edition (1859) reprinted in facsimile, with an introduction by Ernst Mayr (Cambridge, MA: Harvard University Press, 1964), p. 128. Unless otherwise specified, all quotations are from this edition, cited by page number in my text.

16. Quoted in Beer, *Darwin's Plots*, p. 119.

17. Ibid.

18. Rudyard Kipling, *The Jungle Books*, ed. W. W. Robson (Oxford: Oxford University Press, 1992). Page numbers are given in my text.

19. Charles Darwin, *The Descent of Man and Selection in Relation to Sex* (New York: D. Appleton and Co., 1897), p. 18. Page numbers are hereafter given in my text.

20. Robson, in *The Jungle Books*, p. 354.

21. Lisa Lewis, ed., *The Just So Stories for Little Children*, by Rudyard Kipling (Oxford: Oxford University Press, 1995). Page numbers are given in my text.

22. M. E. Boole, *The Preparation of the Child for Science* (Oxford: Clarendon Press, 1904), pp. 151–52.

23. H. G. Wells, *The Island of Dr. Moreau* (Harmondsworth, UK: Penguin, 2005), p. 43. Page numbers are hereafter given in my text.

24. Dr. Seuss [Theodor Seuss Geisel], *On beyond Zebra* (New York: Random House, 1955).

25. Dr. Seuss [Theodor Seuss Geisel], *If I Ran the Zoo* (New York: Random House, 1950).

26. Dr. Seuss [Theodor Seuss Geisel], *And to Think That I Saw It on Mulberry Street* (New York: Random House, 1937).

27. Darwin, *Descent of Man*, pp. 494–96.

28. Dr. Seuss [Theodor Seuss Geisel], *Scrambled Eggs Super* (New York: Random House, 1953).

CHAPTER NINE: *Ill-Tempered and Queer*

1. For a survey of the relationships between philology and biology in the nineteenth century, see Stephen Alter, *Darwinism and the Linguistic Image: Language, Race, and Natural Theology in the Nineteenth Century* (Baltimore: Johns Hopkins University Press, 1999); the quotation from Ernst Haeckel appears on p. 116. For more on these relationships, especially the fascination with both biological and linguistic trees, see Peter Bowler, *Life's Splendid Drama: Evolutionary Biology and the Reconstruction of Life's Ancestry, 1860–1940* (Chicago: University of Chicago Press, 1996).

2. For a general history of these developments, see Maurice Pope, *The Story of Decipherment*, rev. ed. (London: Thames and Hudson, 1999), and the set of handbooks on early inscriptions originally published by the British Museum and collected in J. T. Hooker, ed., *Reading the Past: Ancient Writing from Cuneiform to the Alphabet* (Berkeley and Los Angeles: University of California Press, 1990).

3. The use of the word *nonsense* to apply to humorous verse or forms of playful writing, though it is cited by the *Oxford English Dictionary* as early as 1670, does not become a common notion until the mid-nineteenth century (*OED*, s.v. "nonsense verse"). A letter from John Keats of 17 September 1819, cited by the *OED*, makes clear that this form of writing is associated with childhood and the school: "I cannot get on without writing as boys do at school a few nonsense verses." The editor of the *OED* himself, Sir James A. H. Murray, weighed in on the origins of the term in his comment on the word *limerick* in *Notes and Queries*, 10 December 1898, p. 470 (also cited by the *OED*): "A nonsense verse such as was written by Lear is wrongfully so called. . . . Who applied this

name to the indecent nonsense verse first it is hard to say." Edward Lear called his initial collection of verse *A Book of Nonsense* (first edition, 1846) and wrote in a letter of 1870, "Nonsense is the breath of my nostrils." Quoted in Vivien Noakes, ed., *The Complete Verse and Other Nonsense*, by Edward Lear (Harmondsworth, UK: Penguin, 2001), p. xxii. The entire introduction to this edition (pp. xix–xxxiv), together with the annotations to the poems and the edition itself, constitutes a valuable resource, not just for Lear's work but for the nineteenth-century culture of nonsense as a whole. All quotations from Lear are from this edition, cited by page number in my text. Lear and Carroll have been associated with nonsense verse from the earliest critical assessments. See Carolyn Wells, ed., *A Nonsense Anthology* (New York: Scribner's, 1902), in which the first poem is "Jabberwocky"; Emile Cammaerts, *The Poetry of Nonsense* (London: George Routledge and Sons, 1925); Elizabeth Sewell, *The Field of Nonsense* (London: Chatto and Windus, 1952); and Jean-Jacques Lecercle, *Philosophy of Nonsense: The Intuitions of Victorian Nonsense Literature* (London: Routledge, 1994). For Carroll's nonsense verse in the Alice books, and for a collection of materials bearing on his place in the culture and aesthetics of nonsense, see Martin Gardner, *The Annotated Alice* (New York: Clarkson N. Potter, 1960). All quotations from the Alice books are from this edition, cited by page number in my text.

4. On Scott's place in the *OED* and his reputation for linguistic experimentation and innovation, see John Willinsky, *Empire of Words: The Reign of the OED* (Princeton, NJ: Princeton University Press, 1994). On the philological concerns of Victorian novelists and the place of linguistic experiment, regionalism, and historical awareness in nineteenth-century imaginative writing generally, see Linda Dowling, *Language and Decadence in the Victorian Fin de Siècle* (Princeton, NJ: Princeton University Press, 1986); Cary H. Plotkin, *The Tenth Muse: Victorian Philology and the Genesis of the Poetic Language of Gerard Manley Hopkins* (Carbondale: Southern Illinois University Press, 1989); Dennis Taylor, *Hardy's Literary Language and Victorian Philology* (Oxford: Oxford University Press, 1993); and Seth Lerer, *Error and the Academic Self: The Scholarly Imagination, Medieval to Modern* (New York: Columbia University Press, 2002), pp. 103–74 (on Eliot's *Middlemarch* and Victorian philology).

5. William Makepeace Thackeray, *Vanity Fair* (1847–48; New York: Signet, 1962), pp. 48–49.

6. In addition to the works cited above, I have found the following helpful and stimulating for this chapter: Kathleen Blake, *Play, Games, and Sport: The Literary Works of Lewis Carroll* (Ithaca, NY: Cornell University Press, 1974); Robert Polhemus, "Lewis Carroll and the Child in Victorian Fiction," in *The Columbia History of the British Novel*, ed. John Richetti, pp. 579–607 (New York: Columbia University Press, 1994); and U. C. Knoepflmacher, *Ventures into Childland: Victorians, Fairy Tales, and Femininity* (Chicago: University of Chicago Press, 1998). Among the many biographical studies of Carroll and Lear, I single out Peter Levi, *Edward Lear: A Biography* (London: Macmillan, 1995); and Morton Cohen, *Lewis Carroll: A Biography* (New York: Knopf, 1995).

7. Knoepflmacher, *Ventures into Childland*, esp. pp. 150–227; Thomas Dilworth, "Society and the Self in the Limericks of Lear," *Review of English Studies*, new series, 45 (1994): 42–62.

8. See Hans Aarsleff, *The Study of Language in England, 1780–1860* (Princeton, NJ: Princeton University Press, 1967); Murray Cohen, *Sensible Words: Linguistic Practice in England, 1640–1785* (Baltimore: Johns Hopkins University Press, 1977); and Olivia Smith, *The Politics of Language, 1791–1819* (Oxford: Oxford University Press, 1984).

9. Quoted in Blake, *Play, Games, and Sport*, pp. 70–71.

10. Quoted in Blake, *Play, Games, and Sport*, p. 75.

11. This material is reprinted, with discussion, in Gardner, *The Annotated Alice*, pp. 191–94.

12. Quoted in Cohen, *Lewis Carroll*, p. 511.

13. Gardner, *The Annotated Alice*, p. 193.

14. The word appears twelve times in *Alice in Wonderland* and eight times in *Through the Looking Glass*.

15. *OED*, s.v. "queer," adj. 1.

16. *OED*, s.v. "queer," adj. 1, def. 3, "Queer Street," first attested in a quotation from 1811.

17. Woody Allen, "The Kugelmass Episode," in *Side Effects* (New York: Random House, 1980), p. 55.

18. For the "Nonsense Botany," see Noakes, *Complete Verse*, pp. 251–53; for "The Table and the Chair," see pp. 277–78.

19. Dilworth, "Society and the Self," p. 45.

20. The preceding limericks are on pp. 220–32 in Noakes, *Complete Verse*; the notes to the story are on pp. 503–4.

21. "Illustrations for 'Kathleen O'Moore,'" in Noakes, *Complete Verse*, pp. 59–61; "The Courtship of the Yonghy-Bonghy-Bò," ibid., pp. 324–27.

22. Lecercle, *Philosophy of Nonsense*, p. 202.

23. E. C. Bentley, *Biography for Beginners: Being a Collection of Miscellaneous Examples for the Use of Upper Forms* (London: T. W. Laurie, 1905), p. 1. See also E. Clerihew Bentley with G. K. Chesterton, *The First Clerihews* (Oxford: Oxford University Press, 1982), a facsimile reproduction of the clerihew manuscript notebook, together with discussion.

24. Hugh Lofting, *The Story of Doctor Dolittle* (New York: F. A. Stokes, 1920), chap. 10.

25. Wells, *Nonsense Anthology*, p. xix.

26. Cammaerts, *Poetry of Nonsense*, pp. 2–3.

27. For insights into the relationships among the Dada movement, children's literature, and the fascination with childhood in avant-garde European literary movements, I am indebted to Sara Pankenier, "*In Fant Non Sens*: The Infantilist Aesthetic of the Russian Avant-Garde, 1909–1939" (Ph.D. diss., Stanford University, 2006).

28. Tristan Tzara, "Dada Manifesto," in Barbara Wright, trans., *Seven Dada Manifestos* (London: Calder, 1977).

29. Pankenier, "*In Fant Non Sens*," p. 172.

30. Cammaerts, *Poetry of Nonsense*, p. 31.

31. Antoine de Saint-Exupéry, *The Little Prince*, trans. Katherine Woods (San Diego, CA: Harcourt, 1943), p. 38.

32. See Ruth K. MacDonald, *Shel Silverstein* (New York: Twayne, 1997).

33. Shel Silverstein, *Where the Sidewalk Ends* (New York: Harper and Row, 1974).

34. The song's lyrics are apparently traditional, and different versions abound (e.g., some have "peppermint" instead of "cigarette"). This version is attributed to Harry Mc-Clintock. I quote from memory of the song as sung by Burl Ives, originally recorded in 1949.

35. Johann Wolfgang von Goethe, "Mignon," in *Selected Poems*, ed. Christopher Middleton (Boston: Suhrkamp/Insel, 1983), p. 132; translation mine.

CHAPTER TEN: *Straw into Gold*

1. Cynthia Zarin, Sendak profile, *The New Yorker*, 17 April 2006.

2. For the history of the fairy tale, see Roger Sale, *Fairy Tales and After: From Snow White to E. B. White* (Cambridge, MA: Harvard University Press, 1978); Jack Zipes, *Fairy Tales and the Art of Subversion* (New York: Routledge, 1983); and Maria Tatar, *The Classic Fairy Tales: Texts, Criticism* (New York: Norton, 1999). The publications of Zipes and Tatar, too many to enumerate here, have largely legitimated the study of the fairy tale in academic literary contexts. Both have focused their researches largely on the Grimm Brothers; specific studies will be cited later in this chapter. For a survey of the *conte de fées* in the context of seventeenth-century court culture, see Jean-Marie Apostolidès, "1661: From *Roi Soleil* to *Louis le Grand*," in *A New History of French Literature*, ed. Denis Hollier, pp. 314-20 (Cambridge, MA: Harvard University Press, 1989); and Walter E. Rex, "1704: Sunset Years," in Hollier, *New History of French Literature*, pp. 396-402. For a collection of modern tales and an evocative introduction, see Alison Lurie, ed., *The Oxford Book of Modern Fairy Tales* (Oxford: Oxford University Press, 1993).

3. See Apostolidès, "1661"; and Rex, "1704" (quotation from p. 401). Jack Zipes, Lissa Paul, Lynne Vallone, Peter Hunt, and Gillian Avery, eds., *The Norton Anthology of Children's Literature: The Traditions in English* (New York: Norton, 2005) has a particularly rich selection of fairy tales, together with a detailed introduction and a comprehensive bibliography (see pp. 175-386, 2434-35).

4. Sarah Fielding, *The Governess; Or, The Little Female Academy* (London, 1749); the quotations are from the facsimile edition prepared by Jill E. Grey (London: Oxford University Press, 1968), p. 166.

5. On the Grimms' development of the law of consonant correspondence, see Holger Pedersen, *The Discovery of Language: Linguistic Science in the Nineteenth Century*, trans. John W. Spargo (Bloomington: Indiana University Press, 1962). On the implications of their work for later English and European philology, see Hans Aarsleff, *The Study of Language in England, 1780-1860* (Princeton, NJ: Princeton University Press, 1967). Passow is quoted in German in Aarsleff, p. 255; my translation. Coleridge is quoted in Aarsleff, ibid.

6. James A. H. Murray, "Presidential Address," *Transactions of the Philological Society*, 1884, p. 509.

7. In addition to the studies cited above, see Jack Zipes, *The Brothers Grimm: From Enchanted Forests to the Modern World* (New York: Routledge, 1988); and Maria Tatar, *The Hard Facts of the Grimms' Fairy Tales*, 2nd ed. (Princeton, NJ: Princeton University

Press, 2003). See also the materials from the Grimms' prefaces collected and translated in Maria Tatar, *The Annotated Brothers Grimm* (New York: Norton, 2004). In this chapter, my quotations from the Grimms' tales in German are from *Die Märchen der Brüder Grimm* (Munich: Wilhelm Goldmann Verlag, n.d.). Translations are from Jack Zipes, *The Complete Fairy Tales of the Brothers Grimm* (New York: Bantam, 1992).

8. Tatar, *The Annotated Brothers Grimm*, p. 41.

9. See Lawrence Stone, *The Family, Sex and Marriage in England, 1500–1800* (London: Weidenfeld and Nicolson, 1977), a study that remains one of the most influential works of social history of the last generation. Stone's arguments have been challenged, most systematically by Alan Macfarlane, *Marriage and Love in England: Modes of Reproduction, 1300–1840* (Oxford: Blackwell, 1986), but I think the general claim about the rise of affection still stands. My summary here also draws on Jack Goody, *The European Family: An Historico-Anthropological Essay* (Oxford: Blackwell, 2000), and on the detailed studies collected in David I. Kertzer and Marzio Barbagli, eds., *Family Life in the Long Nineteenth Century, 1789–1913* (New Haven, CT: Yale University Press, 2002).

10. Quoted in Stone, *The Family, Sex and Marriage*, p. 407.

11. Ibid., pp. 450–58.

12. In addition to the material in the work of Zipes and Tatar, see, on this point in particular, Christa Kamenetsky, *The Brothers Grimm and Their Critics* (Athens: Ohio University Press, 1992).

13. See the discussion in Tatar, *Hard Facts*.

14. "Von dem Fischer un syner Fru," in *Märchen*, p. 80.

15. See the discussions in Zipes, *Brothers Grimm*, p. 38; and Kamenetsky, *Brothers Grimm*, p. 167.

16. Jakob Karl Ludwig Grimm, *On the Origin of Language*, trans. Raymond A. Wiley (Leiden: Brill, 1984), p. 20.

17. Quoted in Kamenetsky, *Brothers Grimm*, p. 120.

18. Ibid.

19. On Andersen, see Jack Zipes, *Hans Christian Andersen: The Misunderstood Storyteller* (New York: Routledge, 2005). For a biographical survey, see Jackie Wullschlager, *Hans Christian Andersen: The Life of a Storyteller* (New York: Knopf, 2001). For Andersen's autobiography, see *The Fairy Tale of My Life* (New York: Cooper Square Press, 2000), a facsimile reprinting of the English translation of 1871 (London: Paddington Press).

20. Andersen, *Fairy Tale of My Life*, pp. 11, 19, 20.

21. "The Nightingale," in Zipes et al., *Norton Anthology of Children's Literature*, pp. 215–20.

22. K. M. Elisabeth Murray, *Caught in the Web of Words* (New Haven, CT: Yale University Press, 1977), p. 321.

23. On the turn to paranormal interests, the rise of the ghost story, and the culture of performance in late nineteenth- and early twentieth-century England, see Samuel P. Hynes, *The Edwardian Turn of Mind* (Princeton, NJ: Princeton University Press, 1968). On the rise of the ghost story in the nineteenth century, and for a representative selection of tales, see Michael Cox and R. A. Gilbert, eds., *Victorian Ghost Stories: An Oxford Anthology* (Oxford: Oxford University Press, 1991).

24. Andrew Lang, *The Blue Fairy Book* (London: Longmans Green, 1889).

25. See the discussions in Peter Green, *Beyond the Wild Wood: The World of Kenneth Grahame* (Exeter, UK: Webb and Bower, 1982); and Alison Prince, *Kenneth Grahame: An Innocent in the Wild Wood* (London: Alison and Busby, 1994).

26. Lurie, *Oxford Book of Modern Fairy Tales*, pp. 182–202.

27. Ibid., pp. 203–14.

28. The bibliography on Tolkien—as a children's author, as a philologist, as a cultural icon—is immense. To my mind, the best of the critical materials that bear on the relationship of Tolkien's scholarly and creative work are T. A. Shippey, *The Road to Middle Earth* (London: Allen and Unwin, 1982); Shippey, *J. R. R. Tolkien: Author of the Century* (London: HarperCollins, 2000); and Jane Chance, *Tolkien's Art: A Mythology for England*, rev. ed. (Lexington: University Press of Kentucky, 2001). Still valuable are the essays in Mary Salu and Robert T. Farrell, eds., *J. R. R. Tolkien, Scholar and Storyteller* (Ithaca, NY: Cornell University Press, 1979). Two specific essays I have found valuable for understanding Tolkien's scholarly and critical work are Bruce Mitchell, "J. R. R. Tolkien and Old English Studies: An Appreciation," *Mythlore* 80 (1995): 206–12; and David Sandner, "The Fantastic Sublime: Tolkien's 'On Fairy-Stories' and the Romantic Sublime," *Mythlore* 83 (1997): 4–7. The standard biography is Humphrey Carpenter, *J. R. R. Tolkien: A Biography* (London: Allen and Unwin, 1977). A selection of letters has been edited by Carpenter and Tolkien's son, Christopher Tolkien, *Letters of J. R. R. Tolkien* (London: Allen and Unwin, 1981).

29. J. R. R. Tolkien, "To the Electors of the Rawlinson and Bosworth Professorship of Anglo-Saxon, University of Oxford," 27 June 1925, in Carpenter and Tolkien, *Letters*, pp. 12–13. For a fuller discussion of this letter of application and its place in Tolkien's work, see my *Error and the Academic Self* (New York: Columbia University Press, 2002), pp. 83–85.

30. Tolkien, "On Fairy Stories," originally published in *Tree and Leaf* (London: Allen and Unwin, 1964), reprinted in *The Tolkien Reader* (New York: Ballantine Books, 1966), pp. 33–99; this quotation from p. 46.

31. Ibid., p. 56.

32. Zipes, *Complete Fairy Tales of the Brothers Grimm*, p. 161.

33. E. V. Gordon, *An Introduction to Old Norse*, 2nd ed. (Oxford: Oxford University Press, 1957), p. 196.

34. J. K. Rowling, *Harry Potter and the Sorcerer's Stone* (New York: Scholastic Press, 1998), p. 137.

35. Quoted in Peter Gilliver, Jeremy Marshall, and Edmund Weiner, *The Ring of Words: Tolkien and the Oxford English Dictionary* (Oxford: Oxford University Press, 2006), p. 104.


CHAPTER ELEVEN: *Theaters of Girlhood*

1. J. K. Rowling, *Harry Potter and the Prisoner of Azkaban* (New York: Scholastic Books, 1999), p. 415.

2. See in particular Deborah Gorham, *The Victorian Girl and the Feminine Ideal* (Bloomington: Indiana University Press, 1982); Lynne Vallone, *Disciplines of Virtue: Girls' Culture in the Eighteenth and Nineteenth Centuries* (New Haven, CT: Yale University Press, 1995); and Sally Mitchell, *The New Girl: Girls' Culture in England, 1880-1915* (New York: Columbia University Press, 1995). Studies that offer important assessments of the female audience in children's literature include U. C. Knoepflmacher, *Ventures into Childland: Victorians, Fairy Tales, and Femininity* (Chicago: University of Chicago Press, 1998); Catherine Robson, *Men in Wonderland: The Lost Girlhood of the Victorian Gentleman* (Princeton, NJ: Princeton University Press, 2003); and Beverly Lyon Clark, *Kiddie Lit: The Cultural Construction of Children's Literature in America* (Baltimore: Johns Hopkins University Press, 2003). General histories of the family with an impact on this chapter include Linda A. Pollock, *Forgotten Children: Parent-Child Relationships from 1500 to 1900* (Cambridge: Cambridge University Press, 1983); Carolyn Steedman, *Strange Dislocations: Childhood and the Idea of Human Interiority* (London: Virago, 1995); and Claudia Nelson and Lynne Vallone, eds., *The Girl's Own: Cultural Histories of the Anglo-American Girl, 1830-1915* (Athens: University of Georgia Press, 1994).

3. Michael Fried, *Absorption and Theatricality: Painting and the Beholder in the Age of Diderot* (Berkeley and Los Angeles: University of California Press, 1980).

4. Text references to the fables are by Perry number (see chap. 2, n. 1); Ben Edwin Perry, *Babrius and Phaedrus*, Loeb Classical Library (Cambridge, MA: Harvard University Press, 1965).

5. For the different versions of "Little Red Riding Hood," from Perrault and the Grimms through the reconstruction of a pre-Grimm "original" to twentieth-century transformations, see the selection in Jack Zipes, Lissa Paul, Lynne Vallone, Peter Hunt, and Gillian Avery, eds., *The Norton Anthology of Children's Literature: The Traditions in English* (New York: Norton, 2005), pp. 338-86.

6. Jack Zipes, trans., *The Complete Fairy Tales of the Brothers Grimm* (New York: Bantam, 1992), p. 57.

7. Sigmund Freud, *The Question of Lay Analysis*, in *The Standard Edition of the Complete Psychological Works of Sigmund Freud*, ed. and trans. James Strachey, vol. 20, 1925-26 (London: Hogarth Press, 1959), p. 212. Note that the phrase "dark continent" is in English in Freud's original text.

8. Much of this material appears in such histories of family life as Lawrence Stone, *The Family, Sex and Marriage in England, 1500-1800* (London: Weidenfeld and Nicolson, 1977); and Steven Ozment, *Ancestors: The Loving Family in Old Europe* (Cambridge, MA: Harvard University Press, 2001).

9. Mitchell, *The New Girl*, p. 8.

10. Ibid., p. 6.

11. Mary Cowden Clarke, *The Girlhood of Shakespeare's Heroines in a Series of Tales* (London: Smith, 1851-52). The volumes appeared almost simultaneously in New York, published by Putnam. Subsequent editions and selections are legion. I quote from the two-volume Everyman Library edition (London: J. M. Dent, 1907). Two valuable critical studies are George C. Gross, "Mary Cowden Clarke, 'The Girlhood of Shakespeare's Heroines,' and the Sex Education of Victorian Women," *Victorian Studies* 16 (1972): 37-58; and

Sarah Anne Brown, "The Prequel as Palinode: Mary Cowden Clarke's *Girlhood of Shakespeare's Heroines*," *Shakespeare Survey* 58 (2005): 95–106.

12. The quotations in my text are from Cecily Devereux, ed., *Anne of Green Gables*, by L. M. Montgomery (London: Broadview, 2004), whose introduction and full critical bibliography call attention to the texture of literary and artistic allusions throughout the novel. This edition also reproduces the illustrations from the first edition of 1908. An important collection of essays on the reception and transformations of the novel is Irene Gammel, ed., *Making Avonlea: L. M. Montgomery and Popular Culture* (Toronto: University of Toronto Press, 2002).

13. See Faye Hammill, "'A new and exceedingly brilliant star': L. M. Montgomery, *Anne of Green Gables*, and Mary Miles Minter," *Modern Language Review* 101 (2006): 652–70.

14. Quoted in E. Holly Pike, "Mass Marketing, Popular Culture, and the Canadian Celebrity Author," in Gammel, *Making Avonlea*, p. 247.

15. See Elizabeth R. Epperly, "The Visual Imagination of L. M. Montgomery," in Gammel, *Making Avonlea*, pp. 84–98; the photo is reproduced on p. 96.

16. This desire is noted in Ednah D. Cheney, *Louisa May Alcott: Her Life, Letters, and Journals* (Boston: Roberts, 1892), p. 63. Critics have long noted Alcott's fascination with the theater and the role of theatrical productions in her major novels and short stories. For a review of scholarship and critical readings, see Claudia Mills, "'The Canary and the Nightingale': Performance and Virtue in *Eight Cousins* and *Rose in Bloom*," *Children's Literature* 34 (2006): 109–39. See also the entries for "Acting (Theme)" and "Acting (LMA's)" in Gregory Eiselein and Anne K. Phillips, eds., *The Louisa May Alcott Encyclopedia* (Westport, CT: Greenwood Press, 2001).

17. See Geraldine Brooks, "Orpheus at the Plough," *The New Yorker*, 10 January 2005, pp. 58–65.

18. On the place of the stage in mid-nineteenth-century American moral reform, see Gary A. Richardson, *American Drama: From the Colonial Period through World War I* (New York: Twayne, 1993); and John W. Frick, *Theater, Culture and Temperance Reform in Nineteenth-Century America* (Cambridge: Cambridge University Press, 2003), who cites Twain's comment (p. 12). Much of this material is synthesized in Mills, "'The Canary and the Nightingale'," pp. 109–10.

19. These quotations are from the *Oxford English Dictionary*, s.v. "melodrama."

20. Quoted in Claudia Johnson, "That Guilty Third Tier: Prostitution in Nineteenth-Century American Theaters," *American Quarterly* 26 (1975): 582, quoted and discussed in Mills, "'The Canary and the Nightingale'," p. 110.

21. See Anne Hiebert Alton, ed., *Little Women*, by Louisa May Alcott (London: Broadview, 2001). Quotations in my text are from this edition.

22. The quotations in my text are from Gretchen Holbrook Gerzina, ed., *The Secret Garden*, by Frances Hodgson Burnett (New York: Norton, 2006).

23. Robert Louis Stevenson, *A Child's Garden of Verses* (London: Longmans, Green, 1885).

24. Kenneth Grahame, *The Cambridge Book of Poetry for Children*, 2 vols. (1915, 1916), republished as one volume (Cambridge: Cambridge University Press, 1919), p. 3.

25. L. Frank Baum, *The Wonderful Wizard of Oz*, illustrated by W. W. Denslow (Indianapolis: Bobbs-Merrill, 1900). I quote from the reprint of 1903.

26. Denslow's illustrations dress the wizard in a long frock coat, with a dotted vest and striped trousers. These are the basics that survive in later versions, including John. R. Neill's illustration from *The Patchwork Girl of Oz* (Chicago: Reilly and Britton, 1913), which is discussed in terms of the wizard's resemblance to P. T. Barnum in Suzanne Rahn, *The Wizard of Oz: Shaping an Imaginary World* (New York: Twayne, 1998), pp. 38–39. For a review of the place of the books in Baum's own theatrical aspirations, and a conspectus of critical responses to the Oz tales in the political and social life of early twentieth-century America, see Katharine M. Rogers, *L. Frank Baum, Creator of Oz* (New York: St. Martin's Press, 2002), especially the review of literary criticism, pp. 265–66.

27. See Mark Evan Swartz, *Oz before the Rainbow: L. Frank Baum's "The Wonderful Wizard of Oz" on Stage and Screen to 1939* (Baltimore: Johns Hopkins University Press, 2000).

28. Salman Rushdie, *The Wizard of Oz* (London: British Film Institute, 1992), p. 30.

29. The quotations in my text are from E. B. White, *Charlotte's Web* (New York: Harper and Row, 1952).

CHAPTER TWELVE: *Pan in the Garden*

1. Julia Briggs, "Transitions (1890–1914)," in Peter Hunt, ed., *Children's Literature: An Illustrated History* (Oxford: Oxford University Press, 1995), p. 172.

2. Samuel P. Hynes, *The Edwardian Turn of Mind* (Princeton, NJ: Princeton University Press, 1968), p. 3. This book remains the best synthesis of the literary and social history of the era. I have also drawn on some more recent studies, including Jonathan Rose, *The Edwardian Temperament: 1895–1919* (Athens: Ohio University Press, 1986); Jefferson Hunter, *Edwardian Fiction* (Cambridge, MA: Harvard University Press, 1982); and the volume of reminiscences assembled by Thea Thompson, *Edwardian Childhoods* (London: Routledge and Kegan Paul, 1981). For a brief but incisive reassessment of the Edwardian revivals in post–World War II Britain and their impact on literature and culture, see Tony Judt, *Postwar: A History of Europe since 1945* (New York: Penguin, 2005), pp. 226–30, 768–73.

3. See the discussion in Rose, *Edwardian Temperament*, pp. 181–84.

4. Quoted and discussed in Edmund Morris, *The Rise of Theodore Roosevelt* (New York: Coward, McCann and Geoghegan, 1979), p. xii.

5. See Peter Green, *Beyond the Wild Wood: The World of Kenneth Grahame* (Exeter, UK: Webb and Bower, 1982), pp. 185–86.

6. See the discussion in Rose, *Edwardian Temperament*, pp. 178–79.

7. Hynes, *Edwardian Turn*, p. 134.

8. Ibid., pp. 146–47.

9. Perceval Landon, "Thurnley Abbey," in *Victorian Ghost Stories: An Oxford Anthology*, ed. Michael Cox and R. A. Gilbert, pp. 466–79 (Oxford: Oxford University Press, 1991); this quotation from p. 477. Even though this anthology is titled *Victorian Ghost*

*Stories*, it includes works published up to 1908, and it concludes with a chronological review of stories published up to 1910.

10. Hynes, *Edwardian Turn*, p. 246.

11. See the discussion in Richard Schoch, *Shakespeare's Victorian Stage* (Cambridge: Cambridge University Press, 1998), pp. 183–84. For more reflections on the nineteenth- and early twentieth-century idioms of Shakespearean staging and performance, see Stephen Orgel, *Imagining Shakespeare* (London: Palgrave, 2003).

12. Sir Herbert Beerbohm Tree as Caliban was drawn by Charles A. Buchel and published in the *Tatler* in 1904.

13. See the discussion in Schoch, *Shakespeare's Victorian Stage*, p. 155.

14. But what most critics of the children's literature of this time still address is biography. J. M. Barrie's relationship to the Davies family, Kenneth Grahame's relationship to his son, L. M. Montgomery's life in Prince Edward Island, Francis Hodgson Burnett's move to America—all these factors, and many more, have governed most appreciations of these authors' major works. While I do not dismiss biographical inquiry as enhancing our study of children's literature generally, my purpose in this chapter is to relocate the major works of the Edwardian era in the cultural moment of their composition and to place them in the larger critical arc of my book: its concerns with education and theatricality, with transformations of earlier canonical literature into the realm of the childhood imagination, and with the impact of technology on the experience of nature.

15. Hynes, *Edwardian Turn*, p. 134.

16. Kenneth Grahame, *The Wind in the Willows*, ed. Peter Green (Oxford: Oxford University Press, 1983), p. 72. Quotations in my text are from this edition.

17. All quotations from *Peter Pan* are from the revised, 1928 version of the play as printed in Jack Zipes, Lissa Paul, Lynne Vallone, Peter Hunt, and Gillian Avery, eds., *The Norton Anthology of Children's Literature: The Traditions In English* (New York: Norton, 2005), pp. 1301–1356. Perhaps the most influential critical discussion (influential in that it has spawned perhaps as much criticism as approval) is Jacqueline Rose, *The Case of Peter Pan: or, The Impossibility of Children's Fiction* (London: Macmillan, 1984). For a critical account grounded in notions of Edwardian gender roles, see Amy Billone, "The Boy Who Lived: From Carroll's Alice and Barrie's Peter Pan to Rowling's Harry Potter," *Children's Literature* 32 (2004): 178–202. Outside my scope is a study of the relationships among the various forms the Peter Pan story took in Barrie's work: the play of 1904; the novella, *Peter Pan in Kensington Gardens* (1906); and the novel, *Peter and Wendy* (1911).

18. Jennifer Breen, ed., *Wilfred Owen: Selected Poetry and Prose* (London: Routledge, 1988), pp. 50–51.

19. The bibliography on Grahame is large and growing. For an excellent annotated survey, see the bibliography in Peter Green's edition of *The Wind in the Willows*, pp. xxi–xxiv.

20. Jerome K. Jerome, *Three Men in a Boat (To Say Nothing of the Dog)*, originally published 1889; I quote from the earliest American edition (New York: Hurst and Company, n.d.).

21. Quoted in Jeremy Nicholas, "Three Men in a Boat and on the Bummel—The Story behind Jerome's Two Comic Masterpieces," http://www.jeromekjerome.com/threemen.htm.

22. On the impact of the Romantic poets on Grahame's idiom, see Richard Gillin, "Romantic Echoes in the Willows," *Children's Literature* 16 (1988): 169–74; and David Sandner, *The Fantastic Sublime* (Westport, CT: Archon Books, 1996), pp. 67–81.

23. Kenneth Grahame, *The Cambridge Book of Poetry for Children*, 2 vols. (1915, 1916), republished as one volume (Cambridge: Cambridge University Press, 1919); I quote from the edition of 1919 here.

24. And some of those disguises have a clearly Shakespearean resonance. On Toad as Falstaff, see Nicholas Tucker, "The Children's Falstaff," *The Times Literary Supplement*, 26 June 1969, p. 687.

25. I quote from E. Nesbit, *The Railway Children* (1906; reprint, with original illustrations, San Francisco: Sea Star Books, 2005).

26. C. S. Lewis, *The Chronicles of Narnia* (New York: HarperCollins, 2004). Page numbers are given in my text.

CHAPTER THIRTEEN: *Good Feeling*

1. For the history and details of the Newbery and Caldecott Medal establishment, together with a list of all winners and honor books, see the links at the American Library Association Web site, http://www.ala.org. See also Marjorie Allen, *One Hundred Years of Children's Books in America* (New York: Facts on File, 1996). *Horn Book Magazine* published two volumes detailing the first decades of the awards, complete with citations and (when available) authors' acceptance speeches. See Bertha Mahony Miller and Elinor Whitney Field, eds., *Newbery Medal Books: 1922–1955* (Boston: Horn Book, 1955); and Miller and Field, eds., *Caldecott Medal Books: 1938–1957* (Boston: Horn Book, 1957).

2. Beverly Lyon Clark, *Kiddie Lit: The Cultural Construction of Children's Literature in America* (Baltimore: Johns Hopkins University Press, 2003), pp. 73–75.

3. For a larger history of prizes and the culture of awards in American society, see James F. English, *The Economy of Prestige: Prizes, Awards, and the Circulation of Cultural Value* (Cambridge, MA: Harvard University Press, 2005).

4. See Clark's discussion throughout her chapter 3, "Kiddie Lit in the Academy," pp. 48–76.

5. For a history of the American public library and the role of librarians in shaping aspects of social life, see Dee Garrison, *Apostles of Culture: The Public Librarian and American Society, 1876–1920* (New York: Free Press, 1979); and Lowell A. Martin, *Enrichment: A History of the Public Library in the United States in the Twentieth Century* (Latham, MD: Scarecrow Press, 1998).

6. See Garrison, *Apostles of Culture*, pp. 206–25; and Martin, *Enrichment*, pp. 57–64. On the impact of Anne Carroll Moore on American children's literature and its reception, see Frances Clarke Sayers, *Anne Carroll Moore* (New York: Atheneum, 1972); and Barbara Bader, "*Only* the Best: The Hits and Misses of Anne Carroll Moore," *Horn Book* 73 (1997): 520–29.

7. See Garrison, *Apostles of Culture*, p. 211.

8. English, *The Economy of Prestige*, esp. pp. 28–49. For English's reflections on the Newbery Medal, see pp. 360–61, n. 35.

9. Historical material for the following paragraphs, together with the wording of the Newbery Medal criteria, may be found at the ALA Web site (see n. 1 above).

10. Hendrik Willem Van Loon, *The Story of Mankind* (New York: Boni and Liveright, 1921). All quotations, cited by page number in my text, are from this edition.

11. Moore's reviews were collected three times: in *Roads to Childhood* (1920), *New Roads to Childhood* (1923), and *Crossroads to Childhood* (1926). These volumes were re-edited, with new material, in *My Roads to Childhood* (1939). A new edition of this collection appeared as *My Roads to Childhood: Views and Reviews of Children's Books* (Boston: Horn Book, 1961), from which I quote. Moore's expanded review of *The Story of Mankind* is on pp. 159–60 of this edition.

12. Miller and Field, *Newbery Medal Books*, pp. 11–12. This is the entire selection from *The Story of Mankind* offered here (ellipses are theirs). This passage comes from pp. 463–65 of the original edition (the final pages of the book).

13. Gerard Willem Van Loon, *The Story of Hendrik Willem van Loon* (Philadelphia: J. B. Lippincott, 1972), pp. 123–34; quotations from pp. 128–29, 134.

14. Hugh Lofting, *The Voyages of Doctor Dolittle* (Philadelphia: J. B. Lippincott, 1922).

15. See Miller and Field, *Newbery Medal Books*, pp. 28–241, for publishing details, summaries, author biographies, and author acceptance speeches for the years 1924 to 1943.

16. Esther Forbes, *Johnny Tremain: A Novel for Old and Young* (Boston: Houghton Mifflin, 1943). All quotations in my text are from this edition. See the material in Miller and Field, *Newbery Medal Books*, pp. 242–54. For a list of the top-selling children's books (ranking *Johnny Tremain* sixteenth—and *Charlotte's Web* first), see the Infoplease Web site, at http://www.infoplease.com/ipea/A0203050.html.

17. Quoted in Jack Bales, *Esther Forbes: A Bio-Bibliography of the Author of "Johnny Tremain"* (Latham, MD: Scarecrow Press, 1998), p. 47.

18. Norman Mailer, *The Naked and the Dead* (New York: Rinehart, 1948), p. 3. For a fuller discussion of the language and style of the reporting and literary fiction of the Second World War, see Seth Lerer, *Inventing English: A Portable History of the Language* (New York: Columbia University Press, 2007), pp. 246–57.

19. Miller and Field, *Caldecott Medal Books*, pp. 79–86.

20. Ibid., pp. 83–84.

21. Robert McCloskey, *Make Way for Ducklings* (New York: Viking, 1941).

CHAPTER FOURTEEN: *Keeping Things Straight*

1. Georges-Louis Leclerc, Comte de Buffon, is reported to have uttered this maxim on August 25, 1753, to the Académie française and repeated it in his *Discours sur le style* (1753). The sentiment, however, was a commonplace, attributed to figures as various as the English explorer and poet Sir Walter Raleigh and the French philosopher and critic Charles-Augustin Sainte-Beuve.

2. Heinrich Hoffmann, *Lustige Geschichten und drollige Bilder* (1845), originally offered ten brief tales in verse, each illustrating a particularly bad habit or failure of hygiene or social decorum. The stories were republished in 1858 under the title *Struwwelpeter*.

3. Carlo Collodi, *Le avventure di Pinocchio* (Florence: Flice Paggi Libraio-Editore, 1883). I use the bilingual edition, *The Adventures of Pinocchio*, ed and trans. Nicolas J. Perella (Berkeley and Los Angeles: University of California Press, 1986). Perella's comprehensive introductory essay (pp. 1–75) lays out the origins, early reception, and literary contexts for the work.

4. Collodi, *Avventure / Adventures*, pp. 136–41.

5. St. Augustine, *Confessions*, trans. R. S. Pine-Coffin (Baltimore: Penguin, 1961), bk. 1, chap. 19, p. 39.

6. Ibid., bk. 3, chap. 1.

7. E. B. White, *Stuart Little* (New York: Harper, 1945); Dr. Seuss [Theodor Seuss Geisel], *The Cat in the Hat* (New York: Random House, 1957).

8. William Strunk, Jr., and E. B. White, *The Elements of Style*, 2nd ed. (New York: Macmillan, 1972). Quotations in my text are from this edition.

9. Quoted in Jack Zipes, Lissa Paul, Lynne Vallone, Peter Hunt, and Gillian Avery, eds., *The Norton Anthology of Children's Literature: The Traditions in English* (New York: Norton, 2005), p. 1431.

10. Benjamin Spock, *Baby and Child Care*, 15th ed. (New York: Bantam, 1985), p. 479.

11. William O. Douglas, *The Court Years, 1939–1975: The Autobiography of William O. Douglas* (New York: Random House, 1980), p. 92.

12. Leslie Fiedler, "Come Back to the Raft Ag'in, Huck Honey!" *Partisan Review*, June 1948.

13. William H. Whyte, *The Organization Man* (New York: Doubleday, 1956), p. 6.

14. *The Cat in the Hat* appeared in March 1957; Ginsberg read his poem *Howl* in San Francisco in October 1955; and Elvis Presley appeared on the Ed Sullivan Show in September 1956.

15. Louis Menand, "Cat People: What Dr. Seuss Really Taught Us," *The New Yorker*, December 23–30, 2002.

16. *Bartholomew and the Oobleck* (New York: Random House, 1949); *Green Eggs and Ham* (New York: Random House, 1960); *One Fish, Two Fish, Red Fish, Blue Fish* (New York: Random House, 1960).

17. Robert McCloskey, *Burt Dow, Deep-Water Man* (New York: Viking, 1963).

18. George Selden, *The Cricket in Times Square* (New York: Yearling, 1960).

19. Robert McCloskey, *Make Way for Ducklings* (New York: Viking, 1942); *Blueberries for Sal* (New York: Viking, 1948); *One Morning in Maine* (New York: Viking, 1952).

20. Roald Dahl, *Charlie and the Chocolate Factory* (New York: Knopf, 1964; London: Allen and Unwin, 1967).

21. Roald Dahl, *The Fantastic Mr. Fox* (New York: Knopf, 1970).

22. A. A. Milne, *Winnie-the-Pooh* (New York: E. P. Dutton, 1954), p. 159.

CHAPTER FIFTEEN: *Tap Your Pencil on the Paper*

1. Jon Scieszka, *Summer Reading Is Killing Me!* (New York: Viking, 1998).

2. See Ellen Winner, *The Point of Words: Children's Understanding of Metaphor and Irony* (Cambridge, MA: MIT Press, 1988); and Bettina Kümmerling-Meibauer, "Metalinguistic Awareness and the Child's Developing Concept of Irony: The Relationship between Pictures and Text in Ironic Picture Books," *The Lion and the Unicorn* 23 (1999): 157-83.

3. Jedediah Purdy, *For Common Things: Irony, Trust, and Commitment in America Today* (New York: Knopf, 1999); these quotations from pp. xi–xii.

4. Louise Fitzhugh, *Harriet, the Spy* (New York: Delacorte, 1964; reprint, Random House, 2002). On the social challenges felt at the time, see the review by Ruth Hill Viguers in *Horn Book* 41 (1965): 74–75. See also the discussion in Anne Scott MacLeod, *American Childhood: Essays on Children's Literature of the Nineteenth and Twentieth Centuries* (Athens: University of Georgia Press, 1994), pp. 198–215.

5. Robert Baden-Powell, *Scouting for Boys* (1909), p. 121, quoted in Joseph Bristow, *Empire Boys: Adventures in a Man's World* (London: HarperCollins, 1991), p. 191.

6. Kümmerling-Meibauer, "Metalinguistic Awareness," p. 157.

7. Judy Blume, *Are You There God? It's Me, Margaret* (New York: Simon and Schuster, 1970). On reception contexts and the climate of censorship, see MacLeod, *American Childhood*, pp. 173–86.

8. Purdy, *For Common Things*, pp. 23, 21.

9. Francesca Lia Block, *Weetzie Bat* (New York: HarperCollins, 1989).

10. Louis Sachar, *Holes* (New York: Farrar, Straus and Giroux, 1998).

11. Harry Frankfurt, *On Bullshit* (Princeton, NJ: Princeton University Press, 2005).

EPILOGUE: *Children's Literature and the History of the Book*

1. See my discussion in chapter 1, with the reproduction of the illustration there.

2. See Leslie Webber Jones and C. R. Morey, eds., *The Miniatures of the Manuscripts of Terence prior to the Thirteenth Century* (Princeton, NJ: Department of Art and Archaeology of Princeton University, 1932).

3. See Robert Black, *Humanism and Education in Medieval and Renaissance Italy* (Cambridge: Cambridge University Press, 2001), esp. pp. 40–42.

4. See Nicholas Barker, ed., *Two East Anglian Picture Books: A Facsimile of the Helmingham Herbal and Bestiary and Bodleian MS Ashmole 1504* (London: Bernard Quaritch, 1988).

5. Peter Hunt, ed., *Children's Literature: An Illustrated History* (Oxford: Oxford University Press, 1995).

6. See, for example, Bettina Hürlimann, *Picture-Book World* (London: Oxford University Press, 1968); Ruth S. Freeman, *Children's Picture Books, Yesterday and Today: An Analysis* (Watkins Glen, NY: Century House, 1967); Lyn Ellen Lacy, *Art and Design in Children's Picture Books* (Chicago: American Library Association, 1986); Perry Nodelman, *Words about Pictures: The Narrative Art of Children's Picture Books* (Athens: Uni-

versity of Georgia Press, 1988); and David Lewis, *Reading Contemporary Picturebooks* (London: Routledge, 2001).

7. Ellen Handler Spitz, "Between Image and Child: Further Reflections on Picture Books," *American Imago* 53 (1996): 176–190; this quotation from p. 190. Spitz develops this material in her *Inside Picture Books* (New Haven, CT: Yale University Press, 1999).

8. Jack Zipes, Lissa Paul, Lynne Vallone, Peter Hunt, and Gillian Avery, eds., *The Norton Anthology of Children's Literature: The Traditions in English* (New York: Norton, 2005), color plates (C1–C32) following p. 1097.

9. The citation may be found by following the links at http://www.ala.org. For a survey of Caldecott books, see Lee Kingman, ed., *Newbery and Caldecott Medal Books, 1976–1985* (Boston: Horn Book, 1986).

10. On the French scholarly tradition of *l'histoire du livre*, see Lucien Febvre and Henri-Jean Martin, *L'apparition du livre*, translated by David Gerard as *The Coming of the Book* (London: New Left Books, 1976; originally published in French in 1958); Roger Chartier, *The Order of Books: Readers, Authors, and Libraries in Europe between the Fourteenth and the Eighteenth Centuries*, trans. Lydia Cochrane (Stanford, CA: Stanford University Press, 1994); and Roger Chartier and Henri-Jean Martin, *Histoire de l'édition française*, 4 vols. (Paris: Fayard, 1989).

11. Recent works in book history that bear on my study include Roger Chartier, ed., *The Culture of Print*, trans. Lydia Cochrane (Princeton, NJ: Princeton University Press, 1989); Adrian Johns, *The Nature of the Book* (Chicago: University of Chicago Press, 1999); and the essays collected in Seth Lerer and Leah Price, eds., "The History of the Book and the Idea of Literature," *PMLA*, special issue, 121, no. 1 (2006). For a survey of the field with full bibliography, see Edward L. Bishop, "Book History," in *The Johns Hopkins Guide to Literary Theory and Criticism*, 2nd ed., ed. Michael Groden, Martin Kreiswirth, and Imre Szeman, pp. 131–36 (Baltimore: Johns Hopkins University Press, 2005); and, from a more advanced, scholarly perspective, David Vander Meulen, "How to Read Book History," *Studies in Bibliography* 56 (2003–4): 171–94.

12. On the German traditions of illustrated books and children's literature, see the discussion in Klaus Doderer, *Das Bilderbuch: Geschichte und Entwicklung des Bilderbuchs in Deutschland von den Anfängen bis zur Gegenwart* (Weinheim: Beltz, 1973).

13. For a brief but evocative survey of illustration in the late nineteenth century, see Julia Briggs and Dennis Butts, "The Emergence of Form," in Hunt, *Children's Literature: An Illustrated History*, pp. 162–65. For material on John Harris in particular, see the excellent and detailed entry in Humphrey Carpenter and Mari Prichard, *The Oxford Companion to Children's Literature* (Oxford: Oxford University Press, 1984), pp. 240–42; and the discussion in Mary V. Jackson, *Engines of Instruction, Mischief, and Magic: Children's Literature in England from Its Beginnings to 1839* (Lincoln: University of Nebraska Press, 1989), pp. 191–97. For material on the illustrators Walter Crane, Randolph Caldecott, and Kate Greenaway, see Anne H. Lundin, *Victorian Horizons: The Reception of the Picture Books of Walter Crane, Randolph Caldecott, and Kate Greenaway* (Lanham, MD: Scarecrow Press, 2001).

14. See Joan M. Friedman, *Color Printing in England, 1486–1859* (New Haven, CT: Yale Center for British Art, 1978); and Jay T. Last, *The Color Explosion: Nineteenth-Century American Lithography* (Santa Ana, CA: Hillcrest Press, 2005).

15. See Greg Smith and Sarah Hyde, eds., *Walter Crane, 1845–1915: Artist, Designer, and Socialist* (Manchester: University of Manchester, 1989); and Rodney K. Engen, *Walter Crane as a Book Illustrator* (London: Academy Editions, 1975).

16. See Rodney Engen, *Kate Greenaway, a Biography* (London: Macdonald, 1981); and Ina Taylor, *The Art of Kate Greenaway: A Nostalgic Portrait of Childhood* (London: Webb and Bower, 1991).

17. See Brian Alderson, *Sing a Song for Sixpence: The English Picture Book Tradition and Randolph Caldecott* (Cambridge: Cambridge University Press, 1986); and the immense amount of material assembled at the Web site of the Randolph Caldecott Society, http://www.randolphcaldecott.org.uk.

18. This material, and many other tributes and testimonials, are available at the Caldecott Society Web site: http://www.randolphcaldecott.org.uk/tributes.htm.

19. The Chesterton quotation is available at http://en.wikipedia.org/wiki/Randolph_Caldecott.

20. Zipes et al., *Norton Anthology of Children's Literature*, plate C32, caption.

21. For the history of the pop-up book, or "movable," together with a detailed bibliography, see the excellent essay by Ann Montanaro, "A Concise History of Pop-Up and Movable Books," http://www.libraries.rutgers.edu/rul/libs/scua/montanar/p-intro.htm.

22. Discussions of the Czech contribution to the pop-up book, and the larger environments for Czech children's literature, are available in English on a variety of Web sites keyed to library and university exhibitions, publisher's catalogues, and historical work. See in particular http://www.lib.virginia.edu/small/exhibits/popup/kubasta.html; and http://www.library.unt.edu/rarebooks/exhibits/popup2/kubasta.htm.

23. For his brilliant exposition of the cultural environment of Czechoslovakia in particular and Eastern Europe in general in the mid-twentieth century, I am indebted to Tony Judt, *Postwar: A History of Europe since 1945* (New York: Penguin, 2005). The quotation from Seifert appears on p. 311.

24. Quoted in Andrew Osmond, "Czech Animation: Two Perspectives," *Animation World Magazine*, September 10, 2003.

25. See http://www.janpienkowski.com/.

26. For reviews of Victorian developments in book production, see Allan C. Dooley, *Author and Printer in Victorian England* (Charlottesville: University of Virginia Press, 1992); and Norman Feltes, *Modes of Production of Victorian Novels* (Chicago: University of Chicago Press, 1986). For general remarks on the mechanization of printing and illustrating in the nineteenth century, see D. C. Greetham, *Textual Scholarship* (New York: Garland, 1994), pp. 139–51.

27. For a conveniently available set of reproductions of book designs by Talwyn Morris and Charles Rennie Mackintosh for Blackie, together with a history of the firm, see http://www.fulltable.com/BG/tb.htm. For a survey of the Glasgow school of art, its

relationship to Art Nouveau, and Mackintosh's work in particular, see James Macaulay, *Glasgow School of Art: Charles Rennie Mackintosh* (London: Phaidon, 1993).

28. See the collection of studies and the large number of reproductions in Christian Robin, ed., *Un éditeur et son siècle: Pierre-Jules Hetzel (1814–1886)* (Saint-Sébastien: Société Crocus, 1988), especially the color plates preceding p. 283.

29. See Pierre Amandry, "La libraire Lefèvre et Guérin, 1860–1920," *Revue française d'histoire du livre* 82 (1994): 213–40, especially the discussion and reproductions on pp. 219–24.

30. On the implications of this visual tradition for contemporary notions of aesthetics, see Sianne Ngai, "The Cuteness of the Avant-Garde," *Critical Inquiry* 31 (2005): 811–47.

# Index